PO-0150

THE COLLECTED POEMS OF FRANK O'HARA

THE COLLECTED POEMS OF
FRANK O'HARA

EDITED BY DONALD ALLEN

WITH AN INTRODUCTION BY JOHN ASHBERY

UNIVERSITY OF CALIFORIA PRESS

Berkeley · Los Angeles · London

University of California Press
Berkeley and Los Angeles, California
University of California Press, Ltd.
London, England

First Paperback Printing 1995

Library of Congress Cataloging-in-Publication Data
O'Hara, Frank.
    [Poems]
        The collected poems of Frank O'Hara / edited by Donald Allen ;
    with an introduction by John Ashbery.
            p.   cm.
        ISBN 0-520-20166-3
        1. New York (N.Y.)—Social life and customs—20th century—Poetry.
    2. City and town life—New York (N.Y.)—Poetry.   I. Allen, Donald
    Merriam, 1912–   .   II. Title.
    PS3529.H28A17   1995
    811'.54—dc20   94-24660
                                                            CIP

Some of these poems first appeared in The Nation, Angel Hair, Art News, Audit, "C," Ephemeris II,
Evergreen Review, Fuck You/A Magazine of the Arts, Harper's Bazaar, The Harvard Advocate,
The New American Poetry, The New Republic, New World Writing, The Paris Review, Partisan
Review, Poetry, San Francisco Earthquake, Texas Quarterly, Yügen, Locus Solus, In Transit, Sum,
Fathar, Adventures in Poetry, Folder, Signal #1, Accent, The Bonacker: A collection of Eastern
Long Island Writing, Floating Bear, Generation, Hasty Papers, Iowa Defender, Nomad, Second
Coming, Swank, Semi-colon, Voices. "For Poulenc" is reprinted with permission of the copyright owners,
E. C. Schirmer Music Company, Boston, Mass.
Manufactured in the United States of America.

Printed in the United States of America
08 07 06 05 04 03
9 8 7 6
The paper used in this publication is both acid-free and totally chlorine-free (TCF). It meets the minimum
requirements of ANSI/NISO Z39.48-1992 (R 1997) (Permanence of Paper). ∞

This edition is an attempt to provide a reliable text for all the poems Frank O'Hara published during his lifetime—in individual volumes and in anthologies and periodicals—together with all the unpublished poems he conceivably would have wanted to see in print. In collecting the latter, I have followed every suggestion and clue I could recall from conversations and correspondence with O'Hara, every hint I could find in his papers, and every lead given me by the many poets and painters who knew his work. (We have thought it best to reserve O'Hara's many collaborations with other poets and his translations for a separate volume.)

Five of the volumes of poems he published between 1952 and 1965 are in reality selections from the many hundreds of poems he held in manuscript. His first collection, the unpublished Hopwood Award manuscript, "A Byzantine Place," is a selection from the poems he had written from 1948 to 1951, some of which were included in *A City Winter, and Other Poems* along with poems written later in 1951 and in 1952. *Meditations in an Emergency* reprints some of these poems, together with new work chosen from what he had written before 1959. In the following year, he planned, with my help, a volume to be called "Poems 1956–1960," which was to have included the nine odes, some poems later included in *Lunch Poems,* a number of poems unpublished until the present volume, and those of the *Love Poems* he had written up to that time.

These last poems, written for Vincent Warren, 1959–61, had a characteristically frustrating publishing history: four were included in *The New American Poetry* anthology, several others appear in *Lunch Poems,* another sixteen were chosen for *Love Poems,* and several remained unpublished until the present volume, which now presents the whole series for the first time.

Between 1960 and 1964 O'Hara and I worked intermittently at compiling *Lunch Poems,* which in the end became a selection of work dating from 1953 to 1964. In 1966 he made another selection for a projected volume which was to have been called "In Memory of My Feelings: Selected Poems 1949–1966"; it included poems from *A City Winter* and *Meditations in an Emergency,* both of which were out of print at the time, plus "Second Avenue," and some of the *Love Poems* and *Lunch Poems.*

That Frank O'Hara tended to think of his poems as a record of his life is apparent in much of his work. "What is happening to me, allowing for lies and exaggerations which I try to avoid, goes into my poems," he wrote in his statement for *The New American Poetry.* Yet there is nowhere any clear suggestion that he contemplated anything like a collected volume of his poems. His attitude towards much of his work tended, in my experience, to be rather diffident and tentative, although he was certainly convinced of his genius and knew the excellence of his great poems.

At the same time he apparently did think of his work as a whole, as is evidenced by the fact that he went through his manuscripts on more than one occasion and wrote in the place and date of composition for most, but not all, of his earlier poems. (By 1958 he had made it a practice to type in the date below the completed poem.) A number of poems have survived in several states, and in some cases there are many typed copies of the final version of a poem. On the other hand, as it turned out, O'Hara did not keep copies of a large number of poems which have only survived, as John Ashbery remarks in his Introduction, through the care of friends and collaborators to whom he sent them. There is every reason to expect that other lost poems will surface during the years following the publication of this volume and that some puzzles in the notes to the poems will be solved when more of O'Hara's letters become available.

The compilation and editing of *The Collected Poems of Frank O'Hara* was largely made possible by the kindness of Maureen Granville-Smith, the administratrix of her late brother's estate, who made all of his manuscripts accessible to the editor. O'Hara's many friends have given important leads, most helpful advice, and valuable assistance. I am particularly indebted to: John Ashbery, Bill Berkson, Ted Berrigan, John Button, Jan Cremer, Edwin Denby, Morton Feldman, Hal Fondren, Jane Freilicher, Barbara Guest, Grace Hartigan, Jasper Johns, Kenneth Koch, Al Leslie, Joseph LeSueur, Kynaston McShine, J. J. Mitchell, John Bernard Myers, Ron Padgett, Larry Rivers, Ned Rorem, Aram Saroyan, James Schuyler, Patsy Southgate and Vincent Warren.

I am also indebted to Tom Clark, Lawrence Ferlinghetti, Ron Loewinsohn, David Schaff and Harold Snedcof for suggestions and guidance, and to the following for warmly appreciated assistance: Julien Michel of the University of California (Berkeley) Library; Mary E. Cooley, secretary of The Hopwood Room, University of Michigan; Richard Moore of KQED, San Francisco; John R. Payne of the Academic Center Library, University of Texas, who gave us permission to include "Lines for the Fortune Cookies"; and Minna Rosenberg of the New School for Social Research. Finally, the preparation of this volume was immensely aided by the loyal support of my gifted assistants: Valerie Estes, Andra Lichtenstein, Pamela Millward and Nancy Peters.

D.A.

In preparing this revised edition, I have been greatly aided by the suggestions of the late Alexander Smith, Jr., who vetted THE COLLECTED POEMS while compiling his superb FRANK O'HARA: A COMPREHENSIVE BIBLIOGRAPHY.

D.A.

INTRODUCTION

That *The Collected Poems of Frank O'Hara* should turn out to be a volume of the present dimensions will surprise those who knew him, and would have surprised Frank even more. Dashing the poems off at odd moments—in his office at the Museum of Modern Art, in the street at lunchtime or even in a room full of people—he would then put them away in drawers and cartons and half forget them. Once when a publisher asked him for a manuscript he spent weeks and months combing the apartment, enthusiastic and bored at the same time, trying to assemble the poems. Finally he let the project drop, not because he didn't wish his work to appear, but because his thoughts were elsewhere, in the urban world of fantasy where the poems came from. Donald Allen's task in tracking them down has not been easy. Sometimes poems Frank's friends remembered having seen had simply disappeared. Some survived only in letters. One of his most beautiful early poems, "Memorial Day 1950," exists only because I once copied it out in a letter to Kenneth Koch and Kenneth kept the letter. But, given the instantaneous quality of the poems, their problematical life seems only natural: poetry was what finally mattered to Frank, and even the poems themselves, like the experiences and personal relationships that went into them, were important but somehow secondary. His career stands as an unrevised work-in-progress; the fact that parts of it are now missing or unfinished is unimportant, except as an indicator of the temporal, fluctuating quality that runs through his work and is one of its major innovations.

For his poetry is anything but literary. It is part of a modern tradition which is anti-literary and anti-artistic, and which goes back to Apollinaire and the Dadaists, to the collages of Picasso and Braque with their perishable newspaper clippings, to Satie's *musique d'ameublement* which was not meant to be listened to. At Harvard he majored in music and did some composing, and although he wrote poetry too, he was more influenced by contemporary music and art than by what had been going on in American poetry. The poetry that meant the most to him when he began writing was either French—Rimbaud, Mallarmé, the Surrealists: poets who speak the language of every day into the reader's dream—or Russian—Pasternak and especially Mayakovsky, from whom he picked up what James Schuyler has called the "intimate yell." So it was not surprising that his work should have initially proved so puzzling to readers—it ignored the rules for modern American poetry that had been gradually drawn up from Pound and Eliot down to the academic establishment of the 1940s. To ignore the rules is always a provocation, and since the poetry itself was crammed with provocative sentiments, it was met with the friendly silence reserved for the thoroughly unacceptable guest.

It is true that much of Frank's early work was not only provocative but provoking. One frequently feels that the poet is trying on various pairs of brass knuckles until he finds the one which fits comfortably. It is not just that it is often aggressive in tone—it simply doesn't care. A poet who in the academic atmosphere of the late 1940s could begin a poem

> At night Chinamen jump
> On Asia with a thump

was amusing himself, another highly suspect activity. But these poems, so "French" in the pejorative sense the word so often had in America, were essential in the early, muscle-flexing period of his work. Just as he was constantly interested in a variety of people, in several branches of the arts at once and in an assortment of writers of whom one had never heard (Beckett, Firbank, Jean Rhys and Flann O'Brien were among the then almost unknown writers he was reading when I first met him in 1949), so he was constantly experimenting in his poetry in different ways without particularly caring whether the result looked like a finished poem.

The first four or five years of Frank O'Hara's writing—from about 1947 to 1952—were a period of testing, of trying to put together a tradition to build on where none had existed. Except for some rather pale Surrealist poetry written in England and America during the 1930s, and an occasional maverick poet like John Wheelwright or Laura Riding; except for Hart Crane in his vatic moments and the more abandoned side of Dylan Thomas and the early Auden, there was nothing like a basis for the kind of freedom of expression that Frank instinctively needed. One had to look to France, and even there the freedom was as often as not an encouraging sentiment expressed in poetry (*"Il faut être absolument moderne, plonger au fond du gouffre"*) than as a program actually carried out in search of new poetic forms. Even French Surrealist poetry can be cold and classical, and Breton's call for *"liberté totale"* stopped short of manipulating the grammar and syntax of the sacrosanct French language.

So it was natural for Frank to turn to other branches of the arts, closer to home, where a profounder kind of experimentation was taking place. One of these was American painting, which was just then in what is now called the "heroic period" of Abstract Expressionism. This art absorbed Frank to such a degree, both as a critic for *Art News* and a curator at the Museum of Modern Art, and as a friend of the protagonists, that it could be said to have taken over his life. In return it gave him a conception of art as process which, if not exactly new (it was close to Gertrude Stein's definition of creative thinking, which applied both to her own work and to Picasso's: "Real thinking is conceptions aiming again and again always getting fuller, that is the difference between creative thinking and theorising" *), still had never before been applied in America with such dramatic results. Frank O'Hara's concept of the poem as the chronicle of

* Quoted by Leon Katz in his text for the catalog of the show of the Stein collections, "Four Americans in Paris," Museum of Modern Art, New York, 1970.

the creative act that produces it was strengthened by his intimate experience of Pollock's, Kline's and de Kooning's great paintings of the late 40s and early 50s, and of the imaginative realism of painters like Jane Freilicher and Larry Rivers.*

Frank also listened constantly to music, not only to composers of the recent past as diverse as Rachmaninoff and Schönberg (his elegies to both of them are in this volume) but to contemporary avant-garde composers such as Cage and Feldman. We were both tremendously impressed by David Tudor's performance at a concert on New Year's Day 1952 of John Cage's "Music of Changes," a piano work lasting over an hour and consisting, as I recall, entirely of isolated, autonomous tone-clusters struck seemingly at random all over the keyboard. It was aleatory music, written by throwing coins in a method adapted from the *I Ching*. The actual mechanics of the method escaped me then as it does now; what mattered was that chance elements could combine to produce so beautiful and cogent a work. It was a further, perhaps for us ultimate proof not so much of "Anything goes" but "Anything can come out."

This climate—Picasso and French poetry, de Kooning and Guston, Cage and Feldman, Rachmaninoff, Schubert, Sibelius and Krenek—just about any music, in fact—encouraged Frank's poetry and provided him with a sort of reservoir of inspiration: words and colors that could be borrowed freely from everywhere to build up big, airy structures unlike anything previous in American poetry and indeed unlike poetry, more like the inspired ramblings of a mind open to the point of distraction. The result has been a truly viable freedom of poetic expression which, together with other attempts at technical (Charles Olson) and psychological (Allen Ginsberg) liberation, has opened up poetry for today's generation of young poets. In fact without the contribution of poets like these, and O'Hara in particular, there probably wouldn't be a young generation of poets committed to poetry as something living rather than an academic parlor game.

It is not surprising that there should be experiments which didn't work out among these early poems, considering they were part of an attempt to plot a not-yet-existent tradition with reference to what it was and what it wasn't. The posturing that mars "Oranges" and the obfuscation that makes reading "Second Avenue" such a difficult pleasure were useful because they eventually turned out to be unsatisfactory; it would not be necessary to try them again. That it was nevertheless worthwhile to do so once is proved in poems like "Easter"—an example of what I think of as Frank's "French Zen" period, where the same faults don't impair but rather make the poem—whose form is that of a bag into which anything is dumped and ends up belonging there.

*James Schuyler takes issue with my estimate of the role of painting in Frank's work. He says in a letter to me, "I think you are hampered by a feeling of disapproval, or irritation (also felt by others—Schuyler, Koch . . .) for Frank's exaltation of the New York painters as the climax of human creativity, as something more important than his own work and talent. Perhaps the kindest (and it may even be true) way of seeing it would be along the lines of what Pasternak says about life creating incidents to divert our attention from it so that it can get on with the work it can only accomplish unobserved."

What was needed was a vernacular corresponding to the creatively messy New York environment to ventilate the concentrated Surrealist imagery of poems like "Hatred," "Easter" and "Second Avenue." Though a conversational tone had existed in his poetry from the beginning, it had often seemed a borrowed one—sometimes with overtones of home-grown Surrealism, as in "Poem" ("The eager note on my door . . ."); sometimes veering into Parisian artiness ("Oh! kangaroos, sequins, chocolate sodas!/You really are beautiful!"). It was not yet a force that could penetrate the monolithic slipperiness of the long poems, breaking up their Surreal imagery and partially plowing it under to form in the process a new style incorporating the suggestions and temptations of every day as well as the dreams of the Surrealists. In the poems he was to write during the remainder of his life—from about 1954 to 1966, the year of his death—this vernacular took over, shaping his already considerable gifts toward a remarkable new poetry—both modest and monumental, with something basically usable about it—not only for poets in search of a voice of their own but for the reader who turns to poetry as a last resort in trying to juggle the contradictory components of modern life into something like a livable space.

That space, in Frank O'Hara's case, was not only the space of New York School painting but of New York itself, that kaleidoscopic lumber-room where laws of time and space are altered—where one can live a few yards away from a friend whom one never sees and whom one would travel miles to visit in the country. The nightmares, delights and paradoxes of life in this city went into Frank's style, as did the many passionate friendships he kept going simultaneously (to the point where it was almost impossible for anyone to see him alone—there were so many people whose love demanded attention, and there was so little time and so many other things to do, like work and, when there was a free moment, poetry). The term "New York School" applied to poetry isn't helpful, in characterizing a number of widely dissimilar poets whose work moreover has little to do with New York, which is, or used to be, merely a convenient place to live and meet people, rather than a specific place whose local color influences the literature produced there. But O'Hara is certainly a New York poet. The life of the city and of the millions of relationships that go to make it up hum through his poetry; a scent of garbage, patchouli and carbon monoxide drifts across it, making it the lovely, corrupt, wholesome place New York is.

Another way in which his work differs from that of other New York poets is that it is almost exclusively autobiographical. Even at its most abstract, or even when it seems to be telling someone else's story (see Donald Allen's footnote to the poem "Louise," whose title was suggested to Frank by a louse he says he "found on my own immaculate person") it is emerging out of his life. Yet there is little that is confessional about it—he does not linger over aspects of himself hoping that his self-absorption will make them seem exemplary. Rather he talks about himself because it is he who happens to be writing the poem, and in the end it is the poem that materializes as a sort of monumental backdrop against the random ruminations of a poet seemingly caught up in the business of a New York working day or another love affair. This is the tone in great poems like "In Memory of My Feelings," "For the Chinese New Year and for Bill Berkson"; this is the tone of the Odes, Lunch Poems and Love Poems (love is as important as lunch). Half on contemptuously familiar terms with poetry, half embarrassed or withdrawn before its strangeness, the work seems entirely natural and available to the multitude of big and little phenomena which combine to make that almost unknowable substance that is our experience. This openness is the essence of Frank O'Hara's poetry, and it is why he is read by increasing numbers of those who, in Kenneth Koch's phrase, are "dying for the truth."

—JOHN ASHBERY

1926 Francis Russell O'Hara was born on June 27, in Baltimore, Maryland, the oldest of the three children of Katherine Broderick O'Hara and Russell J. O'Hara (both parents were originally from Worcester, Massachusetts).

1927 The family moved to Grafton, Massachusetts, where they resided at 16 North Street.

1933–40 Attended St. Paul's School in Chatham Street, Worcester. Studied piano and, later, harmony with private teachers in Worcester.

1940–4 Attended St. John's High School, then located in Temple Street, Worcester.

1941–4 Studied piano with Margaret Mason as a special student at the New England Conservatory, Boston.

1944–6 Served as sonarman third class on the destroyer USS *Nicholas*. Stationed at Norfolk, Virginia, in California, and sailed in the South Pacific and to Japan.

1946–50 At Harvard College he first majored in music, then changed his major to English; B.A. 1950. Here he met John Ashbery, Violet (Bunny) Lang, and George Montgomery; and published poems and stories in the *Harvard Advocate*. He was one of the founders of the Poets' Theatre, Cambridge, and worked with the Brattle Theatre as stage apprentice during the summer of 1950. On visits to New York he met Jane Freilicher, Kenneth Koch, Fairfield Porter, and Larry Rivers.

1950–1 Graduate school studies at the University of Michigan, Ann Arbor; M.A. 1951. Received a major Hopwood Award in Creative Writing for "A Byzantine Place," his manuscript of poems, and a verse play *Try! Try!* The judges were Karl Shapiro, Louis Untermeyer, and Peter Viereck. The original version of *Try! Try!* and *Change Your Bedding* were produced by the Poets' Theatre in 1951, along with John Ashbery's masque *Everyman,* for which he composed the incidental music. In the autumn he moved into an apartment at 326 East 49th Street. He worked briefly as private secretary to Cecil Beaton, and was employed on the front desk of the Museum of Modern Art. He met Joseph LeSueur and James Schuyler.

1952 *A City Winter, and Other Poems,* his first book of poems, was published by Tibor de Nagy Gallery. He participated in several panel discussions at The Club of the New York Painters on 8th Street. During this period he met Helen Frankenthaler, Barbara Guest, Grace Hartigan, Joan Mitchell, Edwin Denby, Alfred Leslie, Michael Goldberg, Franz Kline, Elaine and Willem de Kooning,

Philip Guston, Jackson Pollock, Ned Rorem, and many other writer and painter friends.

1953 *Oranges* was issued by Tibor de Nagy on the occasion of the exhibit of Grace Hartigan's *Oranges* paintings. He resigned from the Museum of Modern Art to become an editorial associate of *Art News* (1953–5), to which he contributed regular reviews and occasional articles. The second version of *Try! Try!* was produced by the Artists' Theatre, and he acted in the Living Theater's production of Picasso's *Desire Caught by the Tail* at the Cherry Lane Theatre.

1954–55 His essay "Nature and New American Painting" was published in *Folder* 3.

1955–66 He rejoined the Museum of Modern Art in 1955 as a special assistant in the International Program. He assisted in the organization of many important traveling exhibitions, including *The New American Painting* (the first exhibition of American abstract-expressionism circulated in Europe, 1958–9) and *Twentieth Century Italian Art from American Collections* (shown in Milan and Rome, 1960). In 1960 he was appointed Assistant Curator of Painting and Sculpture Exhibitions for the Museum, in 1965 Associate Curator. He selected U.S. representations for the following international exhibitions: IV International Art Exhibition, Japan, 1957; IV Bienal, São Paulo, Brazil, 1957 (selections comprising a group exhibition of five painters and three sculptors and *Jackson Pollock: 1912–56,* a memorial exhibition which later traveled in Europe, 1958–9); XXIX Venice Biennale, 1958 (Seymour Lipton and Mark Tobey sections); with Porter A. McCray, *Documenta II '59,* Kassel, Germany, 1959; and VI Bienal, 1961, São Paulo, Brazil (Robert Motherwell and Reuben Nakian sections). The following exhibitions were shown at the Museum of Modern Art: *New Spanish Paintings and Sculptures,* 1960; *Robert Motherwell,* 1965; and *Reuben Nakian,* 1966. Other exhibitions under his direction which traveled widely after 1961 include: *Magritte-Tanguy; Abstract Watercolors by 14 Americans; Gaston Lachaise; Drawings by Arshile Gorky; Drawings by David Smith; Franz Kline; Recent Landscapes by 8 Americans; Robert Motherwell: Works on Paper;* and *David Smith.* With René d'Harnoncourt, Director of the Museum, he codirected *Modern Sculpture: U.S.A.* (Paris, Berlin and Baden-Baden, 1965–6). At the time of his death he had begun work on a major retrospective of Jackson Pollock, and he had at last secured Willem de Kooning's agreement to his organizing a large retrospective of his paintings. Throughout this period he formed many friendships with people in music, dance, and the theater, among them: Virgil Thomson, Aaron Copland, Morton Feldman, Ben Weber,

Arthur Gold and Robert Fizdale, Lincoln Kirstein, Arnold Weinstein, Merce Cunningham, and Paul Taylor.

1956   He accepted a one-semester fellowship at the Poets' Theatre in Cambridge, where he produced and acted in John Ashbery's *The Compromise;* and met John Wieners. Back in New York he collaborated with Arnold Weinstein and John Gruen on the musical comedy *Undercover Lover.* Met Norman Bluhm returned from Europe.

1957   Moved with Joe LeSueur to 90 University Place. *Meditations in an Emergency* published by Grove Press. Met Gregory Corso, Allen Ginsberg, and Jack Kerouac.

1958   *Stones,* the lithographs he made with Larry Rivers, were published by Universal Art Editions; "Franz Kline Talking" was published in *Evergreen Review.* Met Kynaston McShine of the Museum of Modern Art, and Alex Katz. First trip to Europe, when he met many Spanish artists whom he was later to include in *New Spanish Painting and Sculpture* exhibition; visited Berlin, Venice Biennale, Rome, and Paris. Met Patsy Southgate.

1959   Moved to 441 East 9th Street. *Jackson Pollock* published by George Braziller; "About Zhivago and His Poems" published in *Evergreen Review;* and "An Interview with Larry Rivers" published in *Horizon. Love's Labor, an eclogue* produced by the Living Theater. Met Vincent Warren, the dancer, LeRoi Jones, Bill Berkson, Frank Lima, and many other young poets.

1960   *Odes,* with five serigraphs by Mike Goldberg, published by Tiber Press; *Second Avenue* published by Totem/Corinth Press; *The New Spanish Painting and Sculpture* published by the Museum of Modern Art. *Awake in Spain* produced by the Living Theater, and published in *Hasty Papers. Try! Try!* (in *Artists' Theatre,* edited by Herbert Machiz) published by Grove Press. In October he painted 26 poem-paintings with Norman Bluhm. Met J. J. Mitchell. Traveled to Spain to organize the exhibition of Spanish painting and sculpture, and to Paris.

1961   Became art editor of the quarterly *Kulchur* and contributed several Art Chronicles. Traveled to Rome and Paris in October.

1962   Received a grant from the Merrill Foundation and took a brief leave from the museum to write.

1963   Taught a poetry workshop course during the spring term at the New School for Social Research. Moved to 791 Broadway. Started a collaboration with Jasper Johns on poems/lithographs. In the fall, traveled to Europe for opening of the Kline exhibition at Stedelijk Museum in Amsterdam, and for a second showing at Museo Civico di Torino. Also went to Antwerp, Paris, Milan, Rome, Copenhagen, Stockholm, Vienna, Zagreb, Belgrade, and

Prague. Was in Prague at the time of President John F. Kennedy's assassination. In Amsterdam he visited studios of young Dutch artists and met the artist and novelist Jan Cremer.

1963–4   Collaborated with Al Leslie on the film *The Last Clean Shirt,* for which he wrote the subtitles.

1964   *Lunch Poems* published by City Lights Books. *Audit/Poetry* published an issue "Featuring Frank O'Hara." *The General Returns from One Place to Another* was produced by Present Stages at the Writer's Stage Theatre; it was published in *Art and Literature* in 1965. *Franz Kline, a Retrospective Exhibition* published by Whitechapel Gallery, London. Interviewed David Smith and Barnett Newman for the National Educational Television *Art: New York* Series. Al Leslie projected a collaboration, a series of animated films to be based on O'Hara's poems, but only the drawings for POEM (The eager note on my door said "Call me,") were completed. They were published with the poem in *In Memory of My Feelings* (1967, edited by Bill Berkson).

1965   *Love Poems* (*Tentative Title*) published by Tibor de Nagy; *Robert Motherwell* published by the Museum of Modern Art; and his "Memoir of Larry Rivers" published in the catalog of the retrospective exhibition by Brandeis University. Interviewed by Edward Lucie-Smith for *Studio International.* Helped choose poets invited to Settimano di Poesia, Spoleto Festival of Two Worlds, in the summer. Collaborated with Al Leslie on the film *Philosophy in the Bedroom,* for which he wrote the subtitles. Featured in the National Educational Television *USA: Poetry* Series.

1966   Wrote the introduction for the *David Smith* catalog published by the Museum of Modern Art; traveled to Europe in the spring for the Smith exhibition in Otterlo, Netherlands. His introduction to the *Nakian* catalog published by the Museum of Modern Art. He collaborated with Joe Brainard on collages and drawings. Worked with Arnold Weinstein and John Gruen on the musical play *The Undercover Lover.*

In the early morning of July 24 he was struck and gravely injured by a beach-buggy on the beach of Fire Island. Taken to Bayview Hospital in Mastic Beach, L.I., he was given massive transfusions and underwent an exploratory operation, but his condition deteriorated and he died at 8:50 the evening of the 25th. On the 28th he was buried in the Springs cemetery, near East Hampton. Larry Rivers, Bill Berkson, Edwin Denby and René d'Harnoncourt, Director of the Museum of Modern Art, delivered eulogies; John Ashbery read from his poems; and Allen Ginsberg and Peter Orlovsky chanted sutras over his grave. On his tombstone is carved "Grace to be born & live . . ."   —D.A.

CONTENTS

THE COLLECTED POEMS OF FRANK O'HARA

HOW ROSES GET BLACK

First you took Arthur's porcelain
pony from the mantel and! dashed
it against the radiator! Oh it was

vile! we were listening to Sibelius.
And then with lighter fluid you wet
each pretty pink floored rose, tossed

your leonine head, set them on fire.
Laughing maniacally from the bath-
room. Talk about burning bushes! I,

who can cut with a word, was quite
amused. Upon reflection I am not.
Send me your head to soak in tallow!

You are no myth unless I choose to
speak. I breathed those ashes secretly.
Heroes alone destroy, as I destroy

you. Know now that I am the roses
and it is of them I choose to speak.

GAMIN

All the roofs are wet
and underneath smoke
that piles softly in
streets, tongues are
on top of each other
mulling over the night.

We lay against each other
like banks of violets
while the slate slips
off the roof into the

garden of the old lady
next door. She is my

enemy. She hates cats
airplanes and my self
as if we were memories
of war. Bah! when you
are close I thumb my
nose at her and laugh.

MADRIGAL FOR A DEAD CAT NAMED JULIA

They never understand
she said they always want pictures
as at a dress rehearsal. O!
the castle is for playing nifty dreams to
yourself
and thinking about asparagus soup.

O, this is no medicine
to drive away fear or ennui, my cat
you have typhus and must die!
You are not just guilty of the castle
rats' deaths
but you ate them afterwards, my sick one.

Better you had slipped
a fin to Roscoe the rabbit and gone
west to be in a musical! you
would have been a slinky number in the chorus, a
hoofer
with light feet, my friend's cat, pretty Julia

who is so difficult
to understand. When you say look me over
I don't know what costume
you mean, except your eyes like empty ballrooms
swallow
the castle and its vague green moat.

1

Black crows in the burnt mauve grass, as intimate as rotting rice, snot on a white linen field.

Picture to yourselves Tess amidst the thorny hay, her new-born shredded by the ravenous cutter-bar, and there were only probably vague lavender flowers blooming in the next field.

O pastures dotted with excremental discs, wheeling in interplanetary green, your brown eyes stare down our innocence, the brimstone odor of your stars sneers at our horoscope!

When she has thrown herself to the brook and you see her floating by, the village Ophelia, recall that she loved none but the everyday lotus, and slept with none but the bull on the hill.

Mercy, mercy, drown her, rain!

2

Is it the truth that she will finally conquer? that smiling her gravel smile with those dark teeth rolling in their sockets, bobbing brown corks in the thick pink sea-trough, she will devour me? Shall my flesh, bitten and mangled by the years, fall, a tired after-birth?

Pan, your flesh alone has escaped. Promise me, god of the attainable and always perfecting fruit, when I lie, whether hidden in livid moisture or exposed on gaudy ceramic to the broiling dust, when my reclining bones have made a profound pattern on the earth and, perverse chameleon, have embarrassed mother-of-pearl with their modest chalk, you will sit in memory of thought by my fragile skull and play into my rain-sweet canals your notes of love!

3

What fire murmurs its seditions beneath the oaks, lisping and stuttering to the shrivelled leaves?

I have lain here screaming for five days!

It is a real pleasure to shatter the supercilious peace of these barked mammals.

I hear you! You speak French!

There is water flowing underneath. The rain is making a river to wash my buttocks. My root takes to water, and eddying the filth falls from me. There is a little pile of excrement at my nape like a Japanese pillow.

O delicious rest!

4

O the changing dialects of our world! that we have loved and known a week is seen one day to be a weed!

Once in bed we thrashed about; I knocked over the flower vase and the hurricane lamp.

I was glad to hear them crash to the floor. Your lungs had become a monotone.

Rain is coming through the roof. Drop and drop on my spine. Paralytic. Let me get underneath.

Speak to me in Mandarin! Talk not of rice and rickshaw!

Thunder was in my ears as she placed the lotus in the bud vase, the glass lipped round the stem tightly; he said, is that right?

Yes.

Ah! his face turned green, a briar wall: but autumn! The leaves are dropping! The petals! he seized me. She was terrified. The storm blew the window in. We all cried.

Cease playing harmonicas, you lizards!

5

Decide what you want of my heart most particularly, eagle, and take it. I defy you! Eat on.

Here on this pinnacle you have known what I lacked; and you have gone on eating. I owe you nothing— not even a sentimental tic.

See! where the bones of Bellini lie mossy under the bridge, and the blood of Isabella d'Este like a scarf thrown beneath them!

Bellini's hair thatches a puddle.

You, my centaur, bear me away with your talons and your hunger. Gods! you have chained me with airy fetters to perpetual flight. Mountainward the wind from the sea is the spume from your nostrils, centaur, the heavy slopes are your panting flanks! I struggle naked under your great eye!

Always the same landscape behind us: girls dropping dead in laundry yards, cripples sunning on the snow, the mangy cat crying, the tiny man at the factory pouring wine into his ear. All these lovers!

And for us always the same terrible mountain, our beautiful flesh and our loathing, to urge us on.

6

The light only reaches half way across the floor where we lie, your hair elaborated by my breath.

Your dolls grovel against you like suckling pigs.

As we roll these pebbles that we picked from the sand years ago I see your eyes grow green.

Hear how our lives were changed by the sea whispering from the shell.

I have ripped your dress! I shall now rip you up the middle and eat your seeds!

And now at last I know you. When we meet in the streets how painfully we shall blush!— but in the fields we shall lie down together inside a bush and play secretly.

We know each other better than anyone else in the world.

And we have discovered something to do.

7

As I waded through inky alfalfa the sun seemed empty, a counterfeit coin hung round the blue throat patched with leprosy.

Then in other fields I saw people walking dreamily in the black hay and golden cockleburs; from the firmament streamed the music of Orpheus! and on earth Pan made vivid the pink and white hunger of my senses!

Snakes twined about my limbs to cool them, and springs cold and light sucked my tongue; bees brushed sweat from my eyelids; clouds washed my skin; at the end of the day a horse squandered his love.

The sun replenishes, mirror and magnifier of my own beauty! and at night through dreams reminds me, moaning, of my daytime self.

8

Where is she?

Thoughts, fabulous and eternal, lie unclaimed in my brain. My feet, tender with sight, wander the yellow grass in search of love.

Drought and famine, blossoming souls!

Once a lady asked for her milk to be changed to water; and once a kindly priest scorched the earth with his piss. O gods of the pagans!

Out of the blue grotto near the dried river I summon Pan, god of our hearts. He bears summer heavy in his arms as a limp virgin, her hair polishes his hooves, and white against his sweaty skin her flesh sticks soft.

For you, Pan, are the fruits of the earth: rocks, mountains, fountains, flagpoles, bear your seed! Companion of the beautiful, questioner of the idle, disrupter of the sly, virtuous inseminator, O beloved pimp of our hot flesh, roam throughout the world seeking the salvation of souls!

He turns aside from the breathing limbs, Orpheus-over-the-hills, to play his pipes.

Everyone! Everywhere! Dance!

9

The lily and the albatross form under your lids. Awaken, love, and walk with me through the green fields. Under the mist we need not fear the sound of wings or sneak of tangled roots; the sun will lift. And until heat of day I'll not disturb the grey pearls hanging on your flesh and hair.

Awaken, love, the horses are grazing at our flanks; the gramophone is damp. I forgot to post your letter yesterday. What shall we have for lunch?

Where you go, I go.

10

What furious and accepted monster is this? I receive and venerate your ambition to die. We are all brothers. You do not have tuberculosis. Kiss me.

And on Sunday— oh the rapture! Only the slightest and meanest of women would stay in bed. You are the soul I never have been and your soul is that of my half-sister, moth-eaten and be-twigged. We must find ourselves before the dawn.

There beneath the pool, glassed like a pheasant, is the soul of my first cousin. That is my soul. That one there. Give it me!

Alice, said the Hare, you are a girl.

When I saw the light I came because I knew you'd need me. I prayed that you'd come. I pray I'll get back safely. Oh.

Night, night with its sulphurous pulsations moans about me! Where is the vision I summoned from yonder deity? Why was it ugly?

Ah!

11

Voyagers, here is the map our dear dead king left us: here the rosary he last spat upon: here his score of *Seraglio*: here his empty purse. Let us pray and meditate always on deep things.

Rhinestones and chancres, twins of our bosoms, Christian constellations, resplendent pins, fly on! Dredge for the gold dust in the snow! The blood beneath the ice! A mad mud-junket!

I have won myself over to this cause. I am yours! You are mine! Light bulb! Holy Ghost!

I make my passport/dossier: a portrait of the poet wrapped in jungle leaves airy on vines, skin tender to the tough wind; I ride a zebra through the scrubby plains which nevertheless now and then bloom with cattleyas and blue hydrangeas. The hollyhock is my favorite flower although I have been known to bleed when stabbed with a yucca. Standing in the photograph, then, filthy and verminous but for my lavender shaving lotion, I must confess that the poor have me always with them, and I love no god. My food is caviar, I love only music and my bed is sin. Protected souls, where love and honor gleam through the window I am a stranger. The beauty within me withers at my glance. I stand upright, whip-handle to jaw, betrayer of my race and mud-guard of the bourgeoisie.

Listen to me, you who are attracted: the other dusk in the streets I was the gentlest person you know—my periwinkle irises dripped like the corners of a jackal's mouth. Love me!

Bring me my doll: I must make contact with something dead.

And now that I am initiated I have only to bury you, my dear doll, before I set out. Here beneath this yew I dig a hole for wooden playthings. Man is nothing but this doggy instinct.

Kiss me, kiss me! doll!

I smother!

12

Marine breeze!

Golden lily!

Foxglove!

In these symbols lives the world of erection and destruction, the dainty despots of society.

Out of the cloud come Judas Agonistes and Christopher Smell to tell us of their earthy woe. By direction we return to our fulfilling world, we are back in the poem.

Across the window-sill lies the body of a blue girl, hair floating weedy in the room. Upon her cypresses dance a Black Mass, the moon grins between their legs, Gregorian frogs belch and masturbate. Around the window morning glories screech of rape as dreadful bees, consummately religious, force their way in the dark. The tin gutter's clogged by moonlight and the rain barrel fills with flesh. Across the river a baboon blesses cannibals.

O my posterity! This is the miracle: that our elegant invention the natural world redeems by filth.

A PRAYER TO PROSPERO

to David Hersey who created him for me

Our father local and famous
you are the motive forever
guide of our consciousness

towards you storms beckon
incident for moral proof
and abide by your decision

with you as upon an island
the beast the butcher and
the fool live harmonious

you are guardian of our
faculties and we owe you
what beauty we attain to

your kingdom always is
manifest in villains virgins
everything we understand

and hazard leads us to you
with its invisible voice
or destroys us apart alone

neglect us not now we are
free our need is difficult
strangers steal our voice

HOMAGE TO RROSE SÉLAVY

Towards you like amphibious airplanes
peacocks and pigeons seem to scoot!

First thing in the morning your two eyes
are shining with all night's funny stories

and every time you sit down during the day
someone drops a bunch of rubies in your lap.

When I see you in a drugstore or bar I
gape as if you were a champagne fountain

and when you tell me how your days and nights
seem to you you are my own stupid Semiramis.

Listen, you are really too beautiful to be true
you egg-beater and the next time I see you

clattering down a flight of stairs like a
ferris wheel jingling your earrings and feathers

a subway of smiling girls a regular fireworks
display! I'll beat you and carry you to Venice!

MELMOTH THE WANDERER

These women are given the
bleeding meat of bulls fresh
killed in fields their work
of charity at night to sing
to tombstones and ships

this is the only food they
need wives of shadows their
cheeks suck inwards the waves

are white and thin you can
smell their breaths as they

wash over the hill blue
eyes shine dimly and the
moon spins in its socket of
comparative stone unable to
decide if this is the night

HE will again appear the
real lighthouse beyond the
sleeping city and the sailors
their voices rise it is a
long time lover since youth

AUTODIOGRAPHIA LITERARIA

When I was a child
I played by myself in a
corner of the schoolyard
all alone.

I hated dolls and I
hated games, animals were
not friendly and birds
flew away.

If anyone was looking
for me I hid behind a
tree and cried out "I am
an orphan."

And here I am, the
center of all beauty!
writing these poems!
Imagine!

THE DRUMMER

Baraban! baraban! this is a quick
stiletto bounced tight in tin casket!
The devil you say! Wicked the way
my aunt had to tell me after uncle
rolled over and over inside the locomotive
bellowing like a walrus's guffaw!

Baraban! Tighten till it pricks through
keen as a blonde feather, the saint!
the rib-tickler! oh!oh! the dromedary
sharp-tooth, swaying its all-muscle belly,
has all the luck. What a whale! it careens
over the tracks, dropping bison cakes.
That's the way it was on the prairies,
with a baraban! every two minutes and
the red men knocking us off like turkeys.

Oh uncle, you died in a roadster coupé
fighting the Pawnees and Banshees, you did,
and I'll drum you over the hill, bumpily,
my drum strongly galumphing, kangaroos
on all sides yelping baraban! for you.

THE MUSE CONSIDERED AS A DEMON LOVER

Once at midnight in the fall
I woke with a shout at a light!

it burned all over the sheets, the
walls were panting with excitement!

a picture fell down! and a collage
peeled into a forest floor! It was

an angel! was I invited to a butterfly
ball? did it want to be in my movie?

It winked and took me by the hand:
"Max Ernst waits for us." "Petulant!"

it cried. It shrugged and listlessly
sat on my typewriter. The light went

out. "Que manges-tu, belle sphinx?"
came roaring through the dark; beau!

I muttered and hid my head, but a
wrenching kiss woke me again with a

"Suis-je belle, ô nausée?" We danced
in the light, that angel and I, sang

"Towards you all anguine conebos seem
to scoot"; oh I'd never let that angel

go! But seriously it said to me "I've
got to get a bun." My feet went blind.

The angel's voice called gaily: "There
are faith, hope, and charity, and

the greatest of these is homily. I
am an angel. Trouvez Hortense!"

POEM

At night Chinamen jump
on Asia with a thump

while in our willful way
we, in secret, play

affectionate games and bruise
our knees like China's shoes.

The birds push apples through
grass the moon turns blue,

these apples roll beneath
our buttocks like a heath

full of Chinese thrushes
flushed from China's bushes.

As we love at night
birds sing out of sight,

Chinese rhythms beat
through us in our heat,

the apples and the birds
move us like soft words,

we couple in the grace
of that mysterious race.

POEM

The eager note on my door said "Call me,
call when you get in!" so I quickly threw
a few tangerines into my overnight bag,
straightened my eyelids and shoulders, and

headed straight for the door. It was autumn
by the time I got around the corner, oh all
unwilling to be either pertinent or bemused, but
the leaves were brighter than grass on the sidewalk!

Funny, I thought, that the lights are on this late
and the hall door open; still up at this hour, a
champion jai-alai player like himself? Oh fie!
for shame! What a host, so zealous! And he was

there in the hall, flat on a sheet of blood that
ran down the stairs. I did appreciate it. There are few
hosts who so thoroughly prepare to greet a guest
only casually invited, and that several months ago.

TODY

Oh! kangaroos, sequins, chocolate sodas!
You really are beautiful! Pearls,
harmonicas, jujubes, aspirins! all
the stuff they've always talked about

still makes a poem a surprise!
These things are with us every day
even on beachheads and biers. They
do have meaning. They're strong as rocks.

CONCERT CHAMPÊTRE

The cow belched and invited me
to breakfast. "Ah" I said "I
haven't written a pastoral for

ages! What made you think of
me?" We rolled in the clover
pleasantly, my! it was nice.

With her great fat tongue she
seemed a giantess of good, not
the old fearsome kind. Sweeping

her lashes at the bees she
looked very grand and not at all
bucolic. "Do you know" I said

"that I once wrote a story,
about a cow? And to think I
didn't even know you then!"

She grinned and bit me (did
I know her?) captiously upon
the knee! "Ouch! you bewilder

me!" Her udder splayed richly
in the green, she crooned
silently and threw a leg

over my shoulder. I leaned my
head against her throat. We
looked admiringly skyward.

Very chummy. "Some day I'll
read you my story" I said.
"It will kill you."

AN 18TH CENTURY LETTER

to V. R. Lang

To you who's friend to my angels (all quarrelling)
I write this breathlessly, marvelling
at the power of communication of the Word,
which is not a mystery but is not bored
at being an attribute of the Good. What
is important to you, the angels & me is: Thought
must somehow touch these larger links
& not relax at movie references to the Sphinx.
& Word must not be shy of Good, but strong;
but not belligerent or painless, that is wrong.

Thus the formula for 100% cognition
is 60% true tribulation 40% anxious ebullition,
is it now? & then if we feel the stars
slipping away further & our course
unalterable, we must only remember the Good.
At this the stars will move sensibly, as our food
or as if we had fallen into a mirror,
towards us with quiet consideration nearer
our hearts, & it will be Thought as
Hero. Our joy will give birth to Word, was
ever a cycle more magical, angels, meant
more? Again we'll be free to puzzle the event
but we'll pay respect to the alleged glory
of Unknown, thought and worded in this Allegory.

Picasso made me tough and quick, and the world;
just as in a minute plane trees are knocked down
outside my window by a crew of creators.
Once he got his axe going everyone was upset
enough to fight for the last ditch and heap
of rubbish.
                    Through all that surgery I thought
I had a lot to say, and named several last things
Gertrude Stein hadn't had time for; but then
the war was over, those things had survived
and even when you're scared art is no dictionary.
Max Ernst told us that.
                    How many trees and frying pans
I loved and lost! Guernica hollered look out!
but we were all busy hoping our eyes were talking
to Paul Klee. My mother and father asked me and
I told them from my tight blue pants we should
love only the stones, the sea, and heroic figures.
Wasted child! I'll club you on the shins! I
wasn't surprised when the older people entered
my cheap hotel room and broke my guitar and my can
of blue paint.
                    At that time all of us began to think
with our bare hands and even with blood all over
them, we knew vertical from horizontal, we never
smeared anything except to find out how it lived.
Fathers of Dada! You carried shining erector sets
in your rough bony pockets, you were generous
and they were lovely as chewing gum or flowers!
Thank you!
                    And those of us who thought poetry
was crap were throttled by Auden or Rimbaud
when, sent by some compulsive Juno, we tried
to play with collages or sprechstimme in their bed.
Poetry didn't tell me not to play with toys
but alone I could never have figured out that dolls
meant death.
                    Our responsibilities did not begin
in dreams, though they began in bed. Love is first of all
a lesson in utility. I hear the sewage singing
underneath my bright white toilet seat and know
that somewhere sometime it will reach the sea:
gulls and swordfishes will find it richer than a river.

And airplanes are perfect mobiles, independent
of the breeze; crashing in flames they show us how
to be prodigal. O Boris Pasternak, it may be silly
to call to you, so tall in the Urals, but your voice
cleans our world, clearer to us than the hospital:
you sound above the factory's ambitious gargle.
Poetry is as useful as a machine!
                                        Look at my room.
Guitar strings hold up pictures. I don't need
a piano to sing, and naming things is only the intention
to make things. A locomotive is more melodious
than a cello. I dress in oil cloth and read music
by Guillaume Apollinaire's clay candelabra. Now
my father is dead and has found out you must look things
in the belly, not in the eye. If only he had listened
to the men who made us, hollering like stuck pigs!

V. R. LANG

You are so serious, as if
a glacier spoke in your ear
or you had to walk through
the great gate of Kiev
to get to the living room.

I worry about this because I
love you. As if it weren't grotesque
enough that we live in hydrogen
and breathe like atomizers, you
have to think I'm a great architect!

and you float regally by on your
incessant escalator, calm, a jungle queen.
Thinking it a steam shovel. Looking
a little uneasy. But you are yourself
again, yanking silver beads off your neck.

Remember, the Russian Easter Overture
is full of bunnies. Be always high,

full of regard and honor and lanolin. Oh
ride horseback in pink linen, be happy!
and with your beads on, because it rains.

A SCENE

Pie, tomatoes, eggs, coffee, spaghetti
clobbered the dusty kitchen toward
Mrs. Bennett Smith, teacher of pianoforte.
"Bah!" her husband, frazzled and frenzied, cried
"Your damnable ennui's aroused the Gods!
I'm through with sitting in my unmade bed
praying on my brass knuckles for guidance!
Why do you tootle for our daily bread, you
messy girl, while I in solitude am wracked
by a thousand demon consciences, all arguing!"

"Oh dear, oh dear. You miserable lout!
Whatever I have cooked for you, you throw at me!
At me, who works all day to keep us free
Of psychopathic hospital and all!
If you don't kiss me quick I'll tear off my
chemise, and tell the judge you threw me out!
Why do you speak so nastily, you beast, I'll not
teach pimply girls pianoforte no more!
If you are going to beat me up like this, I
won't live with you. I'm going to do something!"

Pie, tomatoes, eggs, coffee, spaghetti,
meat balls, dishes, shoes, cups and punches
settled soft as airplanes to the kitchen floor.
"Why do I do these things?" said Mr. Smith.
"I never beat you up. I even love the way
your mother cooks. Right now the gods are telling me
I love you. I'll buy you, dear, a television set."

When music is far enough away
the eyelid does not often move

and objects are still as lavender
without breath or distant rejoinder.

The cloud is then so subtly dragged
away by the silver flying machine

that the thought of it alone echoes
unbelievably; the sound of the motor falls

like a coin toward the ocean's floor
and the eye does not flicker

as it does when in the loud sun a coin
rises and nicks the near air. Now,

slowly, the heart breathes to music
while the coins lie in wet yellow sand.

A WALK ON SUNDAY AFTERNOON

The gulls wheeled
several miles away
and the bridge, which
stood on wet-barked
trees, was broad and
cold. Rio de Janeiro
is just another fishing
village, said George.
The sun boomed calmly
in the wind around
the monument. Texans
and Australians climbed
to the top to look
at Beacon Hill and

the Common. Later we
walked round the base
of the hill to the Navy
Yard, and the black
and white twigs stuck
in the sky above the old
hull. Outside the gate
some children jumped
higher and higher off
the highway embankment.
Cars honked. Leaves
on trees shook. And
above us the elevated
trolley trundled along.
The wind waved steadily
from the sea. Today we
have seen Bunker Hill
and the Constitution,
said George. Tomorrow,
probably, our country
will declare war.

LES ÉTIQUETTES JAUNES

I picked up a leaf
today from the sidewalk.
This seems childish.

Leaf! you are so big!
How can you change your
color, then just fall!

As if there were no
such thing as integrity!

You are too relaxed
to answer me. I am too
frightened to insist.

Leaf! don't be neurotic
like the small chameleon.

A LETTER TO BUNNY

1

Once before I tried to tell you
about the incinerator. Last summer
while I was living in the hot
city. All day long at the theatre
would flash in my mind this thing
and that thing too, but usually
that heavy cave where there were
no flames bothered me. And I
could not tell you, Bunny, then:
there was always my spiral
staircase and the diamond pattern
of the well, the eerie sounds of
a quiet house, le Boeuf sur le Toit
and friends who would fight and
would not kill anyone silently.

2

Now, as if this had bothered me ever
since, I find the words are at the
front of my mind. The incinerator
is clearly horrible, soundless, cold.
I went there too often with those things
dear to us both: the tinsels and the
velvets of the stage, the broken sets
and used drapes and tattered scrims,
and they were not consigned to
any glorious or at least bright
immolation. Just a clean dump. Do
you wonder it's bothered me? you
don't, we troupers in private know
all about carnival gestures. Before,
I wrote, "it's grey and monstrous" which
is false, and fumbled after "hints of
mysticism" or "death's shrewdnesses,"
all notions, all collections of sentiment
that make a poem another burner full of
junk. You enable me, by your least
remark, to unclutter myself, and my
nerves thank you for not always laughing.

3

But I still fear to mention the blue
flowers. They scared me most and I
prolong other talk. There were fields of

them around the place, all blue, all
innocent. The artificial is always innocent.
They looked hand-made, fast-dyed, paper.
They nodded ominously in the sun, right
up to the edge of the concrete ramp, a
million killing abstractions, a romantic
absence of meaning, a distorted prettiness
so thorough that my own eyes rolled up
in fear for their identity and I involuntarily
cried at the thought of tiny mirrors where
the object is lost irretrievably in its own
repetition. Is this how beauty accompanies
fear so it can escape us? Do you think these
flowers could be auctioned tintypes or souls
outside hell? Is blue what they mean by
"shun posterity" and "the price of fame" and
"fear of death"? Have I learned it wrong?

4
When anyone reads this but you it begins
to be lost. My voice is sucked into a thousand
ears and I don't know whether I'm weakened.
Bunny, when I ran to you in the summer
night and upset us both it was mostly this,
though you thought I was going away. See?
I'm away now, but I'm here. And even if the
rose has been ruined for all of us by religion
we don't accept these blue flowers. The sun
and the rain glue things together that are not
at all similar, and we are not taken in
by the nearness, the losses, or the cold.
Be always my heroine and flower. Love, Frank.

A PLEASANT THOUGHT FROM WHITEHEAD

Here I am at my desk. The
light is bright enough
to read by it is a warm
friendly day I am feeling
assertive. I slip a few
poems into the pelican's

bill and he is off! out
the window into the blue!

The editor is delighted I
hear his clamor for more
but that is nothing. Ah!
reader! you open the page
my poems stare at you you
stare back, do you not? my
poems speak on the silver
of your eyes your eyes repeat
them to your lover's this
very night. Over your naked
shoulder the improving stars
read my poems and flash
them onward to a friend.

The eyes the poems of the
world are changed! Pelican!
you will read them too!

POEM

The flies are getting slower now
and a bee is rare. Negroes walk
around the fountain with too many
clothes on and whites have lost
already their faint contact with
the sun. Oh fountain! you'll form
solid arcs and the snow will settle
like a sheet over all live color!

The leaves drift from the trees,
the cowards, so they'll be dead tired
when the snow comes. And the sky
gathers its clouds, intending to
winter elsewhere. Here, as in the
gallery, Henry Koerner's parents
say goodbye forever. The flies crawl
their lonely ways. The light hardens.

        WHE
            EWHEE   ry never
d   W   g   always perhaps
    e   hee whee   n   never always
    a   -ed   J   a   like
    r, wick   as   a   are blue velvet
wicked-   .gold, w   n   fl-   in one wind
      y   o   c   uttering
        o u k n
                                F
                                r
                                e
                                i
        y   l
          o   i
          u   c
                                h   u   t
        a   er yo   e
        r   ,   g
        e   r
        t   l   ry   o
        h   not i   e w   f
        e   be   k v o
        e   oh   e   man,-   t
y   S   pretty,   ,
  o   c   r   my   n
  o   g   heh!e azade   o
  hoo   e   ,   d
  a   n   f   t
  n   r   paint   l   o   t
  g   -   e   i
  o   e   pots   ts   a
  n   r
  t   y   e   p   t
  o   o u r   swe   a
  p   i   really
  e   s   n   for   ever!
  a l   t   please
  r   my

THE SPOILS OF GRAFTON

for my sister

Look! the table, like an arrière-
pensée, trembles on its legs and
totters forwards. The cast-iron savings
bank slides down the bannister!
The hall is dark, winter's just
around the corner. Leaves have
stuck and stopped the bright
erector set that I'd made into a
ferris wheel, and the drain pipe
screams with moonlight, when
the moon comes out. The wind
swoops down the hill without
skis, driving mice into the cellar.
By November they'll be upstairs.

Oh piano! hire a moving van!
Put down Mendelssohn and run!

THE CLOWN

As a child, fleeing, trying his body
among trees, feeling the wind, even
then knowing treasures that surprised

him, he cried "I am glorious! it is a
secret that must not be kept from them!"
and saw his voice in the sky's clamors.

And they heard him full of castles
cannons and sharks as he made up the
illustrations for these people, they

sighed over the spectacle and sent him
compliments lest he make a noise or
scandal. He smiled at their solicitude.

At their insistence he pranced higher,
not happy in their excessive interest,
uneasily older by their seriousness.

They were always crying! he noticed
and turned away to meditate. But now
the tears seemed closer and too loud!

He knelt, his ear next his heart, thus
striking an attitude of insight. Ah!
his heart ached like Niagara Falls!

"What have you done?" he screamed "I was
not like this when you came!" "Alas,"
they sighed, "you were not like us."

ODE ON SAINT CECILIA'S DAY

I
Pan seized the reeds
and bound them quickly.
Ah! they'd escape into the silent lake
and he'd be left in idleness and lust
to polish the horns of his forehead!
He wept as he worked, afraid that desire again
might wither and
the music fail,
that beauty might flee his new assault
in the mirror
or in the trees.

II
Laying his hollow mouth
upon the open reeds Pan
saw another love that memory never
captures or kills, a final abstraction
engaging pursuit in its delight.
The piano had not yet been invented, no one
had ever stood
with violin raised
to kiss a madly erotic maiden.
Pan's melody was
his handiwork.

III

All of us who play at
music fill our empty hearts
and slump beside an indifferent pool
in the passionless gloaming, hearing
in the pure geometry of tones
whatever complicated commentaries we wish.
Our motive's not
despicable, in play
we separate desire from the mirage
of sentiment and
ideal choice.

IV

Those who are not very fond
of the tangible evidences of love
shun music and are quiet, doctored by
memory and the martyrdom of Saint Cecilia.
The rest of us play and are played,
seeking like Pan the pattern of our true desire,
willing to follow
motive anywhere
to the tempo of failure and crime.
I wonder can a
virgin make music?

V

For this is necessary. Memory
is a soundless ruin, a habit of
mourning that builds no bridges or hands.
It sighs, a harp no love can search; memory
is without symmetry, supine and bad.
Even with sandwiches and a pocket flask we die
among its black
houses. My dear!
seek things seriously on your flute!
I want you,
tomorrow!

VI

Here, on the phonograph and
in the hall of mountainous
heroes, Schoenberg praises our beauty
and the difficulty of our best chances.
He sings of Cleopatra, not of you, poor
Cecilia, who knew not even the fragile dream of
Mélisande's fate.
Mean pathos! His

voice is too great, too great, it would
burst your
prudent heart!

VII
Impoverished Cecilia! flowers
sent from heaven mean nothing!
They should have been carelessly picked
and strewn about your head and thighs.
And I don't like your instrument, it
embarrasses Pan and all lovers with its machinery.
Music is
incidental
to your virgin contraption, proud girl!
Ah! Cecilia! you
did not love us!

VIII
Beautiful girl, had you been
more the prodigal, less the saint,
intimate music would have called you close
at hand; no monster chewing fingers and
belching into bottles at an intellectual
remove, would have revealed your virtue's artifice!
Fie, Cecilia!
your instrument
will never lead us in war or love!
Today we hallow
others' songs!

POEM

God! love! sun! all dear and singular things!
I am not bad although I am wicked
perhaps, and not too rare. Beat, yes, liquored
to exhaustion, dead tired in sheets, still sings

to me the thunderous redwood's laughings
at my ears, a lover patient and picked,
and the crooning violet's not panicked
by my bloodshot foreskin, swollen lips, wings,

her tongue stays in my ear and sings. Purple
clouds, doubting, say hello across the lawn
and linen, wondering if I'm too gay

with exits, too abrupt with doors. Away,
far! the scratchy tune "L'amant du peuple":
I see a girl tap-dancing on the dawn.

ANIMALS

Have you forgotten what we were like then
when we were still first rate
and the day came fat with an apple in its mouth

it's no use worrying about Time
but we did have a few tricks up our sleeves
and turned some sharp corners

the whole pasture looked like our meal
we didn't need speedometers
we could manage cocktails out of ice and water

I wouldn't want to be faster
or greener than now if you were with me O you
were the best of all my days

MORNING

I've got to tell you
how I love you always
I think of it on grey
mornings with death

in my mouth the tea
is never hot enough
then and the cigarette
dry the maroon robe

chills me I need you
and look out the window
at the noiseless snow

At night on the dock
the buses glow like
clouds and I am lonely
thinking of flutes

I miss you always
when I go to the beach
the sand is wet with
tears that seem mine

although I never weep
and hold you in my
heart with a very real
humor you'd be proud of

the parking lot is
crowded and I stand
rattling my keys the car
is empty as a bicycle

what are you doing now
where did you eat your
lunch and were there
lots of anchovies it

is difficult to think
of you without me in
the sentence you depress
me when you are alone

Last night the stars
were numerous and today
snow is their calling
card I'll not be cordial

there is nothing that
distracts me music is

only a crossword puzzle
do you know how it is

when you are the only
passenger if there is a
place further from me
I beg you do not go

THE THREE-PENNY OPERA

I think a lot about
the Peachums: Polly
and all the rest are
free and fair. Her jewels
have price tags in case
they want to change
hands, and her pets
are carnivorous. Even
the birds.
        Whenever our
splendid hero Mackie
Messer, what an honest
man! steals or kills, there
is meaning for you! Oh
Mackie's knife has a false
handle so it can express
its meaning as well as
his. Mackie's not one to
impose his will. After all
who does own any thing?

But Polly, are you a
shadow? Is Mackie projected
to me by light through film?
If I'd been in Berlin in
1930, would I have seen you
ambling the streets like
Krazy Kat?
        Oh yes. Why,
when Mackie speaks we

only know what he means
occasionally. His sentence
is an image of the times.
You'd have seen all of us
masquerading. Chipper; but
not so well arranged. Air-
ing old poodles and pre-war
furs in narrow shoes
with rhinestone bows.
Silent, heavily perfumed.
Black around the eyes. You
wouldn't have known who
was who, though. Those
were intricate days.

A NOTE TO JOHN ASHBERY

More beautiful even than wild ducks
paddling among drowned alley cats
your green-ringed words roll
nooses of elephant smells and
hoop fine delicate grunts
of giraffes around our neck.

Where the sun is and how sharp
the tree grows we find ourselves
when you push us into the mangoes
from under your Papageno cape.
If we could keep your words forever
in our heart like a tub of frogs

all the dolors and broken-down Fords
would melt away like Turkish delights!
and we'd waddle happily rosary to
belly-button by the fly-bright fur.
Anyway we crane over the wave gawk
pleasantly and make a scaly leg.

A NOTE TO HAROLD FONDREN

The sky flows over Kentucky and Maryland
like a river of riches and nobility
free as grass. Our thoughts move
steadily over the land of our birth.

Ours is a moral landscape. We
breathe deeply, crowded with values.
We love the world, and it feels a cultivation
like a golden bridle under our touch.

At night the earth gives itself over
into our protecting hands. And the same sun
rises every morning. Our responsibility
is continuous. And painful. But it lingers

just above us and scents everything
like the spoor of a brave animal. We seed
the land and its art without being prodigal
and are ourselves its necessity and flower.

A CAMERA

The going into winter and the never coming out,
the vanquished castle moving towards a tourist's
          deliberative gulp,

all those links that seemed exquisitely separable
when confronted in an apple on its majestic bough:
          they do not break.

Once in dreams, where my innocence was fondled by
my desires, I thought the kiss a blessed phenomenon,
          no neural trap;

but now as I lower my head towards you tenderly a wind
from my own mountains blows hair between our eyes,
          woeful prospect!

and the waves that frighten you are the knives I courted
yesterday, a vision of clouds that descend thickly to my
flutter of dismay.

I observe a heart tangled in the lines of my verse, as
in those surrealist paintings where an object wails of
intended magnificence.

A POEM IN ENVY OF CAVALCANTI

Oh! my heart, although it sounds better
in French, I must say in my native tongue

that I am sick with desire. To be, Guido,
a simple and elegant province all by myself

like you, would mean that a toss of my head,
a wink, a lurch against the nearest brick

had captured painful felicity and all its opaque
nourishment in a near and cosmic stanza, ah!

But I only wither to the earth, my personal
mess, and am unable to utter a good word.

AN IMAGE OF LEDA

The cinema is cruel
like a miracle. We
sit in the darkened
room asking nothing
of the empty white
space but that it

remain pure. And
suddenly despite us
it blackens. Not by
the hand that holds
the pen. There is
no message. We our-
selves appear naked
on the river bank
spread-eagled while
the machine wings
nearer. We scream
chatter prance and
wash our hair! Is
it our prayer or
wish that this
occur? Oh what is
this light that
holds us fast? Our
limbs quicken even
to disgrace under
this white eye as
if there were real
pleasure in loving
a shadow and caress-
ing a disguise!

THE POET IN THE ATTIC

High in th' exciting gloom his eye
is king of Zanzibar visiting Czar
potentate lover of crazy horses
he'll never be embarrassed at

He slides warmly o'er the world
on nationally geographic carpets
never afraid of airsickness oh
what a dog he is for th' exotic

And as Nubian niggers rub
their bellies against his open lips
he fashions a constrictor
out of a dead feather boa

The terrible wasps are hard at
the skylight but don't scare
French sailors away from Frank
Nefertit's had a bellyful of wasps!

The ants upon the leaning door
are Ascot Wimbledon racers!
grandpa's teeth are bracelets worn
by mahouts of th' elephants cemetery

As fast as telegraph service in
the Virgin Isles he finds his gorge
rising in Aetna cloudy heady
festive ah! a pit full of pigs

The most ancient of boards creaks
beneath Frank's mammoth back
and lava bursts o'er the flesh! that
childishly thrusts for lost Pompeii

EARLY MONDRIAN

The flower, the corpse in silhouette
its skeleton caught on a red drop
of yellow teaching ivory tusks
a tougher thinner restraint,
withers against the black draped sea

of the Lowlands. Which is always
encroaching, and will presumably
become black lines to grill us
to its erosive vision.
Love makes it poetic though blue,
and because this cloud tangles

itself in the black lines, becoming
spindrift and ambergris,

the sea is beautiful. The flower,
long since washed into Proteus'
car, so classically! is dead. And
before us from the foam appears
the clear architecture
of the nerves, whinnying and glistening
in the fresh sun. Clean and silent.

NIGHT THOUGHTS IN GREENWICH VILLAGE

O my coevals! embarrassing
memories! pastiches! jokes!
All your pleasaunces and
the vividness of your ills
are only fertilizer for
the kids. Who knows what
will be funny next year?
The days will not laugh
at what we say is dry, but
wheeling ridicule our
meanings. The too young
find the grave silly and
every excess absurd. I,
at twenty four, already
find the harrowing laugh
of children at my heels—
directed at me! the Dada
baby! How soon must we all
get rid of love to save
our energy, how soon our
laughter becomes defensive!
O my coevals! we cannot die
too soon. Art is sad and
life is vapid. Can we thumb
our nose at the very sea?

POEM

All the mirrors in the world
don't help, nor am I moved

by the calm emergence of my
image in the rain, it is not

I who appears or imagines. See,
if you can, if you can make

the unpleasant trip, the
house where shadows of my own

childhood are watered and forced
like overgrown bludgeons, you

must look, for I cannot. I
cannot face that fearful usage,

and my eyes in, say, the glass
of a public bar, become a

depraved hunt for other re-
flections. And what a blessed

relief! when it is some
disgusting sight, anything

but the old shadowy bruising,
anything but my private haunts.

When I am fifty shall my
face drift into those elongations

of innocence and confront me?
Oh rain, melt me! mirror, kill!

POEM

Although I am a half hour
early I just missed you:

the keys are dustless on
the table and the toilet

is still bubbling. What
minute on the subway should
have been a proper goodbye?
If connections had been

better would your sore
throat have let you whisper
"Adieu, sagesse, I'll
stay with you forever"?

I am alone now. Only
my own face stares back
from the window, the
record, this white paper.

I put on my black shirt
and my sneakers, whistle
Glazounoff and try to
pick up the dirty room.

Last night I said "I'm
sick." Today is very windy.
The curtains are pulled
back but the sun goes

somewhere else. I've
seen all the movies. I
think I'm going to cry.
Yes. To kill the time.

POEM

If I knew exactly why the chestnut tree
seems about to flame or die, its pyramids

aquiver, would I tell you? Perhaps not.
We must keep interested in foreign stamps,

railway schedules, baseball scores, and
abnormal psychology, or all is lost. I

could tell you too much for either of us
to bear, and I suppose you might answer

in kind. It is a terrible thing to feel
like a picnicker who has forgotten his lunch.

And everything will take care of itself,
it got along without us before. But god

did it all then! And now it's our tree
going up in flames, still blossoming, as if

it had nothing better to do! Don't we have
a duty to it, as if it were a gold mine

we fell into climbing desert mountains,
or a dirty child, or a fatal abscess?

POEM

Let's take a walk, you
and I in spite of the
weather if it rains hard
                    on our toes

we'll stroll like poodles
and be washed down a
gigantic scenic gutter
                    that will be

exciting! voyages are not
all like this you just put
your toes together then
                    maybe blood

will get meaning and a trick
become slight in our keeping

before we sail the open sea it's
                        possible—

And the landscape will do
us some strange favor when
we look back at each other
                        anxiously

POEM

The clouds ache bleakly
and, when they can manage it,
crush someone's head in
without a sound of anger.
This is a brutal mystery.

We meet in the streets
with our hands in our pockets
and snarl guiltily at each other
as if we had flayed a cloud
or two in our salad days.

Lots of things do blame us;
and in moments when I forget
how cruel we really should be
I often have to bite my tongue
to keep from being guilty.

POEM

The ivy is trembling in the hammock
and the air is a brilliant pink
to which I, straddling brilliantly the hummock,
cry "It is today, I think!"

There are white pillars around me
and the grass has stones hidden in it,
my heart is arching over its "Found me?
I'm coming back!" like the eyebrow of a linnet.

O sweet neurosis of a May jump!
pure oar expecting the sea to be white!
it's your stony tear I accept as a slump
in my heart's internationality at night.

O my darling sculpture garden,
you are sorry I went to Alaska?
and if you aren't I am sorrier than a hardon
that refuses to get hard in Alaska.

The sunset is climbing up I think
and I am coming back or going back,
as our love dries itself like ink
after this long swim, this heart attack.

POEM

The stars are tighter
in New Hampshire
though they are deeper
in New Guinea.

At Key West property
is a pair of earrings;
you hang your wash
out over a cloud.

And at Race Point
purple, indigo,
green and magenta
flash knives on waves;

or like Long Beach
there's a ferris wheel
to pump the sunset
dry. Alcohol! Oh

when I was in
the Philippines
the mud was yellow
as a cocktail

and in the sweet rain
the sky was a thumb!
Now you see how the
sky can be everywhere,

even where we go:
I aboard the Jeroboam,
you in a white regatta,
all bearings are possible.

SONG FOR LOTTA

You're not really sick
if you're not sick with love
there is no medicine

the busy grass can grow
again but love's a witch
that poisons the earth

you're not really sick
if you think of love as
a summer's vacation

I'm going to die unless
my love soon chases
the clouds away

and the azure smiles
and browns my strong
belief that love is.

THE ARGONAUTS

The apple green chasuble, so
cut with gold, spins through
the altar like a buzz saw
while nuns melt on the floor.

A skinny Christ, diffident
and extremity relaxed, leans
lightly into the rose window of
the future, and looks away.

The wind squeezes glass leaves,
staining with mulberry the grey
trodden present. Which presently
is scabbed by the sun's healing

cry, not utterly beatific,
yet not the azure exclusion
they had prayed against. Ah!
to be at vespers with Mediterranean

heroes! the muttering drones
casual as surf in our ears,
the black desert which strangles
into adventure our furious host.

THE LOVER

He waits, and it is not without
a great deal of trouble that he tickles
a nightingale with his guitar.

He would like to cry Andiamo!
but alas! no one has arrived
yet although the dew is perfect

for adieux. How bitterly he beats
his hairy chest! because he is
a man, sitting out an indignity.

The mean moon is like a nasty
little lemon above the ubiquitous
snivelling fir trees, and if there's

a swan within a radius of
twelve square miles let's
throttle it. We, too, are worried.

He is a man like us, erect
in the cold dark night. Silence
handles his guitar as clumsily

as a wet pair of dungarees.
The grass is full of snakespit.
He alone is hot amidst the stars.

If no one is racing towards him
down intriguingly hung stairways,
towards the firm lamp of his thighs,

we are indeed in trouble, sprawling
feet upwards to the sun, our faces
growing smaller in the colossal dark.

THE YOUNG CHRIST

My skull, which like an eye strains
sideways and dives into fluttering hair,
in the nick of time cuts down the apple's noose.

About my ankles crash the slender pillars
of Saint Cecilia, with what fragile earth-
deafening organum dear God! dustless.

The hill my bones fornicate and thatch
screams at the pure azure to get
bloody, at the immaculate ocean to be

purer than the royal motive, ticket
to Rome with a homosexual Pharisee.
Nobody'll be playing on that striped beach.

And on the way in from the country I thought
my skull which like a sow burns fat
was ovoid rectum to a frightened girl

at her mirror. What think you? the grass
grows everywhere, I must be a pansy
myself, they say all the Jews are really.

Then, having left Nazareth once for all,
I'll thrust my skull between king's purple thighs
a burning child, adoring and my Father's pyre.

WOMEN

They sit on the stairs and cry.
They hear accidents a week away
screaming "Pierrot Lunaire! why

am I sitting at home while you are
there?" They let their hands fall over
the bannister with an awed sigh or

clear themselves by moaning "I'm in
this too deep. I'll never see the ring
hit the bottom of the well and heaven

will be denied my kind!" And this
becomes sure for them. Even the grass
gets rusty; cobwebs fill the dark trees.

But strong as a violet some deny order.
Wear no pattern but the hazardous
polka dot or stripe. Eat their emeralds.

THE CRITIC

I cannot possibly think of you
other than you are: the assassin

of my orchards. You lurk there
in the shadows, meting out

conversation like Eve's first
confusion between penises and

snakes. Oh be droll, be jolly
and be temperate! Do not

frighten me more than you
have to! I must live forever.

ORIGINAL SIN

Dense black trees trapped and bound! the hairy skull
and pushed wildly against the door of sky!
the paralyzed flowers, ah! with each eye
shrieking, caught in the web of stars, skillful

seiners! in the pitiless sea of will.
Hysterical telegraph vines cry to
the vacationing sky, monstrous! the blue
mother with her breasts to the wall. The hill

groans in support of them all, saddled! grinds
its great wheels like a riverboat, plunging
and deadly in a smoke of bleeding woods.

Beetles scurry under! ostriches, hinds,
dolphins die in the tumult! The unguent
python waits at the open window, broods.

The only way to be quiet
is to be quick, so I scare
you clumsily, or surprise
you with a stab. A praying
mantis knows time more
intimately than I and is
more casual. Crickets use
time for accompaniment to
innocent fidgeting. A zebra
races counterclockwise.
All this I desire. To
deepen you by my quickness
and delight as if you
were logical and proven,
but still be quiet as if
I were used to you; as if
you would never leave me
and were the inexorable
product of my own time.

TARQUIN

Exactly at one o'clock your arms broach
the middle of the moon; surf finds its ways
barred by the bold light and a rough loon sways,
bumps in night's ear, a clattering stagecoach.

It is the murmur and the moonstruck ouch!
of love, its glitter in the dark of days
and hurricane of knights' and cowboys' hey!s
on the fragrant plaza, on the hard couch.

The loon resounds like a knock on the door
of the flooded heart, o sweet Roman light
in ribbons over the prairie's collapse!

and the middle of the sea calls on night
to lay her sleeping head upon the shore
and herd the clouds, their mountainous eclipse.

YET ANOTHER FAN

It's a great shame
Madame Mallarmé
that to sad us your
hands seem swans
on tortoises drifting
elegant in the sea

While birds whine
at the sun we lay
our aching eyes in
your lap and an iron
balustrade holds
firm round our heart

Gently white planes
rove the horizon
as your wings beat
to earth and trample
our freckles into
coral and grass

A HOMAGE

It's a brave thing
        to know the cheapness of
            the world

and suffer in music
    still
        admiring a thing you know

or two
    Erik Satie
        give me some strength

laughing at tinsel
    to love neon
        and not see bandages when

fresh
    rainy
        lovely

there is a leaf
    right in front of my nose
        and the sun has suddenly

miracle
    become willing to enliven
        my wet eyes

    oh Erik Satie
        our man

A POEM ABOUT RUSSIA

What shall we pray
now that you hate us?
castle last mystic land
of the great split soul

and the rite of spring
whose angels were devils
in my lonely childhood
golden and snowy pals

Your heart my second
homeland was the beating
dance and all music's
most passionate blood

the wind of your steppes
swept my cluttered heart
and made my pettish
tears into savage stones

And my hatreds were your
rich fire of longing of
distance of mystery of
silence and fierce animals

Oh now I cry you black
jellied rivers heaps of
startling lovers tundras
of quick wolves! oh tears

A PROUD POEM

Ah! I know only too well how
black my heart is
how at home I am with snails
and dingleberries and

other dark things. Be sure that
no god turns me
inside out like a supple glove or
nibbles my identity.

I am hopelessly happily conceited
in all inventions and
divertissements. I hardly even notice
hurricanes any more

for the glamor of suspension bridges
alleys and pianolas—
I claim them all for my insufferable
genius my demon my dish

and when I'm cornered at the final
minute by cries "you've
murdered angels with toys" I'll go down
grinning into clever flames.

FEBRUARY

The scene is the same,
and though I try to imagine
plinking starry guitars,

and while I spend my
time listening to a foreign
contralto sing the truth,

the earth is everywhere,
brown and aching. At first
it seemed that this life

would be different: born
again in someone else's
arms, after seasons of childhood

and error and defense,
I thought freshly and tried
to change the color of my

habit. New metrics would be
mine in this excess of
love! but I was a braggart

to hope so. My old hurts
kept attacking me at odd
moments, after too many

songs, on public conveyances,
in the blue light of bars. Ah!
I cried, do not blame me,

save your temper for the
others! and at the same instant
in the same breath cried,

break me! I dare you, for
which of us am I? you will
break yourself! And this

became only too true, the
worst of all possible vistas,
my lone dark land.

A RANT

"What you wanted I told you"
I said "and what you left me
I took! Don't stand around
my bedroom making things cry

any more! I'm not going to
thrash the floor or throw any
apples! To hell with the radio,
let it rot! I'm not going to be

the monster in my own bed
any more!" Well. The silence
was too easily arrived at; most
oppressive. The pictures swung

on the wall with boredom and
the plants imagined us all in
Trinidad. I was crowded with
windows. I raced to the door.

"Come back" I cried "for a minute!
You left your new shoes. And the
coffee pot's yours!" There were no
footsteps. Wow! what a relief!

INTERIOR (WITH JANE)

The eagerness of objects to
be what we are afraid to do

cannot help but move us   Is
this willingness to be a motive

in us what we reject?   The
really stupid things, I mean

a can of coffee, a 35¢ ear
ring, a handful of hair, what

do these things do to us?   We
come into the room, the windows

are empty, the sun is weak
and slippery on the ice   And a

sob comes, simply because it is
coldest of the things we know

RENAISSANCE

Bang your tambourine! kiss
my ass, don't mind if they

say it's vicious—they don't
know what music should do to you.

Now, while the drums are
whacking away and your blond

eyes stammer like two kinds
of topaz knocking together,

we'll wear out all the instruments
they usually beg with—the

hand-organ and ocarina and
dirtied trumpet—and brighten

them up! In the midst of these
mad cholers where love becomes

all that's serious we'll cling
like hunks of voluptuous driftwood,

our heart for a sail, the sea
will sigh with relief and end

its moan to clap us as happy
kids! savages ripe from the trees.

A POSTCARD FROM JOHN ASHBERY

What a message! what a picture!
all pink and gold and classical,
a romantic French sunset for a
change. And the text could not
but inspire—with its hint
of traduction, renaissance, and
Esperanto: verily, The Word! By
what wit do we compound in an
eye "Enée racontant à Didon les
malheurs de la Ville de Troie"
(suburban sexuality and the
milles fleurs that were Rome!)
with "Äneas erzählt Dido das
Missgeschick der Stadt Troya"
(truisms and immer das ewig
Weibliche!) and (garlic oscura,
balliamo! balliamo, my foreign
lover!) "Enea che racconta a
Didone le disgrazie della Città
de Troia" followed by yet an-
other, yet wait! in excess perhaps
but as gleaming as the fandango
that echoes through all of Ravel

"Eneas contando a Dido las desgracias
de la Ciudad de Troya"? (let me
dance! get your hands off me!)
for Guérin was thinking of Moors
and Caramba! flesh is exciting,
even in empirical pictures! No?

POEM

Ivy invades the statue.
Say that it is a bust
of Columbus erected by
Italianate citizens. By

contemplating this figure's
lack of astonishment at
the ambitious vine, I know
how the grass feels under

my feet, what it is doing.
To be always on top! as
the financiers say, is that
too much? The grass does

creep, the ivy does twine,
and this marble is no
more able to smile than
I am, at such simple fear.

DRINKING

This is the feared moment   Light
falters because it's been on so long

and music slips into a briefcase or
satchel hungry for breakfast   My face

flushed with its wit and apprehension
begins to pale when the waitress claims

my glass   And I look at friends haltingly
And I look at strangers   The dawn alone

drains the eye   The dumb heart finds
no neighbor to kill its rising fever

SMOKING

The blue plumes drift and
sway before my eyes—against my

grey skies they are quite blue,
perhaps merely gasps of ether

and disappointment fitfully
escaping from a covered heart—

caught, mirrored instantly, a
breath of these thin tourmalines,

a grey heart's horizon of
silence, a shadowy cancan line—

PANIC FEAR

How obscure can woods get?
I've been walking for hours.
No fiery salamander's wandered

by, and not so much as a
bison turd to mark the way!

The sky may be blue, but not
so blue as it ought to be. And
what good does it do when all
I can see is the deceptive glint of
something else in panting waters?

Lord! I will cry if it comes
this way—and it will because I
expect it—and try to duck into
the boskage. Oh lord! I'll cry, but
what lord? This is Pan's altar

and the leaves are like teeth!

BOSTON

These heavy wings lurch in a gummy sky
on either side of me. And it has been
too shiny all the way, the blinding grin
of clouds, the altitude's deafening sigh.

This time I can pick out the buildings my
friends laugh and sulk interestingly in;
with tears of relief I come roaring, thin
and stinging lonely in the earth's flat eye.

Beside the dumpy airport rotting soon
a once-romantic colonial port
the city guards. They run fast on fences

towards me! Another hour and my senses
would have plunged like Icarus' foot 'tween sun
and sea. Yet now on land, find close consort.

A PASTORAL DIALOGUE

The leaves are piled thickly on the green tree
among them squirrels gallop and chuckle
about their emeralds' raindrops; a buckle
like a piece of sun excites them where he

lies drifting in the grass. Towards him they prance,
dart, riot towards the lovers down the mast
and o'er the bounding sod! and she at last
awakes, wakens him quietly. They dance.

"I love you. Their furry eyes and feathers
are for us riches for a shipwrecked pair,
loving on this seashore this forest's porch."

"My hands beneath your skirt don't find weathers,
charts. Should my penis through dangerous air
move up, would you accept it like a torch?"

POEM

I ran through the snow like a young Czarevitch!
My gun was loaded and wolves disguised

as treed nymphs pointed out where the fathers
had hidden in gopher holes. I shot them right

between the eyes! The mothers were harder to find,
they changed themselves into grape arbors, vistas,

and water holes, but I searched for the heart
and shot them there! Then I ran through paper

like a young Czarevitch, strong in the white and cold,
where the shots hung glittering in air like poems.

Wakening at noon I smelled airplanes and hay
rang wildly on long distance telephone
ah! what a misery abed alone
alas! what is that click? hurry! hurray!

the sky was wheeling under sad and grey
sweet clouds but wickedly ne'ertheless shone
outside my lonely coverlets where gone
oh Operator Eighty-one? today

bring me that breath more dear than Fabergé
your secret puissance Operator loan
to pretty Jane whose paintings like a stone

are massive true and silently risqué:
"How closer than Frank to the cosmic bone
comes the bold painting of Fernand Léger"!

THE ARBORETUM

This tree is black with dry feathers
sprawled as if the sun had smashed it
cluttered with broken bicycles
the river flops on the grassy roots

As the light marches towards us
it pushes the whiskered leaves aside
dust roars down from the highway
two Chinese homosexuals walk by

I am thinking of Jane painting
a bicycle falls into the river
the dust is heavy on my shoulders
and the tree is out of sight

What a hot day it is! for
Jane and me above the scorch
of sun on jungle waters to be
paddling up and down the Essequibo
in our canoe of war-surplus gondola parts.

We enjoy it, though: the bats squeak
in our wrestling hair, parakeets
bungle lightly into gorges of blossom,
the water's full of gunk and
what you might call waterlilies if you're

silly as we. Our intuitive craft
our striped T shirts and shorts
cry out to vines that are feasting
on flies to make straight the way
of tropical art. "I'd give a lempira or two

to have it all slapped onto a
canvas" says Jane. "How like
lazy flamingos look the floating
weeds! and the infundibuliform
corolla on our right's a harmless Charybdis!

or am I seduced by its ambient
mauve?" The nose of our vessel sneezes
into a bundle of amaryllis, quite
artificially tied with ribbon.
Are there people nearby? and postcards?

We, essentially travellers, frown
and backwater. What will the savages
think if our friends turn up? with
sunglasses and cuneiform decoders!
probably. Oh Jane, is there no more frontier?

We strip off our pretty blazers
of tapa and dive like salamanders
into the vernal stream. Alas! they
have left the jungle aflame, and in
friendly chatter of Kotzebue and Salonika our

friends swiftly retreat downstream
on a flowery float. We strike through

the tongues and tigers hotly, towards
orange mountains, black taboos, dada!
and clouds. To return with absolute treasure!

our only penchant, that. And a red-
billed toucan, pointing t'aurora highlands
and caravanserais of junk, cries out
"New York is everywhere like Paris!
go back when you're rich, behung with lice!"

ON LOOKING AT *LA GRANDE JATTE,* THE CZAR WEPT ANEW

I
IIe paces the blue rug. It is the end of summer,
the end of his excursions in the sun. He
may now close his eyes as if they were tired flowers
and feel no sense of duty towards the corridor,
the recherché, the trees; they are all on his face,
a lumpy portrait, a painted desert. He is crying.
Only a few feet away the grass is green, the rug
he sees is grass; and people fetch each other in
and out of shadows there, chuckling and symmetrical.

The sun has left him wide-eyed and alone, hysterical
for snow, the blinding bed, the gun. "Flowers, flowers,
flowers!" he sneers, and echoes fill the spongy trees.
He cannot, after all, walk up the wall. The skylight
is sealed. For why? for a change in the season,
for a refurbishing of the house. He wonders if,
when the music is over, he should not take down
the drapes, take up the rug, and join his friends
out there near the lake, right here beside the lake!
"O friends of my heart!" and they will welcome him
with open umbrellas, fig bars, handmade catapults!
Despite the card that came addressed to someone else,
the sad fisherman of Puvis, despite his own precious
ignorance and the wild temper of the people, he'll try!

2
Now, sitting in the brown satin chair,
he plans a little meal for friends. So!
the steam rising from his Pullman kitchen

fogs up all memories of Seurat, the lake,
the summer; these are over for the moment,
beyond the guests, the cooking sherry and
the gin; such is the palate for sporadic
chitchat and meat. But as the cocktail
warms his courageous cockles he lets
the dinner burn, his eyes widen with
sleet, like a cloudburst fall the summer,
the lake and the voices! He steps into
the mirror, refusing to be anyone else,
and his guests observe the waves break.

3
He must send a telegram from the Ice Palace,
although he knows the muzhiks don't read:
"If I am ever to find these trees meaningful
I must have you by the hand. As it is, they
stretch dusty fingers into an obscure sky,
and the snow looks up like a face dirtied
with tears. Should I cry out and see what happens?
There could only be a stranger wandering
in this landscape, cold, unfortunate, himself
frozen fast in wintry eyes." Explicit Rex.

ANN ARBOR VARIATIONS

I
Wet heat drifts through the afternoon
like a campus dog, a fraternity ghost
waiting to stay home from football games.
The arches are empty clear to the sky.

Except for leaves: those lashes of our
thinking and dreaming and drinking sight.
The spherical radiance, the Old English
look, the sum of our being, "hath perced

to the roote" all our springs and falls
and now rolls over our limpness, a daily
dragon. We lose our health in a love
of color, drown in a fountain of myriads,

as simply as children. It is too hot,
our birth was given up to screaming. Our
life on these street lawns seems silent.
The leaves chatter their comparisons

to the wind and the sky fills up
before we are out of bed. O infinite
our siestas! adobe effigies in a land
that is sick of us and our tanned flesh.

The wind blows towards us particularly
the sobbing of our dear friends on both
coasts. We are sick of living and afraid
that death will not be by water, o sea.

2
Along the walks and shaded ways
pregnant women look snidely at children.
Two weeks ago they were told, in these

selfsame pools of trefoil, "the market
for emeralds is collapsing," "chlorophyll
shines in your eyes," "the sea's misery

is progenitor of the dark moss which hides
on the north side of trees and cries."
What do they think of slim kids now?

and how, when the summer's gong of day
and night slithers towards their sweat
and towards the nests of their arms

and thighs, do they feel about children
whose hides are pearly with days of swimming?
Do they mistake these fresh drops for tears?

The wind works over these women constantly!
trying, perhaps, to curdle their milk
or make their spring unseasonably fearful,

season they face with dread and bright eyes.
The leaves, wrinkled or shiny like apples,
wave women courage and sigh, a void temperature.

3
The alternatives of summer do not remove
us from this place. The fainting into skies

from a diving board, the express train to
Detroit's damp bars, the excess of affection
on the couch near an open window or a Bauhaus
fire escape, the lazy regions of stars, all
are strangers. Like Mayakovsky read on steps
of cool marble, or Yeats danced in a theatre
of polite music. The classroom day of dozing
and grammar, the partial eclipse of the head
in the row in front of the head of poplars,
sweet Syrinx! last out the summer in a stay
of iron. Workmen loiter before urinals, stare
out windows at girders tightly strapped to clouds.
And in the morning we whimper as we cook
an egg, so far from fluttering sands and azure!

4
The violent No! of the sun
burns the forehead of hills.
Sand fleas arrive from Salt Lake
and most of the theatres close.

The leaves roll into cigars, or
it seems our eyes stick together
in sleep. O forest, o brook of
spice, o cool gaze of strangers!

the city tumbles towards autumn
in a convulsion of tourists
and teachers. We dance in the dark,
forget the anger of what we blame

on the day. Children toss and murmur
as a rumba blankets their trees and
beckons their stars closer, older, now.
We move o'er the world, being so much here.

It's as if Poseidon left off counting
his waters for a moment! In the fields
the silence is music like the moon.
The bullfrogs sleep in their hairy caves,

across the avenue a trefoil lamp
of the streets tosses luckily.
The leaves, finally, love us! and
moonrise! we die upon the sun.

A CHINESE LEGEND

Hahahahaha! he laughs briefly
and is for that deepness
the father in a blue sky.

Lizards jangle their machetes
at him, and emeralds get
flaws like common colds.

And then he hits on a
solution, that is, a tiger
has been menacing maidens,

eating up the village
landscape, he must avenge.
So hahahahaha! eat up.

Later, lying on silk pillows
he jiggles a bellyful of
rice and lemon cakes and

saffron sticks and poppy
pellets, sharkfin toothpicks,
whale piss. Too fat?

He lolls till the moon
is up and flopping through
a cloudy sky. Sneaking

behind a warm flat rock
he hears a titter, leaps!
forty feet to grumpy

stripe-ass! scrunches
drat-puss into thick dirt
by the eyebrows! and

old snarl and blooded fang
suffocates thrashingly!
Beneath that full moon.

Pausing to pant and
hesitate, now done, he
knows of good sleep, dear.

How that fat he in
tigerskin wrapt round
grins handstands, holidays!

AFTER WYATT

The night paints inhaling smoke and semen.
   The frail face pulses like a parachute,
   corridors of shakes melting from the boot
   of that surf north breathes bloody in simoon.
On the tide when the galleon is moved
   by the fatal dolor of mariners,
   a cry becomes whole night of war in us;
   I'm wrecked on what's no grunted green behoved
or truly sufferable. The white will
   and jealousy of death beside the sea
   crushes when not all dark and grievable
like the monster who specks the distance, leers,
   collapses, shouts "You can die even me,"
   roaring up, throttles whom he fed for years.

THE SATYR

The trees toss and plunge in a skyblue surf!
an automobile comes whizzing, falls by
as the floor of the lake against my thigh
flings needles and leaves like a kiss or scarf

The bend of the shore where my armpits laugh
runs after the cars that drop from my eye
I'll recapture them all before I die
without losing my limbs in the thick turf

Without fearing the bluejays and pine cones
that rob the sun and torment my cold face
I'll become the Lover of the quick world

For these trees waves and thieves I'm eager! whirled
and drowned in maelstroms of rhododendrons!
full flowers! round eyes! rush upward! rapture! space!

THE TOMB OF ARNOLD SCHOENBERG

The avalanche drifts to earth through giant air
your pure monument's loud windless blizzard,
pianoforte of celestial hazard
strangling the swans of peace with arms of hair,

father of sound whose harp's fallen to earth
in bitterness and snows of savage age.
Ice silences your noble eyes, image
of spring, thus my tears your death gives to birth

over Pacific pines and the blue crouch
of the setting world. This birth screams in gaze
blind with art's crushing defeat. The dull roar

of incessant soldiers muffles the touch
of spherical music with brutal lays.
I weep upon your bier, this glacial shore.

POET

He'd be wispy in a double feature,
is one transfixed before the naked arm
of a lady shirt maker, sings the psalm
at the supper show night before Easter.

Is in a jam and doesn't know the worth,
escapes always and's forever blinded
to the casements there, wrapped behindhand
in railroads and the moony look of earth.

"Does it sting of boyish failure?" or fill
the streets with wilderness and derision?
He's anxiety like a whippoorwill

caught by camera over Canada. Loan
him to rending and wrath, subdivision
of love. It's his international zone.

A MODERN SOLDIER

Essays, boring conversations and vistas
smile in the barracks fire if you march off.
Or the red tapestry of an elbow. Accepting
all the dirt of the camp, it's enough!

you cry, and "if, in the month of dark
December" there are no trollops near
it's the time for preparing acceptances:
to be exceptionally blue with fear,

to kiss a trembling palm from the hatch
of an ascending airplane and be a lover
in the azure cheerfully, in tears, and
listen: such pauses, multifarious thinks!

behind the dark head's ominous gully.
Still carom the outraged source books
and sweaty bellies and soft staring pupils
jetted in the obsessive years of looks

and self-reprimands, sentimental colloquies,
ugh! all that; but the landscape with a gun
in your hand becomes friendly, sucking you
down, "ain't that your idea of good fun?"

because you are the scholar with his feet
in a bottle of earth, your ears are true
I love yous, deaf to the ballast. So you shoot!
ripping into a silence which is already you.

A MEXICAN GUITAR

Actors with their variety of voices
and nuns, those arch campaign-managers,
were pacing the campo in contrasting colors
as Jane and I muttered a red fandango.

A cloud flung Jane's skirt in my face
and the neighborhood boys saw such sights
as mortal eyes are usually denied. Arabian day!
she clicked her rhinestone heels! vistas of lace!

Our shouting knocked over a couple of palm trees
and the gaping sky seemed to reel at our mistakes,
such purple flashing insteps and careers!
which bit with lavish envy the northern soldiers.

Then loud startling deliberation! Violet peered,
hung with silver trinkets, from an adobe slit,
escorted by a famished movie star, beau idéal!
crooning that dejected ballad, "Anne the Strip."

"Give me back my mink!" our Violet cried
"and cut out the heroics! I'm from Boston, remember."
Jane and I plotz! what a mysteriosabelle!
the fandango died on our lips, a wintry fan.

And all that evening eating peanut paste and onions
we chattered, sad, of films and the film industry
and how ballet is dying. And our feet ached. Violet
burst into tears first, she is always in the nick of time.

JANE AWAKE

The opals hiding in your lids
    as you sleep, as you ride ponies
mysteriously, spring to bloom
    like the blue flowers of autumn

each nine o'clock. And curls
    tumble languorously towards
the yawning rubber band, tan,
    your hand pressing all that

riotous black sleep into
    the quiet form of daylight
and its sunny disregard for
    the luminous volutions, oh!

and the budding waltzes
    we swoop through in nights.
Before dawn you roar with
    your eyes shut, unsmiling,

your volcanic flesh hides
    everything from the watchman,
and the tendrils of dreams
    strangle policemen running by

too slowly to escape you,
    the racing vertiginous waves
of your murmuring need. But
    he is day's guardian saint

that policeman, and leaning
    from your open window you ask
him what dress to wear and how
    to comb your hair modestly,

for that is now your mode.
    Only by chance tripping on stairs
do you repeat the dance, and
    then, in the perfect variety of

subdued, impeccably disguisèd,
    white black pink blue saffron

and golden ambiance, do we find
the nightly savage, in a trance.

1951

Alone at night
in the wet city

the country's wit
is not memorable.

The wind has blown
all the trees down

but these anxieties
remain erect, being

the heart's deliberate
chambers of hurt

and fear whether
from a green apartment

seeming diamonds or
from an airliner

seeming fields. It's
not simple or tidy

though in rows of
rows and numbered;

the literal drifts
colorfully and

the hair is combed
with bridges, all

compromises leap
to stardom and lights.

If alone I am
able to love it,

the serious voices,
the panic of jobs,

it is sweet to me.
Far from burgeoning

verdure, the hard way
is this street.

DIDO

Suppose you really do, toward the end, fall away into a sunset which is your own self-ignited pyre? is it any the less a sunset just because you stopped carrying the torch? I must pull myself together tomorrow early, is market dallying and this time I've got something to get rid of, inherited I'd never want. "Like has a way of making everything die." Should I now that the war is over voluntarily about face and shoot things squarely and in the middle to test the steadiness of my rust-covered hand which has been so dependable of late? I do not love hunting or any of the Roman positions, yet foreigners frighten the very shores! Am I too lady luck or nuts?

Once when the bishop's blague had become a kernel I raced to the nearest theatre "babes in arms" and earned some small relaxation, even though they all said it would ruin the babies' eyes. Would they were beggars these days! if only I weren't feeling sentimental, but how else can you get passionate? and I at least know that that's my devoir. Yes, dear heart, gloriously ruined, lamentably grey, the poor tattered plaything with a heart of whale blubber, it to be in Sydney Australia married to an architect! But this is most heartbreaking of all, for the truly grave is the most objective like a joke: you advance unawares while misery surrounds you on the lips in the bars, and it accepts you as the characteristic sibilance of its voice, hitherto somewhat less divine.

I could find some rallying ground like pornography or religious exercise, but really, I say to myself, you are too serious a girl for that. The leaves do not wither because it is winter, but because they stay there and know better, and they want what must happen, they are the lying down kind. If, when my cerise muslin sweeps across the agora, I hear no whispers even if they're really echoes, I know they think I'm on my last legs, "She's just bought a new racing car"

they say, or "She's using mercurochrome on her nipples." They'd like to think
so. I have a stevedore friend who tells everything that goes on in the harbor.

Well all right. But if this doesn't cost me the supreme purse, my very talent,
I'm not the starlet I thought I was. I've been advertising in the Post Office
lately. Somebody's got to ruin the queen, my ship's just got to come in.

BROTHERS

The pursefishers have flaunted their last
red sail and swung in from the sea,
sleeping all the way to Grand Army Plaza for
the sheer underground of it, you could.

The stacked paintings, the half light, dirty
feet and the snore from next door, they
tell how thin a floor can get when you must
work to make succulent the dish that's art.

"Are you dishing art?": John's most sophistical,
Jimmy seriousest, Kenneth large, locomotive,
laughing like Midas of the Closed Fist.
When to the silent generosities I stumble home.

A CITY WINTER

I

I understand the boredom of the clerks
fatigue shifting like dunes within their eyes
a frightful nausea gumming up the works
that once was thought aggression in disguise.
Do you remember? then how lightly dead
seemed the moon when over factories
it languid slid like a barrage of lead
above the heart, the fierce inventories

of desire. Now women wander our dreams
carrying money and to our sleep's shame
our hands twitch not for swift blood-sunk triremes
nor languorous white horses nor ill fame,
    but clutch the groin that clouds a pallid sky
    where tow'rs are sinking in their common eye.

2

My ship is flung upon the gutter's wrist
and cries for help of storm to violate
that flesh your curiosity too late
has flushed. The stem your garter tongue would twist
has sunk upon the waveless bosom's mist,
thigh of the city, apparition, hate,
and the tower whose doves have, delicate,
fled into my blood where they are not kissed.

You have left me to the sewer's meanwhile,
and I have answered the sea's open wish
to love me as a bonfire's watchful hand
guards red the shore and guards the hairy strand,
our most elegant lascivious bile,
my ship sinking beneath the gutter's fish.

3
How can I then, my dearest winter lay,
disgorge the tasty worm that eats me up
falling onto the stem of a highway
whose ardent rainbow is the spoon's flat cup
and in the vilest of blue suited force
enamored of the heated needle's arm
finds the ministrant an own tongue's remorse
so near the blood and still so far from harm,
thus to be eaten up and gobbled down
volcanoes of speedometers, the strike
that heats the iris into flame and flow'rs
the panting chalice so a turning pike:
    you are not how the gods refused to die,
    and I am scarred forever neath the eye.

4
What are my eyes? if they must feed me, rank
with forgetting, in the jealous forest
of lustrous brows, so luminously blank
through smoke and in the light. All faint, at rest,
yet I am racing towards the fear that kills
them off, friends and lovers, hast'ning through tears

like alcohol high in the throat of hills
and hills of night, alluring! their black cheers
falling upon my ears like nails. And there
the bars grow thick with onanists and camps
and bivouacs of bears with clubs, are fair
with their blows, deal death beneath purple lamps
    and to me! I run! closer always move,
    crying my name in fields of dead I love.

5
I plunge me deep within this frozen lake
whose mirrored fastnesses fill up my heart,
where tears drift from frivolity to art
all white and slobbering, and by mistake
are the sky. I'm no whale to cruise apart
in fields impassive of my stench, my sake,
my sign to crushing seas that fall like fake
pillars to crash! to sow as wake my heart

and don't be niggardly. The snow drifts low
and yet neglects to cover me, and I
dance just ahead to keep my heart in sight.
How like a queen, to seek with jealous eye
the face that flees you, hidden city, white
swan. There's no art to free me, blinded so.

ASHES ON SATURDAY AFTERNOON

The banal machines are exposing themselves
on nearby hillocks of arrested color: why
if we are the anthropologist's canapé
should this upset the autumn afternoon?

It is because you are silent. Speak, if
speech is not embarrassed by your attention
to the scenery! in languages more livid than
vomit on Sunday after wafer and prayer.

What is the poet for, if not to scream
himself into a hernia of admiration for all

paradoxical integuments: the kiss, the
bomb, cathedrals and the zeppelin anchored

to the hill of dreams? Oh be not silent
on this distressing holiday whose week
has been a chute of sand down which no
factories or castles tumbled: only my

petulant two-fisted heart. You, dear poet,
who addressed yourself to flowers, Electra,
and photographs on less painful occasions,
must save me from the void's external noise.

FEMALE TORSO

Each night plows instead of no head
nowhere. The gully sounds out
the moonlight, a fresh stream
licks away blood ties they'd touched
my trail by. Clouds pour over engines
and the children log down this chute
who is the vernal rattletrap. See,
much am I missed among the ancients.
Here jerk the cord around my neck
to heel. I'm the path so cut and red.
She shall have her arms again.

IN HOSPITAL

These laboratories and those picnics
swing out over the bay
in a cradle of sleet

and seem indigenous, to the aged.
A bushel of cauliflower dirty
by the bed smells sweet,

like roses that were fed on snow.
Eyes, failing, call immense
suns a cow, a lemon,

and shrivelled lips, soon to be
smothered in earth, kiss men
whose youth's perennial

as letters from nieces. The morning
flows after twilight, a
luminous river,

and who steps ashore upon that
white sheet, need not
imagine permanence.

OVERLOOKING THE RIVER

Clouds or cloudbursts, the haze
reaching for Afghanistan-by-the-Sea,
the willowing weathers for. Now the sighs
darting into a tender fracas leeward and lee

of the trembling bosky shore.
When to the fameless currents of the subway
leathern angels drop their fingers where
they fall scuttling redly, cross Broadway,

and disappear into the Park,
the oar juts fleshily out dripping with
silver, singing its arietta of planks and rock,
while the bracing wind makes a monolith

of my always pushing westward.
The falling water of the starry signs

seeks out that love a child first did in Sherwood
Forest, with rogues, by the mill's pouring turbines.

POEM FOR A PAINTER

The ice of your imagination lends
an anchor to the endless sea of pain,
a harsh cry to the dumb smack who's again
caught in the pitiless tide of hot ends.

Such a trough as I'm in! blind in the rain
the minotaur, hero, struggles. Embrace
engulfs him, and no Muse but the whore. Grace,
you are the flowergirl on the candled plain

with fingers smelled of turpentine. New Year
be shouted, but not by serious you.
Sea and engine crash on the hapless ear

but your ice holds fast, willed art in a nest
of worlds. Hold fast this vessel as your guest,
for fiery spindrift tears me into view.

AN ABORTION

Do not bathe her in blood,
the little one whose sex is
undermined, she drops leafy
across the belly of black
sky and her abyss has not
that sweetness of the March

wind. Her conception ached
with the perversity of nursery
rhymes, she was a shad a
snake a sparrow and a girl's
closed eye. At the supper, weeping,
they said let's have her and
at breakfast: no.

              Don't bathe
her in tears, guileless, beguiled
in her peripheral warmth, more
monster than murdered, safe
in all silences. From our tree
dropped, that she not wither,
autumn in our terrible breath.

SUNSET

You fragile woman whose profile barely discerns
itself at the edge of the penthouse in a shrub,
do you know that the airplanes are in danger of
your thoughts? the nougatines of your fingertips
and tender acanthus which ignores your breasts!
I imagine you have counted the bricks of my eyes.

Across the river the thrashing lunatics quench
and lie as a garbage scow fondles the seventeen bridges,
the blue-eyed batty and their realistic charades
of games and bounty. They're too cold for us. We miles
apart and bravely standing each other's sole possibility,
the violet and strangling hour before sundown

where the punishment we'd been denied at ruby settings
will perhaps, passionate with impatience, decline
our future like a pack of cards. Now you have turned,
tinkling like a wind-bell, your gaze to the East: conquered
the tempestuous bulging of my cloud-borne heart
which strains to burst this slender fist.

The guts that stream out of the needle's eye
of the pigeon cote where the old people rest,
there upon the bird sanctuary the gulled heart
flaps its breezy spieling of nationality.

Praying perhaps for rain and a chess partner
best friends pay off the baby mailman with a bust
and arrest their attention to the feathers falling
from trees that had been in song too long,

oi! prayer, prayer, be mine your lazy latenesses.
And where the path turns its cinders forward in
the face of a jealous trapeze diva, tantamount
glittering in wettest green metal, tzing me,

the west of the passive, upon whose elbow of myrrh
reclines the weight of history, the type who rode
elephants down hillsides into the fray! Those guts
our brains, bashed out in flight against the bridge.

FUNNIES

Deep to Alley Oop
the rocks and hairs
when babyface sucked
in came out a cheek
of newsprint and snow.

Is able a century
whole of crust by files
to find the wetness new
in a tarn of tiptoes
and a cold spa full

of hairy elephants so
they walked right out

of life. The sarong always
such shapely fur near
now. They're not young.

WASHINGTON SQUARE

That arch bestrides me, French
victory! the golden staff of the savior

with blue lids. The soldiers filing
at my feet hiss down their drinks

and are savagely decorated, savagely
turned, their gentle feathers torn to medals

in the air. Gold falls upon them, because
there is no love, and it is not the sun.

Jane and Mark flutter along the plaza
underneath the fainting gingko trees

and are cheered by pearly uniform horses,
still, at parade rest. The guns ejaculate

into clouds abstractedly, and the day
is in danger of passing without wickedness.

ELEGY

Ecstatic and in anguish over lost days
we thrust ourselves upon all poor fish
who came drifting into our starry net
and cost them the supreme price of love

mercilessly, while the sun went out
and the moon sank into a bathos, the
music of the spheres, the deafness of
the heavens we look to for a breather.

Accept, o almighty Dead, the tribute
of our kicks, in the impassioned loosenesses
of your gravel sarongs, and accept
the multifarious timidities of the youthful

whose eating has not yet crystallized
into the compunction of the verdant skies.
Accept the salt seas flowing from our own
precious organs, the whirling notes

which may seem savage to your supine
majesties yet is the fugal diadem of
your dirty virginities. We were lovely.
Now lay for you upon sidereal simplicities.

ELEGY

Salt water. and faces dying
everywhere into forms of fish.
Be unseen by the abandoned flying
machine near the jetty by the bird's
wrist on the empty cliff crying!

From beyond the Atlantic beyond
the sand dunes' leonine crouch
not a mast thrusts up its nose on
the sky's pillow. The mean slouch
of fishermen wakes the falling vagabond.

And our love. it follows them
heaved like dung by tridents on
the ocean floor, our famous men!
and breaks our heart the ascension
to the sea's ferocious surface! then

escaping never into that realm
of shining, the perfect configurations,
the Bear of desire! Could we o'erwhelm
all earth with our heroes these lacerations
still, these waves, gnaw down our helm.

COMMERCIAL VARIATIONS

1
"When you're ready to sell your diamonds
it's time to go to the Empire State Building"
and jump into the 30s like they did in 1929.
Those were desperate days too, but I'd no more
give up our silver mine, Belle, just because gold
has become the world standard look, than all
your grey hairs, beloved New York from whence
all the loathsome sirens don't call. They would like
to take you away from me wouldn't they? now that the fever's
got me and there're rumors of a Rush in California
and pine fields in Massachusetts as yet unindustrialized.
That's how they act to The American Boy
from Sodom-on-Hudson (non-resident membership
in The Museum of Modern Art) as if it weren't the best
little municipality in the U.S. with real estate
rising like a coloratura, no road sighs, and self-plumbing;
and more damned vistas of tundra than Tivoli
has dolce far niente. It's me, though, not the city—
oh my god don't let them take me away! wire The Times.

2
Last year I entertained I practically serenaded
Zinka Milanov when the Metropolitan Opera Company
(and they know a good thing) came to S-on-H, and now
I'm expected to spend the rest of my days in a north-state
greenhouse where the inhabitants don't even know
that the "Jewel Song"'s from *Carmen.* They think oy
is short for oysters. I may be tough and selfish, but
what do you expect? my favorite play is *William Tell.*
You can't tell me the city's wicked: I'm wicked.
The difference between your climate and mine is
that up north in the Aurora Borealis the blame falls like rain.

In the city's mouth if you're hit in the eye it's the sun
or a fist, no bushing around the truth, whatever that is.
I like it when the days are ducal and you worry fearlessly.
Minding the Governor your lover, and the witch your sister,
how they thought of the least common denominator and're dazzling!

3
The sky has opened like a solarium and the artillery
of the pest has peddled into the feathery suffering
its recently published rhymes. How that lavender weeping
and beastly curses would like to claim the soldiers its own,
and turn the "tide" of the war! But they, shining,
mush back to The Trojan Horse, climb up, and ride away.

4
Yes, the mathematicians applauded when the senator
proved that god never sent cablegrams or disappeared
except when voodoo or political expediency flourished,
it being sweet times, in Tammany in the 90s
and before one hated to seem too cocky or too ritzy.
One thought a good deal then of riding for pleasures
and in shrubbery of a casual fistfight Vesuvius smarting
and screaming creamed rubily as if to flush the heavens.
As the glassy fencing of sunrise in a fish market
cries out its Americanism and jingoes and jolts daily
over the icebergs of our historically wispy possum-drowsy
lack of antiquity, we know that art must be vulgar to say
"Never may the dame claim to be warm to the exact,
nor the suburban community amount to anything in any way
that is not a pursuit of the purple vices artsy-craftsy,
the loom in the sitting room where reading is only aloud
and illustrative of campfire meetings beside the Out Doors
where everyone feels as ill at ease as sea-food."

Often I think of your voice against the needles of dawn
when the dampness was operatic in Ann Arbor lilacs
and the gold of my flesh had yet to be regimented in freckles.
Now I must face the glass of whatever sliver's my smile,
each day more demanding me for what I have always tossed aside
like listening to *Erwartung* hanging by your thumbs;
I turn grey over night screaming feverishly scoreful, note
for note as I have always believed, for I know what I love
and know what must be trodden under foot to be vindicated
and glorified and praised: Belle of Old New York
your desperation will never open in *La Forza del Destino*
which was my father's favorite opera when he tried to jump
out a window on New Year's Eve in 1940, thirty days

before I ditched the stable boy who gave me the diamonds
I'm turning in today for a little freedom to travel.

COLLOQUE SENTIMENTAL

"It's too wrestling at the beach the sand
the sand shackles the wrists shunt."

Tired and walking's slighter than grips eye.
"The big book for dinner and after, gin.

I want you to succeed but strap you
beauty befuddled and its soothing filth?"

Grass on the screens and those mosquitoes
humming humming. "Gee I don't know

if bawling really interests me. When I was
Scandinavia sang two days but I three away

all the money." The wind's cold plunging
apart strides into narrow staring caves.

"I love you more than life itself, but what's
most painful is most peaceful and I

I must be punished because I'm popular.
It's wet and your neck is knotted with mine."

PORTRAIT OF GRACE

Her spinning hair webbed lengthening through
amber silk, where the colored plaster and laughter
find division.

Silently, the presence spills
its inviolable distances into the studio. Blue.
Most remote white of a mountain range in hours
of weeping. The trees are felled,
they fed that silken mesh. And now to ocean,
the roses grow. The plaited ordure that sings
its dust into the feet, it shall be snow; she bears
no memory like a mast, nowhere becalmed, enraged,
no spear.
        If each thing become crystal,
"I'll not construct that flaw," to be beauty itself,
then must she take forests in her arms of water
and disappear behind us, while we greet that clarity
of sunrise which is woman's praise, so ripe
in its begrudging. She does not falter, she has gone.

She will darken, decisive as a light bulb, when
the building crumbles. She had thought herself tough,
but now each day, trembling and cloudy she sighs,
feathered, for that virginity which seeks her out.
The harp would flee her pale fingernails,
but the sea may flatten into a smile before she's done
with those bruisings.
               She has not a natural voice.
She's not a star.
             She has ridden sidesaddle to churches,
is no frequenter of palace or barn. Now
celebrate her, for that light which is anguish will
again and again illumine her our shores, coming to her
as a downy bird, but she will not forget the eagle.
Her eyes are not glass children. Let not that firebrand
stolen from the summits mark her brow.

JANE AT TWELVE

Wishing away all her time the little girl faces the window and breathing is
to her words, what words are to an idiot, so are the pears in a nightmare thud-
ding from wet boughs, that speed. So are all the numbers, inexplicably personal
like degrading acquaintances.

    At notion counters and bargain trays the monkeys stare at her disarmingly, tearing their leaves to yellow and green shreds, calling her by a first name her mother has long since forgotten. It is her legend, similar to others, which moves them so and makes them cry. She's proud of the reputation she has with monkeys and their ilk, the parachutes, for she notices that others are ignored, go by, go by.

The door of her wings opens on a gesture of infinitude which must be smiling into laundry bags. She ducks and the tomato hits her in the face. "I am always the end. To grow becomes the merest lassitude in a life of continual streets, parks, boardwalks, elevator men and pencils. When did you get to know me? I have already forgotten your face although the way you thrust your knee between my thighs when we dance seems unmistakably remembered to you. My hair has come out green more and more lately. Is it a change? I know the beach intimately, am wanting a ducking. Ride me. I thought you would need to ask to arrive late and be polite. So you are? do you know? Here is the corner they call mine."

In her own room, dark and damask with pet plants, she wears a turban in the Jewish style, a cheese cloth failing to fly about her shoulders hides necklaces of blown up pink pearls. She faces her mirror and cries till her breasts are stinging neath the stream. "Apples of desire, how find the form will halve your future rent? Astounding mandrills and horses sniff my perfume through the dormer. Shall I one day be the witch who saves men's lives by throwing self beneath a rambling truck? Oh mother, die! for I must be about my business while the going is dewy and all risks mechanical shine fresh in a morning which is mine." And she is not late for the curtain as the theatre explodes in a sheet of flame which is her breathing always.

JANE BATHING

Up to our noses in the cresting wallops we find too busily what is under over ripped screams and sweep up a lighthouse up the pavilion beyond the park where the beltway stays and stays.

Yum, the brine's thick jellyfish sting and your hand is crushed in my gathering manacle since you are night herself and I persuaded you to come in. Not a little your shrieks please when zoom in the spindrift bird's-eye of cities! anonymously for all we know about each other crushing. Speckled. Ordure. Amber. Grit. Aren't we?

Blue wraps itself about the pill we are spitting out anyhow. You say "Babbles, babbles her name, next in that wave, from the high school I pointed. That's Jack. The sky falls so, so monotonous, I sleep at musics, it all goes and goes. I freeze. Tell me when to get out."

For an ambulance has just enfolded one brave swimmer to her dislocated shoulder wrenched over fish, and Jane is scared. No won't tell. Am raked off enough as it is for all the smiling breast plate and piling up of heels. Yet. Yet. Yet. Yet. Yet. Deliriously floundering patina over the vulgar swimmers which will yet ransom us two rats for a dinghy. Bowwow. "Jane! can you hear the bell?" Rolling the grid scale of death we outweigh even the snowy grains of that most painful salty shingle's belly bounding as is as. Smile into the foam.

"I'm keeping no rendezvous, Frank, though the light goes out and the door slams open. I can only think while we're sinking. That neither of us cried out and the night was grinning enough for help and we could only start at not you and not me seizing that trumpet would have made us never again speak these ears if you let go."

Day out on the bus we read headlines ALL THAT'S NEW FITS so we don't fight. We're sneaky enough to stick together, the sky so splendidly compromising in powder puff tweed green. O the glances like nipples! and in every other wave all the we don't desire screaming with envy. Not fear drapes the testy two; a welling in the pupils of the strangers.

LOCARNO

to James Schuyler

Bushes toss on the crowded terrace
like a piano's thunderous onslaught
falls from the cuff, sentimental twilight
of horns. "You saw me last later with kohl
on my lids, you said hello, I know you did.
The next day the skiing instructor cut me.
I had overheard you telling Dorabella and Jo
he wrote. Then be so kind as to cut my heart out
of the doily in the Turkish Ambassadress's V neck.

Alma." And when certain octaves are struck
childhood rears up on its hind legs, billy club
in lob-lolly careening leaden and fat. Blue
tissue nipples like a sunrise in Yokosuka. I
went to the Admiralty, those buggers, with a complaint
that Americans are the ones who are different. Did
I ever feel the traitor, Jesus, my old copperhead;
you know, Miss, I never done delivered no baby before.

There were plenty of fronds and no graveyard. Echo, even. Be not willing, salty, translated and D moll. Toot, toot, o dearest of many many loves and as many crusts on my spring eyelids, octaves of pollen, yes, Arachne.

It is not enough to find you resemble someone older than yourself reading The Author for the first time, and do not speak to me of what you merrily call "astral"; nor do we care for cherries, do we? Well, do we? At night the first time it snowed I felt my privacy invaded, for I can do nothing in the light, I must be always reaching for the chain; the snow illuminated everything from my heart to the North Pole and back so no one could even move. People starved in thousands and many a face went unwashed, the millions dirty and seeded for the Grim Reaper who was said to be gone that year but showed up anyhow.

Then, then I truly wept for the quarrel you inadvertently caused, you trouble maker, with me and my alter ego. The pain it caused me shall not soon wipe itself off the statue of Dante in the little square on the Spanish side of town, nor shall my relatives forget the independence I showed in never closing my eyes to my own distasteful ambitions and hyena-like reserves. Should I be satisfied with the almost accidental deaths that drift onto the flags during one of your wars, is that what art teaches us? Never not in practice, nor indeed in fantasy, nor indeed in the technique which shall down us like a shot. It's not the end, the buds are not scampering, and you can come too if you've a pound of flesh to spare, fuel for the man who cannot make it himself but is some sort of guide they recommend for the ascent.

Do you mind if I turn the score sideways? and may I eat my ham with pus on it and a few dead roaches? for our ensembles must never let down the supreme Decorator, who has habituated the course in stars, those teeth of zippers, pounding pounding down the stretch onto the fanfare's oceanic permanent dip. Lead me always upward, my true darling, and never mind the bus fare. I have a pocket for every hider. As in that moment when one puts his hand on the doorknob of a car that has only half stopped, this kiss will initiate you for the time being. And that is the only time for you and me, because the police come running when they smell a fight and the very air is collapsing under the strain of a mythology which is as yet a secret.

The weight must come at above. It is not blessed to live thus. I was washed in dirty water with the Thief of Egypt. Had you known me sunnier earlier when my flesh was a light coating of dew on blue grass you'd have bitten me eagerly enough, which is what I've always wanted, Now, the wickedness . . .

The wickedness which gains no sanction in failing but strains its glamorous nightly stealth to a winding hideous uproar of stones! I am lost, I have fallen, my lymph cries like a rumor beneath the bushes. On this night the wind falls, the skin of worms. I've had the intentions of a welterweight boxer, but my misery is not so strict. I would be rug of the world, their feet are already in my eyes.

A city of hyenas is giving birth tonight to my immortal French face. I shall be remembered as long as human imagination twitches into the starry smile of boredom—can you imagine a pit in which I do not brace the abyss, like a log lifting the heads of the standees to a rim where they can howl their amusement at being segregated?

The wind now seems to be puking behind the poplars, but I am too tired for companionship, my extremity is one of those glorious upper berths from which the soul cannot claim to be drunk or beg forgiveness and snobbery. Some disinfatuated fisherman will say of me "He just wanted to go somewhere," and indeed it will make for the tears of intimacy to hear. I am truly filthy, and not the most bitchy could guess the whimsicality of my retreats, the arabesque of my faltering. Ah! what do I mean of myself? I find it simple on this rock that smells of camel spit to wallow in foreboding. And I am out on a limb, and it is the arm of God.

THE NEXT BIRD TO AUSTRALIA

Leave there be no weeping
like tails of draught horses dragged
in the dust of our advancement
or long range fear of being tagged

on the spot in the streetlight's bush.
But I don't want to disremember
the heroes who suddenly said "Palms!"
into the teacups of that tan September.

Though I must drift into a gale
and drop only the aroma of lushness
in your basket, you'll find the wake
of the red look merely deliciousness,

as in the story not by the same name.
And "il faut partir" dontcha know,
because it's already sweet die day
and I go where the wild geese go.

DAY AND NIGHT IN 1952

Be not obedient of the excellent, do not prize the silly with an exceptionally
pushy person or orphan. The ancient world knew these things and I am unable
to convey as well as those poets the simplicity of things, the bland and amused
stare of garages and banks, the hysterical bark of a dying dog which is not
unconcerned with human affairs but dwells in the cave of the essential passivity
of his kind. Kine? their warm sweet breaths exist nowhere but in classical
metre, bellowing and puling throughout the ages of our cognizance like roses
in romances. We do not know any more the exquisite manliness of all brutal
acts because we are sissies and if we're not sissies we're unhappy and too busy.
Be not discouraged by your own inept affection. I don't want any of you to
be really unhappy, just camp it up a bit and whine, whineola, baby. I'm talking
to you over there, isn't this damn thing working? You're just the one I'm
talking to. Don't you understand what's going on around here? It's not that
I want you to be so knowing as all that, but I don't want some responsibility
to be shown in the modern world's modernity, your face and mine dashing
across the steppes of a country which is only partially occupied and acceptable,
and is very windy and grassy and rugged. I speak of New Jersey, of course,
the always acceptable and dismal, a farewell view of which might knock you
right on your nose, poor sentimental dear that I know you are. What do you
want of me? or my friends? or all the dopes you make demands of in toilets,
there's no gratuity for you in it. Accept that, my bright turgid little tamarind.
Are you still listening, cutie? you who dresses in pumps for the routine, shorts,
a tuxedo jacket and a sequin tophat? you are delicious I don't mind letting you
know. If we were some sort of friends I might have to bitch you; as it is you
can have whatever you want from anyone else and whatever somewhat in-
accurate cooperation you may care to have from me. I'm not this way with
people I know. And they're not with me. John, for instance, thinks I am the
child of my own old age; Jimmy is cagey with snide remarks while he washes

dishes and I pose in the bathroom; Jane is rescuing herself at the mercy of her ill temper towards me which is expressed only in the riddles of her motival phantasies; what am I to say of Larry? who really resents the fact that I may be conning him instead of Vice and Art; Grace may secretly distrust me but we are both so close to the abyss that we must see a lot of each other, grinning and carrying on as if it were a picnic given by somebody else's church; Kenneth continually goes away and by this device is able to remain intensely friendly if not actually intimate; but the other John catches everyone of my innuendi the wrong way or at the very least obliquely and is never mistaken or ill-tempered, which is what I worry about the most. What can I do? I can

and then I, ravished and indeed under an enormous pressure of circumstance, paced the carpet, opened the casement, plunged my perspiring hands into a basin of iced cologne my mother had thoughtfully left in a corner on a large tea-table, wrinkled and unwrinkled my brow in a ripple of anxiety, and felt desperately ill. The window opened on a broad lawn and behind, as if accidentally, a vista of dunes which were incredibly boring and strange. Do you occasionally wonder at the inscrutable nature of visual experiences, an undeniable and far from optometrical

distance? the bane and bolster of
my primping prissy heart's bane of
anguish! the pressure wheel stone of
desire. I do not want to be victim of
the ability to enthuse myself at or of
and especially kissy people who are of
the darker race. Did I say Dark? of
what comparative device may I avail myself of
pretending to be the Queen of Africa and of
Suez. Perhaps more especially of
Suez, since Aden is most beautiful of
courses, having the famous flamingoes of
Saratoga flown over for that weekend of
mad irregular what else! Of
distances I can only say Paris! you of
the paper route, you fictitious of
all the prancers in my ardent imagination of
which are you not the least and most of
what I think about the world of
no illusion, not an iota! Not hated of
my shuddering pressure and ending, of
my interminable self-disciplines, of
the symbol which is the lover not of
the people who neither care nor of
pleasaunces are chary, an apple-headed putsch of
Vienna and those light-skinned pusses. So of
you I am least proud in mind and most of
my thoughts are blue with miles of

figures and chariots and nudes on paths of
primrose, going down the drain of
modern times like a rhymed heroic tragedienne of
patsies and opening nights and visions of
the madame who cares and knows not what of.

POEM

The distinguished
and freshly dusted Apollodorus-type, he
ravenously branched and crusted blackly peach tree
of so many splendid nights, wished
what to do with so round and woolly blue promontory

of vistas sterile.
The passage of ladies up the chimney o'er
the lawn reminded him of ripe perfume, how it soar
if need be the dankness of puerile
tree-climbers who break the blossoms, bleed, are sore

from tumbling.
Forgetting his dignity and dazzling apple
with flint of random strokes cutting the thick dapple
of heaven's cloudless afternoon rumbling
into the night that proudly tosses, embosses air: apt to fall,

and apt to keep
falling, oh murderous and deeply fruitful,
how slender with rickets onto brown and bountiful
sod the kneeling children now do weep
and sink into a past where peaches bounce and beautiful

in being blonde.
Aristocratically some true the tree approaches
capish and black, rooting the blood, branches and coaches
packed with bloom, hidden stench, beyond
where the amorous and listening eye lifts its reproaches.

Later the pewter listeners disappeared
into the saffron lake which was Sun
swallowing Rascal. The rattlers all
serenaded each other, rapping upon realizing
their loss some minuscule sipper's louse.

Rendering unto the sinking its Lie,
its paraphrase of the biblical camp,
the Making, we practically created a
Musical Comedy, arms entwined and skipping,
like *The Jazz Singer* in reverse.
The four of us seemed quite awful
at the picnic to all those New York friends
who'd just wangled an invitation. But we
were the ones to start hating, weren't we?
Ssssss. The sun, the Sun! didn't refrain
its random capsule to escape us or let
them off.
            Going down into our blood
like the last day of our sweet nearing lives
it cried "Kill! Kill!" and folk from the City
were there to massage the altar of
our fear, forgotten as we ranted and shook,
so golden leeches, leaping and scarlet into the sea.

EASTER

The razzle dazzle maggots are summary
tattooing my simplicity on the pitiable.
The perforated mountains of my saliva leave cities awash
more exclusively open and more pale than skirts.
O the glassy towns are fucked by yaks
slowly bleeding a quiet filigree on the leaves of that souvenir
of a bird chastely crossing the boulevard of falling stars
cold in the dull heavens
drowned in flesh,

it's the night like I love it all cruisy and nelly
fingered fan of boskage fronds the white smile of sleeps.

When the world strips down and rouges up
like a mattress's teeth brushed by love's bristling sun
a marvellous heart tiresomely got up in brisk bold stares
when those trappings fart at the feet of the stars
a self-coral serpent wrapped round an arm with no jujubes
without swish
without camp
floods of crocodile piss and pleasures of driving
shadows of prairie pricks dancing
of the roses of Pennsylvania looking in eyes noses and ears
those windows at the head of science.
I supplicate
dirty blonde mermaids leaning on their elbows
rigor mortis sculpting the figure of those iron tears,
all the feathers falling font a sea of yuccas and blue riddles
every Nevada fantastic has lost his dolorous teeth
when the world, smutty abstract, powders its pearls
the gardens of the ooa's come
a mast of the barcantine lost flaming bearer of hurricanes
a hardon a sequoia a toilet tissue
a reject of poor people
in squeezing your deflowered eyeballs
all the powdered and pomaded balloon passengers
voluntarily burning their orifices to a cinder
a short circuit in the cow eyes' sour milk
eyes sucked by fever
the x-ray night's mercury prophylaxis
women who use cigars
the sea swallowing tumultuous islands
is burnt by the sun like a girl
a sieve of stinking villages
a muff of mosquitoes in the walking dark
pouring demented chinchillas
trumpets fell, many the virulent drapery lids
the murdered raining softly on yellow oranges
violating the opaque sexual privileges of twilight
the big nigger of noon
just as the floor of the ocean crushes pebbles
too eager for the appetites of little feet.

Giving and getting the pubic foliage of precarious hazard
sailors
Silent ripples in a bayou of raffish bumpkin winks
sweet meat packers touting the herb bracelets of pus

kisses! kisses!
fresher than the river that runs like a moon through girls.
And the swamped ship flouncing to the portholes at the eagle hour
earrings

the ship sawed up by the biting asses of stars
at the heaving buttocks of coupling drydocks
and the ship latches onto a sideboard of sourdough
sends telegrams by camel and dodo
an aloof dancer practicing push-ups on top of the mast
all night you see them plunging and swizzling
pouncing elegantly in that jewelled grass
an army of frigates
an army of cocks
an army of wounds
an army of young married couples' vanilla hemorrhages
a spine-tingling detonation nested in leaves
alfalfa blowing against sisters in a hanky of shade
and the tea ship crushes an army of hair
in rampant jaws those streets whose officer deploys a day of
hairs strutting the rosy municipal ruts
hairs brushing the seaflowers and tapestries from the gums
of the shore

birdie, birdie
on the uptown train
dining in the midst of waiters
O the bread of colleens butters the rain.
A minute more and earth would grab the crater's lip
and a wind of diamonds rough up red sultans
and their cast off whores, chemises!
shuffling their shoes to a milky number about sugar
in the gardens of the rainbow planted by anarchists
whose hairy sheets cover the nits of canaries
brushed out by henna specialists.
When the world has walked the tightrope that ties up our eyes
when the world has stretched the rubber skin of sleep
when the world is just a cluttered box for your cluttered box
and charges through the cream of your smiling entrails
like a Pope
sounding box of tomorrow champion box alarm
at the call of mystics and pilots
box raining sadly over Sicily and over the bars
and the weekly tooth brush

furious senses your lianas forest the virgin
O sins of sex and kisses of birds at the end of the penis

cry of a black princess whose mouth founders in the Sun
a million gardens fill the white furry sky
black pillow cast on the retreating flood of night
absurd ice under the hand's breast of dark
bitten by smiles habitual, the giggle
in the blue lidded eyes of prunes
a dawn of justice and magnetic mines
the princess in the clear heart of summer sucks her flower
and honey drowns her in a green valley
she is privately caught in the breeze blown silence
night without eyelids
tied to the jet of my mysterious galley
my cuckoo my boomerang
I have sunk my tongue in the desperation of her blood
strangely her features are Easter
and the balm of Easter floods, my tongue's host
a rivulet of purple blood runs over the wise hands
of sobbing infants.
And the ship shoves off into the heady oceans of love
whose limpidity is the exile of the self
I cry the moon to shower fishes and tears over her
runners through the warring surf of Red Indians
on the California shore, that nausea
not swamp the wind's hand of the Sun
towering afire over the living islands and hairy waves
not forgotten in the silken sound of fruits
proud shout the coyotes and the orchids of the testicles.

Boom of pregnant hillsides
awash with urine
a tambourine relieving the earth beside a hedge
when the fingers tap against the spine it's cherry time
where are the suburbs of powdered corpses dancing
O the amusing audience to all words shivers
before the flashing sword of the thighs of the Sun
like a hangar the sun fries all mumbojumboes
and the rivers scramble like lizards about the ankle
until the ravishing pronunciamento of stone.

Black bastard black prick black pirate whose cheek
batters the heavenly heart
and signs its purple in the ribs of nightly explosion
Sun boom
sleep trooped about by paid assassins mad for kisses
from the bamboo bottle of the Father of Heaven, race
whom I quit as the salamander quits the flame.
The day passes into the powdery light of your embrace

like an Alaskan desert over the basket of Mexico
before the coming of the Spics. River rushing into the Sun
to become golden and drossy drip the fingernails
the molluscs on the underside of the scrotum
embroidered with lice and saliva and berries
the Sun sings in the stones of the savage
when the world booms its seven cunts
like a river plunged upon and perishing
´un, to the feast!
to be pelted by the shit of the stars at last in flood
like a breath.

STEVEN

The little dark haired boy whose black looks
find the rampart a way hung with frosted steel,
he is the poet, he's the one who doolies and duties
in the sand dunes on the empty beach so no one sees.
He will swim past all the landmarks of the heart, a
veritable Maximilian and False Florimel
the world awaits and races hysterically away from.

He is the naturally elegant in nervousness,
he has no checking account and grows no wildflowers
in the toothpick rib-cage of his ripening eyes,
the jewels of which are flatter than a fighter's ears,
little Steven, whose anger has already wrapped us in
its careless kiss that left welts. He absurdly humors
himself to think, for the Loch Ness monster's chosen

him already for a masque to enslave lechery. We
turn his gaze from the window where his father's friends,
limping and flayed by the disinterested, cross each
street that trembles, binding and abandoning themselves
to a future he'll be forced to cut open. It will
not be Steve's fist, but his open hand. Yet thanks
to his wit, we won't be mannequins at a clam bake,

and he won't be hounded by a past that owes him a lot.
As it owes me all the paste diamonds I paid out. As if

he were creditor of the mist we keep trying to fan away
from his feet so he won't bog down around the blue tree
that I tell him gave me blood poisoning, it's like a trip
to the mountains, where Stevie, if he takes it, will find
the still hid; but we must keep him from this talent.

POEM

The hosts of dreams and their impoverished minions
who like guests are departing never, fading always
into something more real and less expensive, sloop
towards the sundown of an early morning, their property.

Is it night or day? The azure mummified minutes
pick their own scent for the surprising occasion,
which is the arrival of Kenneth at the Villa Rivers
in a state of extreme fatigue and harm from California.

Many a week and day had fled horrified and un-
delineated into the bright forest of business where
no postman approaches the hollow stump marked "outgoing"
and Kenneth had no way of knowing his loving companions,

what they were up to and on. Messages were sent
frantically through the shrubbery concerning how much
Kenneth should be told, and indeed it was little enough
equipment for the crisis, pasturing as we were on the backs

of two children who always fling themselves into riptides.
Joseph, of Kenneth, exclaims "Why you!" and swats flies.
Steve sleeps late and thinks nothing but the truth, but
these are children who aren't yet afraid of the languors

which often remove themselves into affectionate distances
towards which no sea's reaches crisply curl. We may wander
coldly in a mirage which Kenneth will spot and point out
and despise us for, if we've been loose and windy and tidal

in his absence which was not our responsibility, yet
which we owe him and ourselves like a vision and beside it

the willowy fountain that nobody saw but everybody was there.
The prayers went up, billowed. Not for Kenneth, but he came.

CHEZ JANE

The white chocolate jar full of petals
swills odds and ends around in a dizzying eye
of four o'clocks now and to come. The tiger,
marvellously striped and irritable, leaps
on the table and without disturbing a hair
of the flowers' breathless attention, pisses
into the pot, right down its delicate spout.
A whisper of steam goes up from that porcelain
urethra. "Saint-Saëns!" it seems to be whispering,
curling unerringly around the furry nuts
of the terrible puss, who is mentally flexing.
Ah be with me always, spirit of noisy
contemplation in the studio, the Garden
of Zoos, the eternally fixed afternoons!
There, while music scratches its scrofulous
stomach, the brute beast emerges and stands,
clear and careful, knowing always the exact peril
at this moment caressing his fangs with
a tongue given wholly to luxurious usages;
which only a moment before dropped aspirin
in this sunset of roses, and now throws a chair
in the air to aggravate the truly menacing.

DUCAL DAYS

A rending. Red whispers. The sailboat dives
upon the viaduct, barely catches

an infant stolen in the hospitals.
Mother is served under the velvet bridge

for the sixth time at the end of the continent.
When shall your golden eyelashes waltz down
round your excellent shoulders on the half past six?
I want to fell your ankles and the water a-keen,

the glancing bubbles of those breaths.
Then passing; so articulate clearly:
"There's the cast-off grillwork of your smile,
which in a better world held down your heart."

TWO SHEPHERDS, A NOVEL

BOOK ONE
"Here he comes now, the big prick-with-ears,
with his pansy smile as if he'd just shit
his pants. Throw a rock at him, pitch!
The sun's going down, isn't it? You
won't be able to see him in a minute."

The sun went down and the boys played on,
each in his own tender and delightful way.

"When I saw your sister, I admit it,
I said to myself 'What boobs!' Jesus,
kid, do you ever get any idea how
she grew them? What it takes, I mean,
special food or something? Do you ever
get a chance to give them a work out? Boy,
would I like to give her a hand job. You
got something on me in that department
and I bet you know how to use it. Baby!"

Then the light of an omnipresent smile
flickered across the unpuddled pavement's flats.

"See this Spanish dyke coming down the
street? She does a flamingo dance in a box
my sister told me about, all those crazy men

crazy for her queer ass. Pretty nifty,
those trousers of hers cost plenty, hah?
There's a lot of dancing going on down here,
I seen what I seen, and you can make a lot
in tips: all over the fucking city,
thousands of couples whirling around, whoosh!
in that flimsy stuff they strain come through,
wow! what a pink sight! it cracks the neon!"

In the elevators there were loud sighs, and
the Municipal Transportation System agreed, nodded.

"When your eye gets better I'll try
to get you a job on my paper route. The sooner
the better. Dress up when you want to be interviewed
and I'll get the idea. What's your first name,
anyway? I don't like your looks much, but
what the hell? They can't be choosey these days.
Watch out for the Mack truck. It's got your number
on it. What a beautiful girl! I hear monkeys."

BOOK TWO
So, running as fast as ever they could,
they snatched at conversations. Ah!
si la jeunesse savait! and perhaps
in the very near future, let it come!
let it come! the pink and yellow flowers
will have exploded into the Empire State
Building like a famous incident, withered
yet smelling of a rare exchange of experiences.
Do you know where the gamins are rounding
their corners now? Haha. And the President
will not find it too inscrutable to say
"Boris and Charlie" or "Maximilian and
Jewie" in an address to the U S Senate
always referring to my selfsame darlings. Now
fame crosses its knees and expectorates,
they do a quick somersault and the Rodeo
seems to think it has come to Town. Lodie!
those son-of-a-guns with their peach kneecaps
are quicker than a fleet of swordswallowers
who gurgle "Stevie and Joe, the coondancers
of Chuckaluck! How the hell are yeah, fellahs?"
They smile, they duck, they beg for butts.

By 1812 they were already part of our colony's
prehistory, a type of embroidered sampler
quite new in conception and execution. To

the petit point of the French had been addended
what I can only term a "larger" licentiousness,
it may have been the feeding! and our Dutch
neatness of proverbiality had lent orgiastic screams-
while-running a sweet reasonableness which
became characteristic of shepherds everywhere.
They were Big Business! But to hear them talk
you'd think they'd never gotten in off the streets.
There were always blue skies, rotten apples,
the savor of geranium cunts, midnight snacks of
milk and powdered cheese, to foster their running
commentary, which became ultimately philosophical.
Thus they retained their glittering pectorals,
and their buttocks stayed firm as hassocks.

"Christ, I worry a lot about becoming a mere
technician, but hell, so long as we grow backwards
younger and make history, what the hell. You
can't sell a blind cow a bicycle. I've got to make out
twice a night or I get irritable, what with
all these fucking flowers where the Chrysler Building
used to be in the good old days. Gee, remember
the Palladium in Hollywood? What a place
to pick up a real razzle-dazzle cunt. Man!"

OCTOBER 26 1952 10:30 O'CLOCK

This minute I've not been able not been
you know simply not been like positively being dead
able to hear your voice though having dialed
you at home at studio at bar. I am not frantic,
I hope, at not being able to catch your sigh
of boredom, not I, not the number who knows all
about the city's darling diversions. I never expected
you to speak to me having once illuminated to me
with your long exotic thumbnail my weakness
which I wear "cross at the war" elegantly.
I hope that your blue eyes are slanting into music
by Ben Weber, because I should have only reminded you of
a cello concerto of our old midsummer anguish,

vieux jeux like falling out of trees into a collector's album.
And upbraided you for my expecting the absence
which like a vulgar newspaper horoscope has happened
to Jane. Where are you? where are you? where are you?

AUBADE

to Jimmy Schuyler

A million stars are dreaming out
the murderous whims of the apples.
Sinking like celestas in the dawn
already growing faint, beyond temples

whose silent throbbing dictates
a green life to my waking heart. Bids
the bones that decorate this shore
become the pearl of loved eyelids'

sunlight, withdrawn until unseen
at night, when like the cat's hand,
the sea, they warmly flutter near
upon the belly of the sable sand.

A meaning of my life volleys
thus into the sky to rest, breathes
upon these vessels by the sea,
to be wrought in the frothing waves.

BAARGELD

". . . he soon gave up painting and all public activity.
He died in 1927 in an avalanche." —Georges Hugnet

It ambleth. And recaptured, that first flight
staring into the snowstand out a hospice,
that leaning wind which makes the blood
back up recovered and bored: they wept,

they did, to be not in slaloms beyond the waving
of smoky tails. Having fallen desperately, as
they say, it occurs to the eye to blacken flaskish
and close. Nothing matters. Or at least the rain

has aerated itself, is light, if care. Then
perhaps a field of dollar bills to the American
who just been come to Switzerland looks up
purely silver as the honking of Wisconsins,

but before this a decade of frozen heartbeats in
Gideon Bibles will cry "The snow! the snow
is my cunning stunt." And the years will roll
on and the Swiss will roll over the Germans

like an Italian funicular. My son, my dearest
son all that bad blood powdered: he, famed skier
first I took traveling in the rued sky and waxed
the chutes. Slowly and more slowly now, the cold war.

BIRDIE

It is after four in my life and the salmon have ceased leaping, though I pretend
that the water's just as disturbed as it ever was. I think of Birdie, and it is not
disturbing, they have certainly gone, thank god, or should I regret this peace-
ful plaza? into which Birdie is even now arranging to emerge patting her a
little in back, herself her hair.

She boards the train, for it awaits her, and immediately her car is full of
waiters dressed in spotted white, manicolored starry mirrors with yellow faces.
They flutter about her, she's a courtesan! clicking their chopsticks and dancing
gan gan gwoo hop hop. Birdie can't help chuckling, for they are truly charm-
ing with their funny little fingers flapping.

And out her windows she peers into the eyes of the city, millions like stars
from a space ship, she's right smack going down Main Street as if it were
Buffalo, New York. Alas, the poignancy of this careening through life in a
vessel of steel so fast that nobody thinks to open a window, and anyway the
air is flipping with soot while two sailors exchange telephone numbers.

When, at the instant of headiest spring, some dark actor dashes on stage and
stabs the heroine, the salmon all scream in their seats, the lights go up hideously
and quick, and quick the great central chandelier plops towards the forward

trembling napes. No one for that moment imagines they are watching *Carmen,* even if, as invariably happens in our courteous age, the villain deigns to wear maquillage; and they aren't, they are in the daylight street and the sun's enjoying this.

Birdie would only have dirtied herself. And anyhow the mountains are running toward her, jumping and flaming, to nestle at her feet with all the naïve elegance of a hermaphrodite who has not yet been put through the mill.

BLOCKS

1

Yippee! she is shooting in the harbor! he is jumping
up to the maelstrom! she is leaning over the giant's
cart of tears which like a lava cone let fall to fly
from the cross-eyed tantrum-tousled ninth grader's
splayed fist is freezing on the cement! he is throwing
up his arms in heavenly desperation, spacious Y of his
tumultuous love-nerves flailing like a poinsettia in
its own nailish storm against the glass door of the
cumulus which is withholding her from these divine
pastures she has filled with the flesh of men as stones!
O fatal eagerness!

2

O boy, their childhood was like so many oatmeal cookies.
I need you, you need me, yum, yum. Anon it became suddenly

3

like someone always losing something and never knowing what.
Always so. They were so fond of eating bread and butter and
sugar, they were slobs, the mice used to lick the floorboards
after they went to bed, rolling their light tails against
the rattling marbles of granulation. Vivo! the dextrose
those children consumed, lavished, smoked, in their knobby
candy bars. Such pimples! such hardons! such moody loves.
And thus they grew like giggling fir trees.

POEM

He can rest. He has blessed him and hurt him
exactly. They start violent under his held smile,
so shy in evil, winningly frank about the bridge
he blew into a snow of subway straps, honestly
confused at the boy's ankle found in his pocket,
his eyes in front of the bed like a green book bag,
sagging helplessly toward the doomed man
who would fill them and whom they untidily contained.

Sweetly he has walked, slender, called down to him
the bungling snow which, on his saffron forehead
under streetlamps, speaks the atonality of thorns.
He has been, once or twice, the true lip on newspaper
behind glass on the muddy feathers, has been called
"Europa's Messenger" and again "Fart in the Hurricane";
So his accomplishments have not been sculpture.

When he has been most rapid with desire the wind
has lifted him like a puppet's jock strap,
the clamored light against his flesh like flags.
Then his pupils narrow to a pinpoint and he dives
into the surf pounding in his throat, his very pestilence.
Oh linen threshold of the Orient whose bamboo smiles
open always onto nipples and come up with hairs,
where is thy encompassing vista of dwarfs and spines
green with becoming lax and wens and nervous wines?
Press me to thy multicolored maggots, for I seize
upon the clapping altitudes, and go blind and white.

OCTOBER

Summer is over,
that moment of blindness
in a sunny wheelbarrow
aching on sand dunes
from a big melancholy

about war headlines
and personal hatreds.

Restful boredom waits
for the winter's cold solace
and biting season of galas
to take over my nerves,
and from anger at time's
rough passage I fight
off the future, my friend.

Is there at all anywhere
in this lavender sky
beside the UN Building
where I am so little
and have dallied with love,
a fragment of the paradise
we see when signing treaties
or planning free radio stations?

If I turn down my sheets
children start screaming through
the windows. My glasses
are broken on the coffee table.
And at night a truce
with Iran or Korea seems certain
while I am beaten to death
by a thug in a back bedroom.

SNAPSHOT FOR BORIS PASTERNAK

I
The wrinkled page of the sky swells
with emptiness like the heart of a man
imprisoned, and the cloudy paragraphs
of his prayer beat my forehead as I
kneel before the translation of your lips.

I am new; shall grow old and die
into the space of one cloud's passing
which is already your immortal sentence.

Nothing changes that into a rainbow,
and I am never funereal with your iron shaft

lodged black in my tangled breast. If
it were here, everything would proclaim:
conqueror whose Asiatic fastnesses grip lips
of sapphire and thoughts dripping with honey.
A photograph must do for greeting in its rain.

2

I eagerly rose that morning! the sunlight
so green, spiders hiding at the edge of trees,
and the glimmering shadows of an irate father
busy in the meadows of my maturing birth.

In the clear and plain air of June
swallows flung themselves from treetops
into the diamond wink of a lake's blue tin,
and a husbandman kissed all his flocks

before he let them appear scattered
on the mirrored pasture or cascading hill.
The sufferings of my childhood were set
among these beauties, subtle as a snake,

and hand in hand with Sally I ran heavily
through the neighbors' formal gardens
stumbling over crocus bulbs and the fragile turds
of pheasants, playing Monopoly on Sundays.

At school in the city my heart fell
for five & ten cent stores, their goldfish,
candy, scolding women, orange scarves and
swinging doors. I was a truant caught

upon the silver screen, an astrologist
of that shadowed fame, kissed by millions.
In interims of tears I strutted Peer Gynt
through the scared sound tracks of bedrooms:

"Gone the low lying wonder of the prairie
looking over a pillow at unbelievable morning.
From now on the rain will slant into my eyes
green and unzipped, like mountain leaves,

flatlands falling, falling like a forever
now, once fertile with bodies beautiful

as the excitement of costume jewelry or
the common importunate grace of dishes;

now falling into a sea of mornings I
never should have awakened to, although
the swell of the heart is not landscape
but the fatal pull of the moon at our roots.

I do not climb you, mountains! you rush
under me, the wave of the future, escalator
and bed, thrusting me into the frigid air
of the sun. Trees here flail myriad arms!

thrust toward the others in my panic
of storms and my leaves flutter open
like the fans of raped Chinese. Look, exiles!
how the clouds fear our reflected loves.

The sea is only a sob to us, alas, now
and the prairie is too plain for us
to love it. Only the special flesh of clouds
draws on the heart that's lived too high!"

and thus was I able to leap from
the pinnacle of adolescence to lie at rest
in the hollow of sexuality, spending years
of youth in the glamorous exchange of vices.

And this became the identical vista
of my childhood because of its quickness
and the sameness of its eyes. Toads strode
through rest rooms at odd moments, and

bats fluttered next my ear to wake me
from nightmares in which I trained in tights
for the black captaincy of Parachute Troops.
Those mornings I fell into algebra, round eyes

and snoring. Only music accepted the errors
of my filling scrapbook, turned the pages
with a cooky smile; leaves fell into my head
the air's flagellation! and I scribbled:

"How violently the wind escapes us!
and in what cavern dwells the Father's will
hidden, obscured from all but the vile ill
and their self fed fire? Oh not to live thus,

I beg, not to die at the heart's own hand
on a pillar of shame! The poison of,
how unerringly sought! prodigal love,
our sea of ether our anxious den, grant"

and, moaning in Wagnerian night, cried
"Father, shall be before your last leb'wohl
a wing spread over our frantic white brow.
Fathoming, flying the feverish blue

you will bless our sick body and sword whole,
purged by desire's wicked search for the new,
found in your Presence, leb'wohl, call you Thou,"
sinking in velvet pity and self hate.

But in my breaking ears the Muse's tongue
then softly claimed, and all the provinces
that I had sought her were my own capable organs
of spirit, clothing her nakedness to me.

3
But all we love and are grows different, weeps,
lying in the tender arms of our gigantic continents.
You cannot know the Prussian lather of the suburbs
here, nor I the bad blood in the crouching Urals;
yours is the barren forest of the haunted patriot
whose birds fly south when his breath writhes cold,
highwayman out of bullets above the timber line,
ambitious in poor country, athletic in snow.

Dear Master, as time pushes us towards the abyss
that's sharp as a sledge hammer, let always
your prayer be perverse and gratuitous, a
volcano in the lengthening bandyleg of truth
so far from fountains that the sun's outdoors
choking on its own white fur and black tongue
and whispered wrist. Do not dismiss me, sad
that I am in your world, as your eyes rip
in the perfect light of fame, as you permit earth
completion in vicarious mortality, like poetry.

THE BATHERS

After the immersion and the stance
how the blood bubbles like a firefly!
and the many flies come clipping through
the cumulus. Paradise melts its wings,

the shingle shows a red flag, lit,
incandescent, and chattering forth.
Crushing as always the pale leaves
of children's feet, the shells crush,

the petals thrash, a lifeguard weeps
for his dead mother who has just sailed on.
Rumpling and rolling over, the rain
dumps its burden of restraint stonily,

without pressure from above. Be it killing
or caressing, the unhappy bathers moan
and remonstrate, hurtling through indifferences
and colors. On the sandbar lovers

hound each other to the salt, afraid of
neither running paralyzed nor trembling
hung, longing only to drift totally
in the garrulous frequency of their immanence.

Striding like statues the tremendous
arches, partially concealed by sunlight,
bounce. From barges grey with carrion
seem to rise the frenzied whimpers of those

who are not thrusting their cheeks
against the wicker chests of heroes and
Desdemonas. Shall they drown that passion
they remember best? glinting and passing,

that discord scratching them a future
white-embossed and streaked? The delicacy
of birds eating fleas, so the sand may have
an eye at last, that crater and that sun.

ALMA

"Est-elle almée? . . . aux premières heures bleues
Se détruira-t-elle comme les fleurs feues. . . ."
  —*Rimbaud*

1

The sun, perhaps three of them, one black one red, you know, and her dancing
all the time, fanning the purple sky getting purple, her fancy white skin quite
unoriental to the dirty children's round eyes standing in circles munching muf-
fins, the cockroaches like nuggets half hid in the bran. Boy! how are you,
Prester John? the smile of the river, so searching, so enamelled.

2

What mention of the King?
the spinning wheel still turns,
the apples rot to the singing,
Alceste on winter sojourns

is nice at Nice. Wander,
my dear sacred Pontiff, do dare
to murder minutely and ponder
what is the bloody affair

inside the heart of the weak
dancer, whose one toe is worth
inestimable, the gang, the cheek
of it! it's too dear, her birth

amidst the acorns with nails
stuck through them by passionate
parents, castanets! Caucasian tales!
their prodigality proportionate:

"Sacred Heart, oh Heart so sick,
make Detroit more wholly thine,
all with greeds and scabs so thick
that Judas Priest must make a sign."

Thus he to bed and we to rise
and Alma singing like a loon.
Her dancing toenails in her eyes.
Her pa was dead on the River Gaboon.

3

Detroit was founded on the great near waterways next to Canada which was
friendly and immediately gained for herself the appellation "the Detroit of
Thermopylaes," a name which has stuck to this day wherever ballroom dancing
is held in proper esteem. Let me remind you of that great wrist movement,

the enjambement schizophrene, a particularly satisfying variation of which may be made by adding a little tomato paste. Great success. While in Detroit accused of starting the Chicago fire. Millions of roses from Russians. Alma had come a long way, she opened a jewelry shop, her name became a household word, she'd invented an arch-supporter.

How often she thought of her father! the castle, the kitchen-garden, the hollihocks and the mill stream beyond curving gently as a parenthesis. Many a bitter tear was shed by her on the boards of this theatre as she pondered the inscrutable meagerness of divine Providence, always humming, always shifting a little, never missing a beat. She guested one season at the height of her nostalgia with the Metropolitan Opera Ballet in *Salammbô;* her father seemed very close in all that oriental splendor of bamboo and hotel palms and stale sweat and bracelets, an engagement of tears. In the snow, in her white fox fur wraps, how more beautiful than Mary Garden!

4
Onward to the West. "Where I came from,
where I'm going. Indian country." Gold.
Oh say can you see Alma. The darling
of Them. All her friends were artists.
They alone have memories. They alone
love flowers. They alone give parties
and die. Poor Alma. They alone.
                                    She died,
and it was as if all the jewels in the world
had heaved a sigh. The seismograph
at Fordham University registered, for once,
a spiritual note. How like a sliver
in her own short fat muscular foot.
She loved the Western World, though
there are some who say she isn't really dead.

EAST RIVER

Homes of aviators suddenly mounting,
General Vivre is poking his fishing rod
into the reeds, murmuring salaciously
"Two, three times your courage hut rises."

Kept necessitates beautiful, final, a sum
shaking night of its vines and its pimps,
expanding their clarity over the streets
in rainy asters, baguettes, evil wishes
flickering their evil wishes on the vendors.

A swallow passes along the kid-strewn sigh
and rents a house, intending to study voice;
catch his graveness as he tcases the kelp!
She parks her purse on the bottom of the river,
a plant of coins and promises to leave.

I understand the song when it screams
and I hear the scream when it sighs,

with my flag I dive into the Hudson
and come up in a deep river near Poughkeepsie,

where is General Vivre living now
that the war is dead and has flagged us?

HATRED

I have a terrible age and I part
my name at the seams of the beast
in a country of robbers who prepare meals
for a velvet church green with stammerers
and with cuckoos, with cormorants and cranes.

I've tucked the rushing earth under my legs
so I won't have to turn my back on Sundays
and the morasses of ritual archers milking,
and I eat in a prison of bread and mortar,
I eat the stuff with the wooden provocations.

But if I'd broken you one of my wings,
shaft darkening over the prairie of your soul,
for the sea's split resistance I'd never snout.
I'd retch up all men. I would give
up America and her twenty twistings of my years.

The footsteps and suspirations of a twig!
and these given me by ransom. America
watches at the feet of my ramparting brow
and in a three thousand of years of brutes
will violate the wistful sphinx of myself

beneath an arch, latched onto poles
like the doors of comrades forced wide open
to the lost wind of a night on its back
supping whatever free entrails. Hounds,
the drab chefs, the menacing drones and icemen

who whirl towards us with bleakest confidence,
I have hounded myself out of the coral mountains
when my flesh quivered controllably upwards
into the chimneys of a black horde
which were the liberty to work beautifully.

I hounded and hounded into being born
my own death and the death of my country
at the stick, aloft and articulate,
so that the wry words of prophetic ravens
recognized themselves in clutching my wounds

and instantly died as I have wished to be dead
lately. For the delivery of the ensign
upon the painless body which is an island
I alone accept the blue breath of princes, for I
have done it. Am General and Ghost.

I have prized those days most dolefully
which saw me able to disrobe in the savage foam
of spears not polished to celebrate marriages.
I have never feared to suck out the soldier's brag
and so return to cadavers resuscitated on other shores

where war and its raptures is the only light,
and more dire than sisters. I don't wish to tear
the Chinese or their dogs into an intellectual smile,
nor does catching the ripe gules of enemy crossfire
upon my eyelashes signify Life in Death to me,

not when the corpses still circle my sweating front
like laurel. There are millions who'd like to see
that they meet the elderly dead in noisy churches
throughout a land that famine wooed garretless:
for these I paint the signs of the rounds of the latrines.

Two by two. They love Force while still hooked
otherward like two flies in a breeze, but let that other
pace the sheep and incense of a streetcorner on night
and they all go down, beneath dust-flower quilts
where the chosen homeland sweats and feels no winds.

But the war. How shall it claw me up?
and rip America sideways into pieces and shreds of blood.
The warriors clash into their ginlike fusillades
and are asleep before any thin arms entwine them,
having betrayed the numbers but never blabbed.

All!   I cry who am all
where the plain bee on my body farms out gold,
do not wish my brittle bones to be dough on the tooth
held like a cleft palate in a bus of silver
by lame emigrants who do not love to go further.

I have resisted my comrades and their parties.
The general reunion called "Kindertoten" and "Jadis"
I'd use as a bomb to salve the voters who read
that youth, that age must rest on the divine.
But where is the first acrobat, and a woman kneeling?

Parting, the sugar in my breast that's fatuous
in moving and in pushing on, who'll shout a name
where mankind is no longer drowning? Hatred itself
can find no railroads into that sublime country
and slavery will not just burst like a volcano.

Yet I hold myself to you. I have the jangling nerves
of legendary people who box each other's ears and if
it is a union of saxophones and harps and heroes
in me you may discover the gossamer draperies
of defecation and death, and a love for the ancient kings.

What delight tricks you into stripping down
like lousy children who give away their few books
avariciously, and find that all their friends are blind?
I am afraid your kisses, so bland, lean against garages
and are worn out in the white nights of superintendents.

The arrest of the poor struggles into posters
and I bleed through a pose of cautious elephant riding,
am caught in brambles fancy as myself as prisoner
of Chillon. It is against this self that I hasten
towards a higher malady in which you appear starred

as aspiration and regret. The world's years
of war turn like walls of bottles and strangled soldiers
in my breast. I speak of liberty as if a girl
had just been eaten by our tribe between two lumps
of flaming coal, sacrifice to the foibles of cannon.

They have shot up the Just and shunted them
past the falls up to the daisied cliff-dwellers
where I merit, against my will, the careerism of
an Apache. Those compromises in the form of a cross
blot from my face the bony verdure of the clouds

and with a vicarious red salute trailing away
into the image in snot of Christ I refrain
from the maize and the manly savors and tongues
that cry hollowing "Aurora" as I fall upon rocks,
hearing always the churches sinking onto the bored earth.

Herons and priests who do not wear guns or skirts
and who infiltrate drunkenly the pillows and barricades
of what were condemned as castles, how may oppression
strongly enough refuse to resign itself to breathing
the silence of the open air and the praised and the careless?

I have been hunted in the purple arms of a lover
whose twilight had been commanded me for the people's sake,
how ridiculous! and they hurled those first stones
which turned our sobs to plums and sank my head
upon the brown flower which is at once Sun and Eagle.

No revolutionary canticle broke the mist
of that casque, and somewhere like a starry curtain
we drifted towards the Outer, where new myths
lay gasping at our white vanquished languor.
As martyr I am able to whip the crowd into shape,

a coronet of renegades dangling gold in the sky
like fountains and arenas on which feasts the cruel azure
of the holiday immediately succeeding the comradeship
of battle, and the endless chants of fishermen
who are heavy with seining for pyramids and swallows

and find the destroyer like a palace in a nightmare
about anarchists. I shall forget forever America,
which was like a memory of an island massacre
in the black robes of my youthful fear of shadows.
So easily conquered by the black torrent of this knife.

HIERONYMUS BOSCH

So he has a funnel instead of a penis
and has put his mediaeval pianist's hands
on the thighs of a contemporary romance
listening to Brubeck at Birdland. It's just
too very very. "That's one for the apple barrel,
you can feel the North Pole kissing the shellac."
I wear a hook in my look to be sexy, the two
of us mucking the fast in a bush. He puts his long
fingers into the wet mandolin precious with lotion
and stringy. Helplessly clandestine, that's
my song that I sing to the dark people, the
confederate spies when I'm singing them code
over the tongue's turnpike, dub-a-dub and
shit for your momma. We thought we were driving them
out of Finland, but St Anthony flew with his herd
of lepers and made us lie down and come. Sic
transit gloria. O make our hearts so like to Thine!
And they dried him out and hung him up. My, he swung.
Blowing his nose for the lovers; forswunken, forswot.

INVINCIBILITY

"In the church of my heart the choir is on fire!"
            —Vladimir Mayakovsky

I

Avarice, the noose that lets oil, oh my dear oh
"La Ronde," erase what is assured and ours, it
resurrects nothing, finally, in its eagerness
to sit under the widely spaced stairs, to be a fabulous
toilette, doesn't imitate footsteps of disappearance

The neighbor, having teased peace to retire, soon
averages six flowering fountains, ooh! spare the men
and their nervous companions that melt and ripen
into a sordid harbor of squid-slipping tarpaulin strips,
quits the sordid arbor of community butchers' girth

The jumping error pins hate on the blossoms of baffles,
densely foraging covered hero-Nero of Maltese, of Moor,

leap, oh leap! against the fame that's in the noose,
sister of yearning, of eclogues without overcoats deeply,
and the trumpet rages over the filigreed prisoners

Now sallies forth the joyousness of being cruel
which is singing of the world needed by the paralyzed wind,
seated and rebeginning, mounting without saying adieu,
never again delicately to entomb a tear,
that mark of suffering in the toughness of the forest

Lepers nest on the surly cats of glistening delirium,
feet of fire drowning in the attitude of relinquishing foreheads
remember always the barriers so cupiditously defended,
no spume breezy enough for the tempestuous sabers
sent reeling into the charades of fears of the nubile

A crisis questions its attendant in the eyelid of Verona
so serious are the lassitudes of a heart turned into a choir
and the fire-escapes tend to ferment against the paynim cheek
of love that's advancing into a maelstrom for a true speech,
succoring the lewd paupers deliberately, spearlike,
the pearl hesitating to come near the arid well

Noose arriving tropically masterful, estimating and caught,
let the crouching ferns release their nascent sonata
and, shaking with a remuneration of flaccid countries,
eat the rum that cruises an immortally non-sequitur finish,
quaint, and having an aspiration as of torrents and cars

Touched by the insensitivity that broods over the boats,
oh halos of startling carpets, canoes and lathes! archers!
a January of feeling seats itself before the young soldiers
and laughs and laughs at those arch-guardians' radiance,
particularly the sneer of fate, habit shaking its white fists

2

Now for some hell, you make a few fast purchases
separated by first nights of yoyo-cartwheel-violences,
ill but yelling and running full of the younger luminosity,
soulful, oh and epic and sort of rouged between the shoulder blades!
which the striding has not succeeded in making a gondola yet
and this has so devastated the murmuring contributions of strangers
in suits under the brilliant heather, although, my soul! it's white
it's painted white as the rain! and have you not taught for clarity,
for that sweet sake, the worldly dream of the son marching outward
always? and whispering of sins in the green clouds

An eagerness for the historical look of the mirror,
the dry smile of knowledge which is faithlessness apologizing
to the Sphinx, and is it not a great fury of horsemen
who make a guided tour of the future and its glasslike tortures?
the odor of evening vibrating across that linear nostalgia
and vouchsafing a plume and a volume of Plato,
purblind water, the earth pitting its stench against the moon's
and accomplishing a serenade, a terrestrial touchdown sigh
in the silence which is not yet formidable or ominous,
resenting the leaves and not yet geared to the undercutting foam

RIVER

Whole days would go by, and later their years,
while I thought of nothing but its darkness
drifting like a bridge against the sky.
Day after day I dreamily sought its melancholy,
its searchings, its soft banks enfolded me,
and upon my lengthening neck its kiss
was murmuring like a wound. My very life
became the inhalation of its weedy ponderings
and sometimes in the sunlight my eyes,
walled in water, would glimpse the pathway
to the great sea. For it was there I was being borne.
Then for a moment my strengthening arms
would cry out upon the leafy crest of the air
like whitecaps, and lightning, swift as pain,
would go through me on its way to the forest,
and I'd sink back upon that brutal tenderness
that bore me on, that held me like a slave
in its liquid distances of eyes, and one day,
though weeping for my caresses, would abandon me,
moment of infinitely salty air! sun fluttering
like a signal! upon the open flesh of the world.

It's cutting into me on its bareback with talons lifted
like a bespectacled carapaceous witch doctor of Rimini
beautifying an adolescent tubbed in entrails of blue cement
rattling his bells and fox tails and teeth in hydrogen peroxide
under a velour hammock swinging to the bubbles of traffic
of silver striated poppy seeds, milky buses ending in screams
their pods! and a hot wind boring into the cellars of sentiment
which is no more than the animal world, isn't it architectural?
panting its appreciation. You are too late, you are violent,
everyone will know how the man furrows his wet beak,
my nerves will get to the air, and more involved in themselves
than an acanthus issue a somewhat sluggish declaration of wah-wah.
They're calling up the drums to find out if my mask has
buffeted sacks of Congo grass to hide my soul. Great bones
of my knees lifting me hillward! who are you?

O loud timber leg of ore listening to the abutting hoots
and the compensatory descriptions of tin in the banks!
The flour and the fuel of white drill presses is ending!
envelops the corvette which is riddling the farming pillow
diving upon the mustang whose whiskers thump their master,
O great soulful scandal in the courtyard of clairvoyance!
O comatose lips of charcoal going down on the horizon!
the barrages are zooming over the pretty flotillas and bandannas.

Doubtful vendors of stick-seats in the doorway of the furnace,
O doubtful verifiers of the quality of cerise-streaked pus
lying luminously obliterated and sure on a circus salary,
knell of the appealing Wednesday rallying against vices,
knell of sobbing fairies retenting their nut farms and moors,
your fenestrations are full of snow!
O coupling of strangers in the longings of grease!
Evoi!
Dropping warriors champing at their derailed perils
down to the main stream of the never engulfed fund of mares,
tough, serious, consummated, tough, serious, pardoned,
pain willfully enfranchising the foreskin and new wizardry
and puking a little into the jar, pulsating as new ambergris,
do you tender the bounty which has availed itself of your pride?

SONNET ON A WEDDING

for Esther and Alfred Leslie

On the glass escarpment of
the city she waits at a streetlamp
in the dawn. Zephyrs ring
her head with curls and a red
balloon, ripe with her tears,
drifts lost in a forest of lightning.

The towers and minarets at
her silky back fall into the blue
as he drives up in a convertible
silent as strings. She clusters
her skirt about her ankles, squats
on her bustle in the rumbling wind.

Her lips are snowy and he,
the black bridegroom in bangs,
keeps his eye on the ribbon. But
it's no taxi, and when the copper
sings "I pr'ounce you one" her little nose
does hurry sneezing to his cheek,

her fingers perch upon his nape like doves.

TO A FRIEND

If you discard me, too late
in a long line of too lates,
sack of cloud in a century
of sentence for pertinent
arrival and the lavender nit,

Then must I part the dark
hairs and tides of confusion,
my tongue tied on the fang, and
wear dresses in public places,
a man silenced who cannot

speak, for clumsy at your
ear can no more feed.

WALKING TO WORK

It's going to be the sunny side
from now
            on. Get out, all of you.

This is my traffic over the night
and how
            should I range my pride

each oceanic morning like a cutter
if I
      confuse the dark world is round
round who
               in my eyes at morning saves

nothing from nobody? I'm becoming
the street.
               Who are you in love with?
me?
      Straight against the light I cross.

GLI AMANTI

"Of course the room is blue" she
said "it's always cool overlooking
the bay do you think the furniture
is too dark?" I undressed and then

stretched full-length on the bed
while she leaned out the window
showing only buttocks between the
billowing drapes. "There" she said

"is your cousin in an elaborate
carriage clutching a white rabbit
to her girlish bosom! my! she is
smiling!" I rose and doused all

my hair with jasmine cologne put
a flower under my arm and hung
my genitals with pearls whistling
jauntily. "No!" she said turning "you

are not my playmate any more" and
bolted from the intimate room. My
desire would have snapped her garters!
I spun in her absence like a wind I

sobbed. I knelt and watched sailboats
on the water and the jasmine floated out
the window. Blood rose now in my eyes.
The pearls dropped loudly to the floor.

JOVE

He was used to guises and masks
and moonlight, he accepted the fear
to be avoided by an oblique descent,
not to fool himself, but her to reassure.

Whether as bull or swan eluctable
he moved with vigor and cruel light
to possess the deep fount where, downy,
impoverished, the penetrable night

seemed no longer Olympic or vague.
And he loved his victory as beast
as much. Was not his true nature,
but the horns set free what lost

in him the godhead did abuse.
That diadem put off, his thighs
how easily in love pressed being
from mere mythical praise;

the elevation of his brow gave way
to tangled smelly curls. There came
the day when he no longer could
repress his lava from that home:

the ambiguity of his parted crown
fell upon clouds and golden showered.
Fell upon his sweating torso
and to earth. He plunged and flowered.

TO LARRY RIVERS

You are worried that you don't write?
Don't be. It's the tribute of the air that
your paintings don't just let go
of you. And what poet ever sat down
in front of a Titian, pulled out
his versifying tablet and began
to drone? Don't complain, my dear,
You do what I can only name.

STUDY FOR WOMEN ON A BEACH

"I see now tigers by the sea
are crouching. And yet, caught up, gull
on the dolorous possibilities of

waves, I find my flesh more free."
Their hairs clutch at billowing
sands, the dry parishes of pearls

sting in folds of their Imperial
Japanese skin. The ocean's tridents
rear to heaven flaming parachutes

of praise, and walruses wear sables
in the afternoon. "How then, can you
fear death? if, in the hot Sunday,

we are so universally bedded?" They
know of no cathedral, enigmatic as are,
where the spindrift doesn't burn

like a mirror. An icy combustion
has swept into several, yet the two
talk on as incense raises its pillars.

THE STARVING POET

I must have leisure, for the leisure bears
me upward on the breasts of art. How high
flight soar before true manna feeds the eye!
This is not food, though: I must plunder airs

of choice and find my source, the mirror's there.
Now, with two holidays I paint the sky,
an opening in the clouds that, thrusting, I
may find a frightened self that's truly fair

and not raped, not fancy and not prelude,
and not woman. The Muse, if such she be
must welcome me herself, not in image,

and strip me boldly my own heights. There, see
if I shall not seize the full hours! ravage,
and force their meat upon the multitude.

Cold, dark, wet, the lanterns
of Chinatown are hung with icicles
and I am standing on a carpet
atop the telephone pole. And

in the near future rumbles
the vehicle of my adventure,
winding its monstrous way as if
I were the waiting minotaur.

Not fast enough to blind the
lives on east and west bulging
with pain, the luminous glass
identifications of their nagging.

In trances, past turbines,
with empty lunch boxes and all
the cracking evening journals
I speed swimmingly to 106th St.

sixty blocks beyond my goal,
and numb with fear of that devil
river, the munching steel wheels,
and beyond, the open mountains.

BARBIZON

The forest sprang up around me
there in the fertile valley where
I lay nakedly spelling the sleep
of flags. A pulsating swan
shook herself on the long waters.
Did she know the nationalities?
I appeared as a bridge over which
the sky was estimating and establishing
as in a distance the road seems to wind.

Do you see each rippling leaf?
The praying mantises are reflecting
and like a bowl the forest murmurs,
clutching me delicately, pale hair.
If a flute sounded it would all disappear
from sheer similarity, the opposite
of childhood. I am flocking to you,
my beloved waves, where you waste
your breath in another part of the country.

SONNET

Lampooning blizzards, how your ocularities
hask at night and drift like sugar in my ears!
Immense plainnesses of smiling, the sky
is for once kind and bathing, just as before
the party my mother would towel me upon the tile
and make me cry to stay with her, out of the wind.
Now the snow has cuffed a last cry from my cheeks
and festers on my lashes as if they were hands.
They are blue! they are bluer than the dead
and in smiling they roll slightly into cosmic
uneasiness which is based on the infancy of the race;
on that particular event on the shore of Asia Minor
in a gilded canoe when a young queen threw herself
after her crown into the deep for the sheer speed
of a tremendously necessary white departure.

HOUSE

They took the cardboard box and covered
it with plaster, dry among the evergreens.
Thinking of the centuries of worship

that went into those cathedrals built (is
it possible to regret that first whiteness
of construction, so fragile and above
the earth?) like a solid cloud that won't plunge
into the surging aquamarine, they swept
the pipes into a large container to be carted
away by horsepower. And then the surrounding hills
looked beautiful in the fading winter,
although the pipes had been rusted veins
of a structure partially decorated by leaves
and full of sweetness. They preferred the hills,
"spaciousness" they said, and "ease." Yet
there were the horses at night, storming
across the porch of the cement house,
and there were crickets and thistles heaving
full of heart, so prudently habituated.

MANIFESTO

Announcing the publication of a new journal:
THE BENJAMIN FRANKLIN REVIEW

Do you know what you have been reading
lately? Do you see the words, are they dancing?
From now on they will be. Throw away
your galoshes and subscribe (contribute!) to
FRANKLIN, the review that's dedicated.

Literature will now open its big face
in the pages of this publication
and slily, in the spirit of FRANKLIN
and with the amusement of his policy which
is foreign, sit on it. The word "savoir" will now
be translated as "to die." No longer will things
be said to be "beautiful," "amusing," "passionate,"
"moving"; the sanction of the gang who appear here,
the Downtown trapezists, will be indicated by
the phrase "killingly funny," and greatness,
whether it be of Michelangelo or of Bebe Daniels,
will not be surprised by the appellation.
A blush, as at a secret enthusiasm, will spread
over the world, the Red World and the White World.

POEM

When your left arm twitches
it's like sunlight on sugar
to me and my tongue seeks
the sea of your skin, its oily
calm of green light on the floor
of the ocean
                          as in parting,
there's a flutter between us
while I haul down a flag and
you look absently out of
my heart so you won't see
what light one fears in the
sea that I don't want you
to know is of you in me

THE OPERA

Free to suffer speechful constraint
to be whipped by mysterious winds
to find your dear friend's smiling eye
dropping like a window on your neck
          its diamonds.

I am wondering if you remember her
as a young girl with several minor operations
walking her dog and humming the poor reindeer
into the glasses of silver intoxicating sighs
          a very sad dress.

There will never be a moment more like it
when the heart sights its whalespout into the throat
and tears like Alps go up austere elevators
into which blue-you never quite disappears
          though again you try to try.

Then the weather changed. There were all
these instruments looking coldly at us.
"When are you going away?" "Instanter."
And the clouds glowered as if they were snow.
"Vous êtes mal. Stay in bed." An orange wall
was removed to disclose a grey one. A gray
one. I remember that my old intimate was very kind
to me last night before I fell down the stairs,
buying me beer after beer as if I were
an old friend met on the rim of a volcano
to whom a push was a kiss. It made me happy
it did indeed make me happy. It made me happy
as I was capable of at the time. If I had had
an ice cream cone, a chocolate one, and a knish
I would have been a little bit more passionately
happy. But you wake up and someone is moving
the walls. Now the room is completely grey
with a white ceiling. She is standing
at the foot of my bed covered with plaster,
and it is about time that I renewed myself
at her Maker's expense, who is in the world
and will not credit the evil of my intentions.

TWO VARIATIONS

Suddenly that body appears: in my smoke
while someone's heavily describing Greece,
that famous monotonous line feels white
against the tensile gloom of life
and I seem intimate with what I merely touch.

I
Now I am not going to face things
because I am not a start
nor fall asleep against a heart
that doesn't burn the wolves away,

hunting and virtue beside an open fire.
And you know if I drift into the sky
it will be heavy as surf.

2

I'm glad that the rock is heavy
and that it feels all right in my heart
like an eye in a pot of humus.
Let's write long letters on grand themes,
fish sandwiches, egg sandwiches and cheese;
or traveling in Mexico, Italy and Australia.
I eat a lot so I won't get drunk and then
I drink a lot so I'll feel excited
and then I've gone away I don't know where
or with whom and can't remember whom from
except that I'm back with my paper bag
and next time my face won't come with me.

VERY RAINY LIGHT, AN ECLOGUE

(*Daphnis & Chloe*)

D: Remembering at best bitterly
    that peacocks are not a hit with
    you. Chinchilla, you are beautiful.
    All that you've given me's at one.
    I'm not chilly thinking or bones.

C: Someone has glued my castanets
    together. And this morning early I
    became aimlessly apparent 'cause
    I woke up first and the dew jetted
    from your armpits of ambergris.
    I smelled burning rubber, I did
    not receive a cable from your Europe
    every being at war at the time.

D: All praise to Juno, she as disaster
    cuts a fine figure. Your diamonds
    are dripping like spit. Am enamored.

C: The whistle of your gaze cuts across
    my hair like spurs. You're the big

breeze in halflight, don't think I
don't know it. At dawn when I'm milking
the aphids I hear your stomach
coming up like thunder. Oh baby.

D: Onto what Nizhni sifts, ja ja,
the appealing moo? Under which
nasty mummer skips the coral rope?
I like you, but perhaps you, fiery,
are no fit companion on field trips?

C: You must come when my throaty heart
traces the wiry meteors to breathe
in your ear its invitation to the beach.
I will scare up the money to chase
you into my arms where, like winter
flowers, you'll find small sentiments
lunging robustly. Warm. Is as if
I am your sheeted will for windward.
I shall leave a jar of powdered coffee
on your tongue. Be wakefully mine.

D: O joy! O joy! today's the day, eh?
I've quit pictures for the grassy knolls
of knees and the apple of your nut.
No more greys for me! You. Artichoke.

C: O infinite languor of railroads!
truly you master a heady scent.

POEM

As you kneel
be a scholar,
wear color and silk,
hold out to all
your newly woven hand.

A bird in bamboo
is curing the village

as it rides
through the dust storm.

Have you seen,
among clouds and waves,
the unknown artist
in the shape of a fan?

He is at sea
with two pine trees
where the Seven Deities
of the Northern Dipper
dance around a toad.

An angler
is playing the flute
in a boat.

Be a waterfall
with your casual advice
which is like
to not understanding
but is a pair
of travelers.

It is ink
on paper love
and I am dead
because I am attributed
to the moods of others
like a peony.

RENT COLLECTING

I hate the revolutionary vision, a sea of navels,
for their collapse is a false numb in the blare
of daguerreotypes, a sort of moccasin, nervous,
and now an encrusted infiltration. She's mild
for the rancid tenebrae, he for her blind
mariposa, the villain courses the count

and fiery grunt infuses sneezes into the mob
of squatting Pernambucoites, beside the rock.
It is significantly to be pierced noisily
by the misfortunates of hasty arrows
and to shunt some, that the belly distends
into blowing lies of cloud, and the world narrows.
Not quite comparatively, as an Old World is stifled
by a giant hardon, the taverners are loose.

SONNET FOR LARRY RIVERS & HIS SISTER

A young man talking to his sister on
the telephone, "Hello, this is Caesar";
that aspect of concentration
around the eyes comes from life, are
they reflecting it always? Then
whatever diametric blushes appear
gaze towards Egypt, and seem often
to call out confusedly and clear
like palms with pigeons on them. "Eyes!
what do you know about Corot? If I get
it anywhere I get it from him. He's
very influential among you skiing and jet
dilettantes." And the operator interrupted,
"Your bagatelle has been accepted."

ROUND ROBIN

Yes, it's true, I arouse strange sights in
the heart of a girl[1] who hasn't yet chosen
which heart is hers, she's very upset.

She calls for the movies the very day he,[2]
in his salt-stained shirtwaist, embarks
for Europe without me on the pier;

he would weep were I there as he wept
without me, all the Michelangelos in Florence
will be merely my nose veiled by rain.

And there's the other[3] so like and unlike him
who is moved by my smile like a public accusation
of homosexuality against the Great Wall of China;

to him my affection's as pleasing as an insult
to a nun. And he's not very jealous of the legendary beauty[4]
who has launched a thousand of my eyes,

for as I race away from her like a smoky train
she assigns me to the brunette[5] with a cold.
I even love children,[6] despise me for culling their feet,

it's as if we were all clouds and a ray of sun
broke beautifully through one of us, and the others said
"Look, a knife has just dropped into the ocean."

SECOND AVENUE

In memory of Vladimir Mayakovsky

I

Quips and players, seeming to vend astringency off-hours,
celebrate diced excesses and sardonics, mixing pleasures,
as if proximity were staring at the margin of a plea . . .

This thoroughness whose traditions have become so reflective,
your distinction is merely a quill at the bottom of the sea
tracing forever the fabulous alarms of the mute
so that in the limpid tosses of your violet dinginess
a pus appears and lingers like a groan from the collar
of a reproachful tree whose needles are tired of howling.
One distinguishes merely the newspapers of a sediment,
since going underground is like discovering something in

[1]Nina Castelli [2]Larry Osgood [3]Larry Rivers [4]Helen Parker [5]Jane Freilicher [6]Joseph & Steven Rivers

your navel that has an odor and is able to fly away.
I must bitterly reassure the resurgence of your complaints
for you, like all heretics, penetrate my glacial immodesty,
and I am a nun trembling before the microphone
at a movie première while a tidal wave has seized the theatre
and borne it to Siam, decorated it and wrecked its projector.
To what leaf of fertility and double-facedness owe I
my persistent adoration of your islands, oh shadowed flesh
of my smiling? I scintillate like a glass of ice
and it is all for you and the boa constrictors who entertain
your doubts with a scarf dance called "Bronx Tambourine."
Grappling with images of toothpaste falling on guitar strings,
your lips are indeed a disaster of alienated star-knots
as I deign to load the hips of the swimming pool, lumber!
with the clattering caporal of destiny's breast-full,
such exhalations and filthiness falling upon the vegetables!
You will say I am supernatural.
Varying your task with immortal plunging justices and fruits,
I suffer accelerations that are vicarious and serene,
just as the lances of an army advance above the heat of the soldiery,
so does my *I* tremble before the getting-out-of-bedness
of that all-encompassing snake warned-off in pocket-books
as "him," and subtitled elsewhere "couch," "marvel," "ears,"
or "fire-escape," "lampooned frigid scalper of an Amazon maid,"
"warrior of either sex in the distances which are American";
and just as it is a miracle to find her in the interrogation
of an escalator, you find yourself racing towards nervousness,
the purée of crime, and your face has fallen like a waffle
and is the velour of Lesbian sandals with nails in the toes;
your lamp will never light without dirt and the speed
increases of moving away from all rapturous ice-floes
as a shaggy white figure approaches and sinks its fangs
upon my brazen throat, so thrust into the wind that a necklace
of fur such as this which drags me beneath the Bering Sea
is the only possible adornment for this burning flight
and the magnificent entrance to be mine as I crash
against the portals of the mistress of chairs, who is
yes, a bearded man suspended by telephone wires from moons
in alternate sexual systems. And then there is the crushing
drop! as the fur falls from me and the man crashes, a crater,
from the heavens which he so adored and which I also decorate
as the forest of my regard. But now I have a larger following.

2

What spanking opossums of sneaks are caressing the routes!
and of the pulse-racked tremors attached to my viciousness
I can only enumerate the somber instances of wetness.

Is it a triumph? and are the lightnings of movedness
and abysmal elevation cantankerous filaments
of a larger faint-heartedness like loving summer? You,
accepting always the poisonous sting of the spine,
its golden efflorescence of nature which is distrustful,
how is one borne to this caprice of a lashing betrayal
whose jewel-like occasion has the clarity of blossoming trees?
is it not the deepest glitterings of love when the head
is turned off, glancing over a stranger's moonlike hatred
and finding an animal kingdom of jealousy in parachutes
descending upon the highway which you are not speeding down?
It is this silence which returns you to the open fields
of blandest red honey where the snake waits, his warm tongue.
Dice! into the lump and crush of archness and token angels
you burn your secret preferments and ancient streaming,

as a gasp of laughter at desire, and disorder, and dying.

3

And must I express the science of legendary elegies
consummate on the Clarissas of puma and gnu and wildebeest?
Blue negroes on the verge of a true foreignness
escape nevertheless the chromaticism of occidental death
by traffic, oh children bereaved of their doped carts
and priests with lips like mutton in their bedrooms at dawn!
and falling into a sea of asphalt abuse which is precisely life
in these provinces printed everywhere with the flag "Nobody,"
and these are the true tillers of the spirit
whose strangeness crushes in the only possible embrace,
is like splintering and pulling and draining the tooth
of the world, the violent alabaster yielding to the sky,
the kiss and the longing to be modern and sheltered and different
and insane and decorative as a Mayan idol too well understood
to be beautiful. Can roses be charming? As the sluice
pours forth its granular flayings a new cloud rises
and interplanetary driftings become simply initiatory gifts
like the circumcision of a black horse. I yield up
my lover to the reveries, completely, until he is taken away
by the demons who then deliver me their bolts from afar
like drunken Magi. It is the appeasement, frieze-style,
of undulant spiritual contamination, to which sainthood
I sacrifice my brilliant dryness, it had been my devoir
and my elegant distinction, a luminous enlacement
of the people through the bars of the zoo, the never fading.
My spirit is clouded, as it was in Tierra del Fuego,
and if the monsters who twirl on their toes like fiery wagons
cannot dismiss the oceanographer of a capricious promptness

which is more ethical than dismal, my heart
will break through to casualness and appear in windows
on Main Streets, "more vulgar but they love more than he
hates, as the apples turn straightway into balloons
and burst." No airship casts its shadow down the Road
of the Golden Arm, over which is folded the Canal
and the Shroud. A mystery appears and doesn't mention
intelligence or death, and is as swiftly gone into the corn
and the ivy fields, all red and grey in the gathering noise.
The houses look old, viscous, and their robes bear
massive pretenses to anxiety, the animal's dream
of successiveness, the paralytic's apprehension of germs,
and then, fleeing! the dancer's nestling into kelp
and the condemned man's amusement at versatility,
the judge's ardent approximation of harrowing languor
in which the pelt of the whole city moves forward as a flame.
One would call upon Apollo as a famous father and tenor
but the prodigious paleness of the insulted disfigures
all ingenuity and the sounds perfidious mountains move
away from with tomblike excitement, the eternal travelers,
so you are silent, aren't you? Well, I shall be older
and uglier than you, and my least motion shall wither
the vertiginous breath which is earth meeting sky meeting sea,
as in the legend of a sovereign who did and who was.
Immense flapping. I hold all of night in my one eye. You.

4

Is your throat dry with the deviousness of following?
I lead you to a stream which will lick you like a wasp,
and there the maidens will uncoil the hemp hunters and wires
so that your body may recline upon boards of starry nudging,
sisters of bar-girls in the haunches of the Himalayas.
Oh aspirations prancing like an elephant in a skirmish!
Or are you altitudes? . . .

5

                          or are you myself,
indifferent as a drunkard sponging off a car window?
Are you effeminate, like an eyelid, or are you feminine,
like a painting by Picasso? You fled when you followed,
and now the bamboo veils of intemperance are flapping down
with tigerish yaps over the paling corduroy doorway
which was once a capacious volute filled with airplanes,
and that was not a distance, that simple roaring and vagueness.
You are lean, achieved, ravished, acute, light, tan,
waving, stolen, lissome in whispering, salivary in intent,
similar to the sole support of a love affair, so artful,
and loyal only to faults. I found myself equal to every . . .

"Oh the droppings from the trees! the little clam shells,
their bosoms thrust into the clouds and kiss-stained!
I met Joe, his hair pale as the eyes of fields of maize
in August, at the gallery, he said you're the first Creon
of 1953, congrats. Your costume, he said, was hand
over fist. If you worked harder you could remake
old Barrymore movies, you're that statuesque, he said.
For when the window, the ice in it, ran, the fish leaped forth
and returned where they wished to return to and from,
as in a rainbow the end keeps leaping towards the middle
which is the shape of all flowers, and of all flowers
the most exotic." Yes! yes! it was cerulean, oh my darling!
"And the simple yet exquisite pertinence of that race
above the airfield, those tubby little planes flopping
competitively into the wind sleeve, was keen as a violin,
as colorless and as intent. It seemed there was no one there
but children, and at each flaming accident a crumbling giggle
tumbleweeded over the flats and into the hangars and echoed.
What must the fliers have thought? a performance
like a plate of ham and eggs eaten with a fur collar on.
I kept jingling the coins in my pocket and patting
the dollar bills that rustled like so many horses' hooves
against my anxious thigh. He was up there,
the one who ruined my sister while she was still a look
of spiritual withdrawal in my maiden aunt's memories
of bathing at Onset. I always win at Japanese bowling.
I won a piano with a flowered shawl draped over it
and a photograph of Anna Sten beside a trembling yellow vase."

Screaming and tearing at her breasts she bent over,
terribly pale and yet trifling with her feelings before him,
the heavy bronze crucifix he had stepped on, quite
accidentally, mistaking it for a moth, tinea pellionella,
which, in its labors against death, another more
vibrantly mournful kind, renders mankind subtly naked;
more than her eyes could stand, she went bloated into the azure
like a shot. Greying even more steadily now he remembered
the afternoon games of marbles beside the firehouse
and how the scum settled on his shoulders as he swam
and the many tasks done and forgotten and famous which,
as a pilot, he had disdained, trusting to luck always.
"Arabella" was the word he had muttered that moment
when lightning had smelled sweet over the zoo of the waves
while he played on and on and on and the women grew hysterical.
Of heldness and of caresses you have become the entrepreneur.
The sea looked like so many amethyst prophets and I,
hadn't the cannery sent forth perfume? would never go back.

And then staggering forward into the astounding capaciousness
of his own rumor he became violent as an auction,
rubbed the hairs on his chest with bottles of snarling
and deared the frying pan that curtained the windows
with his tears. I remember I felt at that moment the elephant
kissing. When paralysis becomes jaundice and jaundice
is blushing, a linen map of ecstasy hangs next the range
where the peas are burning and memories of Swan Lake
aspire like Victoria Falls to a jacket of dust.

You are too young to remember the lack of snow in 1953 showing:
"1 Except that you react like electricity to a chunk of cloth,
it will disappear like an ape at night. 2 Before eating
there was a closing of retina against retina, and ice,
telephone wires! was knotted, spelling out farce
which is germane to lust. 3 Then the historic duel in the surf
when black garments were wasted and swept over battlements
into the moat. 4 The book contained a rosary pressed
in the shape of a tongue. 5 The hill had begun to roll
luminously. A deck appeared among the fir trees. Larry's
uncle sent a missionary to India when he was in grade school
who cried 'Go straight' to the white men there. Forgiveness
of heat. 6 Green lips pressed his body like a pearl shell.
7 It all took place in darkness, and meant more earlier
when they were in different places and didn't know each other.
As is often misprinted." And such whiteness not there!
All right, all right, all right, you glass of coke, empty
your exceptionally neonish newspaper from such left hands
with headlines to be grey as cut WITHER ACCEPTED AS SELLING.
(The western mountain ranges were sneaking along "Who
taps wires and why?" like a pack of dogies and is there much
tapping under the desert moon? Does it look magical
or realistic, that landing? And the riverboat put in there,
keeps putting in, with all the slaves' golden teeth and arms,
self-conscious without their weapons. Joe LeSueur,
the handsome Captain who smuggles Danish perfumes, tied up
at the arroyo and with thunderous hooves swam across a causeway
to make the Honest Dollar. In Pasadena they are calling
"Higho, Silver!" but in the High Sierras they just shoot
movie after movie. Who is "they"? The Westerners, of course,
the tans. Didn't you ever want to be a cowboy, buster?) Big-
town papers, you see, and this great-coated tour of the teens
in (oh bless me!) imagination. That's what the snow said,
"and doesn't your penis look funny today?" I jacked "off."

6

"Nous avons eu lundi soir, le grand plaisir de rencontrer
à l'Hôtel Oloffson où elle est descendue, la charmante

Mlle. Anne R. Lang, actrice du Théâtre Dramatique de Cambridge.
Miss Lang est arrivée à Port-au-Prince le mardi 24 février
à bord d'un avion de la 'Resort Air Line.'
Cette belle artiste a visité les sites de la Capitale
et est enchantée de tout ce qu'elle a vu. Elle est fort
éprise de notre pays." And it's very exciting to be an old friend
of Verlaine and he has his problems, divine dust bag
of pressure chambers which is merely an episode clarifying
what the work really is in relationship with birds and insects
you are sitting on as you drink and think about dancing,
poor dedicated blonde that you are, ma fille, ma soeur,
my fellow airlines provocateur and sandal dropper on the hots.
Do you know which back alley we would park and snot the wimple
in? It is embarrassing to be too rich with black looks,
he would be waiting for you to come in from roaming, slipper
in left hand raised, the famous left hand of the epigraph.
"Ah, oui." Tumbling vipers where your stain, Lar, hot-tranced
into the hydrogen of a backache which is a whole harem
of swaying odors and caravanserai grit, alors! c'est mung,
the middling passionate rapids down where a tender word
rushes to snarl and laugh deliriously into the back of the head
where the hair barnacles its uneasy lay against the nape
so ecstatic, like churchbells against the flanks of horsetails,
sleight of hand, "Ô reine Überschreigung!" of an old lavatory.
It was that way many times, yet the winter seemed prompt.

7
"You come to me smelling of the shit of Pyrrhian maidens!
and I as a fast come-on for fascinating fleas-in-ice
become ravenously casual avec quel haut style de chambre!
and deny myself every pasture of cerise cumulus cries.
You yourself had taken out volumes of rare skies' pillars
and then bowed forth screaming 'Lindy Has Made It!' until
everyone showed their teeth to the neighbors of Uncle,
how embarrassing! the whiteness of the imitation of the glass
in which one elegant pig had straddled a pheasant and wept.
Well enough. To garner the snowing snow and then leave,
what an inspiration! as if suddenly, while dancing, someone,
a rather piratish elderly girl, had stuck her fan up her ass
and then become a Chinese legend before the bullrushes ope'd.
Yet I became aware of history as rods stippling the dip
of a fancied and intuitive scientific roadmap, clarté et
volupté et vif! swooping over the valley and under the lavender
where children prayed and had stillborn blue brothers of
entirely other races, the Tour Babel, as they say, said.
I want listeners to be distracted, as fur rises when most needed
and walks away to be another affair on another prairie,

yowee, it's heaven in Heaven! with the leaves falling
like angels who've been discharged for sodomy
and it all almost over, that is too true to last, that is,
'rawther old testament, dontcha know.' When they bite,
you've never seen anything more beautiful, the sheer fantail
of it and them delicately clinging to the crimson box
like so many squid, for sweetness. Do you have the haveness
of a collapse, of a rummaging albatross that sings? No!
don't even consider asking me to the swimming team's tea-
and-alabaster breakfast. I just don't want to be asked."

The mountains had trembled, quivering as if about to withdraw,
and where the ships had lined up on the frontier waiting for
the first gunshot, a young girl lunched on aspergum. A cow
belched. The sun went. Later in the day Steven farted.
He dropped his torpedo into the bathtub. Flowers. Relativity.
He stayed under water 65 seconds the first time and 84 the second.
Sheer Olympia, the last of the cat-lovers, oh Jimmy!
the prettiest cat in New York. A waiter stole the dollar bill
while the people sang in the Cicada Circle built in 1982
at a cost of three rose petals. She told him she'd miss him
when she went to live in the marshgrass, did Berdie,
and he thought, "You'll miss me like that emerald I have at home
I forgot to give you when I lost my pink Birthday Book
when it was smuggled out of Europe in a box of chocolate-cherries."
Thirty-five cancerous growths were removed from as many breasts
in one great iron-grill-work purple apartment house yesterday,
and this tribute to the toughness of the Air Corps is like rain.

Had not all beautiful things become real on Wednesday?
and had not your own bumbleshoot caressed a clergyman and autos?
To be sure, the furniture was wrinkled, but a cat doesn't wink,
and her motto exists on the Liberian Ambassador's stationery,
"Amor vincit et Cicero vidit" in sachets of morning-glories.

8
Candidly. The past, the sensations of the past. Now!
in cuneiform, of umbrella satrap square-carts with hotdogs
and onions of red syrup blended, of sand bejewelling the prepuce
in tank suits, of Majestic Camera Stores and Schuster's,
of Kenneth in an abandoned storeway on Sunday cutting ever more
insinuating lobotomies of a yet-to-be-more-yielding world
of ears, of a soprano rallying at night in a cadenza, Bill, of
"Fornications, la! garumph! tereu! lala la! vertigo! Weevy! Hah!",
of a limp hand larger than the knee which seems to say "Addio"
and is capable of resigning from the disaster it summoned ashore.
Acres of glass don't make the sign clearer of the landscape

less blue than prehistorically, yet less distant, eager, dead!
and generations of thorns are reconstructed as a mammoth
unstitched from the mighty thigh of the glacier, the Roaring Id.
You remained for me a green Buick of sighs, o Gladstone!
and your wife Trina, how like a yellow pillow on a sill
in the many-windowed dusk where the air is compartmented!
her red lips of Hollywood, soft as a Titian and as tender,
her grey face which refrains from thrusting aside the mane
of your languorous black smells, the hand crushed by her chin,
and that slumberland of dark cutaneous lines which reels
under the burden of her many-darkly-hued corpulence of linen
and satin bushes, is like a lone rose with the sky behind it.
A yellow rose. Valentine's Day. "Imagine that substance
extended for two hours of theatre and you see the inevitable,
the disappearance of vigor in a heart not sufficiently basted
or burnt, the mere apparition of feeling in an empty bedroom.
Zounds!! you want money? Take my watch which is always fast."

Accuracy has never envisaged itself as occurring; rather a
negligence, royal in retreating upwards of the characteristics
of multitudes. "You call me Mamie, but I'm monickered Sanskrit
in the San Remo, and have a divorce inside my lamé left breast,"
so into the headlands where the peaceful aborigines eat the meat
that's always white, no muscles, no liver, no brains, no, no,
tongue, that's it. Weary. Well, forgetting you not is forgetting,
even if I think of you tall the day, and forgetting you is
forgiving you not, for I am weeping from a tall wet dream, oh.
Cantankerous month! have you ever moved more slowly into surf?
Oh Bismarck! Fortitude! exceptional delights of intelligence!
yappings at cloister doors! dimpled marshmallows! oh March!

9
Now in November, by Josephine Johnson. The Heroes,
by John Ashbery. Topper's Roumanian Broilings. The Swimmer.
Your feet are more beautiful than your father's, I think,
does that upset you? admire, I admire youth above age, yes,
in the infancy of the race when we were very upset we wrote,
"O toe!" and it took months to "get" those feet. Render. Rent.
Now more features of our days have become popular, the nose
broken, the head bald, the body beautiful. Marilyn Monroe.
Can one's lips be "more" or "less" sensual? "Ma,
il primo bacio debbo darlo ancora," so which of you banditti
knows? oh braggarts! toothpastes! you motherfuckers! At
lunch in the park the pigeons are like tulips on the trees.

O panic of drying mushrooms! how many gorillas are there
in cages? They are bashing the seals over the head with coke.

As I walked into the Dairy B & H Lunch I couldn't remember
your other eye, I puked. Sunday came, the violet waves crusted.
The sand bristled and with its stinging flashes we dove
screaming into the rocks where pythons nestled and brooded.
Is the nose, for instance, part of the forehead, a strawberry
part of the forest? Bill was married secretly by a Negro justice
over the Savoy on Massachusetts Avenue where I met for beer
my lover on secret Sundays, for we were all very young
and needed a headquarters which became a jazz tree-hut.
Don't forget, you're most alone, Caramba! Optimo!
when you're alone, when yellow and blue lumber's piled on
a sledge and you gee and haw the oxen as the spring circles
warily and the pheasants shit. Jack-in-the-Pulpit. Bailey
Whitney. My father said, "Do what you want but don't get hurt,
I'm warning you. Leave the men alone, they'll only tease you.
When your aunt comes I want you to get down off that horse
and speak like a gentleman, or I'll take it away from you.
Don't grit your teeth at me." A chicken walked by with tail
reared, looking very personal, pecking and dribbling, wattles.
You suddenly got an idea of what black and white poetry
was like, you grinning Simian fart, poseur among idiots
and dilettantes and pederasts. When the chips are in,
yours will spell out in a wealth of dominoes, YOU, and you'll
be stuck with it, hell to anybody else, drowning in lead,
like your brain, of which the French poets wrote, "O fat-assed
configurations and volutions of ribbed sand which the sea
never reaches!" Memories of home, which is an island, of course,
and historical, of course, and full of ass, of course. Yes,
may you trip on a blue fire-escape and go up when it's raining!
what dismal monster cannot be electrocuted? what fool
not rumpled? what miserable wretch not forced upon the happiness
which kills? I witnessed at last the calmness of ordure.

Less comfortable but more decorative. My head covered
by a green cloth. Taxicabs whistling by. Fulgently leaning
from behind, slightly bent. And then the paralyzing rush
of emotion, its fists caught in Venetian blinds, silent,
burgeoning, like a smudge-pot in a tornado. Utica Avenue.
"Arrivaderlà!" Chief Dispursing Officer, Division of
Disbursement. "I'm glad there's something beautiful in his life."
Shall I ever be able to avail myself of the service called
"Same Day Cleaning," and in what face have I fought the Host?

10
The silence that lasted for a quarter of a century. All
the babies were born blue. They called him "Al" and "Horseballs"
in kindergarten, he had an autocratic straw face like a dark

in a de Kooning where the torrent has subsided at the very center
of classicism, it can be many whirlpools in a gun battle
or each individual pang in the "last mile" of electrodes, so
totally unlike xmas tree ornaments that you wonder, uhmmm?
what the bourgeoisie is thinking off. Trench coat. Broken strap.
Pseudo-aggressive as the wife of a psychiatrist. Beating off.
Banging off. It is delicately thorough in laying its leaden sneer
down in Brettschneider's Funeral Home. You'll say I'm supper,
naturally, but one is distinguished by the newspapers of the lips.

"He vaporously nags down the quoits. I might have to suffer
for another year. I might severally dismiss my trysts, la!
as the fire-eaters collide. See, lumbering dimly: the quest
for Japanese deer, lazy, mean, truncated. See not the ray.
Jealousy bans raffles, lumia advances, ditto March's amber,
pending quietly Negro lariat tumbling derailed 'de' whores.
Jumping ripples pour forth Rienzi. A present: community, Alp,
a jiffy immune piping in a boat of vice about dumbness.
My villain accommodates a Chinese scent to jar the bone-on,
maybe jetting beasts parse what we hesitantly choose,
nipping oval appetites changing and quieting in a Paris
of voluptuary chases, lays, choices, what we know and savor.
Perk quietly, don't, pension me and ply me with love that's droll,
noose light harms and nutty bathers, use, nip, alarm and pet,
eat, sup, end, Antinous, lake of comprehension, unless passion
down aimlessly sonorous plusses, denies our doubtful paroles,"

says that the show miserably disturbs, the endurance of water,
and when the pressure asphyxiates and inflames, Grace destroys
the whirling faces in their dissonant gaiety where it's anxious,
lifted nasally to the heavens which is a carrousel grinning
and spasmodically obliterated with loaves of greasy white paint
and this becomes like love to her, is what I desire
and what you, to be able to throw something away without yawning
"Oh Leaves of Grass! o Sylvette! oh Basket Weavers' Conference!"
and thus make good our promise to destroy something but not us.
A green fire-escape, an orange fire-escape, a black, a grey spider.
"Dolores, O hobble and kobble Dolores. O perfect obstruction
on track." See? "Je suis reine de Sparte et celle-là de Troie,
sachant quels gras couchants ont les plus blancs aveux?"
O pain! driftwood and limewood, they kissed, were missing a leg.
And yet the simple endurance of their attraction carried a camel
into the lake formerly placarded "Abyss of Sizzling Tears."

Butter. Lotions. Cries. A glass of ice. Aldebaran and Mizar,
a guitar of toothpaste tubes and fingernails, trembling spear.
Balustrade, tensile, enclosing the surging waters of my heart

in a laughing collapse where the natives tint urine their hair:
trolley cars find cat-eyes in New Guinea where Mozart died,
on the beach fraught with emotion and rotting elephants,
that elephant of a smile which lingers when I lean over and throw.

I I
My hands are Massimo Plaster, called "White Pin in the Arm of the Sea"
and I'm blazoned and scorch like a fleet of windbells down the Pulaski Skyway,
tabletops of Vienna carrying their bundles of cellophane to the laundry,
ear to the tongue, glistening semester of ardency, young-old daringnesses
at the foot of the most substantial art product of our times,
the world, the jongleurs, fields of dizzyness and dysentery
before reaching Mexico, the palace of stammering sinking success
before billows of fangs, red faces, orange eyebrows, green, yes! ears,
O paradise! my airplanes known as "Banana Line Incorporealidad,"
saviors of connections and spit, dial HYacinth 9-9945, "Isn't that
a conundrum?" asked him Sydney Burger, humming "Mein' Yiddisher Mama,"
I emulate the black which is a cry but is not voluptuary like a warning,
which has lines, cuts, drips, aspirates, trembles with horror,
O black looks at the base of the spine! kisses on the medulla oblongata
of an inky clarity! always the earlobes in the swiftest bird's-death
of night, the snarl of expiation which is the skirt of Hercules,
and the remorse in the desert shouts "Flea! Bonanza! Cheek! Teat!
Elbow of roaches! You wear my white rooster like a guerdon in vales
of Pompeiian desires, before utter languorousness puts down its chisel,"
and the desert is here. "You've reached the enormous summit of passion
which is immobility forging an entrail from the pure obstruction of the air."

DOLCE COLLOQUIO

O sentiments sitting beside my bed
what are you thinking? of an ebony vase?
of a pail of garbage? of memorizing Whitman?
You are leaning on my elbow backwards.

What are you doing, my darling sentiments?
You are indeed bored. Can it be that I'm asleep?
Shall you stride on the shingle with an oar
in your hands, or beach my heart, my barnacled?

You would let me lay in bed all day,
free to drown in your wing-beatings as you fled
past and past my glazed, teary-from-the-breezes heart,
which is not going to open up and look out any more.

3 POEMS ABOUT KENNETH KOCH

QUE VIVA MEXICO!

May I tell you how much I love your poems?
It's as if a great pipeline had been illicitly tapped
along which all personal characteristics
are making a hasty departure. Tuba? gin?
"qu'importe où?" O Kenneth Koch!

GALLOP ALONG! OR HURRY BACK

1

Are you getting the beer, Kenneth? Are you
while Janice and I hang from the mistletoe
of surprising indigestion, I mean indiscretion?
Oh what a green cockatoo of a messenger he is!
he can hardly walk, let alone hurry. Oh mercy me!
Well, dear, who's dying of thirst?
We've still got to finish *Le Cid.* Aldebaran!
are you watching him waste his time in the street?
clucking and scolding as you are wont to do, aren't you?
And what will we send him for if you get him back
to us quickly, busybody? Don't stars ever think?

2

I was musing over the king my father and the beer
my brother and the hots the weather down by the old
gassy superintendent's wet laundry the other day
in the dark when suddenly speed sprang to mind,
oh gloriously it evoked the image of Kenneth
lumbering down the stairs while we laughed. But,
that was in another country, I guess. And pa's dead.

3

He never, Kenneth, did an effortless thing
in his life, but it pains us to send him into the world

in a hurry, he might stumble and commit a series!
Under the careful care of our admiration his greatness
appears like the French for "gratuitous act" and we're proud
of our Hermes, the fastest literary figure of his time.
Are you sitting down to write outside the delicatessen?
Get up, man! come home! Who do you think we are?

THE INCA MYSTERY

Don't tell me to smile, oh flamboyant egrets! not
while I'm pining naked on the Spanish Steps
of an amusement at a corpse's Rabbinical youthfulness.
He kicked off in the line of duty, citizen too,
while Kenneth, oh woe! was in the Hotel Imperial Colon,
Mexico City, watching the city gradually vanish.
Oh cuffs of Kenneth, are you weeping a sooty miasma?
He is dangerously close by air, and we expect him
a day before he arrives, delicious day of overcast.
Two dope addicts did him in. Will Kenneth catch them?
Has he learned about addiction in Tamazunchale,
and fiends! are there any left in fragrant Miami?
They are hunting for the dead cop's wife in Jacksonville
but she's secretly in Lexington, Ky., taking the cure.
Oh Kenneth, hurry, I do wish they'd be nicer to the Jews
in Delaware, I don't think the dope fiends are hiding
there, they're disguised as feathers in Philadelphia.
I know and Kenneth will know. Gee, I'm really depressed.
My black back. And now the telephone. "Hello. Kenneth?"

TWO EPITAPHS

I

The two slept in a dark red armory
in the midst of apparitions where a pianist
committed suicide. Art brought them
together, and though they did achingly
stab each other it was into the ground
where no grass grows, so that
to every passerby who peered ironically
through the stakes of their attraction
they assumed the statuesque impossibility
of genius ignited wastefully in daylight.

2
They were afterwards said to have loved
each other from the first moment, and this
took the formal dispersion of excitement.
Their intimacy sweetly bore them upon a pain
which soared when they were together,
yet spent itself upon the scenery when apart.
No one could have guessed their secret pleasures,
that ardent profile whose public expression is hate.

3
Each formed the other like a passion
from his living flesh: the idea
became clearer by the inevitable distances
of their grandeur. Their birth was a volcano;
they went straight into the air with wings of
suffering, and hung over the city as northern lights.

POEM

I
He sighted her at the moment of recall.
The grass tumbled, rounded his feet like trees.
He fell. The lake! His head sank in a dish of perfume.

2
Now there was a Severini mural outside the house
and hollyhocks, his favorite, but they wouldn't bloom
so they could look like huge chairs nobody sat in,

3
and there was a multiplicity of views;
"You enjoy everything awful because you enjoy
each part of everything not–entirely–beautiful."

4
The sobs rang out and rolled through the landscapes,
all of which you could see at the same time, dear.
Like so many silvery blue disks.

5
We both have blue eyes, you see.
How far had we driven each other toward that mood
of the barberry bush, its berries yearly flinging thorns?

6
Everywhere there were arches but we only looked,
everywhere there were dead rabbits at which we smiled, and
everywhere things seemed to be turning but not signalling.

7
I am so hideous that her many faults will disappear
while I am near, like clouds, O clouds!
stop! waste a moment of your love of time!

8
and Jane is anxious.
Only one thing moves and it is the blue Upwards,
as the future of our faces multiplies in tears.

HOMAGE TO ANDRÉ GIDE

I would attend your pleasure's picturesque remorse
        with an insensitive smile
which the umbrellas, plunging over the abyss like a horse,
        would emulate all the while
as the enormous air of the avenue lay pierced by rain,
        if I were vile
and my heart, like a great beaded purse, feeble and vain.

For the vanity of the great is as simple as a car.
Just as a smile, fainting, reclines in its chair
in the weedy garden and the glass drops from its hand,
so go the umbrellas where they are told to go, bland
and colorless and wet, on their entirely imitative errand.
        And if the vile
        see them, they smile.
I would enjoy walking endlessly upon the sand,
        if the windy course
        of an almost Irish remorse

did not imitate you, and insistently beckon me elsewhere,
and my longings had not become centuries, when the air
is reflected by a star.

LIFE ON EARTH

1

Shine, "O world!" don't weary the gulping Pole
deep in drinking this night his mighty syrup of aches.
His song will be calmer when the laughing birds settle on his soul and cling.
When calmness is near, he will lie with his breast on the fountain and scream
"Walking behind me and distributing my joys is a goose!
My darling is a leaf! My leaf is a toad!"
Hearing this echoed, he burns the air with sobs.

Night is knelling her platitudes and tearing his garments of feeling.
"Here am I! these cries are nearly mine!
their loudness is possessing me, I am becoming a leer, the very glass
of millions of things that find me disgusting.
I have thrown myself from the Bridge of Richness throughout the world!"

Misery has always reached itself a helping hand on the river bed,
the sky burgeons with aspirations as the years exhale and inhale.
It is a great feast! those blossoms which are like the Lives of the Saints.
And must he, then, die of longing in his sty?
He has already forgotten the nearness of his youth, its whiteness
in the morbid dances and truncated limbs of the yards.

See yourself then! in the skeleton of moonlight
you are spending your blood like so many ribbons in a tornado,
your desperate remedies are wildly murmuring curses in your mouth,
hear them thrashing in the dusts and the fears!
Yet choose yourself. The great open stare of unconsciousness is a crystal ball.
Your life is pushing us to our feet, O leaf!

2

Herbs' harp, the ring of the rushing moon.
A sigh of strife clusters against the blue wall
of the water which is beckoning its blue lake from the grass.
A man, a hustler, has stabbed himself, having judged
the fine blackness of his stress and wished it open.

Again the sweet dust of fear closes its eyes.
A calendar of remorse begins to flutter over the wind
in hysterical pages, its cold momentary needs.

No! in my heart the golden tongue of love mutters its worldly little tango,
this lotus blossom is like dope, this arm full of tears.
My heart is warm, my eyes are shining, pointed like fox-ears.

All is lost, the weedy loyalties of the rushing stream are drowned,
sleep appears and flees like a trout with rueful gazes and steps,
yes! I wish to be quickened, yes, until I collapse of nervousness,
I wish to whine all the rest of my life like a kite!

Your soft playing has cut into my heart. O shining ring of love!
you break like a storm on the prow of a ship.
O bitterness, you are lost within me. I am the dawn.

3
In the middle of your cluttered touch
a stork starts skimming thin green tents
and he looks like a blown vase of snow.

Wielding a rucksack he tightens the cord
of the brook, its neck of woven jade. Blue.
Blood. A pavilion wades into the clouds.

On the grey heights friends sit, like fleas,
soon cloaked in snow but very bright, very shrill,
munching the shrouded verses of Negroes.

Irritable signposts! glittering like armor!
racks of slenderness's salty misery,
the hiking lust that's deep as a neck.

At your careless touch which is so purposefully gentle
the water flakes all of me into sighs.
I am beautifully painted, the whole surface of me.

All of you is standing erect in my watery head,
a pavilion in the greenness of my love
and your white smiles, like open wounds,

like moons of wholeness, drift over my griefs
which are your caresses turned inward, O friend!
soon cloaked in snow, but very bright.

4

Yes, madness is the flower of the forests,
the bleeding lotus wrenched out of filthy memory.
The black chief is still on the stairs
and the five pink African girls have come back
from Paris, the bushes uprooted and the leaves swinish,
sick, and one another, and necromantic, and shy.
There is a great locomotive tangled in their lives.
Madness, like a hyena outside a tent, settles onto the trees
assuming its bland look that reflects the sun and the silvery gliders
whose sweet eyes are opened wider.

And the zebras flutter across the smiling eyelids like a scythe.
Your poor army is attacking the zebras!
Your famous strength is suffocating in the laughter!
Look! doesn't the most aluminum elevator operator
flare up and burst like a tired sleepy rose?
Within, moonbeams pass each other's place of business
as a cat licks cream while ghosts grin and widen.
Let's trap the youngsters in here!
O coronary thrombosis of a sentimentalist! O rose!
and shower and soften and stain everything.
Over the ratty blossoms and the glazed grasses
horrible stampings "Yeah!" resound like a storm in a sunken lavatory,
"Hey!" suddenly flattening your face white which is a moon,
which is a toilet bowl which is a glob of spit.
So "life" is still at it, "eh, Nutsy?"
God damned sun always weaving shadows!
whose sweet eyes are opened wider.

And the most beautiful jungle of madness being sent
and sent! and sent! and sent! and sent! into oblivion
is the great sensual blinking flag of alarm at night
hearing itself stuffed and hung, as the stars "hear" longing.
In the darkness I am growing larger!
In the darkness I am growing louder!
I am swinging and clanging inside myself like the tongue of a bell!

5

Winding ears, trauma, and the dolors
of a trumpet player, the pitless stomach, the plague.
He drinks, but it is not more deviously followed,
gauntly, with much leaning, and no revolver pointing the roadmarks.
Then the sting in the vein which is death laughing
while the cool soul volleys for a moment and then, then spills.
It is so dreamlike to surrender the mirrored floor!

What do I hear from the night watch? the horses?
A bagel is sitting in a vent.
Itching, fragmentary in-nesses shine, the feelings of the sinuses,
the mirror is always drowning.
The addict twitches "Lark! loan me
won't you? the spoor and the pang of night!"
and from the deepest pit of vomit the glittering throat ascends
upon whose vague singing soft kisses are pressed.

I am full,
just as the enormous tree in the midst of nowhere
clings to the emptiness of living which is his ground
and sinks his roots through to the drenching purity
of the fountains of the moon, the sweat, the firmament.
O sleep will not come to me,
and if it come with its burning wing
I must lurch forth as if spring's needles were blossoming.
I must be alone with life!

6
To die, soon. The shooting hinders the range of the mountains,
disgusting humans everywhere throng the trails like tall animals,
even the sky is like a city at dusk.

Yet, see! how like silver snails we weave a mind
out of the blue waters of the heavens within us!
here, alone, feeling the strong wind's anxiety
grovel beneath the fir trees.
The glacier sings fully and loudly of the centuries which lily our flesh
and pain is blasting an entrance for the sun.
The earth sighs with longing for us.
The blue world has looked upon us and yielded to temptation,
tired mankind is our slave, we lead him home to the red valley
where he will sleep and forget and be glass.
And the youths are already on their witty bellies!
Our spirits parade the unalterable stairway to power which is sight.
The world woefully fidgets in its cerise cummerbund
claiming to be asleep, to dream.

I am standing here with my harp in the frigid light.
I hear you by my side, but where are you? where is your love?
I sense, O my friend, that in the distant air
a great height is descending to make war upon me.
I have been alone for a long time.
I wander wherever the light seems to lead me,
to the edge of the world where white corpses forbid the openness.
O sun! heart! O eternal love forever blue with despair!

you have cut your face into my bleeding marble eyes!
and I am as absent from you as a fragment.
If I could only fear again, then I might die,
but the flames' speech flowers eternally in my posture
as I seek again and again this world that even gluttons hate.

Vile, ghastly, ignorant, I wander through the barriers,
I suck upon rue for my distinguished heart.
I roam through the city in a shirt and get very high.
I will not go away. I will never take a wife.
My heart is my own, the trapped hare belongs to the hour.
The loving earth bleeds out its laughing grunts which are green
and new and, above all! tender! yes, tender!
like the blue light seeping towards you under my closed eyelids,
so evil, and now closed at last in evil! evil! evil!

ON RACHMANINOFF'S BIRTHDAY

Quick! a last poem before I go
off my rocker. Oh Rachmaninoff!
Onset, Massachusetts. Is it the fig-newton
playing the horn? Thundering windows
of hell, will your tubes ever break
into powder? Oh my palace of oranges,
junk shop, staples, umber, basalt;
I'm a child again when I was really
miserable, a grope pizzicato. My pocket
of rhinestone, yoyo, carpenter's pencil,
amethyst, hypo, campaign button,
is the room full of smoke? Shit
on the soup, let it burn. So it's back.
You'll never be mentally sober.

TO MY MOTHER

Oh witness! to be sure,
you are gone in your violet sleeve,
and I am riding in a grey car
through the suburbs of my nose.

Have you escaped your impatience?
I am guilty and the sky is blue
as a restaurant full of tapioca.
And isn't it ordinary?

like the many famous things
that are called "stuff" somewhere
and are on maps with their bloody veins,
I mean, highways somewhere.

Have you escaped yet? if you
haven't I hope you've killed someone,
or suicide's grown curious of someone,
or someone's accidentally died.

TO MY DEAD FATHER

Don't call to me father
wherever you are I'm
still your little son
running through the dark

I couldn't do what you
say even if I could hear
your roses no longer grow
my heart's black as their

bed their dainty thorns
have become my face's
troublesome stubble you
must not think of flowers

And do not frighten my
blue eyes with hazel flecks
or thicken my lips when
I face my mirror don't ask

that I be other than your
strange son understanding
minor miracles not death
father I am alive! father

forgive the roses and me

SNEDEN'S LANDING VARIATIONS

to Robert Fizdale

I

What an oak! the immense expanses of silver,
and the green river below, trembling in rocks,
each leaf like a Russian farmhouse at night
in the Adirondacks where we fed the fox.

And the melancholy oaks have no disease,
they are simply fragile from being bigger,
their leaves like feet hanging in whitewashed air.
The air is calm as a pencil. Order liquor,

and see what happens. The trees are thoughtful,
poor buttery locusts! but not unbendingly serious,
not in the vein of telegraph posts on the Great Divide
to whom a child's pink cry would seem mysterious,

with the subtle yelling of the coyotes
all around among the dark brown horses, water
in the skies, and a sun-bleached wren dead
in the golden leaves. They frown. The haunter

of the Hudson is living on the wrong side,
he is in the view, fate of the beautiful creature.
Alas for the mothers of those telephone calls!
he is rapturously glowing but it is the feature

of every death, the most vivid moment of the leaf,
when it clutches the air like a cigar and blushes,
and the poisoned ivy's luck is as sweet as the ruby's
since it, too, must languish and burn among the rushes

whose fingers hide their murmurs like manure.
All things are something else, aren't they? like a basket
into which the ants have paraded and become lunch?
and of their passionate nourishment become the casket?

like a broken bracelet? My cat missed your house;
she wanted to be fed in the landscape, verdant no longer.
There will be something new about the cat in the city;
like breathing the sooty air, she'll have to be stronger.

2
We ate manure
    for lunch
in a house
    in the city.

3
That the world might be bigger!
we crushed hedges to hide the rocks
so that at night the remembered fox
could sneak in and steal the liquor

or, as he turned his silver back on the water,
we might seem to him more serious,
our formality, entirely white! mysterious.
A distinguished thief addressed the haunter

of our crepitating house, but blushes
enflamed the fragile creature,
he howled, extinguished every feature
of the amorous scene, and leaped into the rushes

brown, nodding and tingling. It was longer,
somehow, that summer, like a basket
of interminable spices, or a green casket,
the flesh of dawn in Irkutsk; and stronger,

as we lay night after night in the silver.
He watched the river pour into night
its historical hay-scented disease
of which the exotic knowledge is air.

He watched; we did not grow thoughtful,
we feared that would divide

us, as the grave persuades the coyotes
to sing their admiration of the dead.
We heard the trees like electricity, the other side
of the river, utter their ink–stained calls.
O autumn! memories of the single leaf
and love, its haunts, which are like the ruby's.

4
What and each in and they their the
and poor not to with all in in.

Of he alas he of when and since
whose all into and like she there like.

5
The air, if shot with golden dust,
screams itself into a snowy rage.
O embarrassments of autumn!
your great blushing exposures
like a chalice kicked over at sunset!

Once a traveler landed in a creek
of these mountainous shores from his ark
and it was called "Discovery of Autumn."
Aren't you sorry the leaves are falling
round your huge nostalgic vessel? O haunter.

I have the map of love at hand and he
was last seen roaming up the river bank
underneath the orange tossing boughs. It
was Henry Hudson airing his discovery,
at twilight, in the smoke from the flaming trees.

Now we are leaving, the wren is buried
in the golden leaves; Major André's Monument
is garlanded for winter, and the cat is in the car.
Goodbye silvery fox of a river, so moonlike!
you were always kissing summer goodbye.

APPOGGIATURAS

1

Hey, you! raining, from your dilapidated pier, the overseas highway and the roses, so salty! O A U, are you a rose dipping its irritable head into the briny?

Babbling Barbara is marrying Barnacle Bill!

2

Babs! the children! help!

3

A fire swept the city, but it was moreorless of a student fire, and it was easily kept under control, at least partially! by everybody screaming.

4

Even the fishes heard that terrible whine and shuddered. "I wonder if we should do anything about it?" they all asked each other. But really, it wasn't mysterious enough to call for thought. They were quite helpful right where they were. Weren't they? "Yes."

5

So he got to know all the ships. He catalogued them by their various business initials as they went in and out of the hat. And as the children grew old and were born, he got to know them too and was delighted by the forms they took, some blond, some rickety, some human.

6

The panorama of feelings which the whole city considered its "vice" never became a famous site for a mannerist painter, and it's a good thing for us it didn't,

7

the history of surprise is disappearance. You don't prefer mussels to oysters, O!

In Mattituck Inlet the trees are very Japanese.

POEM

I am not sure there is a cure,
but I have just cut my fingernails,
anyway. I am in a quarry,
I believe that the sky is a bag
of leaves thrown down, thrown down,
thrown away like a squirrel's brains.

I can barely draw breath any more,
yet the ships keep coming in
and unloading and sighing, sighing.

Clouds! do you see this fist?
I have just put it through you!
Sun! you do well to crouch
and snarl, I have willed you away.

Ah! she has dropped her pearls.
They are like words, vindictive and cold.
I had slit their cord with my fruit scissors,
they are moaning along the drafty floor.

Away, then! if she falls, she falls.

ROMANZE, OR THE MUSIC STUDENTS

I
The rain, its tiny pressure
on your scalp, like ants
passing the door of a tobacconist.
"Hello!" they cry, their noses
glistening. They are humming
a scherzo by Tcherepnin.
They are carrying violin cases.
With their feelers knitting
over their heads the blue air,

they appear at the door of
the Conservatory and cry "Ah!"
at the honey of its outpourings.
They stand in the street and hear
the curds drifting on the top
of the milk of Conservatory doors.

2

They had thought themselves
in Hawaii when suddenly the pines,
trembling with nightfulness,
shook them out of their sibilance.
The surf was full of outriggers
racing like slits in the eye of
the sun, yet the surf was full
of great black logs plunging, and
then the surf was full of needles.
The surf was bland and white,
as pine trees are white when,
in Paradise, no wind is blowing.

3

In Ann Arbor on Sunday afternoon
at four-thirty they went to an organ
recital: Messiaen, Hindemith, Czerny.
And in their ears a great voice said
"To have great music we must commission
it. To commission great music
we must have great commissioners."
There was a blast! and summer was over.

4

Rienzi! A rabbit is sitting in the hedge!
it is a brown stone! it is the month
of October! it is an orange bassoon!
They've been standing on this mountain
for forty-eight hours without flinching.
Well, they are soldiers, I guess,
and it is all marching magnificently by.

THE HUNTER

He set out and kept hunting
and hunting. Where, he thought
and thought, is the real chamois?
and can I kill it where it is?
He had brought with him only a dish
of pears. The autumn wind soared
above the trails where the drops
of the chamois led him further.
The leaves dropped around him
like pie-plates. The stars fell
one by one into his eyes and burnt.

There is a geography which holds
its hands just so far from the breast
and pushes you away, crying so.
He went on to strange hills where
the stones were still warm from feet,
and then on and on. There were clouds
at his knees, his eyelashes
had grown thick from the colds,
as the fur of the bear does
in winter. Perhaps, he thought, I am
asleep, but he did not freeze to death.

There were little green needles
everywhere. And then manna fell.
He knew, above all, that he was now
approved, and his strength increased.
He saw the world below him, brilliant
as a floor, and steaming with gold,
with distance. There were occasionally
rifts in the cloud where the face
of a woman appeared, frowning. He
had gone higher. He wore ermine.
He thought, why did I come? and then,
I have come to rule! The chamois came.

The chamois found him and they came
in droves to humiliate him. Alone,
in the clouds, he was humiliated.

Joyous you should be,
of all things sweet the most constant and most pure,
eager for what might be obtained—

Luck and life and hideous certainty preventing,
ease and certainty inclining to neglect,
so that real world, blue in the eye! this
umber sky about us drowns. And where
emptiness appears bounding along, of
unrest the most diligent athlete and keenest mate,
remember the pleasure, even there, your beauty affords.

GRAND CENTRAL

The wheels are inside me thundering.
They do not churn me, they are inside.
They were not oiled, they burn
with friction and out of my eyes
comes smoke. Then the enormous bullets
streak towards me with their black tracers
and bury themselves deep in my muscles.
They won't be taken out, I can still
move. Now I am going to lie down
like an expanse of marble floor
covered with commuters and information:
it is my vocation, you believe that,
don't you? I don't have an American
body, I have an anonymous body, though
you can get to love it, if you love
the corpses of the Renaissance; I am
reconstructed from a model of poetry,
you see, and this might be a horseless
carriage, it might be but it is not,
it is riddled with bullets, am I.
And if they are not thundering into me
they are thundering across me, on

the way to some devastated island
where they will eat waffles with the
other Americans of American persuasion.
On rainy days I ache as if a train
were about to arrive, I switch my tracks.

During the noon-hour rush a friend
of mine took a letter carrier across
the catwalk underneath the dome
behind the enormous (wheels! wheels!)
windows which are the roof of the sun
and knelt inside my cathedral, mine
through pain! and the thundering went on.
He unzipped the messenger's trousers
and relieved him of his missile, hands
on the messenger's dirty buttocks,
the smoking muzzle in his soft blue mouth.
That is one way of dominating the terminal,
but I have not done that. It will be
my blood, I think, that dominates the trains.

LARRY

Watching the muddy light attack
some resemblances, you took
my letters from your drawers and said
"You were careful to me." Some look.

Outside in white trousers the night
works. A bus signals into oblivion
and is already at the boundary. If
we lower ourselves by rope ydown

in front over the marquee we won't
get burned by the neon and it'll be
sheer agony. The mountain kind. I wished
already some bar chirruping, aknee

with painters' molls hep to genius.
So we're great friends constant and true

to not being sure of your being sure
of my being sure of your being sure of you.

LEBANON

Perhaps he will press his warm lips
to mine in a phrase exceptionally historic,
which seemed to have lived on lips
in Galilee now that I have already felt

its sting. The sweet fetid dust
of his breath will linger upon my lips
as if my understanding were affected and a soul
of passion and arrogant surmise had my lips

for a moment and then passed through my lips
into the rendering azure of the temple.
It was coolly dawning and his lips
opened, "I'll go with you to the other country,

no matter that my all is here,
my childhood on the plains' grapelike lips,
my father's handkerchief, my mother's tomb,
my memory of games; they go up like lips

in a stadium; all that comes from my white lips
and shall ease you on the unnecessary journey."
And thus the day did blanch upon his lips
despite the dirty windowpanes and cold air.

He did go to the mountains and perhaps I
shall be daily upon those wooded sloping lips,
so that as he is fleetly hunting goats
my breath will find its altar in those lips.

POEM

Now it is light, now it is the calm
yellow after the night goes to sleep.

A goat picks its way down 14th Street
through the briars of the cadenza of dull things

which the moon had summoned with
its guitarlike gutters—Sit down, boy!

I say Waldo, sit down!—resting
his curly head on the curb the sailor

finds his ship is dragging him slowly
into the harbor, where the oil scum

fills his tearless eyes with a
nonchalant reflection, sunless, harmless.

Captain, it's not day yet, but you
are pulling out. And as the sun comes up

the yellow dies into a glaring white
which is only the night's reflection.

THE APRICOT SEASON

There comes a moment in anxiety
when a run in the ceiling spreads
its ladders across the orange sunset
and the clock tower shows no monkeys.
Swooping through dazed eyes the blood
couples go by like years of sadness,
that sadness which signs itself "together"
and is not of the slit-skirt air or airs.

No distance appears at the head of the stairs
to provoke the next partner to move

and pull out his pencil, no lattices
break. Loosing a brooch is like losing
a fleet. A fingernail's worth a loaf
of meat. The girl in the grey wool suit
turns on the bar stool and looks brightly
where the effeminate men in trench coats
pick their noses and suck their glasses' rims.
She can't keep her eyes off them nor can
they keep her eyes off them. It's all over

when it's over, and again a suited figure
stands in the spacious panes of twilight
waiting for the clock's lights to go on
so it will sweat its wrist band across the sky
downtown. His white shirt and black pants
are heaped with lavender pyramids, are crowded
like a view of Venice. There's the plaza where
St Mark was found and summoned to be someone
not much better in the world of painting.

The tires mourn onto the edge of the error
and as they vote they spread an odor of glass
over the brown drape which has dropped from,
like an evening handkerchief, the Milky Way,
so poorly conceived and so inconvenient. Let
him wave to the growing grass as he goes up, green
which cupped his open mouth ignorantly for years
while his tears burnt its roots and weakened him.

NEWSBOY

And so to be near
and so to be far
to be a shrill bird
silly in its tree

to be a blooming whale
and infinitely sad
it is no burden
to be free from fear

but the daring
amasses its red strips
and some are nearer
than others

THE SPIRIT INK

Prince of calm, treasure of fascinating cuts on my arm,
an x ill-aims its roguish atonal bliss of "ment"
and hatted is the viper whose illness I hated having to puke,
April in the lavatory trouble, inside the air he deceives.

Rover! cheat the scholars, Dubonnet Sir Pint,
oust his slick offer to bow, eat, touch your eyes upon.
Park the lily and quietly knit the loose air of a purse,
tough ass, dissembler and fool, O syrup of mammoths!

THE AFTERNOON

In sensuality I find a harvest dawn
    thundering through my hand, it's red
        from obstinacy! and already blood is holding
            a man against the earth with dank feelers.

Is it me? and around in the fields
    horses still wander without suffering,
        their virtue abbreviated by the frosty streams
            and yet they're not tired of the kingdom of innerness.

They laugh when I describe the ghosts
    and through the trees their bravery tumbles
        like a note struck on a piano in a hall, purple
            halls of men so full of fruit and vindictiveness.

sowing absence as if it would grow up
　　to be a golden freedom of the mind and air.
　　　　You are a joy to me, aren't you? and irritable
　　　　　　like the lucky beasts of the field who have a weediness

you seek? you do want to be a rose, don't you?
　　and lose your petals and be free for all the weeds?
　　　　Blueness is gagging me, and whole tiers
　　　　　　of constellations are designing me new clothes.

I am lucky, too, for I lie down without
　　a womb and am not in danger from the herd.
　　　　There's no light in my breast to get an angel
　　　　　　in trouble, no one has ever mistaken me for a window.

I'm not at all like a plant though I love dirt,
　　and the stars I mention are not roots, unless I'm
　　　　upside down, which would be more habit than prospect.
　　　　　　Oh forgive me, I am an army without a battle!

You are too great! O sky machine zipping
　　and empyrean! in storms you heat the day
　　　　and then you sever it from god's bosom there
　　　　　　with a large vague breadknife of wax, beeswax,

I think. Yet it's necessary to step on one
　　neck, just any one, to be a free and witty monk.
　　　　I have a starry lap for you while you are stepping
　　　　　　on my face, O flattering memories of being held!

And lest you die of a broken heart or foot,
　　I am another and you are kneeling before your family
　　　　though you're a man without a country
　　　　　　and the horses are amusing themselves with me.

Look, fields! look, sky! my paramours who
　　stay and stay and are lucky in the sorrows
　　　　of love, as a garden is lucky to a wanderer
　　　　　　whom it recognizes and trips on his homeward

journey. With you I'm again alone, doesn't
　　it please you, that you have me all to yourself
　　　　like the sea? And as terrible times bare the heart,
　　　　　　I am baring my heart, so summon terrible times!

I loathe disinterest and the sensual stars.
　　I am more powerful than the heavens and more true.

O I hate observances, and the decorum of the senses!
like a beautiful horse grazing at my running feet.

TO THE POEM

Let us do something grand
Just this once   Something

small and important and
unAmerican   Some fine thing

will resemble a human hand
and really be merely a thing

Not needing a military band
nor an elegant forthcoming

to tease spotlights or a hand
from the public's thinking

But be   In a defiant land
of its own a real right thing

ANACROSTIC

Elf, forbidden word, heart within me
leaning on a doorstep, talking things over,
able to sigh in the summer air and walk and walk!—
is that the measure of my passion for your every thought?
never being more than my immeasurable self,
enchanting the yellow trees with my emptiness,

doubting each auburn branch and my own
easy recognition of each several branched alliance?

Knocking quietly on the door of trees, by
oceans of affections left awash with dour light,
over your shoulder I watch the future like a virtuoso
nearing, in the dawn of crowded voices, its piano;
in your knowledge you are the night, its inscrutable
noisy laughter of witticisms dropped into a well, soon
gone, like each succeeding breath of air, in my breast.

ON A PASSAGE IN BECKETT'S *WATT*
& ABOUT GEO. MONTGOMERY

There was someone, my life there at that time,
where I'd read this presence out without doubt
and that piercer would quickly overclimb
from what we'd undergone, so blear without,
and what we'd known was in me of our life
and suddenly had trebled and shook clear
at the words' excessive Keatsness. No knife
glancing off both, in hearts, now, even here.
And can I have unburdened me it was?
where must have borne my life beyond all else
who must have knouted feelings as he does
who knells to crime the peasants with his bells.
    I can't remember. No, all, Sinbad, place,
    of clarity, member, redness, or face.

UNICORN

Lingering, vying, fearing, and flowers and fruit,
I parallel the few trees that remain.

An eagle, lo, China! quick faun, a brig.
There run the rapids, there breathe the halls.

Donkeys flee me in the forest of the fruit of aimlessness
and a horn, a tangent, leads me to rest,
quite other than the gentlemen who bear me down.

POEM

The little roses, the black majestic sails
of their promise! or is it a dove paralyzing the air?
Where vessels fled across the waters, there
a railroad was constructed by the few remaining birds
and it was called "Heliotrope, Aldebaran, Cous-cous."
For the time, for the afternoon of their accomplishment,
the roses rested—and that they were doves resting on the waves
became known to them, as the sail knows the air it fills.

LINES WRITTEN IN *A RAW YOUTH*

I have the lame dog with me and the cloud,
cirrus feathering to Europe for spring,
lion at my ear black and gold and loud,
and the brown waves crushing white what they fling.
In a minute the sun will go down and
the wind will sharpen at my throat, its door,
now troubled with breath and raw with brine, sand
in my eyes, at my knees the muscled roar.
Further out my heart's yielding up its food
to fishes hunting coastward with the foam
and as the tents of jellyfish do brood
so brood I on my brutal cold black home.
I plunge again against the pow'rful sea
of my desires and win and force them free.

1

The cold snow, the silver tomb, separates
my thoughts, and a misty drawing of a house
in which are horses and the fighting boys—

        beyond brown hedges
        there are thoughts of rain,
        the voluptuous uncertainty
        of the monotonous sea,

and the cold snow is falling on the windowpanes
within the ocean's warm metallic languor. My boots
are bloody at the heel, dogs howl, the sirens

are abandoning the rocks, yet storms
don't drive us inland. There's a warmth alive
to danger and the lines of mist rising

        are ever sharpening
        accommodate our lives
        together or apart; wild
        horses do not take the bit.

2

An African statue freezes in the snow.
Along the beach pipelines from Arabia
are torn, shattered and thrown by storms,
and sedimentary deposits of ground black pearls
cake my face, so frozen in its smiling.
The millionth artifact of a culture, these
particular pieces of driftwood and these
irreprovably beautiful stones and shells,
collectors' items like the snarl of a boy
or the hem of a waitress, proof that we love
anonymity even more than promiscuity. It is all
so German. "I don't think you really want
to go shooting with me." "I want to go shooting,
all right." And in between the marvellous,
call them pieces, call them works, of
this great museum with its sun strengthening
toward February and an unseasonably hot
pleasant day effervescing for miles
and miles of what, in a better world, we
would call surf, stroll the boxers, the

beagles, an Afghan hound and a schipperke,
and a lame man with his cane and mutt.
And the sea's insatiable ease keeps moaning
its smoky morning-in-a-roundhouse message
of relaxation and contempt, and pain.

3
A seventy years young man
was driving in his roadster,
his lights were glowing dimly,
he swerved to miss a toad, sir,

when suddenly before his brow
a maiden in red shoes
leaped across the highway
as if searching for her ewes.

Then forty paces onward,
or thirty revolutions,
a handsome youth in the gutter
performed some dark ablutions;

the car screeched to a halt
of the septuagenarian,
"Yes, I do need a lift
though I'm not necessarily Aryan."

Skin like ink, eyes open
like the moon, lips white
with sullen foam, and loudly
his wet knuckles bite

as he flicks his razor
open without a leer
and handles the old head
and slits it from ear to ear.

Now instead of the motor
he hears the cries of the waves,
as the moon shrinks even higher
the live man smokes and raves.

4
Sky smoldering with snow, and the light grey
taupe claws asseverating the solid air, so
imperious in definition, knowing the evergreens
will go envious in months soon and indeterminate;

yet never a leaf falls into the moody sea
and, like a cube, the air is stuck upon the dire,
the barren trees, screaming and giving birth,
not to summer but to itself, inside out and backwards.

Or rightside up and forwards, perhaps for the first
time, as a tree takes fifty years to know its roots
from its branches and then reestablishes the horizon.
Along Toylesome Lane came five dogs, four masters,
and a little girl crying "Bridges! and of the world, sic!
an estimate. Don't say it's lovely, say something I
can understand, what you mean" as the snow falls
and fell away from the earth into the mixed up air.

Screams stride through the house, piercing
and blasting the cellar. A child dreams he's stabbed
and the walls fall away and assassins arrive
in jeeps and attack all who have heard the wisdom
of the child, for the world knows every secret
and when it squeals on a German General the path
to his heel becomes crowded with Secret Police; and then,
in a moment, emptiness: the statues removed to museums.

All the pleasures of Paris are not so pertinent
as the dry mockery of one winter cloud refusing to fall,
though full to bursting with human cries and able,
just barely, to contain our pain like a white mother
of dark children. I am on the sand, in the snow,
knee-deep in the paralyzing sea of numbness
which is excessive passion, foolish, unnecessary, despicable;
yet in this snow alone I find the drowsy splendor of the sun.

THE PIPES OF PAN

A calmness is enforced by moving light
and even more than I can hear or know
first flowers breathed me with their freckled sight
beneath grey grass where I no longer go.
My life was then a winter hot with needs,
just then! and now, so careless of its own,

my will relaxes with the fresh green reeds
which spring arrogantly though they're not sown.
Indeed, they want no wind. They are a lake,
and bend when they wish and do not invite
the sun. They flay the air and do not break;
indifferently they disappear at night,
    and just as calmly earth's of them bereft.
    They found earth mute and passionless, and left.

MRS BERTHA BURGER

A widow. She has lived so many lives
and each is like an ember glowing now.
On days of darkness like so many knives
she feels each fullness press her breast and brow.
Each life, protected, prized and coveted
and thought through for the wisdom of events
she sees again as she is buffeted:
delicate ships know well their own torments,
and she knows well the dignity of storms.
She offers in a chance remark her fate
and her reflections are not flights or calms.
Her life is beautiful, and free from hate;
    to know her is to know how rarely one
    may love, as one again beholds the sun.

HOMOSEXUALITY

So we are taking off our masks, are we, and keeping
our mouths shut? as if we'd been pierced by a glance!

The song of an old cow is not more full of judgment
than the vapors which escape one's soul when one is sick;

so I pull the shadows around me like a puff
and crinkle my eyes as if at the most exquisite moment

of a very long opera, and then we are off!
without reproach and without hope that our delicate feet

will touch the earth again, let alone "very soon."
It is the law of my own voice I shall investigate.

I start like ice, my finger to my ear, my ear
to my heart, that proud cur at the garbage can

in the rain. It's wonderful to admire oneself
with complete candor, tallying up the merits of each

of the latrines. 14th Street is drunken and credulous,
53rd tries to tremble but is too at rest. The good

love a park and the inept a railway station,
and there are the divine ones who drag themselves up

and down the lengthening shadow of an Abyssinian head
in the dust, trailing their long elegant heels of hot air

crying to confuse the brave "It's a summer day,
and I want to be wanted more than anything else in the world."

TO JANE; AND IN IMITATION OF COLERIDGE

All fears, all doubts and even dreams
that parody my slender frame
are driven from me, and their screams,
        by the mere thought of fame.

When I stare and brood, and I do often,
I walk again through mountain air
where terrible winds did suddenly soften
        at invisible music there,

or far at sea I once more capture
men and cities and whales in rain,

yet can't make serious with my rapture
        slyly thoughtful, smiling Jane,

who does not feel the sky's a clock
nor that the sea will swallow me—
though she would feel alone, in shock,
        if I did drown, could no more see

her smiling face that sorrows leave
whenever she despatches care,
and she can not unless I grieve
        that she's preoccupied there.

She thinks of me as melancholy,
I think of her as bright and sad,
often my pretentious folly
        makes me self-ashamed and bad

but never to her, never to Jane
"with downcast Eyes and modest Grace";
I could from fame's blue heights refrain
        but never from her blue-lit face.

Her slender hands accomplish more
in moving from sheet to telephone
than all the burning shields knights bore,
        dull blows or slashings to the bone.

I never tell her this because
embarrassment is far more fatal
than shrouding verse in Romantic gauze
        or voyagings foolish and prenatal.

And I am all at sea, at war,
if I ever had a chance I left it
there on the iron deck, my star:
        I stride upon, but cannot heft it.

But I should be master of my ship
not just a member of the crew!
though she may think that I will slip
        into insanity and the blue,

I will not, for I more and more
am master of myself each day,
and sometimes from a savage shore
        plunge into surf and swim away,

and sometimes on my sulking face
a green and sunny look I see
and I fight towards it o'er what space
  the deck's obstruction thrusts at me.

And if her face, my sky, hold fast,
do not abandon nor disdain!
the vessel shall be mine at last,
  as if my life were after Jane.

I do not know how in the South
I managed to content myself
with salt and Mozart in my mouth
  on the Pacific like a shelf

crowded and lonely and overreachable,
low the clouds and light the moon,
low as heaven and as teachable
  as Christianity in its June,

or how in New England where I grew
and tried both to fight and to escape,
I thrived without her intimate view
  always before me, my seascape;

for as the war, art, dissipation,
led me on and made me sane,
I find a world of sweet sensation
  leading me now, and it is Jane.

She is the Lady of my Lake,
the Lily of my sordid life,
hatred within me, for her sake,
  noiselessly empties like a fife

played often but above her hearing
not her tranquility to alarm,
rather t' oppose, by scale endearing,
  the extremity of her charm.

Never her bosom, that soft booty,
's seen in the sea of a sheltered bay,
but that the daughters of Albion's beauty
  in pure consciousness fades away;

she half incloses worlds in her eyes,
she moves as the wind is said to blow,

she watches motions of the skies
        as if she were everywhere to go.

" 'Twas partly Love, and partly Fear,
And partly 'twas a bashful Art"—
the poet cannot hope to near
        the mysterious clarity of her heart;

she is not dangerous or rare,
adventure precedes her like a train,
her beauty is general, as sun and air
        are secretly near, like Jane.

TO A POET

I am sober and industrious
and would be plain and plainer
for a little while
                    until my rococo
self is more assured of its
distinction.
            So you do not like
my new verses, written in the
pages of Russian novels while I do
not brood over an orderly
childhood?
            You are angry
because I see the white-haired
genius of the painter more beautiful
than the stammering vivacity

                            of
your temperament. And yes,
it becomes more and more a matter
of black and white between us

and when the doctor comes to
me he says "No things but in ideas"
or it is overheard
                    in the public
square, now that I am off my couch.

AUS EINEM APRIL

We dust the walls.
And of course we are weeping larks
falling all over the heavens with our shoulders clasped
in someone's armpits, so tightly! and our throats are full.
Haven't you ever fallen down at Christmas
and didn't it move everyone who saw you?
isn't that what the tree means? the pure pleasure
of making weep those whom you cannot move by your flights!
It's enough to drive one to suicide.
And the rooftops are falling apart like the applause

of rough, long-nailed, intimate, roughened-by-kisses, hands.
Fingers more breathless than a tongue laid upon the lips
in the hour of sunlight, early morning, before the mist rolls
in from the sea; and out there everything is turbulent and green.

DEATH

1
If half of me is skewered
by grey crested birds
in the middle of the vines of my promise
and the very fact that I'm a poet
suffers my eyes
to be filled with vermilion tears,

2
how much greater danger
from occasion and pain is my vitality
yielding, like a tree on fire!—
for every day is another view
of the tentative past
grown secure in its foundry of shimmering
that's not even historical; it's just me.

3
And the other half
of me where I master the root
of my every idiosyncrasy
and fit my ribs like a glove,

4
is that me who accepts betrayal
in the abstract as if it were insight?
and draws its knuckles
across the much-lined eyes
in the most knowing manner of our time?

5
The wind that smiles through the wires
isn't vague enough for an assertion
of a personal nature, it's not for me,

6
I'm not dead. Nothing remains, let alone "to be said,"
except that when I fall backwards
I am trying something new and shall succeed, as in the past.

SPLEEN

I know so much
about things, I accept
so much, it's like
vomiting. And I am
nourished by the
shabbiness of my
knowing so much
about others and what
they do, and accepting
so much that I hate
as if I didn't know
what it is, to me.
And what it is to
them I know, and hate.

LINES WHILE READING
COLERIDGE'S "THE PICTURE"

I have no kindness left
and no more tenderness,
that weakness's torn from me—
it once surrounded my desire
as petals fringe the center
of a flower, and now it's
gone to seed, delicate wings
in the wind! and where it
falls to welcoming earth
I don't know yet, but I will
recognize the first frail
shoot and greet it then
as tenderly as the rain,
knowing that each successive
flower's more beautiful,
the more passionately short-lived.

KITVILLE

Sands, sunset, toilets,
O the charities!
the little asylums
of the verities

Once I was humbled
amidst the flowers
and her crushed books
were like bloomers!

She was reading clear
by the coffee lake
and its bitter springs
were a bubbling brook,

and garish her lips
as they parted! a piano
of grassy incidents
twined with the liana

of her wet arms!
behind the bath house
sweet as a wash basin,
her smilings, her pathos.

ON RACHMANINOFF'S BIRTHDAY

Blue windows, blue rooftops
and the blue light of the rain,
these contiguous phrases of Rachmaninoff
pouring into my enormous ears
and the tears falling into my blindness

for without him I do not play,
especially in the afternoon
on the day of his birthday. Good
fortune, you would have been
my teacher and I your only pupil

and I would always play again.
Secrets of Liszt and Scriabin
whispered to me over the keyboard
on unsunny afternoons! and growing
still in my stormy heart.

Only my eyes would be blue as I played
and you rapped my knuckles,
dearest father of all the Russias,
placing my fingers
tenderly upon your cold, tired eyes.

ON RACHMANINOFF'S BIRTHDAY

I am so glad that Larry Rivers made a
statue of me

and now I hear that my penis is on all
the statues of all the young sculptors who've
seen it

instead of the Picasso no-penis shep-
herd and its influence—for presence is
better than absence, if you love excess.

Oh now it is that all this music tumbles
round me which was once considered muddy

and today surrounds this ambiguity of
our tables and our typewriter paper, more
nostalgic than a disease,

soft as one's character, melancholy as
one's attractiveness,

offering the pernicious advice of dreams.
Is it too late for this?

I am what people make of me—if they
can and when they will. My difficulty is
readily played—like a rhapsody, or a fresh
house.

POEM IN JANUARY

March, the fierce! like a wind of garters
its calm kept secret, as if eaten!
and sipped at the source tainted, taut.

Vagrants, crushed by such effulgence,
wrap their mild twigs and bruises in straws
and touch themselves tightly, like buttered bees,

for the sun is cold, there, as an eyeglass
playing with its freshly running sinuses,
swampy, and of a molasses sweetness on the cheek.

Turn, oh turn! your pure divining rod
for the sake of infantile suns and their railing
and storming at the deplorably pale cheeks

and the hemlocks not yet hung up.
Do we live in old, sane, sensible cries?
The guards stand up and down like a waltz

and its strains are stolen by fauns
with their wounded feet nevertheless dashing
away through the woods, for the iris! for autumn!

Oh pure blue of a footstep, have you stolen
March? and, with your cupiditous baton
struck agog? do you feel that you have, blue?

Ah, March! you have not decided whom you train.
Or what traitors are waiting for you to be born,
oh March! or what it will mean in terms of diet.

Take my clear big eyes into your heart, and then
pump my clear big eyes through your bloodstream, and!
stick my clear big eyes on your feet, it is cold,

I am all over snowshoes and turning round
and round. There's a trail of blood through
the wood and a few shreds of faun-colored hair.

I am troubled as I salute the crocus.
There shall be no more reclining on the powdered roads,
your veins are using up the redness of the world.

Now what we desire is space.
To turn up the thermometer and sigh.

    A village had gone under the water
of her smile, and then, quickly, it froze clear
so that the village could know our whereabouts.
And had you intended it?

I found a string of pearls in the tea bags
                        and gave them her
with what love?

                With the love of the camelopard
for the camel, for the leopard.

                    Oh space!
you never conquer desire, do you?

You turn us up and we talk to each other
and then we are truly happy as the telephone
rings and rings and buzzes and buzzes,

    so is that the abyss? I talk, you talk,
he talks, she talks, it talks.

                At last!
You are warm enough, aren't you?
And do you miss me truly dear, as I miss you?
    I don't think I'll return to the zoo.

THREE RONDELS

I
Dreaming that there's a sea god!
with barnacles on his toes.
He lies stretched out beside me
like water he's turned green

with lust and cold with sperm.
I hear his heart shouting, it's
a shell being smashed against—

dreaming that there's a sea god!
a rock. The rock? that's me
and wouldn't it be wonderful if
he were a ship? Then there'd be sailors
dreaming that there's a sea god!

2
Ill fate? no! In fainting you volunteer your tears.
Ill, but never "nuts"; never pleasantly nor jumpily
"gone." An attendant, Venus-like, touches your cells
and you grow dizzy, cry "I am! Bring me untouchables!"

"Intentionally alluring, patient? The sounds are gourds."
Oh the pee and the lightning! The aimless ailments!
Ill fate? no! In fainting you volunteer your tears.

"Intentionally alluring vices? These caves have sheets."
Gone, ill for a peso, tone deaf and immured, he tells
his illness is not venial. Amiability is a horse;
and jumping into the pavilion of the demiurges,
ill fate? no! In fainting you volunteer your tears.

3
Door of America, mention my fear to the cigars!
dance the ch' Indian and quit the covers;
the cigars owe you for toy-chanting to them,
joke used up, having petty symbols.

Lake roses, surrounding the plural natal mates,
eat the nugget of blank fate and then drop the
door of America. Mention my fear to the cigars!

Plural moments are trapped by the passing ravishments.

The Muse becomes a comrade who poses for you
when you are bivouacked and want to get out of the aura:
set rhythms quit, vapid, and flies grow pale.
Door of America, mention my fear to the cigars!

If, jetting, I committed the noble fault
turning in air fell off the balcony
to refountain myself I'd force the port!
violate the piers and their bushy moorings
      you bores! you asses!

geology?   that's hefting the crop
rats like me so profoundly trust;
if I jet into the azure breeze
to multiply the roses there
      I'm roseate myself, aren't I?

and if I jet a grinning conspiracy
to melt everyone into syrup
and feel sure I am that second volcano
and decide that I'm Vesuvius
      you'll say "Itself?"

if I'm jetting rather putridly one
day, you'll say "give me your volcanic
papers, Frank, make peace" but
I'll be dangerous as bread that day,
      I discovered penicillin

or if I'm lying in the harbor quietly
jetting on my back and a refrigerator ship
sails in "for the love of God, Frank
make me your little igloo, I'm on fire!"
      you'd hate my compassion

you'd quit because you can't appreciate
how rich the volcanic appetite, essentially, is—
in regulating my soul's beneficence
I've kayoed your popular cant
      I'd rather jet!

I'm laughing like an old bedspring;
a rather glamorous priest behind the curtains
is groping for benignity, ha! he can't take
that away from me—*Miserere, Domine*
      what a grumbler!

for if you have duennas of children
or of ugliness, I just give up, I throw

myself back into the bay—the sun spits
and I spit back, or maybe we both pour:
    "That's no furnace, that's my heart!"

HOMAGE TO PASTERNAK'S CAPE MOOTCH

"The mind is stifled." Very little sky
is visible through the ailanthus,
and through the ailanthus is the red brick
and the grey brick, and the smell of the cats

in the courtyard. My left hand falls
on a tea bag, humid like the lightless air.
It is morning and a whole day starts
stepping daintily along my sweaty flesh.

Yearning grasses growing from my eyes
to this music do you lean, shallow and wet
like a pebble? I roll the tea into a cylinder
and it's like marijuana beside a pool,

not like a good American cigarette
with its delicate twigs flaring up now
and then beside the nose. In this room
there is suddenly a pool. Drops of water,

slightly chlorinated, fall from my nose
onto the cigarette as I heavily breathe
from swimming through the wood of this parquet
which is deep brown, the tall trunk of hell.

ODE

An idea of justice may be precious,
one vital gregarious amusement . . .

What are you amused by? a crisis
like a cow being put on the payroll
with the concomitant investigations and divinings?
Have you swept the dung from the tracks?
        Am I a door?
If millions criticize you for drinking too much,
the cow is going to look like Venus and you'll make a pass
yes, you and your friend from High School,
the basketball player whose black eyes exceed yours
as he picks up the ball with one hand.
        But doesn't he doubt, too?

        To be equal? it's the worst!
        Are we just muddy instants?

No, you must treat me like a fox; or, being a child,
kill the oriole though it reminds you of me.
Thus you become the author of all being. Women
        unite against you.

It's as if I were carrying a horse on my shoulders
and I couldn't see his face. His iron legs
hang down to the earth on either side of me
like the arch of triumph in Washington Square.
I would like to beat someone with him
but I can't get him off my shoulders, he's like evening.

Evening! your breeze is an obstacle,
        it changes me, I am being arrested,
        and if I mock you into a face
and, disgusted, throw down the horse—ah! there's his face!
and I am, sobbing, walking on my heart.

        I want to take your hands off my hips
        and put them on a statue's hips;

then I can thoughtfully regard the justice of your feelings
for me, and, changing, regard my own love for you
as beautiful. I'd never cheat you and say "It's inevitable!"
        It's just barely natural.
        But we do course together
like two battleships maneuvering away from the fleet.
I am moved by the multitudes of your intelligence
and sometimes, returning, I become the sea—
in love with your speed, your heaviness and breath.

Am I to become profligate as if I were a blonde? Or religious as if I were French?

Each time my heart is broken it makes me feel more adventurous (and how the same names keep recurring on that interminable list!), but one of these days there'll be nothing left with which to venture forth.

Why should I share you? Why don't you get rid of someone else for a change?

I am the least difficult of men. All I want is boundless love.

Even trees understand me! Good heavens, I lie under them, too, don't I? I'm just like a pile of leaves.

However, I have never clogged myself with the praises of pastoral life, nor with nostalgia for an innocent past of perverted acts in pastures. No. One need never leave the confines of New York to get all the greenery one wishes—I can't even enjoy a blade of grass unless I know there's a subway handy, or a record store or some other sign that people do not totally *regret* life. It is more important to affirm the least sincere; the clouds get enough attention as it is and even they continue to pass. Do they know what they're missing? Uh huh.

My eyes are vague blue, like the sky, and change all the time; they are indiscriminate but fleeting, entirely specific and disloyal, so that no one trusts me. I am always looking away. Or again at something after it has given me up. It makes me restless and that makes me unhappy, but I cannot keep them still. If only I had grey, green, black, brown, yellow eyes; I would stay at home and do something. It's not that I'm curious. On the contrary, I am bored but it's my duty to be attentive, I am needed by things as the sky must be above the earth. And lately, so great has *their* anxiety become, I can spare myself little sleep.

Now there is only one man I love to kiss when he is unshaven. Heterosexuality! you are inexorably approaching. (How discourage her?)

St. Serapion, I wrap myself in the robes of your whiteness which is like midnight in Dostoevsky. How am I to become a legend, my dear? I've tried love, but that hides you in the bosom of another and I am always springing forth from it like the lotus—the ecstasy of always bursting forth! (but one must not be distracted by it!) or like a hyacinth, "to keep the filth of life away," yes, there, even in the heart, where the filth is pumped in and slanders and pollutes and determines. I will my will, though I may become famous for a mysterious vacancy in that department, that greenhouse.

Destroy yourself, if you don't know!

It is easy to be beautiful; it is difficult to appear so. I admire you, beloved, for the trap you've set. It's like a final chapter no one reads because the plot is over.

"Fanny Brown is run away—scampered off with a Cornet of Horse; I do love that little Minx, & hope She may be happy, tho' She has vexed me by this Exploit a little too. —Poor silly Cecchina! or F:B: as we used to call her. —I wish She had a good Whipping and 10,000 pounds." —Mrs. Thrale.

I've got to get out of here. I choose a piece of shawl and my dirtiest suntans. I'll be back, I'll re-emerge, defeated, from the valley; you don't want me to go where you go, so I go where you don't want me to. It's only afternoon, there's a lot ahead. There won't be any mail downstairs. Turning, I spit in the lock and the knob turns.

TO THE MOUNTAINS IN NEW YORK

Yes! yes! yes! I've decided,
I'm letting my flock run around,
I'm dropping my pastoral pretensions!
and leaves don't fall into a little halo
on my tanned and worried head.
Let the houses fill up with dirt.
My master died in my heart.
On the molten streets of New York
the master put up signs of my death.
I love this hairy city.
It's wrinkled like a detective story
and noisy and getting fat and smudged
lids hood the sharp hard black eyes.
America's wandering away from me
in a dream of pine trees and clouds
of pubic dreams of the world at my feet.
The moon comes out: languorous
in spite of everything, towards all
its expectancy rides a slow white horse.
I walk watching, tripping, alleys

open and fall around me like footsteps
of a newly shod horse treading the
marble staircases of the palace
and the light screams of the nobility
oblige invisible bayonets. All
night I sit on the outspread knees
of addicts; their kindness
makes them talk like whores to
the sun as it moves me hysterically
forward. The subway shoots onto a ramp
overlooking the East River, the towers!
the minarets! The bridge. I'm lost.
There's no way back to the houses
filled with dirt. My master died
in my heart on the molten streets.

2

Everyone is drinking and falling
and the sour smiles of the wheels
and the curses of ambitious love.
I remember Moscow
I remember two herdsmen in fur caps
and they were lying down together
in the snow of their natural ferocity
which warded off the wolves.
But now no kisses reassure the animals
of my tent, and they wander drunkenly away
and I wander drunkenly here, clouded,
and I see no face to follow down the streets
through the gates of a great city
I was building to house the myth of my love.
I take a flowery drop of gin upon my tongue
and it receives the flaming sibilance
of the Volga. I am murmuring
past my own banks, rushing, floundering and black
at last, into the cleft of the filth.
My head is hot here in the snow and I dart
rebellious looks into the severely hidden
bootless snow. My own youth has narrowed
like a knife which cures the pleasures of life.

I shall never return! though I twist, come back,
grow pale, as the receding waves seem to lick the shore.
I cannot give myself now, I can only rush
towards you, engulf you, and pour forth!
The moon is desirous of detaining me, you,
but you are gone, and I follow.

3
I feel the earth pulsing against my heart.
They call me The Dirt Eater. The Gambler.
I can't rise, I'm so filthy! so heavy!
at last I have my full stench, I've rediscovered
you. That's why you went away, isn't it?
I could have stayed forever in your arms.
But then I'd have become you. Now I've become the earth!
You died, and the tempestuous blue of my eyes
filled the sails of your funeral barque
which, I remember, was filled with walnuts.
It is raining. Shall I grow trees or flowers?

3 REQUIEMS FOR A YOUNG UNCLE

1
Brilliant uncle incarnadine
too, nuance posing dark van

nuance of roadster crash
nuance of care for recklessness
and a deaf girlfriend's big nose

2
Etruria!
leap, ream, eye, Irving, nude.

3
   I haven't seen a curly head in a toilet. See?
you sea-of-the-forehead dice, quit ailing. End, moo,
smile, but leave destiny its Persian quizzicalness
of a permanent interventionist. In your blood, to
object? ditch irritants! owe, but with resignation.
Dance in a vest allocated to the servants of the
harrowing chortle's end.

MAYAKOVSKY

1
My heart's aflutter!
I am standing in the bath tub
crying. Mother, mother
who am I? If he
will just come back once
and kiss me on the face
his coarse hair brush
my temple, it's throbbing!

then I can put on my clothes
I guess, and walk the streets.

2
I love you. I love you,
but I'm turning to my verses
and my heart is closing
like a fist.

Words! be
sick as I am sick, swoon,
roll back your eyes, a pool,

and I'll stare down
at my wounded beauty
which at best is only a talent
for poetry.

Cannot please, cannot charm or win
what a poet!
and the clear water is thick

with bloody blows on its head.
I embraced a cloud,
but when I soared
it rained.

3
That's funny! there's blood on my chest
oh yes, I've been carrying bricks
what a funny place to rupture!
and now it is raining on the ailanthus
as I step out onto the window ledge
the tracks below me are smoky and

glistening with a passion for running
I leap into the leaves, green like the sea

4
Now I am quietly waiting for
the catastrophe of my personality
to seem beautiful again,
and interesting, and modern.

The country is grey and
brown and white in trees,
snows and skies of laughter
always diminishing, less funny
not just darker, not just grey.

It may be the coldest day of
the year, what does he think of
that? I mean, what do I? And if I do,
perhaps I am myself again.

FOR JANICE AND KENNETH TO VOYAGE

Love, love, love,
honeymoon isn't used much in poetry these days

and if I give you a bar
of Palmolive Soap
it would be rather cracker-barrel
of me, wouldn't it?

The winds will wash you out your hair, my dears.
Passions will become turrets, to you.

I'll be so afraid
without you.
The penalty of the Big Town
is the Big Stick,

yet when you were laughing nearby
the monsters ignored me like a record player

and I felt brilliant
to be so confident
that the trees
would walk back to Birnam Wood.

It was all you, your graceful white smiles
like a French word, the one for nursery, the one for brine.

TWO BOYS

A FAVORITE
Just as he's about to rise, he erupts;
or he is showing you the repetitions of his rifle,
enjoying the clatter of his tongue upon surrounding mouths.

HIS YOUNGER BROTHER
Short as he is, he's nearer
to touching you honestly,
eager to flare up with
veracity, an almost
enormous pride in sight.

A HILL

Yes, it's disgusting
when you lose
control, but my
wilderness is love

of a kind, no?
And the purity
of my confusion is
there, it's poetry

in love with you
along with me,
both of us love you
in the same "My!"

Yes, but don't be
scared; poetry
is intangible and
there's no purity

in me
outside of love,
which you can easily wreck
and I can lose.

Clouds pass in
my notorious eye
but you, through
all, I see.

[I KISS YOUR CUP]

I kiss your cup
which will not be used again
till you come back

Loud as a swan's transport
is your voice
amplified by the distance in your eyes

Snow of thought
I am on my back to you
and my lids twitch

I dreamt
that I was mysteriously murdered
with narcotics

And the dust
that makes a Rubens out of you
makes me a serpent

PORTRAIT

Not to be gathered again   across a solemn couch
my lilies, your powders
                        upon the smoky air
            while glassy eyes pursue their indifferent way
                        into the glassy past
and twitch with the utterability of dreams
                        induced by dope

O certainties
        of being despised and sick
                        you are light for the blind
                        and blindness to the poet

Where I walked quietly with my flute among enormous thistles
        a mirage disappeared
        of beasts following me to a bar
                        muscularity had found its window
opening onto a bazaar
                        carrying a cross
        buying fresh cut flowers
        carrying them in a baseball glove

Endless narratives
                        you are told me
                        I believe you
        and the salt is licking across the land

        Soon there will be a wound
        and belief will be able to leave its station

ON THE WAY TO THE SAN REMO

        The black ghinkos snarl their way up
        the moon growls at each blinking window
        the apartment houses climb deafeningly into the purple

A bat hisses northwards
the perilous steps lead to a grate
suddenly the heat is bearable

The cross-eyed dog scratches a worn patch of pavement
his right front leg is maimed in the shape of a V
there's no trace of his nails on the street a woman cajoles

She is very old and dirty
she whistles her filthy hope
that it will rain tonight

The 6th Avenue bus trunk-lumbers sideways
it is full of fat people who cough as at a movie
they eat each other's dandruff in the flickering glare

The moon passes into clouds
so hurt by the street lights
of your glance oh my heart

The act of love is also passing like a subway bison
through the paper-littered arches of the express tracks
the sailor sobers he feeds pennies to the peanut machines

Though others are in the night
far away lips upon a dusty armpit
the nostrils are full of tears

High fidelity reposed in a box a hand on the windowpane
the sweet calm the violin strings tie a young man's hair
the bright black eyes pin far away their smudged curiosity

Yes you are foolish smoking
the bars are for rabbits
who wish to outlive the men

IN THE MOVIES

Out of the corner of my eyes
a tear of revulsion sighs,
it's the point of intersection a foot in front of me,

I call it my cornea, my Muse.
I hurl myself there— at whatever fatal flowery flourish!
flower? flower?
if that face is flourishing, it's toes of tin!
Well, but there is a face there, a ravine of powder and gasps,
I can see it, I must caress it.
I give it one of my marine caresses since it is inferior, petulant.
And the clear water of my head pours over that face.

Flowers. Flowers.
Just because the day is as long and white as a camel
you'll see my head leaning against this masseur of a seat
and the blood in my pants mounts to the stars
as I ponder the silver square.

Flowers. Flowers,
every afternoon at one, why not caress the wind
which passes from the air conditioning to my seat?
as the waters underneath Times Square
pour through my eyes onto the silver screen.
I'm here, pale and supple as a horse-shrine.

Ushers! ushers!
do you seek me with your lithe flashlights?
enveloping me like the controlled current of the air?
There seems to be a ghost up there,
brushing off his gems and plumes.
It's a great feathery candle glowing in the rain
of my fine retrieving gaze,
the large feathered prick that impaled me in the grass.
It was an organ that announced a certain destiny.
And as the plumes flutter in the current they spell out *****
but I don't believe my eyes, it's only a ghost's habit.
I bought a ticket so I could be alone. With the plumes.
With the ushers.
With my own prick,
and with my death written in smoke
outside this theatre where I receive my mail.
Guts? my gut is full of water, like the River Jordan.

The pressure of my boredom is uplifting and cool,
I feel its familiar hands on my buttocks.
And we depend on the screen for accompaniment,
its mirrors
its music
because I've left everything behind but a leaf
and now a dark hand lifts that from my thighs

(out of the corner of my eyes
a tear of revulsion sighs).
No, I've never been in a cotton field in South Carolina.
My head is lost between your purple lips.
Your teeth glitter like the Aurora Borealis.

Cerise trees are plunging through my veins
and not one lumberjack is drowned in my giant flesh.
This stranger collects me like a sea-story
and now I am part of his marine slang.
Waves break in the theatre
and flame finds a passage through the stormy straits of my lips.

In my hands a black cloud of soft winds
pulses forth the error of my blood and my body,
like a poem written in blackface,
his flower opens and I press my face into the dahlialike mirror
whose lips press mine with the grandeur of a torrent,
it is flooding the cleft of my rocklike face
which burns with the anguish of a plaster beast!
I am said to have the eyes of a camelopard
and the lips of an oriole,
it's my movie reputation—
so now you've found my germinal spontaneity
and you are my voyage to Africa.

I love your naked storms.
I contemplate you with the profound regard of a scriptwriter.
The serene horse of your forgetfulness is a crater
in which I bathe the pride of my race,
as we splash away the afternoon
in the movies
and in the mountains.

Reflect a moment on the flesh in which you're mired:
I'm the white heron of your darkness,
I'm the ghost of a tribal chief killed in battle
and I bear proudly the slit nose of your victories.

Suffer my cornea to adopt a verbal blueness,
for you are the sick prince of my cerise innovations,
and my seriousness.
I bear you mirrors
and I kiss the sill of your porcelain fountain,
dreaming midst the flamingo plumes of your penis.

Seized by flames!
seized by winds!
sea of my sex and your red domination!
(red is for my heart and for the wind of my islands)
which envelops this insect, my self,
and salutes your loins
as the shadowy horses increase
and I pale with butterfly aspirations.

Do you feel the hairs that fill my mouth like aigrettes,
as moss fills the stone with longing no hands can tear away?
do you feel your sword imbedded in the legendary rock?
the repose of rivers,
the source of warriors,
warriors of the stars which are my sighs
and my sighs are black
because my blood is black with your love,
the love of the jungle for its secret pools.

We take the silver way along the rocks
and with my head upon your chocolate breast
the screen is again a horizon of blood.
The drapes flutter around us like cement.
In your drowning caresses I walk the sea.
I am gilded with your sweat
and your hair smells of herbs
from which I do not care to peer.

If love is born from this projection in the golden beehive like a swan,
I love you.
I am lighting up the evening which is yours,
I implore you;
and the smoke of my death will have blown away by now,
as my ghosts are laid along your glittering teeth.

[JULY IS OVER AND THERE'S VERY LITTLE TRACE]

July is over and there's very little trace
of it, though the Bastille fell on its face—

and August's gotten orange, it will drop on
the edge of the world like a worm-eaten sun.

The trees are taking off their leaves. So
the purity of the streets is coming, low,

in white waves. In the summer I got good and sunburnt,
winter, so I wouldn't miss the wet brunt

of your storms. Then it was sand from the surf
in my bathing trunks; now snow fills up my scarf.

MUSIC

　　If I rest for a moment near The Equestrian
pausing for a liver sausage sandwich in the Mayflower Shoppe,
that angel seems to be leading the horse into Bergdorf's
and I am naked as a table cloth, my nerves humming.
Close to the fear of war and the stars which have disappeared.
I have in my hands only 35¢, it's so meaningless to eat!
and gusts of water spray over the basins of leaves
like the hammers of a glass pianoforte. If I seem to you
to have lavender lips under the leaves of the world,
　　I must tighten my belt.
It's like a locomotive on the march, the season
　　of distress and clarity
and my door is open to the evenings of midwinter's
lightly falling snow over the newspapers.
Clasp me in your handkerchief like a tear, trumpet
of early afternoon! in the foggy autumn.
As they're putting up the Christmas trees on Park Avenue
I shall see my daydreams walking by with dogs in blankets,
put to some use before all those coloured lights come on!
　　But no more fountains and no more rain,
　　and the stores stay open terribly late.

210

TO JOHN ASHBERY

I can't believe there's not
another world where we will sit
and read new poems to each other
high on a mountain in the wind.
You can be Tu Fu, I'll be Po Chü-i
and the Monkey Lady'll be in the moon,
smiling at our ill-fitting heads
as we watch snow settle on a twig.
Or shall we be really gone? this
is not the grass I saw in my youth!
and if the moon, when it rises
tonight, is empty—a bad sign,
meaning "You go, like the blossoms."

POEM

Tempestuous breaths! we watch a girl
walking in her garden— no flowers, a wintry shrub
and the cold clouds passing over. To
each dark check a chapped panting mouth is pressed

and through the cloth against her flesh
she feels the flashes of our heat. One breath,
heavier than the rest, is penetrating
the folds where her cool limbs join each other
in careless reception of the celebration.

She is listening to music. And I, I
have joined that torso to that thigh with this,
my breath, soot from a volcano, watching her walk.

There's no holly, but there is
the glass and granite towers
and the white stone lions
and the pale violet clouds. And
the great tree of balls in
Rockefeller Plaza is public.

Christmas is green and general
like all great works of the
imagination, swelling from minute
private sentiments in the desert,
a wreath around our intimacy
like children's voices in a park.

For red there is our blood
which, like your smile, must be
protected from spilling into
generality by secret meanings,
the lipstick of life hidden
in a handbag against violations.

Christmas is the time of cold air
and loud parties and big expense,
but in our hearts flames flicker
answeringly, as on old-fashioned
trees. I would rather the house
burn down than our flames go out.

2 POEMS FROM THE OHARA MONOGATARI

I
My love is coming in a glass
the blood of the Bourbons

saxophone or cornet
qu'importe où?

green of glass flowers *dans le Kentucky*

and always the same handkerchief
at the same nose of damask

turning up my extravagant collar
tossing my scarf about my neck

the Baudelaire of Kyoto's never-ending pureness
is he cracked in the head?

2
After a long trip to a shrine
in wooden clogs so hard on the muscles
the tea is bitter and the breasts are hard
so much terrace for one evening

there is no longer no ocean
I don't see the ocean under my stilts
as I poke along

hands on ankles feet on wrists
naked in thought
like a whip made from sheerest stockings

the radio is on the cigarette is puffed upon
by the pleasures of rolling in a bog
some call the Milky Way
in far-fetched Occidental lands above the trees
where dwell the amusing skulls

TO GIANNI BATES

Like a piano concerto your black
and white eyes, your white face and bright black hair.
And then, reclining in silence, you're there
with a hall of echoes arching your back
and forcing you to sigh. In me the lack
of sound is merely that I hear your stare.
And when you leave there isn't any air;
though I should stay aloft, I have the knack.
But you leave. There isn't any reason

to be silent; in halls the audience
disperses as the instrument's wheeled off
and through jet tears and wet mascara scoff
the year, boring heart-and-concert season.
Too, I've not been silent again, or since.

FOR GRACE, AFTER A PARTY

You do not always know what I am feeling.
Last night in the warm spring air while I was
blazing my tirade against someone who doesn't
interest
        me, it was love for you that set me
afire,
        and isn't it odd? for in rooms full of
strangers my most tender feelings
                                writhe and
bear the fruit of screaming. Put out your hand,
isn't there
        an ashtray, suddenly, there? beside
the bed? And someone you love enters the room
and says wouldn't
                you like the eggs a little
different today?
                And when they arrive they are
just plain scrambled eggs and the warm weather
is holding.

LOVE

A whispering far away
heard by the poet in a bower
of flesh his limbs stir

is it sadness or the perfection
of eyes that clutches him?

And a parade of lamenting
draws near a wave of angels
he is drowning in the word

POEM

I watched an armory combing its bronze bricks
and in the sky there were glistening rails of milk.
Where had the swan gone, the one with the lame back?

      Now mounting the steps
      I enter my new home full
      of grey radiators and glass
      ashtrays full of wool.

Against the winter I must get a samovar
embroidered with basil leaves and Ukranian mottos
to the distant sound of wings, painfully anti-wind,

      a little bit of the blue
      summer air will come back
      as the steam chuckles in
      the monster's steamy attack

and I'll be happy here and happy there, full
of tea and tears. I don't suppose I'll ever get
to Italy, but I have the terrible tundra at least.

      My new home will be full
      of wood, roots and the like,
      while I pace in a turtleneck
      sweater, repairing my bike.

I watched the palisades shivering in the snow
of my face, which had grown preternaturally pure.
Once I destroyed a man's idea of himself to have him.

      If I'd had a samovar then
      I'd have made him tea

and as hyacinths grow from
a pot he would love me

and my charming room of tea cosies full of dirt
which is why I must travel, to collect the leaves.
O my enormous piano, you are not like being outdoors

though it is cold and you
are made of fire and wood!
I lift your lid and mountains
return, that I am good.

The stars blink like a hairnet that was dropped
on a seat and now it is lying in the alley behind
the theater where my play is echoed by dying voices.

I am really a woodcarver
and my words are love
which willfully parades in
its room, refusing to move.

POEM

to James Schuyler

There I could never be a boy,
though I rode like a god when the horse reared.
At a cry from mother I fell to my knees!
there I fell, clumsy and sick and good,
though I bloomed on the back of a frightened black mare
who had leaped windily at the start of a leaf
and she never threw me.

I had a quick heart
and my thighs clutched her back.
I loved her fright, which was against me
into the air! and the diamond white of her forelock
which seemed to smart with thoughts as my heart smarted with life!
and she'd toss her head with the pain
and paw the air and champ the bit, as if I were Endymion
and she, moonlike, hated to love me.

All things are tragic
when a mother watches!
and she wishes upon herself
the random fears of a scarlet soul, as it breathes in and out
and nothing chokes, or breaks from triumph to triumph!

I knew her but I could not be a boy,
for in the billowing air I was fleet and green
riding blackly through the ethereal night
towards men's words which I gracefully understood,

and it was given to me
as the soul is given the hands
to hold the ribbons of life!
as miles streak by beneath the moon's sharp hooves
and I have mastered the speed and strength which is the armor of the world.

TO THE HARBORMASTER

I wanted to be sure to reach you;
though my ship was on the way it got caught
in some moorings. I am always tying up
and then deciding to depart. In storms and
at sunset, with the metallic coils of the tide
around my fathomless arms, I am unable
to understand the forms of my vanity
or I am hard alee with my Polish rudder
in my hand and the sun sinking. To
you I offer my hull and the tattered cordage
of my will. The terrible channels where
the wind drives me against the brown lips
of the reeds are not all behind me. Yet
I trust the sanity of my vessel; and
if it sinks, it may well be in answer
to the reasoning of the eternal voices,
the waves which have kept me from reaching you.

HERMAPHRODITE

How he, reclining on the limp edge of
wet dawn, divines rhetorically the stem
of his life which purports a kissing wind,
baguettes, managerial consistency, and
he is seen by too many people. It is
understood by those green trembling faces,
those flatterers.
        He tries desperately
not to notice the necessity of a manner
which is opaque, and dependent on
the rolling branches of blue convolvulus
which, like seeing-eye dogs, are saying
"Ay yeah. Surely. Of course."
              Winter
for instance, compares him to the ancients,
the anemone, the mammoth and his tusky friends,
some beautiful and driven as snow, alone
and each. Unmasking him, unmanning him,
stripping him down and cutting off his breasts
in the style of those Arab outrages, this
would be supremely satisfying to the hoodlums
who are his only audience, the believing ones
he would like to make weep. And yet, poor,
he has no circus smile, he is deep, and
just as a mirror grows hairy with weariness
considering all that remains hidden, he
tabulates ponderously the details of his own
decorum, faints, and then looks quickly up
hoping to recognize the curiosity
of the breakers. He is cold but cannot,
because it would hide his sex.
        Presenting him
always in a summery light is his personality,
the gross pretender to nature and relaxation.
Bedecked with jewels, he's invisible among leaves,
does not think it mean to cry "Pooh! Pho!" at
the hunters and scamper off, although they are
in tears of vacation, they feel queer. Bus,
he must take a bus, he thinks, no parasite he.
They can always check on him through the company.

His hair will not grow thick enough to braid
and hide, leaves are spreading far and high,

he should be curled up tight in the airless ransom,
the sea, whose vibration ceases at the instant
of his need. How brave he is! anxious but silky,
the most lovable echo, the most diffuse alarm. There:
no hello, no goodbye pressing its moist lips
against a thin sky, so still infuriated. "Ah!"

POEM

Pawing the mound with his hairy legs
under the hot hose and the striped sun,
he stuck his head in the sand, a white
triangle. The ball turned blue in his hand
and silver stitching appeared, blinding
the bleachers.
                 Yes! he unwound, the catcher
lost a hand. A bat splintered into a shrine.
A batter went to a sanitarium (they were
the enemy!), and this is not sports.
Whenever a great event occurs, there's a
pitcher and a catcher. The in-between
explodes from burning like the lice
in *All Quiet on the Western Front.* And
quickly the field is filled with crosses,
white and waving their arms and shouting,
and poppies.
                 What happens to the blue world
with its necklace of lights and arteries
and nerves, throbbing through air
so ill-intentioned and other-directed?

A little batboy finds the ball in secret
and he puts it on his bureau underneath the
kerchief of a juvenile delinquent he admires.

An impression of waves mounting the shore
is left on the roots of the pines on the hill
where the vegetation is stammering and failing
underneath the incessant pricks of weather.

Hebdomadaire? Aeons of longing go into one perfect
aridity. The Indians prove that that void alone
is perfectible, the image of lasting in memory,
who wears the bison horns on the higher plateau.

A posse of wild horses drums over the roof
of Canada. Thieves creep in the mineral cellar
like Mexican jumping-beans, gourdless
yet rhythmically noisy. They assume the profundity

of splashing water over rocks is this: to mash
together all the noises in a white nutrition
and wear the fur when it comes alive and is killed
in August. And the trees lose, too; either above

the line of propriety where the oxygen fails
and the weather is callous, or below with the ants,
all building pyramids of sawdust unmemorial
though the wind has died down. Still across the floor

of the continent dead souls are blown, souls
of Indians in dire nomadic hootings: they fell
to earth and did not grow and could not rest
in the cactus heimat. Fire water!   the vulgar buckaroos

in shirts, whipping their pintos on to the waterhole
where they drink calamitously and throw their four legs
up. And the souls of horses must be shod, as the glacier
must roar; as trees must shed their shadows to gain rest.

ON SAINT ADALGISA'S DAY

The geraniums and rubber plants
bend over the dusty sun. With pants

of stiff beige clay, relax
as if they stood beside an axe.

It's prematurely hot today
and no rain in sight for the hay,

for the yellow asphalt on the wall
and underfoot as, in the hall

of avarice, I pace the city.
Spring is never purity

here, all grey, but weakness,
make-up, passing now for chicness

now for humor. In the heavens
radio announcers choose their sevens

and are glad to see me go
to work although I'm tired, so,

they can have the apartment and
turn off the morning music, no hand.

As the sun sits on my bed
with news, with news they fill its head.

CHOSES PASSAGÈRES

à John Ashbery

J'écorche l'anguille par la queue, peut-être un noeud
      d'anguille, ou il y a anguille sous roche,
je ne fais que toucher barres.
Chapeaux bas! mais, il n'y avait pas un seul chapeau,
et moi; j'avais beaucoup travaillé dans le temps.
J'avais souffert un grand échec, mystérieusement.
Qui se sent galeux se gratte!

Hébergement? je suis à la hauteur d'une île, c'est du
      hasard, et je ne suis pas une haridelle,
plein d'impudicité, non, non, j'imprime un mouvement
      à une machine,
la semaine des quatre jeudis, du temps que la reine
      Berthe filait.

J'aime partout les kinkajous.
Hier soir, j'étais un labadens; maintenant? je suis
      un lavabo.
Je mange les morilles moresques, quelle suffisance!
Je suis un homme qui se noie, montant un cheval à nu, et
      mon ciel est couvert de nuances.
Est-ce que j'ai un bel organe, hein? je fais ses orges
      très bien, pourquoi pas?

Ce fruit est du poison tout pur, c'est la pure vérité,
      et pourquoi pas?
ça ne nous rajeunit pas! La rouille ronge le fer,
      c'est un souvenir soviétique.
La trébuchage, le tric-trac, vous vous trompez! dites
      voir turlututu chapeau pointu!
Ce drap est d'un bon user,
pour trouver l'usurpateur utérin. Oui, mais, je suis seul.
Par monts et par vaux, le valet de bourreau vient,
c'est un wattman vulcanien, et j'ai peur.
Il pleut. Je mange un xiphias.
Il n'y gagnera rein, je suis une yole, un you you, moi.
Tu es un homme zélateur, donc? Mon ange, tu as un oeil
      qui dit zut à l'autre.

SONNET

The blueness of the hour
when the spine stretches itself
into a groan, then the golden cheek
on the dirty pillow, wrinkled by linen.
Odor of lanolin, the flower
pressed between thundering doubts of self,
cleaving fresh air through the week
and loading hearts to the millennium.
Go, sweet breath! come, sweet rain,
bewildering as a tortoise
embracing the Indian ocean,
predictable as a porpoise
    diving upon his mate in cool
    water which is not a pool.

The eyelid has its storms. There is the opaque fish-
scale green of it after swimming in the sea and then sud-
denly wrenching violence, strangled lashes, and a barbed
wire of sand falls to the shore.

Or, in the midst of sunset, the passive grey lips: a
virile suffusion of carmine! itching under a plague of
allergies and tears, memories of the first soothing oint-
ment press the cornea to desperate extremity, the back of
the head, like a pool pocket, never there when you stare
steadily and shoot.

A man walked into the drugstore and said "I'd
like one hazel eye and a jar of socket ointment, salted.
My mother has a lid that's black from boredom and though
we're poor—her tongue! profundity of shut-ins!
And oh yes, do you have a little cuticle scissors?"

Purchase to dream, green eyeshadow, kohl, gonorrhea,
of the currents at the bottom of the Gulf of Mexico.

AT THE OLD PLACE

Joe is restless and so am I, so restless.
Button's buddy lips frame "L G T TH O P?"
across the bar. "Yes!" I cry, for dancing's
my soul delight. (Feet! feet!) "Come on!"

Through the streets we skip like swallows.
Howard malingers. (Come on, Howard.) Ashes
malingers. (Come on, J.A.) Dick malingers.
(Come on, Dick.) Alvin darts ahead. (Wait up,
Alvin.) Jack, Earl and Someone don't come.

Down the dark stairs drifts the steaming cha-
cha-cha. Through the urine and smoke we charge
to the floor. Wrapped in Ashes' arms I glide.

(It's heaven!) Button lindys with me. (It's
heaven!) Joe's two-steps, too, are incredible,
and then a fast rhumba with Alvin, like skipping
on toothpicks. And the interminable intermissions,

we have them. Jack, Earl and Someone drift
guiltily in. "I knew they were gay
the minute I laid eyes on them!" screams John.
How ashamed they are of us!   we hope.

A WHITMAN'S BIRTHDAY BROADCAST WITH STATIC

Pas la jeunesse à moi,
ni delicacy, ich kann nicht, ich kann nicht, keines
    Vorsprechen!
Ugly on the patio, silly on the floor, unkempt,
dans le vieux parc je m'asseois, et je ne vois pas
    à droite ni à gauche.
Personne! mais des bruits, des vagues particulières,
    und ich habe Kummer, es könnte ihm ein Schaden
    zustossen, lacht der Kundschafter.
And then someone comes along who's sick and I say
    "Tiens, ça! c'est las de l'amour, c'est okay!"
    and fall.
Da, ich bin der Komponist, und ich bin komponiert.

NOCTURNE

There's nothing worse
than feeling bad and not
being able to tell you.
Not because you'd kill me
or it would kill you, or
we don't love each other.

It's space. The sky is grey
and clear, with pink and
blue shadows under each cloud.
A tiny airliner drops its
specks over the U N Building.
My eyes, like millions of
glassy squares, merely reflect.
Everything sees through me,
in the daytime I'm too hot
and at night I freeze; I'm
built the wrong way for the
river and a mild gale would
break every fiber in me.
Why don't I go east and west
instead of north and south?
It's the architect's fault.
And in a few years I'll be
useless, not even an office
building. Because you have
no telephone, and live so
far away; the Pepsi–Cola sign,
the seagulls and the noise.

POEM

Johnny and Alvin are going home, are sleeping now
are fanning the air with breaths from the same bed.

The moon is covered with gauze and the laughs
are not in them. The boats honk and the barges heave

a little, so the river is moved by a faint breeze.
Where are the buses that would take them to another state?

standing on corners; a nurse waits with a purse
and a murderer escapes the detectives by taking a public

conveyance through the summer's green reflections.
There's too much lime in the world and not enough gin,

they gasp. The gentle are curious, but the curious
are not gentle. So the breaths come home and sleep.

GOODBYE TO GREAT SPRUCE HEAD ISLAND

to Anne and Fairfield Porter

Behind the firs, black in the white and air,
wind fills itself with sun and flaps on the world's
        hour of hearing, almost lavender hour, cold as a
canal pouring through the September of an orchard.
Fall, measured and prolonged as was the voice of Turandot,
        tower of the Orient, as look these trees

now leaning toward northwest from last year's storms with
bough of silver kneeling to the bristling bay some,
        around us gathers nearness and moves in,
between a summer of deep diving and clear heart, a
screen's external cold from the sea, dividing
        ground of all that means and is beyond our leisure.

Defy the fall with bare accepting foot and hotly
eye the curious access to a seriousness, untanned,
        vain, like fish? It will push in, tear limbs like
leaves into a brown tapestry until the snow, reversing,
receives, a grounded white which formerly was the air.
        Rain warms the blanket where the flowers grow,

way of the troubadour flesh in beds on bluffs, when
ray strikes far out the ocean and, cool and passion-
        crossed, lips casually leap in the sun—not to
arcade in winter which is Mondays all far from horn and
shade. To witness brightness and move on! its
        lost, its freckled night, the covered by the cold.

TO AN ACTOR WHO DIED

As the days go, and they go fast on this island
where the firs grow blue and the golden seaweed
clambers up the rocks, I think of you, and death comes
not, except a sea urchin's dropped and cracked

on the rocks and falling bird eats him to rise
more strongly into fog or luminous purple wind. So
to be used and rest, the spiny thing is empty, still
increasing decoration on the craggy slopes above

the barnacles. Lightly falls the grieving light
over the heel of Great Spruce Head Island, like cool
words turning their back on the bayness of the bay
and open water where the swell says heavy things

and smoothly to the nonreflective caves. Clover lies,
in its mauve decline, to the butterflies and bumblebees
and hummingbirds and hornets finding not their sucking
appetites attractive in its stirring dryness, robbed

out of succulence into fainting, rattling noise. Only
the child loves noise, your head is clear as a rock
in air above the fish hawk's habitual shriek at menace
already moving away, above the fish which will not leave the weir

once there as the tide has pulled them. The holy land
outside of nature nothing feeds, as rocks address no sun.

WITH BARBARA AT LARRÉ'S

Fall faces who have lunched on other
Wednesdays at the flattering
bar. They are not turned by a change
of suit not touched by noon, they could be

oscillating with hope, its cigarette-ish
pallor. We pour Martinis in our ears, listening
for each other's silence.
"I ate here with an Englishman

who ordered skate." Demitasses bang together
in the Fall behind the door.
It is the scene of many disasters, how
we wait, as stamps pile up in postal boxes.

"This is quite an aërial table,
isn't it?" To such a tryst we cannot come
so frequently, guarding the effervescent from
the air, the air from all the burning conversation.

FOR JAMES DEAN

Welcome me, if you will,
as the ambassador of a hatred
who knows its cause
and does not envy you your whim
of ending him.

For a young actor I am begging
peace, gods. Alone
in the empty streets of New York
I am its dirty feet and head
and he is dead.

He has banged into your wall
of air, your hubris, racing
towards your heights and you
have cut him from your table
which is built, how unfairly
for us! not on trees, but on clouds.

I speak as one whose filth
is like his own, of pride
and speed and your terrible
example nearer than the sirens' speech,
a spirit eager for the punishment
which is your only recognition.

Peace! to be true to a city
of rats and to love the envy
of the dreary, smudged mouthers
of an arcane dejection
smoldering quietly in the perception
of hopelessness and scandal
at unnatural vigor. Their dreams

are their own, as are the toilets
of a great railway terminal
and the sequins of a very small,
very fat eyelid.
                    I take this
for myself, and you take up
the thread of my life between your teeth,
tin thread and tarnished with abuse,
you still shall hear
as long as the beast in me maintains
its taciturn power to close my lids
in tears, and my loins move yet
in the ennobling pursuit of all the worlds
you have left me alone in, and would be
the dolorous distraction from,
while you summon your army of anguishes
which is a million hooting blood vessels
on the eyes and in the ears
at that instant before death.
                    And
the menials who surrounded him critically,
languorously waiting for a
final impertinence to rebel
and enslave him, starlets and other
glittering things in the hog-wallow,
lunging mireward in their inane
mothlike adoration of niggardly
cares and stagnant respects
paid themselves, you spared,
as a hospital preserves its orderlies.
Are these your latter-day saints,
these unctuous starers, muscular
somnambulists, these stages for which
no word's been written hollow
enough, these exhibitionists in
well-veiled booths, these navel-suckers?

Is it true that you high ones, celebrated
among amorous flies, hated the
prodigy and invention of his nerves?
To withhold your light
from painstaking paths!
your love
should be difficult, as his was hard.

Nostrils of pain down avenues
of luminous spit-globes breathe in

the fragrance of his innocent flesh
like smoke, the temporary lift,
the post-cancer excitement
of vile manners and veal-thin lips,
obscure in the carelessness of your scissors.

Men cry from the grave while they still live
and now I am this dead man's voice,
stammering, a little in the earth.
I take up
the nourishment of his pale green eyes,
out of which I shall prevent
flowers from growing, your flowers.

THINKING OF JAMES DEAN

Like a nickelodeon soaring over the island from sea to bay,
two pots of gold, and the flushed effulgence of a sky Tiepolo
and Turner had compiled in vistavision. Each panoramic second, of
his death. The rainbows canceling each other out, between martinis

and the steak. To bed to dream, the moon invisibly scudding
under black-blue clouds, a stern Puritanical breeze pushing at
the house, to dream of roaches nibbling at my racing toenails,
great-necked speckled geese and slapping their proud heads

as I ran past. Morning. The first plunge in dolorous surf
and the brilliant sunlight declaring all the qualities of the world.
Like an ant, dragging its sorrows up and down the sand to find
a hiding place never, here where everything is guarded by dunes

or drifting. The sea is dark and smells of fish beneath its
silver surface. To reach the depths and rise, only in the sea;
the abysses of life, incessantly plunging not to rise to a face
of heat and joy again; habits of total immersion and the stance

victorious in death. And after hours of lying in nature, to nature,
and simulated death in the crushing waves, their shells and heart

pounding me naked on the shingle: had I died at twenty-four as he, but
in Boston, robbed of these suns and knowledges, a corpse more whole,

less deeply torn, less bruised and less alive, perhaps backstage
at the Brattle Theatre amidst the cold cream and the familiar lice
in my red-gold costume for a bit in *Julius Caesar*, would I be
smaller now in the vastness of light? a cork in the monumental

stillness of an eye-green trough, a sliver on the bleaching beach
to airplanes carried by the panting clouds to Spain. My friends
are roaming or listening to *La Bohème*. Precisely, the cold last swim
before the city flatters meanings of my life I cannot find,

squeezing me like an orange for some nebulous vitality, mourning
to the fruit ignorant of science in its hasty dying, kissing
its leaves and stem, exuding oils of Florida in the final glass of
pleasure. A leaving word in the sand, odor of tides: his name.

MY HEART

I'm not going to cry all the time
nor shall I laugh all the time,
I don't prefer one "strain" to another.
I'd have the immediacy of a bad movie,
not just a sleeper, but also the big,
overproduced first-run kind. I want to be
at least as alive as the vulgar. And if
some aficionado of my mess says "That's
not like Frank!", all to the good! I
don't wear brown and grey suits all the time,
do I? No. I wear workshirts to the opera,
often. I want my feet to be bare,
I want my face to be shaven, and my heart—
you can't plan on the heart, but
the better part of it, my poetry, is open.

Not you, lean quarterlies and swarthy periodicals
with your studious incursions toward the pomposity of ants,
nor you, experimental theatre in which Emotive Fruition
is wedding Poetic Insight perpetually, nor you,
promenading Grand Opera, obvious as an ear (though you
are close to my heart), but you, Motion Picture Industry,
it's you I love!

In times of crisis, we must all decide again and again whom we love.
And give credit where it's due: not to my starched nurse, who taught me
how to be bad and not bad rather than good (and has lately availed
herself of this information), not to the Catholic Church
which is at best an oversolemn introduction to cosmic entertainment,
not to the American Legion, which hates everybody, but to you,
glorious Silver Screen, tragic Technicolor, amorous Cinemascope,
stretching Vistavision and startling Stereophonic Sound, with all
your heavenly dimensions and reverberations and iconoclasms! To
Richard Barthelmess as the "tol'able" boy barefoot and in pants,
Jeanette MacDonald of the flaming hair and lips and long, long neck,
Sue Carroll as she sits for eternity on the damaged fender of a car
and smiles, Ginger Rogers with her pageboy bob like a sausage
on her shuffling shoulders, peach-melba-voiced Fred Astaire of the feet,
Eric von Stroheim, the seducer of mountain-climbers' gasping spouses,
the Tarzans, each and every one of you (I cannot bring myself to prefer
Johnny Weissmuller to Lex Barker, I cannot!), Mae West in a furry sled,
her bordello radiance and bland remarks, Rudolph Valentino of the moon,
its crushing passions, and moonlike, too, the gentle Norma Shearer,
Miriam Hopkins dropping her champagne glass off Joel McCrea's yacht
and crying into the dappled sea, Clark Gable rescuing Gene Tierney
from Russia and Allan Jones rescuing Kitty Carlisle from Harpo Marx,
Cornel Wilde coughing blood on the piano keys while Merle Oberon berates,
Marilyn Monroe in her little spike heels reeling through Niagara Falls,
Joseph Cotten puzzling and Orson Welles puzzled and Dolores del Rio
eating orchids for lunch and breaking mirrors, Gloria Swanson reclining,
and Jean Harlow reclining and wiggling, and Alice Faye reclining
and wiggling and singing, Myrna Loy being calm and wise, William Powell
in his stunning urbanity, Elizabeth Taylor blossoming, yes, to you

and to all you others, the great, the near-great, the featured, the extras
who pass quickly and return in dreams saying your one or two lines,
my love!
Long may you illumine space with your marvellous appearances, delays
and enunciations, and may the money of the world glitteringly cover you

as you rest after a long day under the kleig lights with your faces
in packs for our edification, the way the clouds come often at night
but the heavens operate on the star system. It is a divine precedent
you perpetuate! Roll on, reels of celluloid, as the great earth rolls on!

PEARL HARBOR

I belong here. I was born
here. The palms sift their fingers
and the men shove by in shirts,
shaving in underwear shorts.
They curse and scratch the wet hair
in their armpits, and spit. Whores
spread their delicate little germs
or, indifferently, don't, smiling.
The waves wash in, warm and salty,
leaving your eyebrows white and
the edge of your cheekbone. Your ear
aches. You are lonely. On the
underside of the satin leaf, hot
with shade, a scorpion sleeps. And
one Sunday I will be shot brushing
my teeth. I am a native of this island.

ON SEEING LARRY RIVERS'
WASHINGTON CROSSING THE DELAWARE
AT THE MUSEUM OF MODERN ART

Now that our hero has come back to us
in his white pants and we know his nose
trembling like a flag under fire,
we see the calm cold river is supporting
our forces, the beautiful history.

To be more revolutionary than a nun
is our desire, to be secular and intimate
as, when sighting a redcoat, you smile
and pull the trigger. Anxieties
and animosities, flaming and feeding

on theoretical considerations and
the jealous spiritualities of the abstract,
the robot? they're smoke, billows above
the physical event. They have burned up.
See how free we are! as a nation of persons.

Dear father of our country, so alive
you must have lied incessantly to be
immediate, here are your bones crossed
on my breast like a rusty flintlock,
a pirate's flag, bravely specific

and ever so light in the misty glare
of a crossing by water in winter to a shore
other than that the bridge reaches for.
Don't shoot until, the white of freedom glinting
on your gun barrel, you see the general fear.

RADIO

Why do you play such dreary music
on Saturday afternoon, when tired
mortally tired I long for a little
reminder of immortal energy?
                              All
week long while I trudge fatiguingly
from desk to desk in the museum
you spill your miracles of Grieg
and Honegger on shut-ins.
                          Am I not
shut in too, and after a week
of work don't I deserve Prokofieff?

Well, I have my beautiful de Kooning
to aspire to. I think it has an orange
bed in it, more than the ear can hold.

STATUE

Alone in the dusk with you
while music by Ravel washes over us
and I clasp you in my arms,
your cool white plaster face
is warm against my stubbled cheek
and your arms seem to tremble.
Are you troubled, emotionally troubled?

What things we have heard together!
and afterwards, most of all, what you tell me
of artistic modesty Your waist feels rough,
rough as the skin that keeps us apart
from each other. I shall be nude
against you, close as we can come.

SLEEPING ON THE WING

Perhaps it is to avoid some great sadness,
as in a Restoration tragedy the hero cries "Sleep!
O for a long sound sleep and so forget it!"
that one flies, soaring above the shoreless city,
veering upward from the pavement as a pigeon
does when a car honks or a door slams, the door
of dreams, life perpetuated in parti-colored loves
and beautiful lies all in different languages.

Fear drops away too, like the cement, and you
are over the Atlantic. Where is Spain? where is
who? The Civil War was fought to free the slaves,
was it? A sudden down-draught reminds you of gravity
and your position in respect to human love. But
here is where the gods are, speculating, bemused.
Once you are helpless, you are free, can you believe
that? Never to waken to the sad struggle of a face?
to travel always over some impersonal vastness,
to be out of, forever, neither in nor for!

The eyes roll asleep as if turned by the wind
and the lids flutter open slightly like a wing.
The world is an iceberg, so much is invisible!
and was and is, and yet the form, it may be sleeping
too. Those features etched in the ice of someone
loved who died, you are a sculptor dreaming of space
and speed, your hand alone could have done this.
Curiosity, the passionate hand of desire. Dead,
or sleeping? Is there speed enough? And, swooping,
you relinquish all that you have made your own,
the kingdom of your self sailing, for you must awake
and breathe your warmth in this beloved image
whether it's dead or merely disappearing,
as space is disappearing and your singularity.

AIX-EN-PROVENCE

*"Les concerts ont lieu dans la cour de l'Archevêchê (1), à l'Hôtel de Maynier
d'Oppède (2), dans la cour de l'Hôtel de Ville (3), au cloître Saint-Louis (4), et aux
Baux-de-Provence (5)."—Arts, du 4 au 10 mai, 1955*

Dreamy city where I will doubtless never go
as one never goes to Chinatown, it's too expensive,
too far for the restless poet writing ballads of money
and then there would be the expense of tickets.

Where do you go if you don't go to Aix? you
go to the Remo and talk to Chester by the espresso
machine, watching the drawer where the rubber hoses
wait—we have the Met, too, and the City Center

and the great Rodin near the weeping birches.
But where did the glamor go and the summer music
and the traveling to hear it? Tanglewood, huh!
and it takes hours to get to Jacob Riis Park by bus.

But I'll go, I'll go, putting thoughts of you
in the sand and digging them up again, and with them
thoughts of *La Mouette* and *La Tempête,* musique de
Sauguet and, above all! *Spectacle de ballets* and you.

All of a sudden all the world
is blonde. The Negro on my left
is blonde, his eyes are brimming
like a chalice, he is melting
the gold.
      Beside me, passed out
on the floor, a novelist burns a hole
in my pants and he is blonde,
even the cigarette is. Some kind
of Russian cigarette.
            Jean Cocteau
must be blonde too. And the music
of William Boyce.
            Yes, and what
comes out of me is blonde.

JOSEPH CORNELL

Into a sweeping meticulously-
detailed disaster the violet
light pours. It's not a sky,
it's a room. And in the open
field a glass of absinthe is
fluttering its song of India.
Prairie winds circle mosques.

You are always a little too
young to understand. He is
bored with his sense of the
past, the artist. Out of the
prescient rock in his heart
he has spread a land without
flowers of near distances.

I
Easy to love, but
difficult to please, he
walks densely as a child
in the midst of spectacular
needs to understand.

Desire makes our
enchanter gracious, and
naturally he's surprised to
be. And so are you to be
you, when he smiles.

II
Eagerness doesn't
dare interrupt him when he
works;   the kitten mustn't
interrupt his thoughtful knee,
not if it twitches.

Dusk falls behind his
eventful eyes like a thread
nearing the many-toed busy
beast who leaves red
yarns of thought in stitches.

III
Egregious?   not he!
does he see
what you think
in this sink
New York? oh? glamor?

Deep in its clamor
enough is too plain,
nothing's like pain:
beautiful blue eyes,
you should see only skies.

IV
Embarcadero, aren't you
dying to see him in a
white suit, as a friend saw him once
in Italy, a white shoe
nearing the Spanish Steps?

Don't deny that you're
erotic. Isn't he like a
narrator in Conrad, leaving you, a dunce,
busy with moods of
your own Adriatic transports?

v
Echoes of inspirations
decorate his palm, and winds
which are like a Cardinal's voice
inscribe themselves where
no other gestures stay.

Dying, as I almost did,
eating Swiss chocolates afterwards,
not counting the trees of my life
but sitting in them in a fog,
yellow and white I was lifted into the air.

CAMBRIDGE

It is still raining and the yellow-green cotton fruit
looks silly round a window giving out on winter trees
with only three drab leaves left. The hot plate works,
it is the sole heat on earth, and instant coffee. I
put on my warm corduroy pants, a heavy maroon sweater,
and wrap myself in my old maroon bathrobe. Just like Pasternak
in Marburg (they say Italy and France are colder, but
I'm sure that Germany's at least as cold as this) and,
lacking the Master's inspiration, I may freeze to death
before I can get out into the white rain. I could have left
the window closed last night? But that's where health
comes from! His breath from the Urals, drawing me into flame
like a forgotten cigarette. Burn! this is not negligible,
being poetic, and not feeble, since it's sponsored by
the greatest living Russian poet at incalculable cost.
Across the street there is a house under construction,
abandoned to the rain. Secretly, I shall go to work on it.

THE BORES

Detraction is their game.
Like parrots, they caw forth
the ennui of the last time
that was theirs, and always
will be, empty. Unaware of what
is, or what's moving toward,
with their sharp wings over
their eyes and tongue on palate
and beak on seat, they take each
singular event for someone's
dear convention. Use an eraser
to take notes for their article.
The difficult is foreign and
the simple vulgar, to them.
They entertain each other.

DIALOGUES

1
You find me tentative and frivolous, don't you?
and I don't own anything. Oh yes, you are in doubt.
Perhaps I own the snow, grown dirty and porous now
and disappearing from the feet of trees
into the grey grasses, so dry in the bright air.

2
You say it is to gain simplicity that I have stripped
all the useful faiths from me, leaf by leaf,
and I am nearly breathless. You call me Mr. de Winter
behind my back, smiling, not without gentleness.

3
You have seen me standing beneath a bird
at midnight, staring at the moon's fullness.
I reminded you of a pot in which someone planted
a lot of hairs. And then a small cry! is it me?
Or is the pot where the nightingale's child lives?

4
Make believe you are happy, for you are dining on my image.

5
There was a house, once. I told you about it
once when I was drunk. There, love reclined
beneath the pianos, and the river repeated
its odd little lyrics, and the mailman spoke French.

6
I am not interested in good. It is all like looking
in the mirror mornings. You exclaim, good heavens,
I am handsome! and then, but not quite as handsome
as all the others, especially the dead
                            Beauty,
description, finality, love, but never merely life.

7
And there comes a dawn for you, too, comes one
like spring, like water in spring and merry birds,
where the heart feels openly as the eye sees,
ultimate place, an instant of this world's bloody love.

STAG CLUB

A prickly beer's like
snow on your asshole—
all the asphodels farting
through a poem by Robert Burns.
Joys of interminable beers!
teeth green as grass, the kiss
under the table upside down
mushrooming and sweet sun
over the bitches, their pears.

"That's right, eat, you
pig! it's all you're good
for"— and the sobs
come out of the man
and in it goes,
and it fattens him
as you watch what
a terrible life it is,
and he is a big man.

KATY

They say I mope too much
but really I'm loudly dancing.
I eat paper. It's good for my bones.
I play the piano pedal. I dance,
I am never quiet, I mean silent.
Some day I'll love Frank O'Hara.
I think I'll be alone for a little while.

LISZTIANA

A ribbon is floating in the air,
spring breeze, yellow, white ribbon,
tossing and catching on itself,
panting like a Maltese terrier.
Now it has discovered the earth's
warm cleavage and drifts slowly down.

Are you crying over what we've lost
by not being near each other, hardly
at all?
          Thunderously silent then,
when the horses of snow seemed slower
and more fragile than this ribbon,
pointlessly aimed at the other
instead of simply finding it
under you, earth and cold.
                              And now again
it is drifting, like a kiss on the air,
emblem of our losing, while the white
horses neigh and stomp upon the Arctic.

ON A MOUNTAIN

1
Rocks with lichen on,
rattling leaves and rotting snow

I shall live to finish this cigarette
and the turnpike roars up a lesser hill,
gleams the nether pond and the wire towers
          on the horizon.

A foot away in the dead sun
a handkerchief lies dirty as the snow.
It's the one Molly Bloom pulled off her
          boyfriend into.

I'm smoking a Picayune
"the worst cigarette," press lips upon
          the handkerchief
          and it is warm.

2
If you were with me
a sweet and winning word might be heard
          out of me,

the bare trees under and the visible jet planes
the enormous telegraph paths and grassy snow
the pale photographic sky, the tangled air
crackling above heaving marshes into the day

     would all be leaves
around the depth of your voice,
owning me yours, not naturally so, beyond the barrier.

     Here is where I
       have come, so high
to find this true and all the sounds
of lovers, and the pleasant cold.

POEM

*"Two communities outside Birmingham, Alabama, are
still searching for their dead."*   —News Telecast

And tomorrow morning at 8 o'clock in Springfield, Massachusetts,
my oldest aunt will be buried from a convent.
Spring is here and I am staying here, I'm not going.
Do birds fly? I am thinking my own thoughts, who else's?

     When I die, don't come, I wouldn't want a leaf
     to turn away from the sun—it loves it there.
     There's nothing so spiritual about being happy
     but you can't miss a day of it, because it doesn't last.

So this is the devil's dance? Well I was born to dance.
It's a sacred duty, like being in love with an ape,
and eventually I'll reach some great conclusion, like assumption,
when at last I meet exhaustion in these flowers, go straight up.

POEM

     Instant coffee with slightly sour cream
     in it, and a phone call to the beyond
     which doesn't seem to be coming any nearer.

"Ah daddy, I wanna stay drunk many days"
on the poetry of a new friend
my life held precariously in the seeing
hands of others, their and my impossibilities.
Is this love, now that the first love
has finally died, where there were no impossibilities?

SPRING'S FIRST DAY

Made a "human fly" escape with their baby from a smoke
or call your local travel agent,
any sofa and couch restyled-rebuilt, everything included— nothing
trims close around the beds. Automatic governor foot-operated starter,
carried only the message "When can I go to work?"

    BEANS   TUNAFISH
    regularly 2 cans 35¢   regularly 2 cans 35¢

He has uncovered another windfall in the same kind of transaction.

Any date, quaint, printed, detail, comes in one of the Kay last week,
four hospitals, seven nursing stations, two boarding schools, plane service,
guided missile is the answer, fly high in the stratosphere near
bus ride with William, rock so soft saw
and snow cannot justifiably understand the difficulty with which a marathon
runner maintains training under such conditions; however

and got home ahead of Native Dancer in the Derby, Derby winner Determine
says he, "All the Olympic talk is about Landy, the Hungarians, the English."
All this merchandise has been and will go on FIRE SALE at this EVENT
at the Saturday morning show and every afternoon except Saturday.
The Brighter Day. This Is Nora Drake. Aunt Jenny, drama.

"He doesn't know I'm alive—but I'm going to help him,"

lovely 4 rm. furnished cottage, plus a 3 rm. that is already rented,
immediate opening for switchboard-receptionist with clerical
horizontal boring mill, turret lathe, radial drill borer machine.
'55 Chev., '53 Chev., '51 Ford, '53 Willys, '55 Chev., '50 Chrysler.

Interview by appointment any place, any time at your convenience.

RETURNING

Coming down the ladder
you can hardly remember the plane was like a rabbit
                              the air above the clouds
                              that settling into the earth
                  was like diving onto the sea on your belly,
there are so many similarities you have forgotten.

Well, there are a lot of things you haven't forgotten,
walking through the waiting room you know you should go
to bed with everyone who looks at you because the war's not over,
no assurance yet that desire's an exaggeration
and you don't want anyone to turn out to be a ruined city, do you?

As Marilyn Monroe says, it's a responsibility being a sexual symbol,
and as everyone says, it's the property of a symbol to be sexual.
Who's confused? Dead citizen or survivor, it's only your cock or your ass.
They do what they can in gardens and parks,
                              in subway stations and latrines,
as boyscouts rub sticks together who've read the manual,
                              know what's expected of death.

        LIKE

        It's not so much,
        abstractions are available:
        the lofty period of the mind
        ending a sentence while the pain endures:
        departures, absences.

        And you are still on the dock,
        the smoke hasn't cleared from the last blast
        but the ship is already in The Narrows.

        At noon I sit in Jim's Place waiting for George
        who is mopping the stage up,
        while two girls cry in the last row.

I think they got laid last night.
But who didn't? it was a spring night.
Probably George did, too.

And now the ship has gone
beyond come, sheets, windows, streets, telephones, and noises:
to where I cannot go,
not even a long distance swimmer like my self.

TO JOHN WIENERS

You walk into a theatre in the semidark
a tiny stage holding up a candle
a few actors are pacing from shadow to shadow
mouthing some misty emblematic rhetoric
about incest and a garden that has telescopes

But you hear something and look
a stout lady in furs is pouting over
a script and the director
is fondling his braces' purple
the prop man is commiserating with a girlfriend on the telephone
and a character actor is explaining the ticket tax
to a voluptuary usherette who's bleached
the producer has his feet up on the row in front
it's none of these, is it? ticking away
the lead is patting her hair and picking her teeth
and a pale young man in a muffler sits erect in the last row

Whose heart is beating in this shell? the pulse
of poetry, although the sound-girl's at a funeral

And one day weeks later the muffler grey and old
for one so young unwraps its sheaf of poems
heard already among the sets under the worklight
a voice is heard though everyone was mumbling
now so silent that the dark is all blown up

She has exposed her bosom in its late disguise
under a muffler, it could be St. Petersburg or Cambridge
and the snow and theatre, like Philip Sparrow, nestle there

FOUR LITTLE ELEGIES

1   WRITTEN IN THE SAND AT WATER ISLAND AND REMEMBERED

James Dean
actor
made in USA
eager to be everything
stopped short

Do we know what
excellence is? it's
all in this world
not to be executed

2   LITTLE ELEGY

Let's cry a little while
    as if we're at a movie
and not think of all life's
    fun for a little while
and how it is to be alive.
    Look at the clouds a
minute, hairy and golden,
    and the sky's pink lips
pouting as it passes, they
    passing like that, and
the night's coming on, the
    night that finishes.
He mumbled and scratched
    as if speech were too
awesome a gift and beauty
    a thing you keep moving.
He lunged and rolled always,
    not to be too far off
earth. And how do we know
    where he is and what
he's pretending? there in
    the sand under stones.

3   OBIT DEAN, SEPTEMBER 30, 1955

Miss Lombard, this is a young
movie actor who just died
in his Porsche Spyder sportscar
near Paso Robles on his way
to Salinas for a race. This is
James Dean, Carole Lombard. I hope
you will be good to him up there.

He was not ill at all. He died
as suddenly as you did. He was
twenty-four. Although he acted first
on Broadway in *See the Jaguar,*
is perhaps best known for films
in which he starred: *East of Eden,*
Rebel without a Cause and *Giant.*
In the first of these he rocketed
to stardom, playing himself and us
"a brooding, inarticulate adolescent."

Born on February 8, 1931, in
Marion, Indiana, he grew up in
nearby Fairmount, Indiana, on
a farm where he was raised
by an aunt and uncle, his
mother having died in 1940. Left
the agricultural community after
High School. Went to Hollywood
to try to crack the movies. "Byron
James." No success. He had
a line or two in *Has Anybody*
Seen My Gal and in *Fixed Bayonets*
said "It's a rear guard coming back."

In New York he went to three films
daily, spent the $150 he'd saved up,
studied acting with Lee Strasberg
at the Actor's Studio, waited for a
break. He had also studied law.
When the breaks came, they came thick
and fast. Back to Hollywood as
a star. He opposed the film colony's
hostility with sullenness, refused
to pose for movie-mag photographers or
talk about his dates, fought with directors,
insulted columnists, rode his sickle,
played his drum and raced his car.
One Sunday at Palm Springs he came in third.

He had hoped to be a writer. Ad-
mired Malaparte, Jean Genet, Colette.
His last two pictures are yet to be
released. He looked sad on the set of
Giant in his horn-rimmed glasses,
planned to return to the Broadway
theatre sometime in 1956.

In New York today it's raining. If
there's love up there I thought that you
would be the one to love him. He's
survived by all of us, and so are you.

4A   A CEREMONY FOR ONE OF MY DEAD
Lying on the river bank the cool sun is ruffling the waters
and the grass is scratching its fresh color tenderly. Behind me
the sad tires pound along the highway, whining, shrieking,
and beating like so many gypsy girls who fell dead
for love at their tar-haired lovers' polished feet.

Now when the scullers are calmly competing and the new
buds open their eyes to a first sun, your photographs
are turning into parchment and dropping to floors. It is
the autumn of your remembrance. Other drivers are racing
on superior speedways and salt flats in shinier cars.

Your name is fading from all but a few marquees, the big red
calling-card of your own death. And there's a rumor that you live,
hideously maimed and hidden by a conscientious studio.

    4B
    Yes, I am no
                longer going out
                            into the world.
    I used to be
                 with it so much
                            of the time.
    For so long, it
                 hasn't cared to ask
                            what is my name?
    maybe it would
                 like to think
                            I'm already dead.
    But then, wouldn't
                 it ask? Well,
                            it doesn't matter.
    It doesn't matter
                 that I'm really dead
                            to it, not living,
    it doesn't even matter
                 if it thinks me
                            among the early dead.
    I can't really tell
                 that I'm alive, except
                            I name the world.

I can't deny it,
                    I am among the noble
                              dead, the famous,
most of the time—
                    and this world named
                              them for me.
I'm not at peace
                    though I am out
                              of this world.
I fail to find rest,
                    the place is so
                              unnaturally quiet!
I think I am in
                    the heavens! waiting
                              to be formed,
to have my love
                    and my self given
                              a name, at last.

4C
I breathe in the dust
                              in my lonely room.
It may be a tree
                              then why is there no bird?
There is no hand, pruning.
                              Can you think of the sneeze
as a lovely thing? an apostrophe?
                              Love is not gentle,
like the dust of a room;
                              love is a thing that happens
in a room, and becomes dust.
                              I breathe it in. Is that poetry?

                    4D
                    It's night. Am
                    I awake?
                    I am in heaven.
                    Stars are steering,
                    and the heavens
                    are not smiling
                    their crescents.
                    All right, my
                    thoughts are pitch.
                    It is my fault,
                    the beating of
                    my heart. No
                    extraordinary
                    pain is mine.

The stars are there
at night. Weakness
falls away, like
mankind on
its endless knee
to the night.
I shall not see
another night,
low, like this.

HUNTING HORNS

How nice it is to take up
a familiar sound again
and draw new lines
from the traditional mouth
to the still-wet ear

They were always hearing you
go by as a vague menace
or the rustle of leaves
above the lovers where they lay
and the cold husband returning

A slightly military funeral
resembling the setting sun
with children running into it
they still hunt but they don't
blow the horns any more

IN MEMORY OF MY FEELINGS

to Grace Hartigan

I
My quietness has a man in it, he is transparent
and he carries me quietly, like a gondola, through the streets.
He has several likenesses, like stars and years, like numerals.

My quietness has a number of naked selves,
so many pistols I have borrowed to protect myselves
from creatures who too readily recognize my weapons
and have murder in their heart!
                              though in winter
they are warm as roses, in the desert
taste of chilled anisette.
                    At times, withdrawn,
I rise into the cool skies
and gaze on at the imponderable world with the simple identification
of my colleagues, the mountains. Manfred climbs to my nape,
speaks, but I do not hear him,
                          I'm too blue.
An elephant takes up his trumpet,
money flutters from the windows of cries, silk stretching its mirror
across shoulder blades. A gun is "fired."
                              One of me rushes
to window #13 and one of me raises his whip and one of me
flutters up from the center of the track amidst the pink flamingoes,
and underneath their hooves as they round the last turn my lips
are scarred and brown, brushed by tails, masked in dirt's lust,
definition, open mouths gasping for the cries of the bettors for the lungs
of earth.
          So many of my transparencies could not resist the race!
Terror in earth, dried mushrooms, pink feathers, tickets,
a flaking moon drifting across the muddied teeth,
the imperceptible moan of covered breathing,
                                    love of the serpent!
I am underneath its leaves as the hunter crackles and pants
and bursts, as the barrage balloon drifts behind a cloud
and animal death whips out its flashlight,
                                whistling
and slipping the glove off the trigger hand. The serpent's eyes
redden at sight of those thorny fingernails, he is so smooth!
                                    My transparent selves
flail about like vipers in a pail, writhing and hissing
without panic, with a certain justice of response
and presently the aquiline serpent comes to resemble the Medusa.

2

The dead hunting
and the alive, ahunted.
                    My father, my uncle,
my grand-uncle and the several aunts. My
grand-aunt dying for me, like a talisman, in the war,
before I had even gone to Borneo
her blood vessels rushed to the surface

and burst like rockets over the wrinkled
invasion of the Australians, her eyes aslant
like the invaded, but blue like mine.
An atmosphere of supreme lucidity,
                              humanism,
the mere existence of emphasis,
                              a rusted barge
painted orange against the sea
full of Marines reciting the Arabian ideas
which are a proof in themselves of seasickness
which is a proof in itself of being hunted.
A hit? *ergo* swim.
                 My 10   my 19,
my 9,   and the several years. My
12 years since they all died, philosophically speaking.
And now the coolness of a mind
like a shuttered suite in the Grand Hotel
where mail arrives for my incognito,
                              whose façade
has been slipping into the Grand Canal for centuries;
rockets splay over a *sposalizio,*
                          fleeing into night
from their Chinese memories, and it is a celebration,
the trying desperately to count them as they die.
But who will stay to be these numbers
when all the lights are dead?

3
The most arid stretch is often richest,
the hand lifting towards a fig tree from hunger
                                    digging
and there is water, clear, supple, or there
deep in the sand where death sleeps, a murmurous bubbling
proclaims the blackness that will ease and burn.
You preferred the Arabs? but they didn't stay to count
their inventions, racing into sands, converting themselves into
so many,
              embracing, at Ramadan, the tenderest effigies of
themselves with penises shorn by the hundreds, like a camel
ravishing a goat.
                 And the mountainous-minded Greeks could speak
of time as a river and step across it into Persia, leaving the pain
at home to be converted into statuary. I adore the Roman copies.
And the stench of the camel's spit I swallow,
and the stench of the whole goat. For we have advanced, France,
together into a new land, like the Greeks, where one feels nostalgic
for mere ideas, where truth lies on its deathbed like an uncle

and one of me has a sentimental longing for number,
as has another for the ball gowns of the Directoire and yet
another for "Destiny, Paris, destiny!"

               or "Only a king may kill a king."

How many selves are there in a war hero asleep in names? under
a blanket of platoon and fleet, orderly. For every seaman
with one eye closed in fear and twitching arm at a sigh for Lord Nelson,
he is all dead; and now a meek subaltern writhes in his bedclothes
with the fury of a thousand, violating an insane mistress
who has only herself to offer his multitudes.

                     Rising,
he wraps himself in the burnoose of memories against the heat of life
and over the sands he goes to take an algebraic position *in re*
a sun of fear shining not too bravely. He will ask himselves to
vote on fear before he feels a tremor,

                  as runners arrive from the mountains
bearing snow, proof that the mind's obsolescence is still capable
of intimacy. His mistress will follow him across the desert
like a goat, towards a mirage which is something familiar about
one of his innumerable wrists,

                and lying in an oasis one day,
playing catch with coconuts, they suddenly smell oil.

4
Beneath these lives
the ardent lover of history hides,

                  tongue out
leaving a globe of spit on a taut spear of grass
and leaves off rattling his tail a moment
to admire this flag.

            I'm looking for my Shanghai Lil.
Five years ago, enamored of fire-escapes, I went to Chicago,
an eventful trip: the fountains! the Art Institute, the Y
for both sexes, absent Christianity.

              At 7, before Jane
was up, the copper lake stirred against the sides
of a Norwegian freighter; on the deck a few dirty men,
tired of night, watched themselves in the water
as years before the German prisoners on the *Prinz Eugen*
dappled the Pacific with their sores, painted purple
by a Naval doctor.

             Beards growing, and the constant anxiety
over looks. I'll shave before she wakes up. Sam Goldwyn
spent $2,000,000 on Anna Sten, but Grushenka left America.
One of me is standing in the waves, an ocean bather,
or I am naked with a plate of devils at my hip.

to be born and live as variously as possible. The conception
of the masque barely suggests the sordid identifications.
I am a Hittite in love with a horse. I don't know what blood's
in me I feel like an African prince I am a girl walking downstairs
in a red pleated dress with heels I am a champion taking a fall
I am a jockey with a sprained ass-hole I am the light mist
                                        in which a face appears
and it is another face of blonde I am a baboon eating a banana
I am a dictator looking at his wife I am a doctor eating a child
and the child's mother smiling I am a Chinaman climbing a mountain
I am a child smelling his father's underwear I am an Indian
sleeping on a scalp
                    and my pony is stamping in the birches,
and I've just caught sight of the *Niña,* the *Pinta* and the *Santa Maria.*
            What land is this, so free?
                                        I watch
the sea at the back of my eyes, near the spot where I think
in solitude as pine trees groan and support the enormous winds,
they are humming *L'Oiseau de feu!*
                    They look like gods, these whitemen,
and they are bringing me the horse I fell in love with on the frieze.

5
And now it is the serpent's turn.
I am not quite you, but almost, the opposite of visionary.
You are coiled around the central figure,
                                        the heart
that bubbles with red ghosts, since to move is to love
and the scrutiny of all things is syllogistic,
the startled eyes of the dikdik, the bush full of white flags
fleeing a hunter,
                    which is our democracy
                                        but the prey
is always fragile and like something, as a seashell can be
a great Courbet, if it wishes. To bend the ear of the outer world.

                            When you turn your head
can you feel your heels, undulating? that's what it is
to be a serpent. I haven't told you of the most beautiful things
in my lives, and watching the ripple of their loss disappear
along the shore, underneath ferns,
                            face downward in the ferns
my body, the naked host to my many selves, shot
by a guerrilla warrior or dumped from a car into ferns
which are themselves *journalières.*
                    The hero, trying to unhitch his parachute,
stumbles over me. It is our last embrace.

                    And yet
I have forgotten my loves, and chiefly that one, the cancerous
statue which my body could no longer contain,

                                        against my will
                                        against my love

become art,
                I could not change it into history
and so remember it,
                        and I have lost what is always and everywhere
present, the scene of my selves, the occasion of these ruses,
which I myself and singly must now kill
                        and save the serpent in their midst.

A STEP AWAY FROM THEM

It's my lunch hour, so I go
for a walk among the hum-colored
cabs. First, down the sidewalk
where laborers feed their dirty
glistening torsos sandwiches
and Coca-Cola, with yellow helmets
on. They protect them from falling
bricks, I guess. Then onto the
avenue where skirts are flipping
above heels and blow up over
grates. The sun is hot, but the
cabs stir up the air. I look
at bargains in wristwatches. There
are cats playing in sawdust.
                        On
to Times Square, where the sign
blows smoke over my head, and higher
the waterfall pours lightly. A
Negro stands in a doorway with a
toothpick, languorously agitating.
A blonde chorus girl clicks: he
smiles and rubs his chin. Everything
suddenly honks: it is 12:40 of
a Thursday.

Neon in daylight is a
great pleasure, as Edwin Denby would
write, as are light bulbs in daylight.
I stop for a cheeseburger at JULIET'S
CORNER. Giulietta Masina, wife of
Federico Fellini, *è bell' attrice.*
And chocolate malted. A lady in
foxes on such a day puts her poodle
in a cab.

       There are several Puerto
Ricans on the avenue today, which
makes it beautiful and warm. First
Bunny died, then John Latouche,
then Jackson Pollock. But is the
earth as full as life was full, of them?
And one has eaten and one walks,
past the magazines with nudes
and the posters for BULLFIGHT and
the Manhattan Storage Warehouse,
which they'll soon tear down. I
used to think they had the Armory
Show there.

       A glass of papaya juice
and back to work. My heart is in my
pocket, it is Poems by Pierre Reverdy.

QU'EST-CE QUE DE NOUS!

for Marcellin

La crise, non plus en tout plein
les beaux sourires d'un ténébreux

comme un fric-frac des anges morbides
où les citrons fleurit, j'en suis

près de la peau, la présence des morts
et les aveugles ronronnent sonore

Embrasse-moi, l'heure est grise
et la chasse entraîne une calme maîtrise

de soi-toi-même à chaque réunion
il est très rare, d'ailleurs, le cri atroce

car dans ce monde où de plus en plus
j'ai moi-même reçu une homélie furibonde

A RASPBERRY SWEATER

to George Montgomery

It is next to my flesh,
that's why. I do what I want.
And in the pale New Hampshire
twilight a black bug sits in the blue,
strumming its legs together. Mournful
glass, and daisies closing. Hay
swells in the nostrils. We shall go
to the motorcycle races in Laconia
and come back all calm and warm.

LISZTIANA, MUCH LATER

I sit in your T shirt
with its spots of paint
as a certain fierceness pours
outside, perhaps, too, on you.

I'm smoking a Camel now
and I have a big hole in my
shoulder from washing away
a lot of dirt. Are you there?

there, are you? I am here
and the storm is not enough,

it should crash in and wet,
there should be maelstrom where

a privileged host is smiling.
And naked in debris I there
should be, but, being here, should
bend to you, pick out of rubble

a scrap of painted shirt
as if it were soiled ivory from
a grand piano, possessed of us
both, and ruined now by storms.

DIGRESSION ON *NUMBER 1*, 1948

I am ill today but I am not
too ill. I am not ill at all.
It is a perfect day, warm
for winter, cold for fall.

A fine day for seeing. I see
ceramics, during lunch hour, by
Miró, and I see the sea by Léger;
light, complicated Metzingers
and a rude awakening by Brauner,
a little table by Picasso, pink.

I am tired today but I am not
too tired. I am not tired at all.
There is the Pollock, white, harm
will not fall, his perfect hand

and the many short voyages. They'll
never fence the silver range.
Stars are out and there is sea
enough beneath the glistening earth
to bear me toward the future
which is not so dark. I see.

[IT SEEMS FAR AWAY AND GENTLE NOW]

It seems far away and gentle now
the morning miseries of childhood
and its raining calms over the schools

Alterable noons of loitering
beside puddles watching leaves swim
and reflected dreams of blue travels

To be always in vigilance away
from the bully who broke my nose
and so I had to break his wristwatch

A surprising violence in the sky
inspired me to my first public act
nubile and pretentious but growing pure

as the whitecaps are the wind's
but a surface agitation of the waters
means a rampart on the ocean floor is falling

And will soon be open to the tender
governing tides of a reigning will
while alterable noon assumes its virtue

WHY I AM NOT A PAINTER

I am not a painter, I am a poet.
Why? I think I would rather be
a painter, but I am not. Well,

for instance, Mike Goldberg
is starting a painting. I drop in.
"Sit down and have a drink" he
says. I drink; we drink. I look
up. "You have SARDINES in it."
"Yes, it needed something there."

"Oh." I go and the days go by
and I drop in again. The painting
is going on, and I go, and the days
go by. I drop in. The painting is
finished. "Where's SARDINES?"
All that's left is just
letters, "It was too much," Mike says.

But me? One day I am thinking of
a color: orange. I write a line
about orange. Pretty soon it is a
whole page of words, not lines.
Then another page. There should be
so much more, not of orange, of
words, of how terrible orange is
and life. Days go by. It is even in
prose, I am a real poet. My poem
is finished and I haven't mentioned
orange yet. It's twelve poems, I call
it ORANGES. And one day in a gallery
I see Mike's painting, called SARDINES.

MILITARY CEMETERY

"Ô toi, mon bien aimé!"
                                    —Dalila

We've got to get our war memorials corrected.
At the time of the great Fatigue of 1949
I found that all the names were spelled wrong
in the cemetery rosters and on the very stones,
that is, there was but one man in every grave,
the selfsame troubadour with egrets and looks,
"good looks" they're called by cemetery people.

The political situation has certainly gotten splendid
enough for us both to take action on this matter,
that is, to get him out of all the graves but his own
and then kill the others, they've been romping too long,
and pop them into the graves that have been so
falsely filled for these many years like the mirror
trick. If this gets to the newspapers first
there'll be a mad scramble for the position of collector,

but then, there always is. To be public spirited, alas!
is to seem mysterious to the very people
you are trying to fill the graves with. They get away.

Now we will get a caravan of movie stars
to consecrate our cemetery, and a hair lotion heiress
will donate the Great-Immovable-Daytime-Light
which is to guard the tombs like a monkey;
there will be a different person in each grave.
And the wind will again whisper through the poplars
when we plant them, and we'll be able to concentrate
on the green stains we get on our trousers when
we lean against the stones in springtime reading books.

AGGRESSION

I think of Cairo and all tossing date palms and a girl,
    what is her name? it is Merrie, arriving at the
    airport down the light aluminum stairway and step-
    ping daintily on a sandbag, with her slender ankle-
    bracelet slipping over tendrils

of blonde hair and her red lips part. O series of smiles!
    and smiles in series from under stern little mustaches
    which get tangled at night in milky teeth. She has
    knees, it seems, and toes,

and Merrie walks dreamily along the fronded streets with
    their Cubist light like maidenfern. Up in the air
    she had seen men marching slowly through the sand.
    What sand! what long shadows, and they had big knees.
    "They seem very young" she had sighed, because of the
    knobby shadows of their heads and their rifles above
    and behind like Indian feathers. Or

feelers. It is always apt to seem calm to Merrie. She strolls
    and smiles and her lipstick begins to get tired. A
    bomb falls, but everyone is cheerful and the stores
    stay open. The British come and the French. She thinks
    of the water, how thin it is inland.

The Israeli Army is at the door and wingèd parachute-troopers
       rush around and nobody is scared while several die,
       among them a handsome stranger who had smiled and she
       had started loving. But isn't everyone a stranger?
       Merrie thought, and then felt shallow. Now the dust
       blew in

and the Israeli Army outside was choking, but the British
       and French were in drinking Vichy water. No, it is now,
       and the Israeli Army cannot seem to reach a city, it
       gets darker and darker like old parchment on which
       something indecipherably sexual is written and lost.
       Merrie smiles because she is inside and cannot get
       outside, any more than you can shoot a dog.

A little shopping and she is tired, she is looking for the
       Suez Canal. She is wrapped in someone's arms and he
       is sweating. "Amer," she murmurs and kisses him after
       a day of fighting. He is handsome, he does not fight
       at night. Everyone seems handsome, she reflects, but
       he handsomest.

She wipes herself off and walks, smiling, back to her
       hotel. She is pale and the wind frees her hair,
       full of cries and smoke and bloody medicines. The
       lift is very old and open as it sags to her floor.
       Inside her room she switches on the fan and wipes
       her wig off, dark, dark, the glamorous insurgence
       of pain and a feeling

almost, of defeat. She falls on the bed and cries and
       writes in her message the name "Amer," and sleeps.
       The Israeli Army marches in like a chorale, through
       vanishing streets and high yelps from corrugated
       burnooses. "They are always coming" she smiles with-
       out waking, and her sleep deepens as the miles be-
       come intimate, and deaths appear, and they are the
       right deaths.

At last you are tired of being single
the effort to be new does not upset you nor the effort to be other
you are not tired of life together

city noises are louder because you are together
being together you are louder than calling separately across a tele-
          phone one to the other
and there is no noise like the rare silence when you both sleep
even country noises—a dog bays at the moon, but when it loves the
          moon it bows, and the hitherto frowning moon fawns and slips

Only you in New York are not boring tonight
it is most modern to affirm some one
(we don't really love ideas, do we?)
and Joan was surprising you with a party for which I was the decoy
but you were surprising us by getting married and going away
so I am here reading poetry anyway
and no one will be bored tonight by me because you're here

Yesterday I felt very tired from being at the FIVE SPOT
and today I felt very tired from going to bed early and reading ULYSSES
but tonight I feel energetic because I'm sort of the bugle,
like waking people up, of your peculiar desire to get married

It's so
original, hydrogenic, anthropomorphic, fiscal, post-anti-esthetic,
          bland, unpicturesque and WilliamCarlosWilliamsian!
it's definitely not 19th Century, it's not even Partisan Review, it's
          new, it must be vanguard!

Tonight you probably walked over here from Bethune Street
down Greenwich Avenue with its sneaky little bars and the Women's De-
          tention House,
across 8th Street, by the acres of books and pillows and shoes and
          illuminating lampshades,
past Cooper Union where we heard the piece by Mortie Feldman with "The
          Stars and Stripes Forever" in it
and the Sagamore's terrific "coffee and, Andy," meaning "with a cheese
          Danish"—
did you spit on your index fingers and rub the CEDAR's neon circle for
          luck?
did you give a kind thought, hurrying, to Alger Hiss?

It's the day before February 17th
it is not snowing yet but it is dark and may snow yet
dreary February of the exhaustion from parties and the exceptional de-
            sire for spring which the ballet alone, by extending its run,
            has made bearable, dear New York City Ballet company, you are
            quite a bit like a wedding yourself!
and the only signs of spring are Maria Tallchief's rhinestones and a
            perky little dog barking in a bar, here and there eyes which
            suddenly light up with blue, like a ripple subsiding under a
            lily pad, or with brown, like a freshly plowed field we vow
            we'll drive out and look at when a certain Sunday comes in May—
and these eyes are undoubtedly Jane's and Joe's because they are ad-
            vancing into spring before us and tomorrow is Sunday

This poem goes on too long because our friendship has been long, long
            for this life and these times, long as art is long and un-
            interruptable,
and I would make it as long as I hope our friendship lasts if I could
            make poems that long

I hope there will be more
more drives to Bear Mountain and searches for hamburgers, more evenings
            avoiding the latest Japanese movie and watching Helen Vinson
            and Warner Baxter in *Vogues of 1938* instead, more discussions
            in lobbies of the respective greatnesses of Diana Adams and
            Allegra Kent,
more sunburns and more half-mile swims in which Joe beats me as Jane
            watches, lotion-covered and sleepy, more arguments over
            Faulkner's inferiority to Tolstoy while sand gets into my
            bathing trunks
let's advance and change everything, but leave these little oases in
            case the heart gets thirsty en route
and I should probably propose myself as a godfather if you have any
            children, since I will probably earn more money some day
            accidentally, and could teach him or her how to swim
and now there is a Glazunov symphony on the radio and I think of our
            friends who are not here, of John and the nuptial quality
            of his verses (he is always marrying the whole world) and
            Janice and Kenneth, smiling and laughing, respectively (they
            are probably laughing at the Leaning Tower right now)
but we are all here and have their proxy
if Kenneth were writing this he would point out how art has changed
            women and women have changed art and men, but men haven't
            changed women much
but ideas are obscure and nothing should be obscure tonight
you will live half the year in a house by the sea and half the year in
            a house in our arms

we peer into the future and see you happy and hope it is a sign that we
will be happy too, something to cling to, happiness
the least and best of human attainments

JOHN BUTTON BIRTHDAY

Sentiments are nice, "The Lonely Crowd,"
a rift in the clouds appears above the purple,
you find a birthday greeting card with violets
which says "a perfect friend" and means
"I love you" but the customer is forced to be
shy. It says less, as all things must.

                              But
grease sticks to the red ribs shaped like a
sea shell, grease, light and rosy that smells of
sandalwood: it's memory! I remember JA
staggering over to me in the San Remo and murmuring
"I've met someone MARVELLOUS!" That's friendship
for you, and the sentiment of introduction.

And now that I have finished dinner I can continue.

What is it that attracts one to one? Mystery?
I think of you in Paris with a red beard, a
theological student; in London talking to a friend
who lunched with Dowager Queen Mary and offered
her his last cigarette; in Los Angeles shopping
at the Supermarket; on Mount Shasta, looking . . .
above all on Mount Shasta in your unknown youth
and photograph.
                       And then the way you straighten
people out. How ambitious you are! And that you're
a painter is a great satisfaction, too. You know how
I feel about painters. I sometimes think poetry
only describes.
                       Now I have taken down the underwear
I washed last night from the various light fixtures
and can proceed.

And the lift of our experiences
together, which seem to me legendary. The long subways
to our old neighborhood the near East 49th and 53rd,
and before them the laughing in bars till we cried,
and the crying in movies till we laughed, the tenting
tonight on the old camp grounds! How beautiful it is
to visit someone for instant coffee! and you visiting
Cambridge, Massachusetts, talking for two weeks worth
in hours, and watching Maria Tallchief in the Public
Gardens while the swan-boats slumbered. And now,
not that I'm interrupting again, I mean your now,
you are 82 and I am 03. And in 1984 I trust we'll still
be high together. I'll say "Let's go to a bar"
and you'll say "Let's go to a movie" and we'll go to both;
like two old Chinese drunkards arguing about their
favorite mountain and the million reasons for them both.

ANXIETY

I'm having a real day of it.
                    There was
something I had to do. But what?
There are no alternatives, just
the one something.
                    I have a drink,
it doesn't help—far from it!
                                        I
feel worse. I can't remember how
I felt, so perhaps I feel better.
No. Just a little darker.
                              If I could
get really dark, richly dark, like
being drunk, that's the best that's
open as a field. Not the best,

but the best except for the impossible
pure light, to be as if above a vast
prairie, rushing and pausing over
the tiny golden heads in deep grass.

But still now, familiar laughter low
from a dark face, affection human and often even—

motivational? the warm walking night
                                        wandering
amusement of darkness, lips,
                          and
the light, always in wind. Perhaps
that's it: to clean something. A window?

WIND

to Morton Feldman

Who'd have thought
                        that snow falls
it always circled whirling
like a thought
                  in the glass ball
around me and my bear

Then it seemed beautiful
                              containment
snow whirled
              nothing ever fell
nor my little bear
                    bad thoughts
imprisoned in crystal

beauty has replaced itself with evil

And the snow whirls only
                              in fatal winds
briefly
                        then falls

it always loathed containment
                              beasts
I love evil

BLUE TERRITORY

to Helen Frankenthaler

Big bags of sand   until they came,
            the flattering end
of the world
            the gulls were swooping and gulping and filling
the bags
        as helpful creatures everywhere were helping
to end
        the world
                so we could be alone together at last, one by one

        Who needs an ark? a Captain's table?
                                and the mountains
never quite sink, all blue, or come back
                                up, de-
sire, the Father of the messness of all
                        cut the glass
and make it grass
                under teat and horn, it's not moss
it's turf
        get back on the boat, Boris! we love you,
you
    don't have to stay . . .
                        lobsters
                        bees
                        barbs
                        taboos
                "Where slug you, then
the flinty boos?"
            a *peut-être* of crapey sacredity
                                of isness
unpropitious
        blasted like o roses

                T H E S E R P E N T

Here I am!
        blue, blue
                whoops!   the gull is making a pomander
pouring pestilence of hollow sweet smells
                                no, I'm drinking
sweat and piss, yum yum, signed
                    "The human Briar"
                                smiling pale

270

wailing is swinging, sit is up, on, fleece is "Irememberhairflowers"
and the curling anemones of the thigh, art-noveau kissings

                              brush yo teef Archielee! mayam?

                do I or don't I
care-package it
                ?be swizzled like a growling thicksea rain bollixing,
we hate
          the lot where the Indians run and run and ride and never fuck
there
          there are no green eyelids advancing into the sea

POEM

to Franz Kline

I will always love you
though I never loved you

a boy smelling faintly of heather
staring up at your window

the passion that enlightens
and stills and cultivates, gone

while I sought your face
to be familiar in the blueness

or to follow your sharp whistle
around a corner into my light

that was love growing fainter
each time you failed to appear

I spent my whole self searching
love which I thought was you

it was mine so briefly
and I never knew it, or you went

I thought it was outside disappearing
but it is disappearing in my heart

like snow blown in a window
to be gone from the world

I will always love you

JE VOUDRAIS VOIR

an immense plain full of nudes
and roses falling on them from the green air
a smile of utter simplicity speaking to the soldiers
of the camel corps, so brief and smelly

listen to the wind in no trees
how ardently it adds and subtracts lives
I am a man of a very ancient race and vengeful
so, to my words do not answer
                              as the sea has ears

and beneath one kind of trembling there is another kind of laughter

do you feel disinterred?

a stream of loud silvery water naked of fish
and a large metallic construction in which a girl sits sweating
she is covered with grass
mater dolorosa
                    the darkness of my glistening skin
"shades" of . . .

shit and its wild air
I would alert Aetna and the moon of Manakura
to help celebrate my serious misgivings

CAPTAIN BADA

Yes, a long cool vindt is pacing over the plains and beside it Captain
      Bada struts, shouting Hup! 1 2 3 4 like an elephant with hot nuts

it is the Captain's way of praising the sky (ja, das meer ist blau, so blau)
      into which his kepi gently pokes as he lumbers along under his baton

in the season of perennial marching. Even on 5th Avenue in États-Unis, they
      march in March, but lo! it is May already and the Captain's in his

cocky shorts, as the sweaty breeze his hairy chest which is as dense with
      curly black and stubby grey-green greasy hairs as a certain portion

of the veldt where even the zebras are slowed down in their perennial
      chasing of each other. Speaking of perenniality, Captain Bada thinks

of the day he saw the zebras fucking. "Much more powerful than a Picabia,"
      he thinks, "with that big black piston plunging and exuding from

the distended grin of its loved one's O," and blushes at the soldiers who
      are grinning at him because of a certain other baton he has unthinkingly

grabbed before it gets tangled in a nearby tree they are being marched past.
      No privacy in the Army! but then, it is the life Captain Bada loves

as he loves his kepi and his cock and they love him. The swarthy face of CB
      wrinkles with zebraic openness and energy as he thinks, "P for Possession."

LOUISE

Sometimes I think I see a tiny figure
sidling through the Bush. Yes, there
at the edge of the forest, blinking in
new light. It must have wandered up
from Down Under. I believe it's Maldoror!

And now, having decided, it starts
the weary trek across the rolling plain,
pausing occasionally beneath a shade

or on the gently sloping rise. It rests,
too, on the crater of a long defunct
volcano, lying down for a time in its
wrinkles.
        Then onward again, through
the valley bounded by Twin Peaks, pink
in the sunlight, with the scattered
forests coming down right to the edge
of the pass.
        Disappearing for almost
a day, or is it night? the toiling figure
suddenly finds itself in a clearing.
(Suddenly to me!) Then there is an upheaval
rather like an earthquake. It clings
for dear life to the nearest overhanging
branch.
        There it is stranded in the blue
gaze. And the gaze is astonished, eye
to eye: a speck, and a vastness staring
back at it. Why it's Louise! Hi, Louise.

FAILURES OF SPRING

I'm getting rather Lorcaesque lately
and I don't like it.
        Better if my poetry were,
instead of my lives. So many aspects of a star,

the Rudolph Valentino of sentimental reaction
to dives and crumby ex-jazz-hangouts.
                          I
put on my sheik's outfit and sit down
at the pianola,
        like when I first discovered
aspirin.
        And I shall never make my LORCAESCAS
into an opera. I don't write opera.
              So hot,
so hot the night my world
            is trying to send up
        its observation satellite.

"Hungry winter, this winter"
                              meaningful hints at dismay
                          to be touched, to see labeled as such
perspicacious Colette and Vladimirovitch meet with sickness and distress,

    it is because of sunspots on the sun

        MOCK POEM
        One pentative device, and then reheat
        To knead the balm, prepucible depense,
        Be undezithered pouncenance; for face
        Devapive hoods and blow the pentagon;
        Foe, steal communion from the Tyche, bless
        Myth less uncertainty, and when repeal,
        On bloated regents pour the sacred boonion.

                        *

                  I clean it off with an old sock
and go on:

    And blonde Gregory dead in Fall Out on a Highway with his Broadway wife,
the last of the Lafayettes,
                            (How I hate subject matter! melancholy,
        intruding on the vigorous heart,
                            the soul telling itself
you haven't suffered enough ((Hyalomiel))
                            and all things that don't change,
photographs,
            monuments,
                    memories of Bunny and Gregory and me in costume

bowing to each other and the audience, like jinxes)

    nothing now can be changed, as if
                            last crying no tears will dry
and Bunny never change her writing of
                            the Bear, nor Gregory bear me
any gift further, beyond liking my poems
                            (no new poems for him.) and
a large red railroad handkerchief from the country in his sportscar

so like another actor:

LITTLE ELEGY

Let's cry a little while
    as if we're at a movie
and not think of all life's
    fun for a little while
and how it is to be alive.
    Look at the clouds a
minute, hairy and golden,
    and the sky's pink lips
pouting as it passes, they
    passing like that, and
the night's coming on, the
    night that finishes.

He mumbled and scratched
    as if speech were too
awesome a gift and beauty
    a thing you keep moving.
He lunged and rolled always,
    not to be too far off
earth. And how do we know
    where he is and what
he's pretending? there in
    the sand under stones.

                    *

For sentiment is always intruding on form,

                        the immaculate disgust of the mind
beaten down by pain and the vileness of life's flickering disapproval,

            endless torment pretending to be the rose
of acknowledgement (courage)
                    and fruitless absolution (hence the word: "hip")
to be cool,
        decisive,
                precise,
                    yes, while the barn door hits you in the face
each time you get up
                because the wind, seeing you slim and gallant, rises

    to embrace its darling poet. It thinks *I'm* mysterious.

All diseases are exchangeable.

        ENVOI
        Wind, you'll have a terrible time
        smothering my clarity, a void

behind my eyes,
              into which existence
continues to stuff its wounded limbs

as I make room for them on one
after another filthy page of poetry.

              And mean it.

TWO DREAMS OF WAKING

1
I stumble over furniture, I fall into a gloomy hammock
on a rainy day in Cape Cod years ago. It is a black hardoy chair.
I reach the kitchen and Joe is making coffee in the dark.
I can't face him, because we both have to go to work
and we hate work. I look into the corner of a shelf. "Work
interrupts life," he is muttering as he splashes in the sink.
I can't remember what he's doing, just that his back
was pale gold. I don't look at it. Two white mice, big,
are running through the hole in the sleeve of my raspberry sweater.
They seem to be harming it. I shout at them. I appeal, "it's already wearing out,"
to Joe. He looks at me coldly. "Leave them alone. They're
playing. They have to live, too, don't they?"
I have a hangover, and he hates me for it, and we start for work,

          2
          I stagger out of bed
          and there are flashes
          of light. I stand naked
          in a certain posture.
          It is Larry welding a
          figure and he says, "I'm
          glad you're developing breasts.
          I want you to pose for
          the legs of this thing."
          I look and I am the same.
          "It's all the same," he
          says, "I just looked at Jane's
          breasts. She's menstruating

and the veins beneath the
hair on your chest are
just like those on her breasts."
I get scared. "I'm not
menstruating, I'm peeing."
I am. There is a chamber pot
forming a triangle with
my feet and the arc of my
pee slopes like a thigh.
It reminds me of a nude in
a painting I can't remember.
I get scared again. "You think,"
Larry says, "that you're safe
because you have a penis. So
do I, but we're both wrong."
He starts banging on the steel
again and the sound puts me
to sleep standing up. I feel
that years are going by
and I can't talk to them or anything.

A YOUNG POET

full of passion and giggles
                    brashly erects his first poems
and they are ecstatic
                    followed by a clap of praise
                                        from a very few hands
belonging to other poets.
                    He is sent! and they are moved to believe, once
more, freshly
                    in the divine trap.
                                        Two years later he has possessed
his beautiful style,
                    the meaning of which draws him further down
into passion
                    and up in the staring regard of his intuitions.
                                                        He stays up
three days in a row,
                    works "morning, noon and night"
                                        and then towards dawn

strolls out into the street
                          to look at City Hall
                                            and
feel the noise of art abate
                          in the silence of life.
                                            He is tired,
hysterical,
          he is jeered at by thugs
                                and taken for a junky or a pervert
by police
        who follow him,
                        as he should be followed, but not by them. He
has started his little
                      magazine, and plans a city issue
                                                    although he's scared
to death.
          Where is the castle he should inhabit on a promontory
while
      his elegies are dictated to him by the divine prosecutor?
                                                              It is
a bank on 14th Street.
                      While we are seeing *The Curse of Frankenstein* he
sits in
        the 42nd Street Library, reading about the Sumerians.
                                                            The threats
of inferiors are frightening
                            if you are a Negro choosing your own High School,
or a painter too drunk
                      to fight off a mugging,
                                            or a poet exhausted by
the insight which comes as a kiss
                                and follows as a curse.

SONG OF ENDING

    Berdie, Berdie
    where are you, and why?

    sometimes I see you in the earth
    sometimes in the sky. Berdie,

a history of childhood where
we thought that birds never died,

just grew more numerous and some
day would fill the sky.

They don't, and falling they
don't cover the earth like leaves,

the fragile saffron wings
of death. They disappear with one

last cry, not echoing, and then
the emptiness is full of light.

Berdie, not to be sad and crazy,
all birds hide what they have lost.

ODE ON NECROPHILIA

*"Isn't there any body you want back from
the grave? We were less generous in our time."*
   —Palinurus (not Cyril Connolly)

Well,
   it is better
      that

          O M E O N
         S love them E

and we
   so seldom look on love
         that it seems heinous

We shall have everything we want and there'll be no more dying
    on the pretty plains or in the supper clubs
for our symbol we'll acknowledge vulgar materialistic laughter
    over an insatiable sexual appetite
and the streets will be filled with racing forms
and the photographs of murderers and narcissists and movie stars
    will swell from the walls and books alive in steaming rooms
    to press against our burning flesh not once but interminably
as water flows down hill into the full-lipped basin
and the adder dives for the ultimate ostrich egg
and the feather cushion preens beneath a reclining monolith
    that's sweating with post-exertion visibility and sweetness
    near the grave of love
                             No more dying

We shall see the grave of love as a lovely sight and temporary
    near the elm that spells the lovers' names in roots
and there'll be no more music but the ears in lips and no more wit
    but tongues in ears and no more drums but ears to thighs
as evening signals nudities unknown to ancestors' imaginations
and the imagination itself will stagger like a tired paramour of ivory
    under the sculptural necessities of lust that never falters
    like a six-mile runner from Sweden or Liberia covered with gold
as lava flows up and over the far-down somnolent city's abdication
and the hermit always wanting to be lone is lone at last
and the weight of external heat crushes the heat-hating Puritan
    who's self-defeating vice becomes a proper sepulchre at last
    that love may live

Buildings will go up into the dizzy air as love itself goes in
    and up the reeling life that it has chosen for once or all
while in the sky a feeling of intemperate fondness will excite the birds
    to swoop and veer like flies crawling across absorbèd limbs
that weep a pearly perspiration on the sheets of brief attention
and the hairs dry out that summon anxious declaration of the organs
    as they rise like buildings to the needs of temporary neighbors
    pouring hunger through the heart to feed desire in intravenous ways
like the ways of gods with humans in the innocent combination of light
and flesh or as the legends ride their heroes through the dark to found
great cities where all life is possible to maintain as long as time
    which wants us to remain for cocktails in a bar and after dinner
    lets us live with it
                             No more dying

POEM

To be idiomatic in a vacuum,
it is a shining thing! I

see it, it's like being inside
a bird. Where do you live,

are you sick?
I am breathing the pure sphere

of loneliness and it is sating.
Do you know young René Rilke?

He is a rose, he is together, all
together, like a wind tunnel,

and the rest of us are testing
our wings, our straining struts.

ODE ON LUST

Asking little more than
a squeal of satisfaction
from a piece of shrapnel,
the hero of a demi-force
pounces cheerfully upon
an exhalted height which shall
hereafter be called Bath

Where in the magnified panorama of hysterical pageantry upon the heights
stands Bath? he is standing in a lovely crater near the topmost peak!

Mildly frowning Bath adjourns
to the crystal lake of his
conception, but
if he imitates his father he
is bathed in sin no matter

how high he climbs and bends
he loses his pearls on the
slopes he finds them again
"meanwhile, back at the crater"
Poor Bath! and poorer still
are his pursuers, seeking only
the momentary smile of clouds
and underneath, a small
irresponsible glory that fits

In pursuing glory are they not wise to take the path of pale eschewment?
for who seeks Bath is the lover of lightning, burnt rather than burning

The avoidance of misery and
pity is a harrowing task for
one who must picture humanity
upside down and singing   A
smile then freezes in its charcoal
and, like a girl in Conrad,
one is the slave of an image
or, like Aïda, begins a slave
and ends singing under a stone
where only the other was to sing

Who has tears for any but these, though they hate them, these whose greed
is simply an overprodigal need of dispersal, whose individuality is silver,
whose attention is solely upon the fragments of love as they die, one by one?
who, like Theodora, are stripped of their seeds by the whiteness of doves
till they stand with their arms spread, nude in the arena; become Empresses

ODE TO WILLEM DE KOONING

Beyond the sunrise
where the black begins

an enormous city
is sending up its shutters

and just before the last lapse of nerve which I am already sorry for,
that friends describe as "just this once" in a temporary hell, I hope

I try to seize upon greatness
which is available to me

                through generosity and
                lavishness of spirit, yours

not to be inimitably weak
and picturesque, my self

                but to be standing clearly
                alone in the orange wind

while our days tumble and rant through Gotham and the Easter narrows
and I have not the courage to convict myself of cowardice or care

for now a long history slinks over the sill, or patent absurdities
and the fathomless miseries of a small person upset by personality

and I look to the flags
in your eyes as they go up

                on the enormous walls
                as the brave must always ascend

into the air, always the musts
like banderillas dangling

and jingling jewellike amidst the red drops on the shoulders of men
who lead us not forward or backward, but on as we must go on

                out into the mesmerized world
                of inanimate voices like traffic

noises, hewing a clearing
in the crowded abyss of the West

        2
        Stars of all passing sights,
        language, thought and reality,
        "I am assuming that one knows
        what it is to be ashamed"
        and that the light we seek
        is broad and pure, not winking
        and that the evil inside us
        now and then strolls into a field
        and sits down like a forgotten rock
        while we walk on to a horizon
        line that's beautifully keen,
        precarious and doesn't sag
        beneath our variable weight

        In this dawn as in the first
        it's the Homeric rose, its scent

that leads us up the rocky path
into the pass where death
can disappear or where the face
of future senses may appear
in a white night that opens
after the embattled hours of day

And the wind tears up the rose
fountains of prehistoric light
falling upon the blinded heroes
who did not see enough or were not
mad enough or felt too little
when the blood began to pour down
the rocky slopes into pink seas

3
Dawn must always recur

              to blot out stars and the terrible systems
of belief
      Dawn, which dries out the web so the wind can blow it,
          spider and all, away

Dawn,
      erasing blindness from an eye inflamed,
                    reaching for its
morning cigarette in Promethean inflection
                 after the blames
and desperate conclusions of the dark
               where messages were intercepted
by an ignorant horde of thoughts
             and all simplicities perished in desire

A bus crashes into a milk truck
            and the girl goes skating up the avenue
with streaming hair
        roaring through fluttering newspapers
and their Athenian contradictions
            for democracy is joined
with stunning collapsible savages, all natural and relaxed and free

as the day zooms into space and only darkness lights our lives,
with few flags flaming, imperishable courage and the gentle will
which is the individual dawn of genius rising from its bed

"maybe they're wounds, but maybe they are rubies"
                each painful as a sun

I live above a dyke bar and I'm happy.
The police car is always near the door

in case they cry
or the key doesn't work in the lock. But

he can't open it either. So we go to Joan's
and sleep over,

Bridget and Joe and I.

I meet Mike for a beer in the Cedar as
the wind flops up the Place, pushing the leaves
against the streetlights. And Norman tells about

the geste,

with the individual significance of a hardon
like humanity.

We go to Irma's for Bloody Marys,

and then it's dark.
We played with her cat and it fell asleep. We
seem very mild. It's humid out. (Are they spelled "dikes"?)
People say they are Bacchantes, but if they are

we must be the survivors of Thermopylae.

TO EDWIN DENBY

I'm so much more me
that you are perfectly you.
What you have clearly said
is yet in me unmade.

I'm so much more me
as time ticks in our ceilings
that you are perfectly you,
your deep and lightning feelings.

And I see in the flashes
what you have clearly said,

that feelings are our facts.
As yet in me unmade.

ABOUT COURBET

I

The angriness of the captive is felt,
is very plain, it is a large feeling
like a light in a toe, a voice of the sky;
now it has yielded all its bars, its robes,
and become the gentle sentiment of a class.
A girl plucks skulls in the arbor of hummingbirds,
and to the smiles of the hills a light
is yielding, yes, dark, towering eyes.

Delving into the rouges nightmares of nudes
was an eventide for other laughter. The hero,
in his traitorous assumption of herbs,
of ribboned mustaches and of pendulous routes,
of reflections in the vague trees so
thickly studded with almond pleasures
and the holidays of the not-so-rich tables,
became as pumice to the poetry of buckles
and leonine knives, accumulating terror
in an ocean of cartwheels where there had been
only desperation and a sense of nightness.

Isn't it delightful to be a woodchopper
among elegants? O fires of impatience!
aren't you smothered by the protecting mountains?
His insights were lice specimens exchanged
for the Academy in the style of Cicero.
Traffic signs became big suddenly, and primary.
The fashion is to sit by the sea and think
and think, and catch a faint whiff of lilac
from New York, it is the French with French
incessant noses, the hell in the nostril
uncapping its Angelus and crying "Fuir!"
but he had taken off his hat, patted his beard.
How sweet it is to be anywhere in the sunlight!

287

2

The alarms of summer have capsized the night.
Silken frills which are more leaf than tresses
seem to be the tears of a medallion that's blushing.
Advancing towards the pot-bellied stoves, we doffed
our galoshes and hissed "True! it's not!" Smell
that honeysuckle? It's not a prison, it's an arbor!
it's not a prism, it's an eye! O Gustavus Adolphus!
O Dreyfus! Seals are whinnying in the Seine
while a soprano in leg o' muttons goes into hysterics.
It's the yachting season, and we feel "well off."

3

Ill, though, and rather stuffily conceited,
he pushed a fumbling stiffness through the waters
where no mother would entrust a heart of hers
so thickly did the passions well. And sweetness
seemed the barker of some inner disaster
about to become national, as the facers often
are a glance of hatred towards the turf. Hadn't
the distinction of pushing everything together
won him for its? Carrying him further and further,
beyond ingenuity, and intuition, and facility,
and boredom, and the paralysis of air. Oh hat!

do you know what a head is? the worm, does he know
the flesh that is streaming past, never to be?

4a   THE SONGS OF COURBET

"Buns, a pleasant journey to the hub,
is all the obliging junk can jam;
she dumps her eyelashes into a tub
and ruptures her umbrella on a tram,

oh isn't it a maid with lewd supports
that's dashing on the boardwalk bare?
Nanette or Charleyhorse, those sports,
with leather flowers in their hair?

Isn't it enough to be middle–age
and French? do we have to be sage?"

4b   A NOSEGAY

Mouth paint. Cigar. Toughs. Obelisks. Noose. Arm.
    Pratfall. Disgust. Heavy winds and bugs. Armistices.
  Teeth in the grass. Windowpanes. A bust. Eat.

Dice. Expectoration brown. Rummaging cheese.
Table linen. Swings.
Arbutus.
Tarts.
Yes.
Yes.
No,
no,
no,
oh!

5

Fire sputtering in the fingerbowl. A bowl, eh?
of air buckling up its lymph, its mignonettes.

I assume you speak of the age in which great forms
appear, only to be taken apart ten years later,

is it that grand sickle your life's a history of?
so impersonal a lust? so demimondaine an aspiring?

that clutch at the throat of all that's artistic
and flimsy and truly moving? down with slow speech!

long works! trips to the zoo! subsidized opera!
up with adolescence and gin and kitchen matches!

Oh my dear, it's not what you do, it's how you do it!
Do you do it? I hope the sea will wash it all away.

6

Beside the sea, green mammoths with frothing lips,
the long razor of the air, the pomposity of the sun,
the man is gone. Only his voice booms like blood vessels
bursting in the eyes. A century of suffering came out
of his work, no Rimbaud he. At supper we eat beef
and at breakfast tears, there's no fort for the heart
to injure itself upon, no capital punishment
for the monks. Our father's fortune is dwindling,
and even he, we remember, didn't like our looks much.
A woman of crepe is standing before the fireplace.

Now speak, delicate green bird of lust, before
you plunge towards the flesh that spreads its steppe
across Europe and Asia and is itself remembering:
"To be a master is that death, affront to nature,
like one child vomiting upon its father's future."

You are someone
who's crazy about a
violinist in the New York Philharmonic.

Week after week, how
much more meaningful
the music is with that
nostril flaring over the bow, that

slipper-black head
bending.
           Don't cry,
it isn't me you love
when I pull out a handkerchief
and wipe the sweat away.

ODE TO MICHAEL GOLDBERG ('S BIRTH AND OTHER BIRTHS)

I don't remember anything of then, down there around the magnolias
        where I was no more comfortable than I've been since
        though aware of a certain neutrality called satisfaction
        sometimes

and there's never been an opportunity to think of it as an idyll
as if everyone'd been singing around me, or around a tulip tree

a faint stirring of that singing seems to come to me in heavy traffic
but I can't be sure that's it, it may be some more recent singing
from hours of dusk in bushes playing tag, being called in, walking
        up onto the porch crying bitterly because it wasn't a veranda
"smell that honeysuckle?" or a door you can see through terribly clearly,
            even the mosquitoes saw through it
suffocating netting
or more often being put into a brown velvet suit and kicked around
perhaps that was my last real cry for myself
in a forest you think of birds, in traffic you think of tires,
            where are you?
in Baltimore you think of hats and shoes, like Daddy did

I hardly ever think of June 27, 1926
when I came moaning into my mother's world
and tried to make it mine immediately
by screaming, sucking, urinating
and carrying on generally
it was quite a day

I wasn't proud of my penis yet, how did I know how to act? it was 1936
"no excuses, now"

    Yellow morning
                  silent, wet
                         blackness under the trees over stone walls
hay, smelling faintly of semen
                    a few sheltered flowers nodding and smiling
at the clattering cutter-bar
                of the mower ridden by Jimmy Whitney
"I'd like to put my rolling-pin to her"   his brother Bailey
leaning on his pitchfork, watching
                  "you shove it in and nine months later
it comes out a kid"
                Ha ha   where those flowers would dry out
and never again be seen
                except as cow-flaps, hushed noon drinking cold
water in the dusty field   "their curly throats"   big milk cans

      full of cold spring water, sandy hair, black hair

        I went to my first movie
        and the hero got his legs
        cut off by a steam engine
        in a freightyard, in my second

        Karen Morley got shot
        in the back by an arrow
        I think she was an heiress
        it came through her bathroom door

        there was nobody there
        there never was anybody
        there at any time
        in sweet-smelling summer

I'd like to stay
        in this field forever
                and think of nothing

but these sounds,
                    these smells and the tickling grasses
                                    "up your ass, Sport"

                    Up on the mountainous hill
                    behind the confusing house
                    where I lived, I went each
                    day after school and some nights
                    with my various dogs, the
                    terrier that bit people, Arno
                    the shepherd (who used to
                    be wild but had stopped), the
                    wire-haired that took fits
                    and finally the boring gentle
                    cocker, spotted brown and white,
                    named Freckles   there,

                    the wind sounded exactly like
                    Stravinsky
                            I first recognized art
                    as wildness, and it seemed right,
                            I mean rite, to me

                    climbing the water tower I'd
                    look out for hours in wind
                    and the world seemed rounder
                    and fiercer and I was happier
                    because I wasn't scared of falling off

                    nor off the horses, the horses!
                    to hell with the horses, bay and black

        It's odd to have secrets at an early age, trysts
    whose thoughtfulness and sweetness are those of a very aggressive person
            carried beneath your shirt like an amulet against your sire
                what one must do is done in a red twilight
                    on colossally old and dirty furniture with knobs,
                and on Sunday afternoons you meet in a high place
                    watching the Sunday drivers and the symphonic sadness
                stopped, a man in a convertible put his hand up a girl's skirt
            and again the twitching odor of hay, like a minor irritation
        that gives you a hardon, and again the roundness of horse noises

                    "Je suis las de vivre au pays natal"
                        but unhappiness, like Mercury, transfixed me

292

there, un repaire de vipères
and had I known the strength and durability
of those invisible bonds I would have leaped from rafters onto prongs
then
and been carried shining and intact
to the Indian Cemetery near the lake
but there is a glistening
blackness in the center
if you seek it
here . . .   it's capable of bursting
into flame or merely
gleaming profoundly in
the platinum setting
of your ornamental
human ties and hates
hanging between breasts
or, crosslike, on a chest of hairs
the center of myself is never silent
the wind soars, keening overhead
and the vestments of unnatural safety
part to reveal a foreign land
toward whom I have been selected to bear
the gift of fire
the temporary place of light, the land of air

down where a flame illumines gravity and means warmth and insight,
where air is flesh, where speed is darkness
and
things can suddenly be reached, held, dropped and known

where a not totally imaginary ascent can begin all over again in tears

A couple of specifically anguished days
make me now distrust sorrow, simple sorrow
especially, like sorrow over death

it makes you wonder who you are to be sorrowful
over death, death belonging to another
and suddenly inhabited by you without permission

you moved in impulsively and took it up
declaring your Squatters' Rights in howls
or screaming with rage, like a parvenu in a Chinese laundry

disbelieving your own feelings is the worst
and you suspect that you are jealous of this death

YIPPEE! I'm glad I'm alive
                    "I'm glad you're alive
        too, baby, because I want to fuck you"
                                you are pink
        and despicable in the warm breeze drifting in the window
and the rent
            is due, in honor of which you have borrowed $34.96 from Joe
        and it's all over but the smoldering hatred of pleasure
        a gorgeous purple like somebody's favorite tie
            "Shit, that means you're getting kind of ascetic, doesn't it?"

                    So I left, the stars were shining
                    like the lights around a swimming pool

                    you've seen a lot of anemones, too
                    haven't you, Old Paint? through the
                    Painted Desert to the orange covered
                    slopes where a big hill was moving in
                    on L A and other stars were strolling
                    in shorts down palm-stacked horse-walks
                    and I stared with my strained SP stare
                    wearing a gun
                                    the doubts
            of a life devoted to leaving rumors of love for new
from does she love me to do I love him,
                                    sempiternal farewell to hearths
        and the gods who don't live there

                    in New Guinea a Sunday morning figure
                    reclining outside his hut in Lamourish languor
                    and an atabrine-dyed hat like a sick sun
                    over his ebony land on your way to breakfast

                    he has had his balls sewed into his mouth
                    by the natives who bleach their hair in urine
                    and their will; a basketball game and a concert
                    later if you live to write, it's not all advancing
                    towards you, he had a killing desire for their women

        but more killing still the absence of desire, which in religion
                                    used to be called hope,
    I don't just mean the lack of a hardon, which may be sincerity
                    or the last-minute victory of the proud spirit over flesh,
            no: a tangerinelike sullenness in the face of sunrise
                    or a dark sinking in the wind on the forecastle
        when someone you love hits your head and says "I'd sail with you any
                            where, war or no war"

who was about
            to die a tough blond death
                                    like a slender blighted palm
in the hurricane's curious hail
                        and the maelstrom of bulldozers
            and metal sinkings,
                            churning the earth
even under the fathomless deaths
                        below, beneath
                                    where the one special
            went to be hidden, never to disappear
                not spatial in that way

        Take me, I felt, into the future fear of saffron pleasures
crazy strangeness and steam
                    of seeing a (pearl) white whale, steam of
being high in the sky
                opening fire on Corsairs,
                                    kept moving in berths
where I trade someone *The Counterfeiters* (I thought it was about personal
freedom then!) for a pint of whiskey,
                        banana brandy in Manila, spidery
steps trailing down onto the rocks of the harbor
                                and up in the black fir, the
pyramidal whiteness, Genji on the Ginza,
                        a lavender-kimono-sized
loneliness,
        and drifting into my ears off Sendai in the snow Carl
T. Fischer's *Recollections of an Indian Boy*
                            this tiny overdecorated
rock garden bringing obviously heart-shaped
                            the Great Plains, as is
my way to be obvious as eight o'clock in the dining car
                                of the
20th Century Limited (express)
                        and its noisy blast passing buttes to be
Atchison-Topeka-Santa Fé, Baltimore and Ohio (Cumberland),
                                        leaving
beds in Long Beach for beds in Boston, via C- (D,B,) 47 (6)
pretty girls in textile mills,
                        drowsing on bales in a warehouse of cotton
listening to soft Southern truck talk
                        perhaps it is "your miraculous
low roar" on Ulithi as the sailors pee into funnels, ambassadors of
        green-beer-interests bigger than Standard Oil in the South
Pacific, where the beaches flower with cat-eyes and ear fungus

warm as we never wanted to be warm, in an ammunition
dump, my foot again crushed (this time by a case of 40 millimeters)

"the

only thing you ever gave New Guinea was your toenail and now
the Australians are taking over"   . . . the pony of war?

to "return" safe who will never feel safe
and loves to ride steaming in the autumn of
centuries of useless aspiration towards artifice
        are you feeling useless, too, Old Paint?
I am really an Indian at heart, knowing it is all
all over but my own ceaseless going, never
to be just a hill of dreams and flint for someone later
but a hull laved by the brilliant Celebes response,
empty of treasure to the explorers who sailed me not

King Philip's trail,
                lachrymose highway of infantile regrets and cayuse
meannesses,
                Mendelssohn driving me mad in Carnegie Hall like greed
grasping
                Palisades Park smiling, you pull a pretty ring out of the pineapple
and blow yourself up
                        contented to be a beautiful fan of blood
                        above the earth-empathic earth

        Now suddenly the fierce wind of disease and Venus, as
when a child
        you wonder if you're not a little crazy, laughing
because a horse
        is standing on your foot
                        and you're kicking his hock
with your sneaker, which is to him
                        a love-tap, baring big teeth
laughing . . .
        thrilling activities which confuse
                        too many, too loud
too often, crowds of intimacies and no distance
                        the various cries
and rounds
        and we are smiling in our confused way, darkly
in the back alcove
                of the Five Spot, devouring chicken-in-the-basket
and arguing,
        the four of us, about loyalty

wonderful stimulation of bitterness
to be young and to grow bigger
more and more cells, like germs
or a political conspiracy

and each reason for love always
a certain hostility, mistaken
for wisdom
                exceptional excitement
which is finally simple blindness
(but not to be sneezed at!) like
a successful American satellite . . .

Yes, it does, it would still
keep me out of a monastery if
I were invited to attend one

                        from round the window, you can't
      see the street!
                you let the cold wind course through
and let the heart pump and gurgle
                in febrile astonishment,
                        a cruel world
to which you've led it by your mind,
                bicycling no-hands
                    leaving it gasping
there, wondering where you are and how to get back,
                      although you'll never let
          it go

         while somewhere everything's dispersed
at five o'clock
            for Martinis a group of professional freshnesses meet
and the air's like a shrub—Rose o' Sharon? the others,
                      it's not
a flickering light for us, but the glare of the dark
                too much endlessness
stored up, and in store:
                "the exquisite prayer
                to be new each day
                brings to the artist
                only a certain kneeness"

I am assuming that everything is all right and difficult,
                        where hordes
      of stars carry the burdens of the gentler animals like our-
selves with wit and austerity beneath a hazardous settlement

which we understand because we made
                                        and secretly admire
        because it moves
yes! for always, for it is our way, to pass the teahouse and the ceremony
        by and rather fall sobbing to the floor with joy and freezing
        than to spill the kid upon the table and then thank the blood

        for flowing
                        as it must throughout the miserable, clear and willful
life we love beneath the blue,
                                a fleece of pure intention sailing like
a pinto in a barque of slaves
                                who soon will turn upon their captors
lower anchor, found a city riding there
                                        of poverty and sweetness paralleled
        among the races without time,
                                        and one alone will speak of being
        born in pain
                        and he will be the wings of an extraordinary liberty

THREE AIRS

to Norman Bluhm

1
So many things in the air! soot,
elephant balls, a Chinese cloud
which is entirely collapsed, a cat
swung by its tail
                        and the senses
of the dead which are banging about
inside my tired red eyes

2
In the deeps there is a little bird
and it only hums, it hums of fortitude

and temperance, it is managing a foundry

how firmly it must grasp things! tear them
out of the slime and then, alas! it mischievously

drops them into the cauldron of hideousness

there is already a sunset naming
the poplars which see only, watery, themselves

3
Oh to be an angel (if there were any!), and go
straight up into the sky and look around and then come down

not to be covered with steel and aluminum
glaringly ugly in the pure distances and clattering and
                              buckling, wheezing

but to be part of the treetops and the blueness, invisible,
the iridescent darknesses beyond,
                              silent, listening to
                the air becoming no air becoming air again

GOOD FRIDAY NOON

It's as good a day as any
to decide whether you like
myth or Minuit. Is myth
drag-assed and scarred or
is it lip-to-lip with Manhattan?
I don't know, I just like
Wagner, that's all, I'd put
up with anything if the
orchestra's big enough.

Is it still bleeding? Naw,
it's hard as an acorn squash.
Haven't you held that street-
light up long enough? Naw,
there wouldn't *be* any light
if I left off. Well, you are
sort of a service to mankind,
no wonder you don't like
anything but leather boots,
jackets and Kundry-type belts.

To humble yourself before a radio on a Sunday
it's amusing, like dying after a party
"click"/and you're dead from fall-out, hang-over
        or something hyphenated

(hello, Western Union? send a Mother's Day message to Russia: SORRY
NOT TO BE WITH YOU ON YOUR DAY LOVE AND KISSES TELL THE CZAR LA GRANDE
JATTE WASNT DAMAGED IN THE MUSEUM OF MODERN ART FIRE /S/ FRANK)

the unrecapturable nostalgia for nostalgia
for a life I might have hated, thus mourned

but do we really need anything more to be sorry about
wouldn't it be extra, as all pain is extra

(except that I will never feel CONTEST: WIN A DREAM TRIP pertains to
me, somehow   Joe, I wouldn't go, probably)

for God's sake fly the other way
leave me standing alone crumbling in the new sky of the Wide World
without passage, without breath

a spatial representative of emptiness

if Joan says I'm wounded, then I'm wounded
and not like La Pucelle or André Gide
not by moral issues or the intercontinental ballistics missile
        or the Seer of Prague

(you're right to go to Aaron's PIANO FANTASY, but I'm not up to it this
time, too important a piece not to punish me
                      and it's raining)

it's more like the death of a nation
henceforth to be called small

although its people could say "Mare nostrum" without fear of hubris
and the air saluted them
            (air of the stars) ashore or leaning on the prow

TO RICHARD MILLER

Where is Mike Goldberg? I don't know,
he may be in the Village far below
or lounging on Tenth Street with the gang
of early-morning painters (before noon)
as they discuss the geste or jest
of action painting, whether it's Yang
or Yin and related to the sun or moon

Maybe he is living sketches of an ODE
ON SEX which I do not intend to write
in his abode or drinking bourbon in the light
of his be-placticked skylight. I will goad
him into Tibering and hope all's for the best

JUNE 2, 1958

Oh sky over the graveyard, you are blue,
you seem to be smiling! or are you sneering?
under the captured moss a little girl
is climbing, come closer! why it's Maude,
or Maudie as she's sometimes called. I think
she is looking for her turtle. Meanwhile,
back at Patsy Southgate's, two grown men
are falling off a swing into a vat of Bloody Marys.
It's Sunday and the trains run on time. What
a wonderful country it is, so black and blue
airy green, leaning out a window
thinking of the sea and the uncomfortable sand!

There is the sense of neurotic coherence

you think maybe poetry is too important and you like that

suddenly everyone's supposed to be veined, like marble

it isn't that simple but it's simple enough

the rock is least living of the forms man has fucked

and it isn't pathetic and it's lasting, one towering tree

in the vast smile of bronze and vertiginous grasses

Maude lays down her doll, red wagon and her turtle
takes my hand and comes with us, shows the bronze JACKSON POLLOCK
gazelling on the rock of her demeanor as a child, says running
away hand in hand "he isn't under there, he's out in the woods" beyond

and like that child at your grave make me be distant and imaginative
make my lines thin as ice, then swell like pythons
the color of Aurora when she first brought fire to the Arctic in a sled
a sexual bliss inscribe upon the page of whatever energy I burn for art
and do not watch over my life, but read and read through copper earth

not to fall at all, but disappear or burn! seizing a grave by throat
which is the look of earth, its ambiguity of light and sound
the thickness in a look of lust, the air within the eye
the gasp of a moving hand as maps change and faces become vacant
it's noble to refuse to be added up or divided, finality of kings

                              and there's the ugliness we seek in vain
through life and long for like a mortuarian Baudelaire working for Skouras
inhabiting neighborhoods of Lear! Lear! Lear!
                              tenement of a single heart

for Old Romance was draping dolors on a scarlet mound, each face
a country of valorous decay, heath-helmet or casque, *mollement, moelleusement*
and all that shining fierce turned green and covered the lays with grass
as later in *The Orange Ballad of Cromwell's Charm Upon the Height "So Green"*
as in the histories of that same time and earlier, when written down at all
sweet scripts to obfuscate the tender subjects of their future lays

to be layed at all! romanticized, elaborated, fucked, sung, put to "rest"
is worse than the mild apprehension of a Buddhist type caught halfway up
the tea-rose trellis with his sickle banging on the Monk's lead window, moon
not our moon
                        unless the tea exude a little gas and poisonous fact
to reach the spleen and give it a dreamless twinge that love's love's near

    the bang of alertness, loneliness, position that prehends experience

not much to be less, not much to be more
                                                alive, sick; and dead, dying
like the kiss of love meeting the kiss of hatred
                                                "oh you know why"
each in asserting beginning to be more of the opposite
                                                what goes up must
come down, what dooms must do, standing still and walking in New York

let us walk in that nearby forest, staring into the growling trees
in which an era of pompous frivolity or two is dangling its knobby knees
and reaching for an audience
                        over the pillar of our deaths a cloud
heaves
        pushed, steaming and blasted
                                love-propelled and tangled glitteringly
                has earned himself the title *Bird in Flight*

FANTASIA (ON RUSSIAN VERSES)
FOR ALFRED LESLIE

Harder nails
a companion of the facts
an appearance before doors
"to piss out of my window over the moon"

"people are ships"
acceptance of acne
the easel disappearing

"a certain ebony king"
an angel but which
the abyss with red cheeks
hanging out from the wall

Manny prepares for the storm
I'm not going to die
"Port Arthur has already surrendered"

Petersburg night
lately knowing
"the lie sat down with us"
hatred in February

up
"confuse the funeral"

"Muravia, that ancient place"
oxymoron
excessive frigidity
"Kirov goes walking through the town"

danger from dogs
"threatening the palace"
what Elvis saw
"Spontaneous in the sea of corn"

"my mouth of stone"
Bowling Green
a lonely cuss
another history for every
flop
aspirins

"out of my hairy belly"
greeting linear pilots
my body
legs
to be not what one seems

the laughing boy goes to sleep
mirage guiding the messenger
to be culpable
the river returns

From near the sea, like Whitman my great predecessor, I call
to the spirits of other lands to make fecund my existence

do not spare your wrath upon our shores, that trees may grow
upon the sea, mirror of our total mankind in the weather

one who no longer remembers dancing in the heat of the moon may call
across the shifting sands, trying to live in the terrible western world

here where to love at all's to be a politician, as to love a poem
is pretentious, this may sound tendentious but it's lyrical

which shows what lyricism has been brought to by our fabled times
where cowards are shibboleths and one specific love's traduced

by shame for what you love more generally and never would avoid
where reticence is paid for by a poet in his blood or coaring to be

blood! blood that we have mountains in our veins to stand off jackals
in the pillaging of our desires and allegiances, Aimé Césaire

for if there is fortuity it's in the love we bear each other's differences
in race which is the poetic ground on which we rear our smiles

standing in the sun of marshes as we wade slowly toward the culmination
of a gift which is categorically the most difficult relationship

and should be sought as such because it is our nature, nothing
inspires us but the love we want upon the frozen face of earth

and utter disparagement turns into praise as generations read the message
of our hearts in adolescent closets who once shot at us in doorways

or kept us from living freely because they were too young then to know
what they would ultimately need from a barren and heart-sore life

the beauty of America, neither cool jazz nor devoured Egyptian heroes, lies in
lives in the darkness I inhabit in the midst of sterile millions

the only truth is face to face, the poem whose words become your mouth
and dying in black and white we fight for what we love, not are

A TRUE ACCOUNT OF TALKING
TO THE SUN AT FIRE ISLAND

The Sun woke me this morning loud
and clear, saying "Hey! I've been
trying to wake you up for fifteen
minutes. Don't be so rude, you are
only the second poet I've ever chosen
to speak to personally
                            so why
aren't you more attentive? If I could
burn you through the window I would
to wake you up. I can't hang around
here all day."
                    "Sorry, Sun, I stayed
up late last night talking to Hal."

"When I woke up Mayakovsky he was
a lot more prompt" the Sun said
petulantly. "Most people are up
already waiting to see if I'm going
to put in an appearance."
                            I tried
to apologize "I missed you yesterday."
"That's better" he said. "I didn't
know you'd come out." "You may be
wondering why I've come so close?"
"Yes" I said beginning to feel hot
wondering if maybe he wasn't burning me
anyway.
            "Frankly I wanted to tell you
I like your poetry. I see a lot
on my rounds and you're okay. You may
not be the greatest thing on earth, but
you're different. Now, I've heard some
say you're crazy, they being excessively
calm themselves to my mind, and other
crazy poets think that you're a boring
reactionary. Not me.
                        Just keep on
like I do and pay no attention. You'll
find that people always will complain
about the atmosphere, either too hot
or too cold too bright or too dark, days
too short or too long.

                    If you don't appear
at all one day they think you're lazy
or dead. Just keep right on, I like it.

And don't worry about your lineage
poetic or natural. The Sun shines on
the jungle, you know, on the tundra
the sea, the ghetto. Wherever you were
I knew it and saw you moving. I was waiting
for you to get to work.

                    And now that you
are making your own days, so to speak,
even if no one reads you but me
you won't be depressed. Not
everyone can look up, even at me. It
hurts their eyes."
                    "Oh Sun, I'm so grateful to you!"

"Thanks and remember I'm watching. It's
easier for me to speak to you out
here. I don't have to slide down
between buildings to get your ear.
I know you love Manhattan, but
you ought to look up more often.
                    And
always embrace things, people earth
sky stars, as I do, freely and with
the appropriate sense of space. That
is your inclination, known in the heavens
and you should follow it to hell, if
necessary, which I doubt.
                    Maybe we'll
speak again in Africa, of which I too
am specially fond. Go back to sleep now
Frank, and I may leave a tiny poem
in that brain of yours as my farewell."

"Sun, don't go!" I was awake
at last. "No, go I must, they're calling
me."
        "Who are they?"
                    Rising he said "Some
day you'll know. They're calling to you
too." Darkly he rose, and then I slept.

PLACES FOR OSCAR SALVADOR

EL ESCORIAL

After a sun lunch the burning landscape
from a stone and Saint Theresa's heated
manuscripts the inks as dry as yesterdays so
many clothes for priests to wear and tombs

it is a vault of sweet martinis and sangrìa
we talk about things and the other tongues
make a basilica of privacy around us like monks
the lissome afternoon of a confession on the Spanish plain

in the Greco martyrdom we occupy so little space
that no one notices a sad chance of immanence come true
except a crazy artist gentler than a dog is blind
hears a guitar string snap it is our space he hears

PLAZA DE ESPAÑA

You cannot do a thing you cannot do
although sand goes with flowers cold
asparagus café with solo
we are one single park in a windy bar
looking over another park from a great height

then at night with the river flowing down
and the careless lights on the road to Portugal
we're not a park anymore no more a plaza
I don't know an enormous multiform past
comes crushing down in its astute immobility

we have quixotically become a building
no longer growing or bearing the horns of day
waiting to become ruins who have never housed a revolution
or a banquet or a case of typhus yet I love it
more than I will ever love the past I love our waiting

PONTE FABRICIO

Lonely and only going halfway
surrounded by green like a storm cloud that didn't break
here the river quickens and the children never swim
I stand here the oldest in Rome not used to traffic
a figure of scorn to myself to others a memory
the pain of my faulty joinings doesn't subside in the rapids
I think I will not be rebuilt

I think I have started to fall and will end in the sea
I think half-thoughts I do not reach the other shore

POEM

Today the mail didn't come
and Berlin was happy!
there was no bad news

a student with a mustache was repairing the façade of the Hotel Kempinski
with glass that was falling apart
and it suddenly started raining

and people kept right on walking
with the hopelessness of leisure
and the light improved and the student wouldn't stop working

TO GOTTFRIED BENN

Poetry is not instruments
that work at times
then walk out on you
laugh at you old
get drunk on you young
poetry's part of your self

like the passion of a nation
at war it moves quickly
provoked to defense or aggression

unreasoning power
an instinct for self-declaration

like nations its faults are absorbed
in the heat of sides and angles
combatting the void of rounds
a solid of imperfect placement
nations get worse and worse

but not wrongly revealed
in the universal light of tragedy

WITH BARBARA GUEST IN PARIS

Oh Barbara! do you think we'll ever
have anything named after us like
rue Henri-Barbusse or
canard à l'Ouragan?

have infected a pale white
moonish bateau-frigidaire
with our melancholy lights
and vaguely proud dissemblings?

Care for the lap of Mallarmé
and the place where heroes fell down
is right in our Pushkinesque enclosure
as greatness sleeps outside
      smiles and bears
      the purple city air

FAR FROM THE PORTE DES LILAS
AND THE RUE PERGOLÈSE

to Joan Mitchell

Ah Joan!   there
you are
surrounded by paintings
as in another century you would be wearing lipstick
(which you wear at night to be old-fashioned, of it!
    with it!   out!

and the danger of being Proustian
and the danger of being Pasternakesque
and the cops outside the BALAJO frisking Algerians
who'd been quietly playing "surf" with their
    knuckles

gee, if I don't stop being so futuristic Elsa Triolet
    will be after me!

a dream of immense sadness peers through me
as if I were an action poem that couldn't write
and I am leaving for another continent which is the
    same as this one
goodby

HEROIC SCULPTURE

We join the animals
not when we fuck
            or shit
not when tear falls

but when
            staring into light
we think

LOVE

To be lost
                the stars go out a broken chair
                is red in the dark a faint lust
                stirs like a plant in the creased rain

                                        where the gloom
                                        swells into odor
                                        like earth in the moon

lightness the arrow ears its sigh of depth and its sorrows
                        of snow

                BERDIE

                It has suddenly rained
                on Second Avenue and
                we are thinking of you
                as the small thoughts of
                the rain drum on tin
                and soot runs down the
                windows we always do
                in the rain it's no more
                different than the rain
                you went there honorably as
                stone becomes sand and
                the sad shore falls
                into the unwilling sea

TWO RUSSIAN EXILES: AN ODE

Like a cat who pushes and flexes forelegs
with half-sheathed claws
      before fucking
or deciding to sit down on someone

you pace and sheathe your breath
before the motive's uttered
      of longing
and the bitterness of knowing it sweet

bitterest of all to know sweetness as longing
exiled on the heights of joy
      creation
which is not the comfortable abyss that sympathies
cloud-rack men in off from their own lost kind

but the joy
     which all must envy and is mortal
inducing ennui in animals and hatred in friends
and can be heard from a mountain as a wind
and can be felt from a mouth as a sob of knowing

all that appears is two large eyes
      and snow in them
and underneath an oracle of sadness
      counting
at the moment of joy an interminable desolation
for everything is present for joy
no anticipation
    no heroic advance
      no hope
a wild instantaneous fullness accepts being
alone in irreparable stillness
     as a nation
hates the exile in its heart
     receives royalty
from you as exile in our alternating climate
of doors and crags which you have sent
and seen
   as one moves from the Ural's eaglish
clearness towards the muddy heart of Moscow
from joy the simple animals ignore to strident
  pity foreign to his heights and painfully warm
  pity foreign to his enemies and painfully dark

O foreign

to be exile in your homeland
is far worse than the concert emigration of a thousand sounds
at night in the open air when the airplanes crash
and the sleeping poet wakes

to write for tragedy its obvious ode
and birdlike rite
to carry the pianist past
her knack of loving into joyous night
music must die but poetry is silent joy

THANKSGIVING

The heat rises, it is not the pressure
of an old tired remembrance

but the bored hello of an extra alliance of tedious sanct.
Goodby
I am saying
hello, hello hello
who am I? it is a mess, my life, old father time
has said his last hello . . .

The anxiety of the future is only equalled by the tiresomeness of
the present

Lean it
but don't
learn it

eat it
but don't
kiss it

learn it
but don't
study it

And then you find that the mysterious mandarin

                                          is pooped

cut down

         the yews
           the appletrees
           the chasms

                      it is a saintly mess of pulpitude and hash
it is an acceptable pie of walking meat, gristle and bone
     and tomorrow we will put a bullet through your red hide

[MELANCHOLY BREAKFAST]

Melancholy breakfast
blue overhead blue underneath

the silent egg thinks
and the toaster's electrical
           ear waits

the stars are in
"that cloud is hid"

the elements of disbelief are very strong in the morning

GREGORY CORSO: *GASOLINE*

I see you standing in the clear light
of what is soon to become day, or night

it is your standing that counts, the ineluctable nonsleeping
                                 and nonpolishing, you
are not a stitcher of the wing to sandaled verse

poems discrete, admirable, scandal-free, sweet and disruptable
they are scandalous as stars
                              because the meanness of souls cannot be assuaged
though it can be eradicated
                              which no tyrannous power has ever thought of
because tyranny has never known
                    real powers

        and what with the leverage of chance and all
        the false rear their many-colored sheet
     but at last we are liberated
                              from the psychology of the nonesuch
                not ignorant of your sailing

Stance is the gift of the poet
                              the tiger looking out of the clean-shaved face
the book of the greater book
                              just above the outstretched hand as it moves
an element of disaster which will never fall
                                        in tawdry skirmishing
and the brazen supposition of a few mistakes that turn out right, as
        under New-Yorkless Paris' night a nude falls open to fire
          and Zizi laughs at last
        but Bird no longer wails at the Open Door, no Open Door

It's to be a meal for the world
                              yet selfish and grudging of appetite
be it true appetite or the avaricious
                                        sapping of timorous quail
so the sun will become mouthless
                              observing the Haarlem miracles
as the angels go under
                    your angels, because they don't look and then not look
as you have told them

Thanks for the not-memory of choosing a world
                                          choosing sides for your side
while the academy burgeons on blundering wages

        Now it is GASOLINE
                        "a dark arriviste, from a dark river within"
refined in the heat of Measure
                              as in the desert a blood-clotted satyr
becomes bone and whiteness for the silent sun
                                        through Corso "vision agent"
not creating "a" world, but choosing *the* world

What Corso is doing
                    is surrounding the world with
the positive question
                    of his own value
          crazy question for the frightened, life for the poet
      accepting frail music for the ultimate answer
          an ode for the tie-tree of his Saint Sebastian
      Coit Tower, where all memories grow into childhood
          and the poet takes up the knives of his wounds to catch the light

THE "UNFINISHED"

In memory of Bunny Lang

As happiness takes off the tie it borrowed from me
and gets into bed and pretends to be asleep-and-awake
or pulls an orange poncho over its blonde Jay-Thorped curls
and goes off to cocktails without telling me why
it's so depressing,
                    so I will be as unhappy as I damn well
please and not make too much of it because I am
really here and not in a novel or anything or a jet plane
as I've often gone away on a ladder, a taxi or a jet plane

        everybody thinks if you go, you go up
but I'm not so sure about that because the fault of my generation
is that nobody wants to make a big *histoire* about anything
and I'm just like everybody else, if an earthquake comes
laughingly along and gulps down the whole of Madrid
including the Manzanares River and for dessert all the royal tombs
in the Escorial I'd only get kind of hysterical about one person
no Voltaire me
                    and isn't it funny how beautiful Sibelius sounds
if you haven't found him for a long time? because if we didn't all
hang onto a little self-conscious bitterness and call it intelligence
and admire it as technique we would all be perfectly truthful
and fall into the vat of longing and suffocate in its suet
except for the two Gregorys
                            Lafayette who was so pointlessly handsome
and innocently blond that he cheerfully died
                                    and Corso
too lustrously dark and precise, he would be excavated and declared

a black diamond and hung round a slender bending neck
in the 26th Century when the Court of the Bourbons is reinstated
and heaven comes to resemble more closely a late Goya

      this isn't bitterness, it's merely a tremor of the earth
I'm impersonating some wretch weeping over a 1956 date book and of course
I pull myself together and then I wipe my eyes and see that it's my own
              (date book, that is)
and everything becomes history: when Lennie Bernstein conducted it
on TV last week he called it my Symphony Number One, my "Unfinished"
that sort of thing can give you a terrible feeling that you've
             accomplished something

meanwhile, back at the Paris branch of contemporary depression, I
am dropping through the famous blueness like a pearl diver, I am
looking for Gregory who lives on Heart-Bed Street and I sit with Ashbery
in the Flore because of his poem about himself in a flower-bed
and we look for Gregory in the Deux Magots because I want to cry with him
about a dear dead friend, it's always about dying, never about death
I sometimes think it's the only reason that any of us love each other
it is raining, Ashes helps me finish my gall and seltzer, and we go

     the casual reader will not, I am sure, be averse to a short
     digression in this splendid narrative by which the nature
     of the narrator can be more or less revealed and all sorts
     of things subsequently become clearer if not clear: picture
     a person who one day in a fit of idleness decides to make
     a pomander like the one that granny used to have around the
     house in old New England and so he takes an orange and sticks
     a lot of cloves in it and then he looks at it and realizes
     that he's killed the orange, his favorite which came from
     the Malay Archipelago and was even loved in Ancient China,
     and he quickly pulls out all the cloves, but it's too
     late! Orange is lying bleeding in my hand! and I
     suddenly think of the moon, hanging quietly up there
     ever since the time of Keats, and now they're shoot-
     ing all those funny-looking things at her, that's
     what you get, baby (end of digression)

and back in New York Gregory is back in New York and we are still missing
each other in the Cedar and in hotel lobbies where Salvador Dali is
supposed to be asleep and at Anne Truxell's famous giggling parties
until one fine day (*vedremo*) we meet over a duck dinner, good god
I just remembered what he stuffed it with, you guessed it: oranges!
and perhaps, too, he is the true narrator of this story, Gregory

no, I must be, because he's in Chicago, and after all those months
including Madrid where it turns out there wasn't any earthquake
and also the TV broadcast was cancelled because Bernstein had a sore
thumb, I'm not depressed any more, because Gregory has had the same
experience with oranges, and is alive

     where all memories grow into childhood
     and mingled sound and silence drifts up to the rooftop
     where a bare-legged boy stares into the future
     takes up the knives of his wounds to catch the light
     foreseeing his epic triumph in the style of Cecil B. De Mille
     when one day the Via del Corso is named after him
     the principal street of Rome
     which is better than the Nobel Prize
     better than Albert Schweitzer, Pablo Casals and Helen Keller
     PUT TO GETHER

DREAM OF BERLIN

     Night (blue)
     along the long way (out)
     Alexander Blok (wept)
     acceptability (*sic*)
     in sui generis (is)
     ate (sadly)
     upon the floor (of)
     a maggot (rose)

     a day passes (if)
     in a complete circle (nothing)
     and a dream releases (to)
     its poems of Ceylon (route)
     where dwell (dead)
     unArctic fish (for)

     combine (at)
     exceptional movements (under)
     your broken glass (love)
     your captured spoor (hair)
     and the decay (kiss)
     of your ferocity (pleases)

sweet and (not)
palatable (lust)
is the sale (free)
of defeat (knee)

these (hairs)
are the soldiers (armor)
of Fidelio (dark)
Yoicks! (feet)
hunting in the abyss (parade)
what's in the sky (reversed)
they blink (smiling)
they like to (feel)

a girl (disguised)
goes down (further)
with a tag (gilded)
on her hip (heroine)
it is her hand (on)
feathers (burning)

THE LAY OF THE ROMANCE OF THE ASSOCIATIONS

to Kenneth Koch

High above Manhattan's towers
gilded like Camelot in every weather
I heard the cries of the Park Avenue and the Fifth Avenue Associations
trying to get together.

If only, if only, cried the Fifth Avenue Association
being the less élite of the two, and therefore
the first to come on, I weren't so rushed all the time!
I have so much to say to you but we are far apart.

I hear you, yodeled the Park Avenue Association
in Westchester accents cracked with emotion,
and I too am harried even in my very center and a strange
throb of emotion fills the towering Seagram Building
with a painful foretaste of love for you. But alas,
that bourgeois Madison Avenue continues to obstruct
our free intercourse with each other.

Intercourse!

cried Fifth Avenue, all I want to do is kiss you, kiss
your silver grey temples and your charming St. Bartholomew's
ears. What would Saks think, and De Pinna, much less Tishman
if such things were to go on in the middle of Manhattan?
You must not be untrue to your upbringing, even if
your suit is torn and your tailor hasn't delivered the new one.

Suit-shmuit, said Park Avenue, our joining will fecundate
this otherwise arid and sterile-towered metropolis!
the alliance of aristocrat with parvenue has always been
the hope of democracy, not to mention bureaucracy. You
don't think I need you, my plants are green. But look!
I don't have many plants. And you, even in the depths of
winter, are covered with lights under which like basking collies
grow your tender evergreens of love and commerce. Come!

I can't, for stern Madison Avenue has me in thrall
and won't divorce me even though I've offered "no settlement."
Why don't we rendezvous in Central Park behind a clump of cutthroats
near the reservoir and there we'll kiss and hold each other
sweatily as in a five o'clock on a mid-August Friday in the dusk
and after, languorously bathe, to sweeten city water for all time.

ON RACHMANINOFF'S BIRTHDAY

It is your 86th birthday
and I am sitting crying at the corner
of Ninth Street and Avenue A
one swallow doesn't make a summer
this coffee is terribly tepid

sometimes the 2nd Symphony sounds like Purcell
sometimes it sounds like *Wozzeck*'s last act

where is J.F. Donnelly and his Russian wolfhounds?
where is his wife, Helen? where is the cigar-smell
and the hootings in the studio while I practice?

a day of dismay is a day to remember
night doesn't come, and feeling dissipates

as the disgusting blackness of light
refuses to go off and leave melancholy
to nourish its roots of perversity
perhaps it will turn green like a potato

the ability to sing is ordinary
the ability to play is exceptional

where we can shroud ourselves in the
mechanized clarity of emotional vandalism we
do not see your owlish obstinacy staring back

FOR BOB RAUSCHENBERG

Yes, it's necessary, I'll do
what you say, put everything
aside but what is here. The frail
instant needs us and the cautious
breath, so easily drowned in Liszt
or sucked out by a vulgar soprano.

Why should I hear music? I'm not
a pianist any more, and in truth
I despise my love for Pasternak,
born in Baltimore, no *sasha* mine,
and an adolescence taken in hay
above horses—
    what should I be
if not alone in pain, apart from
the heavenly aspirations of
Spenser and Keats and Ginsberg,
who have a language that permits
them truth and beauty, double-coin?
exercise, recreations, drugs—
      what
can heaven mean up, down, or sidewise
who knows what is happening to him,
what has happened and is here, a
paper rubbed against the heart
and still too moist to be framed.

[THE SAD THING ABOUT LIFE IS]

The sad thing about life is
that I need money to write poetry
and If I am a good poet
nobody will care how I got it
and If I am a bad poet
nobody will know how I got it

IMAGE OF THE BUDDHA PREACHING

I am very happy to be here at the Villa Hügel
and Prime Minister Nehru has asked me to greet the people of Essen
and to tell you how powerfully affected we in India
have been by Germany's philosophy, traditions and mythology
though our lucidity and our concentration on archetypes
puts us in a class by ourself
                              "for in this world of storm and stress"
—5,000 years of Indian art! just think of it, oh Essen!
is this a calmer region of thought, "a reflection of the mind
through the ages"?
                  Max Müller, "primus inter pares" among Indologists
remember our byword, Mokshamula, I rejoice in the fact of 900 exhibits

I deeply appreciate filling the gaps, oh Herr Doktor Heinrich Goetz!
and the research purring onward in Pakistan and Ceylon and Afghanistan
soapstone, terracotta-Indus, terracotta-Maurya, terracotta-Sunga,
       terracotta-Andhra, terracotta fragments famous Bharhut Stupa
Kushana, Gandhara, Gupta, Hindu and Jain, Secco, Ajanta, Villa Hügel!

Anglo-German trade will prosper by Swansea-Mannheim friendship
waning now the West Wall by virtue of two rolls per capita
and the flagship BERLIN is joining its "white fleet" on the Rhine
though better schools and model cars are wanting, still still oh Essen
       Nataraja dances on the dwarf
       and unlike their fathers
       Germany's highschool pupils love the mathematics

       which is hopeful of a new delay in terror
       I don't think

Tradewinds where are you blowing
Allen and Peter why haven't you come back
I am walking along the sidewalk
and I see a puddle and it's god, greedy god
always adding to yourself with raindrops and spit
we don't like that, god
and the rainbow is slooping over the Chrysler Building
like a spineless trout, ugly and ephemeral
it is no sign of hope when things get ugly

I am leaping towards the charnel-basket
of a 6th Avenue conscience as the wave
remurmurs an abdication of Moriarty's chops
and the slender Ziegfeld-Egyptian tobacco
smiles and (roll your own) rolls on
where it makes the puddle even browner
not as skin is brown but as souls go bad
a limburger prescience under the clear (no rainbow)

now it is dark on 2nd Street near the abattoir
and a smell as of hair comes up the dovecotes
as the gentleman poles a pounce of pigeons
in the lower East Sideness rippling river
where have you gone, Ashes, and up and out
where the Sorbonne commissions frigidaires
from Butor and Buffet and Alechinsky storages
Beauty! said Vera Prentiss-Simpson to Pal Joe
and the hideaway was made secure against the hares

you see me but you don't care
like in an illuminated manuscript
it is nothing
except a small religious flashlight to light fires
and under the crimson welt of Number 16 East 11th
little cross-hatches were imposed by workmen
to espalier the sighs of the parrot Chum
as he dug his toes into the TV set
and commenced his airy *Cara nome*
dropping as much as he could on the floor
as the air-puddles drop us to our knees in storms

THE DAY LADY DIED

It is 12:20 in New York a Friday
three days after Bastille day, yes
it is 1959 and I go get a shoeshine
because I will get off the 4:19 in Easthampton
at 7:15 and then go straight to dinner
and I don't know the people who will feed me

I walk up the muggy street beginning to sun
and have a hamburger and a malted and buy
an ugly NEW WORLD WRITING to see what the poets
in Ghana are doing these days
                                        I go on to the bank
and Miss Stillwagon (first name Linda I once heard)
doesn't even look up my balance for once in her life
and in the GOLDEN GRIFFIN I get a little Verlaine
for Patsy with drawings by Bonnard although I do
think of Hesiod, trans. Richmond Lattimore or
Brendan Behan's new play or *Le Balcon* or *Les Nègres*
of Genet, but I don't, I stick with Verlaine
after practically going to sleep with quandariness

and for Mike I just stroll into the PARK LANE
Liquor Store and ask for a bottle of Strega and
then I go back where I came from to 6th Avenue
and the tobacconist in the Ziegfeld Theatre and
casually ask for a carton of Gauloises and a carton
of Picayunes, and a NEW YORK POST with her face on it

and I am sweating a lot by now and thinking of
leaning on the john door in the 5 SPOT
while she whispered a song along the keyboard
to Mal Waldron and everyone and I stopped breathing

RHAPSODY

515 Madison Avenue
door to heaven? portal
stopped realities and eternal licentiousness

or at least the jungle of impossible eagerness
your marble is bronze and your lianas elevator cables
swinging from the myth of ascending
I would join
or declining the challenge of racial attractions
they zing on (into the lynch, dear friends)
while everywhere love is breathing draftily
like a doorway linking 53rd with 54th
the east-bound with the west-bound traffic by 8,000,000s
o midtown tunnels and the tunnels, too, of Holland

where is the summit where all aims are clear
the pin-point light upon a fear of lust
as agony's needlework grows up around the unicorn
and fences him for milk- and yoghurt-work
when I see Gianni I know he's thinking of John Ericson
playing the Rachmaninoff 2nd or Elizabeth Taylor
taking sleeping-pills and Jane thinks of Manderley
and Irkutsk while I cough lightly in the smog of desire
and my eyes water achingly imitating the true blue

a sight of Manahatta in the towering needle
multi-faceted insight of the fly in the stringless labyrinth
Canada plans a higher place than the Empire State Building
I am getting into a cab at 9th Street and 1st Avenue
and the Negro driver tells me about a $120 apartment
"where you can't walk across the floor after 10 at night
not even to pee, cause it keeps them awake downstairs"
no, I don't like that "well, I didn't take it"
perfect in the hot humid morning on my way to work
a little supper-club conversation for the mill of the gods

you were there always and you know all about these things
as indifferent as an encyclopedia with your calm brown eyes
it isn't enough to smile when you run the gauntlet
you've got to spit like Niagara Falls on everybody or
Victoria Falls or at least the beautiful urban fountains of Madrid
as the Niger joins the Gulf of Guinea near the Menemsha Bar
that is what you learn in the early morning passing Madison Avenue
where you've never spent any time and stores eat up light

I have always wanted to be near it
though the day is long (and I don't mean Madison Avenue)
lying in a hammock on St. Mark's Place sorting my poems
in the rancid nourishment of this mountainous island
they are coming and we holy ones must go
is Tibet historically a part of China? as I historically
belong to the enormous bliss of American death

SONG

Is it dirty
does it look dirty
that's what you think of in the city

does it just seem dirty
that's what you think of in the city
you don't refuse to breathe do you

someone comes along with a very bad character
he seems attractive. is he really. yes very
he's attractive as his character is bad. is it. yes

that's what you think of in the city
run your finger along your no-moss mind
that's not a thought that's soot

and you take a lot of dirt off someone
is the character less bad. no. it improves constantly
you don't refuse to breathe do you

AT JOAN'S

It is almost three
I sit at the marble top
sorting poems, miserable
the little lamp glows feebly
I don't glow at all

I have another cognac
and stare at two little paintings
of Jean-Paul's, so great
I must do so much
or did they just happen

the breeze is cool
barely a sound filters up
through my confused eyes

I am lonely for myself
I can't find a real poem

if it won't happen to me
what shall I do

ADIEU TO NORMAN,
BON JOUR TO JOAN AND JEAN-PAUL

It is 12:10 in New York and I am wondering
if I will finish this in time to meet Norman for lunch
ah lunch! I think I am going crazy
what with my terrible hangover and the weekend coming up
at excitement-prone Kenneth Koch's
I wish I were staying in town and working on my poems
at Joan's studio for a new book by Grove Press
which they will probably not print
but it is good to be several floors up in the dead of night
wondering whether you are any good or not
and the only decision you can make is that you did it

yesterday I looked up the rue Frémicourt on a map
and was happy to find it like a bird
flying over Paris et ses environs
which unfortunately did not include Seine-et-Oise which I don't know
as well as a number of other things
and Allen is back talking about god a lot
and Peter is back not talking very much
and Joe has a cold and is not coming to Kenneth's
although he is coming to lunch with Norman
I suspect he is making a distinction
well, who isn't

I wish I were reeling around Paris
instead of reeling around New York
I wish I weren't reeling at all
it is Spring the ice has melted the Ricard is being poured
we are all happy and young and toothless
it is the same as old age

the only thing to do is simply continue
is that simple
yes, it is simple because it is the only thing to do
can you do it
yes, you can because it is the only thing to do
blue light over the Bois de Boulogne it continues
the Seine continues
the Louvre stays open it continues it hardly closes at all
the Bar Américain continues to be French
de Gaulle continues to be Algerian as does Camus
Shirley Goldfarb continues to be Shirley Goldfarb
and Jane Hazan continues to be Jane Freilicher (I think!)
and Irving Sandler continues to be the balayeur des artistes
and so do I (sometimes I think I'm "in love" with painting)
and surely the Piscine Deligny continues to have water in it
and the Flore continues to have tables and newspapers and people under them
and surely we shall not continue to be unhappy
we shall be happy
but we shall continue to be ourselves everything continues to be possible
René Char, Pierre Reverdy, Samuel Beckett it is possible isn't it
I love Reverdy for saying yes, though I don't believe it

JOE'S JACKET

Entraining to Southampton in the parlor car with Jap and Vincent, I
see life as a penetrable landscape lit from above
like it was in my Barbizonian kiddy days when automobiles
were owned by the same people for years and the Alfa Romeo was
only a rumor under the leaves beside the viaduct and I
pretending to be adult felt the blue within me and the light up there
no central figure me, I was some sort of cloud or a gust of wind
at the station a crowd of drunken fishermen on a picnic Kenneth
is hard to find but we find, through all the singing, Kenneth smiling
it is off to Janice's bluefish and the incessant talk of affection
expressed as excitability and spleen to be recent and strong
and not unbearably right in attitude, full of confidences
now I will say it, thank god, I knew you would

an enormous party mesmerizing comers in the disgathering light
and dancing miniature-endless, like a pivot

I drink to smother my sensitivity for a while so I won't stare away
I drink to kill the fear of boredom, the mounting panic of it
I drink to reduce my seriousness so a certain spurious charm
can appear and win its flickering little victory over noise
I drink to die a little and increase the contrast of this questionable moment
and then I am going home, purged of everything except anxiety and self-distrust
now I will say it, thank god, I knew you would
and the rain has commenced its delicate lament over the orchards

an enormous window morning and the wind, the beautiful desperation of a tree
fighting off strangulation, and my bed has an ugly calm
I reach to the D. H. Lawrence on the floor and read "The Ship of Death"
I lie back again and begin slowly to drift and then to sink
a somnolent envy of inertia makes me rise naked and go to the window
where the car horn mysteriously starts to honk, no one is there
and Kenneth comes out and stops it in the soft green lightless stare
and we are soon in the Paris of Kenneth's libretto, I did not drift
away I did not die I am there with Haussmann and the rue de Rivoli
and the spirits of beauty, art and progress, pertinent and mobile
in their worldly way, and musical and strange the sun comes out

returning by car the forceful histories of myself and Vincent loom
like the city hour after hour closer and closer to the future I am here
and the night is heavy though not warm, Joe is still up and we talk
only of the immediate present and its indiscriminately hitched-to past
the feeling of life and incident pouring over the sleeping city
which seems to be bathed in an unobtrusive light which lends things
coherence and an absolute, for just that time as four o'clock goes by

and soon I am rising for the less than average day, I have coffee
I prepare calmly to face almost everything that will come up I am calm
but not as my bed was calm as it softly declined to become a ship
I borrow Joe's seersucker jacket though he is still asleep I start out
when I last borrowed it I was leaving there it was on my Spanish plaza back
and hid my shoulders from San Marco's pigeons was jostled on the Kurfürstendamm
and sat opposite Ashes in an enormous leather chair in the Continental
it is all enormity and life it has protected me and kept me here on
many occasions as a symbol does when the heart is full and risks no speech
a precaution I loathe as the pheasant loathes the season and is preserved
it will not be need, it will be just what it is and just what happens

Vaguely I hear the purple roar of the torn-down Third Avenue El
it sways slightly but firmly like a hand or a golden-downed thigh
normally I don't think of sounds as colored unless I'm feeling corrupt
concrete Rimbaud obscurity of emotion which is simple and very definite
even lasting, yes it may be that dark and purifying wave, the death of boredom
nearing the heights themselves may destroy you in the pure air
to be further complicated, confused, empty but refilling, exposed to light

With the past falling away as an acceleration of nerves thundering and shaking
aims its aggregating force like the Métro towards a realm of encircling travel
rending the sound of adventure and becoming ultimately local and intimate
repeating the phrases of an old romance which is constantly renewed by the
endless originality of human loss the air the stumbling quiet of breathing
newly the heavens' stars all out we are all for the captured time of our being

POEM

The fluorescent tubing burns like a bobby-soxer's ankles
the white paint the green leaves in an old champagne bottle
and the formica shelves going up in the office
and the formica desk-tops over the white floor
what kind of an office is this anyway
I am so nervous about my life the little of it I can get ahold of
so I call up Kenneth in Southampton and presto
he is leaning on the shelf in the kitchen three hours away
while Janice is drying her hair which has prevented her from hearing
my voice through the telephone company ear-blacker
why black a clean ear
Kenneth you are really the backbone of a tremendous poetry nervous system
which keeps sending messages along the wireless luxuriance
of distraught experiences and hysterical desires so to keep things humming
and have nothing go off the trackless tracks
and once more you have balanced me precariously
on the wilderness wish
of wanting to be everything to everybody everywhere

as the vigor of Africa through the corridor
the sands of Sahara still tickle in my jockey shorts
the air–conditioner grunts like that Eskimo dad
and the phone clicks as your glasses bump the receiver
to say we are in America and it is all right not to be elsewhere

SAINT

Like a pile of gold that his breath
is forming into slender columns
of various sizes, Vincent lies all
in a heap as even the sun must rest

and air and the noises of Manhattan
he thinks he is not a de Paul yet
the market is sagging today and he
doesn't mind, he is waiting for his sofa

to arrive from Toronto, that's what
he thinks and of whether Maxine
would like a pair of jet earrings
well she would, emotionally at least

and what other way is there to like
in the sea in the salt ease
he founders childlike and aggressive
until the tow draws him out

and scared he swims for it
parting the breakers with strokes
like a rapist pushing through
stormy wheat and he is safe and serious

on the sand like his hair
so night comes down upon
the familial anxieties of Vincent
he sleeps like a temple to no god

"L'AMOUR AVAIT PASSÉ PAR LÀ"

Yes
like the still center of a book on Joan Miró
blue red green and white
a slightly over-gold edition of Hart Crane
and the huge mirror behind me blinking, paint-flecked
they have painted the ceiling of my heart
and put in a new light fixture
and Arte Contemporáneo by Juan Eduardo Cirlot
and the Petit Guide to the Musée National Russe
it is all blankly defending its privacy
from the sighing wind in the ceiling
of the old Theatre Guild building
on West 53rd Street
near the broken promises of casualness
to get to the Cedar to meet Grace
I must tighten my moccasins
and forget the minute bibliographies of disappointment
anguish and power
for unrelaxed honesty
this laissez-passer for chance and misery, but taut
a candle held to the window has two flames
and perhaps a horde of followers in the rain of youth
as under the arch you find a heart of lipstick or a condom
left by the parade
of a generalized intuition
it is the great period of Italian art when everyone imitates Picasso
afraid to mean anything
as the second flame in its happy reflecting ignores the candle and the wind

POEM

Hate is only one of many responses
true, hurt and hate go hand in hand
but why be afraid of hate, it is only there

think of filth, is it really awesome
neither is hate
don't be shy of unkindness, either
it's cleansing and allows you to be direct
like an arrow that feels something

out and out meanness, too, lets love breathe
you don't have to fight off getting in too deep
you can always get out if you're not too scared

an ounce of prevention's
enough to poison the heart
don't think of others
until you have thought of yourself, are true

all of these things, if you feel them
will be graced by a certain reluctance
and turn into gold

if felt by me, will be smilingly deflected
by your mysterious concern

POEM

I don't know as I get what D. H. Lawrence is driving at
when he writes of lust springing from the bowels
or do I
it could be the bowels of the earth
to lie flat on the earth in spring, summer or winter is sexy
you feel it stirring deep down slowly up to you
and sometimes it gives you a little nudge in the crotch
that's very sexy
and when someone looks sort of raggedy and dirty like Paulette Goddard
in *Modern Times* it's exciting, it isn't usual or attractive
perhaps D.H.L. is thinking of the darkness
certainly the crotch is light
and I suppose
any part of us that can only be seen by others
is a dark part
I feel that about the small of my back, too and the nape of my neck
they are dark

they are erotic zones as in the tropics
whereas Paris is straightforward and bright about it all
a coal miner has kind of a sexy occupation
though I'm sure it's painful down there
but so is lust
of light we can never have enough
but how would we find it
unless the darkness urged us on and into it
and I am dark
except when now and then it all comes clear
and I can see myself
as others luckily sometimes see me
in a good light

PERSONAL POEM

Now when I walk around at lunchtime
I have only two charms in my pocket
an old Roman coin Mike Kanemitsu gave me
and a bolt-head that broke off a packing case
when I was in Madrid the others never
brought me too much luck though they did
help keep me in New York against coercion
but now I'm happy for a time and interested

I walk through the luminous humidity
passing the House of Seagram with its wet
and its loungers and the construction to
the left that closed the sidewalk if
I ever get to be a construction worker
I'd like to have a silver hat please
and get to Moriarty's where I wait for
LeRoi and hear who wants to be a mover and
shaker the last five years my batting average
is .016 that's that, and LeRoi comes in
and tells me Miles Davis was clubbed 12
times last night outside BIRDLAND by a cop
a lady asks us for a nickel for a terrible
disease but we don't give her one we
don't like terrible diseases, then

we go eat some fish and some ale it's
cool but crowded we don't like Lionel Trilling
we decide, we like Don Allen we don't like
Henry James so much we like Herman Melville
we don't want to be in the poets' walk in
San Francisco even we just want to be rich
and walk on girders in our silver hats
I wonder if one person out of the 8,000,000 is
thinking of me as I shake hands with LeRoi
and buy a strap for my wristwatch and go
back to work happy at the thought possibly so

POST THE LAKE POETS BALLAD

Moving slowly sweating a lot
I am pushed by a gentle breeze
outside the Paradise Bar on
          St. Mark's Place and I breathe

and bourbon with Joe he says
did you see a letter from Larry
in the mailbox what a shame I didn't
          I wonder what it says

and then we eat and go to
The Horse Riders and my bum aches
from the hard seats and boredom
          is hard too we don't go

to the Cedar it's so hot out
and I read the letter which says
in your poems your gorgeous self-pity
          how do you like that

that is odd I think of myself
as a cheerful type who pretends to
be hurt to get a little depth into
          things that interest me

and I've even given that up
lately with the stream of events

going so fast and the movingly
    alternating with the amusingly

the depth all in the ocean
although I'm different in the winter
of course even this is a complaint
    but I'm happy anyhow

no more self-pity than Gertrude
Stein before Lucey Church or Savonarola
in the pulpit Allen Ginsberg at the
    Soviet Exposition am I Joe

NAPHTHA

Ah Jean Dubuffet
when you think of him
doing his military service in the Eiffel Tower
as a meteorologist
in 1922
you know how wonderful the 20th Century
can be
and the gaited Iroquois on the girders
fierce and unflinching-footed
nude as they should be
slightly empty
like a Sonia Delaunay
there is a parable of speed
somewhere behind the Indians' eyes
they invented the century with their horses
and their fragile backs
which are dark

we owe a debt to the Iroquois
and to Duke Ellington
for playing in the buildings when they are built
we don't do much ourselves
but fuck and think
of the haunting Métro
and the one who didn't show up there

while we were waiting to become part of our century
just as you can't make a hat out of steel
and still wear it
who wears hats anyway
it is our tribe's custom
to beguile

how are you feeling in ancient September
I am feeling like a truck on a wet highway
how can you
you were made in the image of god
I was not
I was made in the image of a sissy truck–driver
and Jean Dubuffet painting his cows
"with a likeness burst in the memory"
apart from love (don't say it)
I am ashamed of my century
for being so entertaining
but I have to smile

SEPTEMBER 14, 1959 (MOON)

Serenity lopes along like exhaustion
only windier and silver-eyed
where fragments of distress in hunks
lay like the plaster in the bedroom
when the bed fell down, greenly
murmuring a phrase from the Jacksonville
Chamber of Commerce of the Pacific
yes no, yes no, yes, yes, yes

an agate breeze pours through the gate
of reddish hair there is a summer
of silence and inquiry waiting there
it is full of wildness and tension
like a *gare,* the warmly running trains
of the South escape to sweet brooks
and grassy roadbeds underneath the
thankful and enlightening Russian moon

VARIATIONS ON PASTERNAK'S
"MEIN LIEBCHEN, WAS WILLST DU NOCH MEHR?"

Walls, except that they stretch through China
like a Way, are melancholy fingers in the snow
of years
            time moves, but is not moving in its strange grimace
the captive fights the distances within a flower of wire
and seldom wins a look from the dull tin receptacle he decorates

      not that anything is really there
the country is the city without houses, the city
merely a kissed country, a hamster of choices
whether you own forty cats or just three snakes you're rich
as you appear, miraculous appearance, I had forgotten
that things could be beautiful in the 20th Century under the moon

the drabness of life peels away like an old recording by Lotte Lenya
it is not lucky to be German and you know it, though doom has held off
      perhaps it is waiting like a smile in the sky
      but no, it's the moon drifting and trudging
         and the clouds are imitating Diana Adams

                              now the rain comes
and your face, like a child's soul, is parting its lids
      pouring down the brown plaster faces over doors and windows
over the casual elegancies of the last century and the poor
      over the lintels and the sniffs and the occasional hay fever
      to where nothing
                              appears to be watering the city trees
                              though they live, live on, as we do

what do you think has happened
that you have pushed the wall and
                              stopped thinking of Bunny
      you have let death go, you have stopped
      you are not serene, you desire something, you are not ending
it is not that the world expects the people, but it does
the brassiness of weeds becomes sculptural and bridal
everything wants to be you and wisdom is unacceptable
      in the leaden world of fringes and distrust and duty

I have discovered that beneath the albatross there is a goose
      smiling
         a centenarian goes down the street and sees
      George Balanchine, that makes the day for him
just as the sight of you, no wall, no moon, no world, makes
                              everything day to me

Khrushchev is coming on the right day!
                                        the cool graced light
is pushed off the enormous glass piers by hard wind
and everything is tossing, hurrying on up
                            this country
has everything but *politesse,* a Puerto Rican cab driver says
and five different girls I see
                        look like Piedie Gimbel
with her blonde hair tossing too,
                                as she looked when I pushed
her little daughter on the swing on the lawn it was also windy

last night we went to a movie and came out,
                                    Ionesco is greater
than Beckett, Vincent said, that's what I think, blueberry blintzes
and Khrushchev was probably being carped at
                                    in Washington, no *politesse*
Vincent tells me about his mother's trip to Sweden
                                        Hans tells us
about his father's life in Sweden, it sounds like Grace Hartigan's
painting *Sweden*
                so I go home to bed and names drift through my head
Purgatorio Merchado, Gerhard Schwartz and Gaspar Gonzales, all
        unknown figures of the early morning as I go to work

where does the evil of the year go
                                when September takes New York
and turns it into ozone stalagmites
                                deposits of light
                        so I get back up
make coffee, and read François Villon, his life, so dark
    New York seems blinding and my tie is blowing up the street
I wish it would blow off
                        though it is cold and somewhat warms my neck
as the train bears Khrushchev on to Pennsylvania Station
    and the light seems to be eternal
    and joy seems to be inexorable
    I am foolish enough always to find it in wind

GETTING UP AHEAD OF SOMEONE (SUN)

I cough a lot (sinus?) so I
get up and have some tea with cognac
it is dawn
                    the light flows evenly along the lawn
in chilly Southampton and I smoke
and hours and hours go by I read
van Vechten's *Spider Boy* then a short
story by Patsy Southgate and a poem
by myself it is cold and I shiver a little
in white shorts the day begun
so oddly not tired not nervous I
am for once truly awake letting it all
start slowly as I watch instead of
grabbing on late as usual
                              where did it go
                              it's not really awake yet
                              I will wait

and the house wakes up and goes
to get the dog in Sag Harbor I make
myself a bourbon and commence
to write one of my "I do this I do that"
poems in a sketch pad
                         it is tomorrow
though only six hours have gone by
each day's light has more significance these days

IN FAVOR OF ONE'S TIME

The spent purpose of a perfectly marvellous
life suddenly glimmers and leaps into flame
it's more difficult than you think to make charcoal
it's also pretty hard to remember life's marvellous
but there it is guttering choking then soaring
in the mirrored room of this consciousness
it's practically a blaze of pure sensibility

and however exaggerated at least something's going on
and the quick oxygen in the air will not go neglected
will not sulk or fall into blackness and peat

an angel flying slowly, curiously singes its wings
and you diminish for a moment out of respect
for beauty then flare up after all that's the angel
that wrestled with Jacob and loves conflict
as an athlete loves the tape, and we're off into
an immortal contest of actuality and pride
which is love assuming the consciousness of itself
as sky over all, medium of finding and founding
not just resemblance but the magnetic otherness
that that that stands erect in the spirit's glare
and waits for the joining of an opposite force's breath

so come the winds into our lives and last
longer than despair's sharp snake, crushed before it conquered
so marvellous is not just a poet's greenish namesake
and we live outside his garden in our tempestuous rights

TO YOU

What is more beautiful than night
and someone in your arms
that's what we love about art
it seems to prefer us and stays

if the moon or a gasping candle
sheds a little light or even dark
you become a landscape in a landscape
with rocks and craggy mountains

and valleys full of sweaty ferns
breathing and lifting into the clouds
which have actually come low
as a blanket of aspirations' blue

for once not a melancholy color
because it is looking back at us

there's no need for vistas we are one
in the complicated foreground of space

the architects are most courageous
because it stands for all to see
and for a long long time just as
the words "I'll always love you"

impulsively appear in the dark sky
and we are happy and stick by them
like a couple of painters in neon allowing
the light to glow there over the river

LES LUTHS

Ah nuts! It's boring reading French newspapers
in New York as if I were a Colonial waiting for my gin
somewhere beyond this roof a jet is making a sketch of the sky
where is Gary Snyder I wonder if he's reading under a dwarf pine
stretched out so his book and his head fit under the lowest branch
while the sun of the Orient rolls calmly not getting through to him
not caring particularly because the light in Japan respects poets

while in Paris Monsieur Martory and his brother Jean the poet
are reading a piece by Matthieu Galey and preparing to send a *pneu*
everybody here is running around after dull pleasantries and
wondering if *The Hotel Wentley Poems* is as great as I say it is
and I am feeling particularly testy at being separated from
the one I love by the most dreary of practical exigencies money
when I want only to lean on my elbow and stare into space feeling
the one warm beautiful thing in the world breathing upon my right rib

what are lutes they make ugly twangs and rest on knees in cafés
I want to hear only your light voice running on about Florida
as we pass the changing traffic light and buy grapes for wherever
we will end up praising the mattressless sleigh-bed and the
Mexican egg and the clock that will not make me know
        how to leave you

LEAFING THROUGH FLORIDA

It is sad and unimaginable that I can be
happy outside Fla. and it is just as sad
that you can and I hope you are but how
lovely it was under the low moon crooning
about hurricanes and cane chairs and *Ulysses*
and sand bags and wet washing and magnolias

for a moment on Cabaña Street I thought
I'd had a vision of true happiness but it
was to wait for the war to be over and grow
like a vine around the new melancholy
of luxurious Mahler with the sun shining
through a Chinese resignation about death

not to be morbid to be beautiful at everything
you do is a rather special gift he got from
Austria and you were given by Florida in '38

DANCES BEFORE THE WALL

My love is like a strong white foot
on a board that gives little gasps of dust
as the lights go up flicker and die down
a monotonous revery of space is growing
like an early Greek statue I forget how B.C.

suddenly everybody gets excited and starts
running around the Henry St. Playhouse which is
odd I don't care whose foot it is and Midi
Garth goes tearing down the aisle towards Fred
Herko while Sybil Shearer swoons in the balcony
which is like a box when she's in it and Paul
Taylor tells Bob Rauschenberg it's on fire
and Bob Rauschenberg says what's on fire and

by that time it is all over but the plangent
memory of a rainy evening in lower Manhattan
the people file into their smoke-filled slickers
and Doris Hering says Doris Hering was here
we go to Edwin Denby's and quietly talk all night

POEM

Now it is the 27th
of this month
which would have been my birthday
if I'd been born in it
but I wasn't
would have made me a
Scorpion
which symbolizes silver, money, riches
firm in aim, coldblooded in action
loving the Bull
smelling of sandalwood
I do anyway

instead of
Cancer
which symbolizes instability, suggestibility, sensibility
all the ilities like a clavichord
only an interior firmness
favoring good and evil alike
loving Capricorn
with its solitudinous research

but how could I love other
than the worldly Virgin
my force is in mobility it's said
I move
towards you
born in the sign which I should only like
with love

POEM

to Donald M. Allen

Now the violets are all gone, the rhinoceroses, the cymbals
a grisly pale has settled over the stockyard where the fur flies
and the sound
                    is that of a bulldozer in heat stuck in the mud
where a lilac still scrawnily blooms and cries out "Walt!"
so they repair the street in the middle of the night
and Allen and Peter can once again walk forth to visit friends
in the illuminated moonlight over the mists and the towers
having mistakenly thought that Bebe Daniels was in *I Cover the Waterfront*
instead of Claudette Colbert it has begun to rain softly and I walk
slowly thinking of becoming a stalk of asparagus for Hallowe'en
      which idea Vincent poopoos as not being really 40s
so the weight
                of the rain drifting amiably is like a sentimental breeze
and seems to have been invented by a collapsed Kim Novak balloon

yet Janice is helping Kenneth appeal to The Ford Foundation in
her manner oft described as The Sweet Succinct and Ned is glad
      not to be up too late
                              for the sake of his music and his ear
          where discipline finds itself singing and even screaming away

I shall not dine another night like this with Robin and Don and Joe
as lightly as the day is gone but that was earlier
                                a knock on the door
my heart your heart

      my head and the strange reality of our flesh in the rain
so many parts of a strange existence independent but not searching in the night
                    nor in the morning when the rain has stopped

      POEM V (F) W

      I don't know if you doubt it
      but I think you do
      I am independent of the Cabaret Voltaire

the Café Grinzing the Black Cat
the anubis
two parallel lines always meet
except mentally
which brings on their quarrels
and if I sit down I admit
it is not at a table
underneath elms
to read

you were walking down a street softened by rain
and your footsteps were quiet
and I came around the corner
inside the room
to close the window
and thought what a beautiful person
and it was you
no I was coming out the door
and you looked sad
which you later said was tired
and I was glad
you had wanted to see me
and we went forward
back to my room
to be alone in your mysterious look

among the relics of postwar hysterical pleasures
I see my vices
lying like abandoned works of art
which I created so eagerly
to be worldly and modern
and with it
what I can't remember
I see them with your eyes

CROW HILL

I put down *Firecrackers*
and take up *Hymns to St. Geryon*
thinking evil of Herakles

I put down the hymns
and take up *Firecrackers* again
I finish *Hymns to St. Geryon*
with its three bodies and its wings
and finish *Firecrackers* and sleep

the stilted houses all dark
rise over the hill of Worcester, Massachusetts
and the highway pours by its feet
in alleys I furtively make my way
with a truncheon and a small knife
the only other member of my gang alive
is Joe and he follows with a chain
we reach aware of being trailed
the abandoned settlement house
and hide there knowing we are known
through a chink in the wall the leader
of the rival gang whispers
that I will die tonight
but Joe will wait till tomorrow
so I send him down Bedford Street
and up Crow Hill where he can see what
he will be up against at dawn
and possibly escape into the sky
and I wait with the chains the knife
a belt and a big stack of pipes
there because we expected trouble
as I expect to die they are closing in

I wake up terrified and think
how much fun it would be to write a pornographic novel
immediately a cosmic man and woman are 69ing in the sky
he raises his head and says my mouth
is just the right distance from my nose to bring this off
she presses her nipples to his inner hips
and avoids being suffocated by his squeezing thighs
through a surging willessness like the air above Crow Hill

POEM

"À la recherche d' Gertrude Stein"

When I am feeling depressed and anxious sullen
all you have to do is take your clothes off
and all is wiped away revealing life's tenderness
that we are flesh and breathe and are near us
as you are really as you are I become as I
really am alive and knowing vaguely what is
and what is important to me above the intrusions
of incident and accidental relationships
which have nothing to do with my life

when I am in your presence I feel life is strong
and will defeat all its enemies and all of mine
and all of yours and yours in you and mine in me
sick logic and feeble reasoning are cured
by the perfect symmetry of your arms and legs
spread out making an eternal circle together
creating a golden pillar beside the Atlantic
the faint line of hair dividing your torso
gives my mind rest and emotions their release
into the infinite air where since once we are
together we always will be in this life come what may

VARIATIONS ON THE "TREE OF HEAVEN"

(In the Janis Gallery)

Sitting in a corner of the gallery
I notice that Albers scratches a tiny A
in the lower right corner with the date
and the paintings are like floodlights
on my emptiness
that I am out of context waiting
for the place where my life exists like a tree
in a meadow
the warm traffic going by is my natural scenery
because I am not alone there
as the sky above the top floor of a tenement
is nearer

which is what the ancients meant by heaven
to be with someone
not just waiting wherever you are

POEM

Light   clarity   avocado salad in the morning
after all the terrible things I do how amazing it is
to find forgiveness and love, not even forgiveness
since what is done is done and forgiveness isn't love
and love is love nothing can ever go wrong
though things can get irritating boring and dispensable
(in the imagination) but not really for love
though a block away you feel distant the mere presence
changes everything like a chemical dropped on a paper
and all thoughts disappear in a strange quiet excitement
I am sure of nothing but this, intensified by breathing

HÔTEL TRANSYLVANIE

Shall we win at love or shall we lose
                                        can it be
that hurting and being hurt is a trick forcing the love
we want to appear, that the hurt is a card
and is it black? is it red? is it a paper, dry of tears
chevalier, change your expression! the wind is sweeping over
the gaming tables ruffling the cards/they are black and red
like a Futurist torture and how do you know it isn't always there
waiting while doubt is the father that has you kidnapped by friends

        yet you will always live in a jealous society of accident
you will never know how beautiful you are or how beautiful
the other is, you will continue to refuse to die for yourself

you will continue to sing on trying to cheer everyone up
and they will know as they listen with excessive pleasure that you're dead
        and they will not mind that they have let you entertain
at the expense of the only thing you want in the world/you are amusing
as a game is amusing when someone is forced to lose as in a game I must

                oh *hôtel,* you should be merely a bed
surrounded by walls where two souls meet and do nothing but breathe
breathe in breathe out fuse illuminate confuse *stick* dissemble
but not as cheaters at cards have something to win/you have only to be
as you are being, as you must be, as you always are, as you shall be forever
no matter what fate deals you or the imagination discards like a tyrant
as the drums descend and summon the hatchet over the tinselled realities

you know that I am not here to fool around, that I must win or die
I expect you to do everything because it is of no consequence/no duel
you must rig the deck you must make me win at whatever cost to the reputation
of the establishment/sublime moment of dishonest hope/I must win
for if the floods of tears arrive they will wash it all away
                                        and then
you will know what it is to want something, but you may not be allowed
to die as I have died, you may only be allowed to drift downstream
to another body of inimical attractions for which you will substitute/distrust
and I will have had my revenge on the black bitch of my nature which you
                love as I have never loved myself

but I hold on/I am lyrical to a fault/I do not despair being too foolish
where will you find me, projective verse, since I will be gone?
for six seconds of your beautiful face I will sell the hotel and commit
an uninteresting suicide in Louisiana where it will take them a long time
to know who I am/why I came there/what and why I am and made to happen

POEM

        Wouldn't it be funny
        if The Finger had designed us
        to shit just once a week?

                all week long we'd get fatter
                and fatter and then on Sunday morning
                while everyone's in church
                                ploop!

POEM

So many echoes in my head
that when I am frantic to do something
about anything, out comes "you were wearing . . ."
or I knock my head against a wall
of my own appetite for despair and come
up with "you once ran naked toward me/Knee
deep in cold March surf" or I blame it
on Blake, on Robert Aldrich's *Kiss Me,
Deadly,* on the "latitude" of the stars

but where in all this noise
am I waiting for the clouds to be blown
away away away away away into the sun
(burp), I wouldn't want the clouds to be
burped back by that hot optimistic cliché, it
hangs always promising some nebulous
healthy reaction to our native dark

I will let the sun wait till summer
now that our love has moved into the dark
area symbolizing depth and secrecy and mystery
it's not bad, we shall find out
when the light returns what the new
season means/when others' interpretations
have gotten back up onto the pedestals
we gave them
                    so long as we are still
wearing each other when alone

PRESENT

The stranded gulch
                    below Grand Central
the gentle purr of cab tires in snow
and hidden stars
                    tears on the windshield

torn inexorably away in whining motion
and the dark thoughts which surround neon

in Union Square I see you for a moment
red green yellow searchlights cutting through
falling flakes, head bent to the wind
wet and frowning, melancholy, trying

I know perfectly well where you walk to
and that we'll meet in even greater darkness
later and will be warm
                        so our cross
of paths will not be just muddy footprints
in the morning
                        not like celestial bodies'
yearly passes, nothing pushes us away
from each other
                        even now I can lean
forward across the square and see
your surprised grey look become greener
as I wipe the city's moisture from
your face
                and you shake the snow
off onto my shoulder, light as a breath
where the quarrels and vices of
estranged companions weighed so bitterly
and accidentally
                        before, I saw you on
the floor of my life walking slowly
that time in summer rain stranger and
nearer
                to become a way of feeling
that is not painful casual or diffuse
and seems to explore some peculiar insight
of the heavens for its favorite bodies
in the mixed-up air

POEM

That's not a cross look it's a sign of life
but I'm glad you care how I look at you
this morning (after I got up) I was thinking

of President Warren G. Harding and Horace S.
Warren, father of the little blonde girl
across the street and another blonde Agnes
Hedlund (this was in the 6th grade!)   what

now the day has begun in a soft grey way
with elephantine traffic trudging along Fifth
and two packages of Camels in my pocket
I can't think of one interesting thing Warren
G. Harding did, I guess I was passing notes
to Sally and Agnes at the time he came up
in our elephantine history course everything

seems slow suddenly and boring except
for my insatiable thinking towards you
as you lie asleep completely plotzed and
gracious as a hillock in the mist from one
small window, sunless and only slightly open
as is your mouth and presently your quiet eyes
your breathing is like that history lesson

SUDDEN SNOW

While a company of dancers hoots whistles stomps
                                        carries on
in front of a palatial TV set with crystalline cobalt goblets surmounting it
        about Rita Hayworth, Bette Davis, Jack Cole, Busby Berkeley, Marc Platt

snow is falling on the sidewalk
                                and two girls arrive who'd fallen
                on their asses in the street-ice, crossing First
                                                        it is
                        the first sign of reality at night, snow

                avenues are made for crossing
                the fur-bearers often do slip
                just as your cheeks have a little darker
                down on the cheekbones under lashes
                and the more tired the more cheerful
                so long as among friends' quips

tenderness and interest continues to falter
not brazen like a pompadour-bomb 40s

there is a window giving on the bedroom
in it a tall dark figure
sits like Asta Nielsen in *Hamlet,* a girl lies
on a pink pillow on the floor giggling about an Equity meeting
all of *us* understand why Lucille Ball is such a success
for a moment I realize how happy I am to be beside you on the floor
and my heart nearly bursts
so to avoid embarrassment I make a vile remark about sweet Janet Blair
and you look kind of cross, no
you are proud of my mean tongue
and the snow like Charles Olson working on one of his ABC poems
is quietly and bitterly falling
but we don't know that yet, you drink more tea
your arm feels a little bit thinner

this morning two ladies from Jehovah's Witnesses came to call
on me in my dungarees, explaining their 3,750,000 copies printed
in Cinyanja, Cishona, English, Ilocano, Tagalog and Twi, Marathi,
Pangasinan, Papiamento, Silozi, Xhosa, Zulu and Finnish
so all day I think of the terrible limitations of poetic style "as we
know it"
till you take me to the movies which reach everywhere
and remind me that you understand me better than I understand you
and I am happy
yes, it's time to go

love is like the path in snow we are making
though no one else can follow, leading us only
to the ocean's sure embrace of summer, serious and free
as you tell me you've got to have eggs for breakfast
and we divert our course a little without fear

AVENUE A

We hardly ever see the moon any more
so no wonder
it's so beautiful when we look up suddenly

and there it is gliding broken–faced over the bridges
brilliantly coursing, soft, and a cool wind fans
          your hair over your forehead and your memories
               of Red Grooms' locomotive landscape
I want some bourbon/you want some oranges/I love the leather
               jacket Norman gave me
                                   and the corduroy coat David
     gave you, it is more mysterious than spring, the El Greco
heavens breaking open and then reassembling like lions
                              in a vast tragic veldt
     that is far from our small selves and our temporally united
passions in the cathedral of Januaries

     everything is too comprehensible
these are my delicate and caressing poems
I suppose there will be more of those others to come, as in the past
                         so many!
but for now the moon is revealing itself like a pearl
                         to my equally naked heart

NOW THAT I AM IN MADRID AND CAN THINK

I think of you
and the continents brilliant and arid
and the slender heart you are sharing my share of with the American air
as the lungs I have felt sonorously subside slowly greet each morning
and your brown lashes flutter revealing two perfect dawns colored by New York

see a vast bridge stretching to the humbled outskirts with only you
               standing on the edge of the purple like an only tree

and in Toledo the olive groves' soft blue look at the hills with silver
               like glasses like an old lady's hair
it's well known that God and I don't get along together
it's just a view of the brass works to me, I don't care about the Moors
seen through you the great works of death, you are greater

you are smiling, you are emptying the world so we can be alone

DÉRANGÉ SUR UN PONT DE L'ADOUR

Where is John with the baggage checks anyway
and why is all this mud pouring out of beautiful Bayonne
it is April 12th and I am still a fool
northern lights are falling into the Hôtel Farnié

A LITTLE TRAVEL DIARY

Wending our way through the gambas, angulas,
the merluzas that taste like the Sea Post on Sunday
and the great quantities of huevos they take off
Spanish Naval officers' uniforms and put on plates,
and reach the gare de Francia in the gloaming
with my ton of books and John's ton of clothes bought
in a wild fit of enthusiasm in Madrid; all jumbled
together like life is a Jumble Shop

                              of the theatre
in Spain they said nothing for foreigners
and we head in our lovely 1st class coach, shifting
and sagging, towards the northwest, while in other compartments
Dietrich and Erich von Stroheim share a sandwich of chorizos
and a bottle of Vichy Catalan, in the dining car
the travelling gentleman with linear mustache and many
many rings rolls his cigar around and drinks Martini y
ginebra, and Lillian Gish rolls on over the gorges
with a tear in her left front eye, comme Picasso,
through the night through the night, longitudinous
and affected with stars; the riverbeds so far below look
as a pig's tongue on a platter, and storms break over
San Sebastian, 40 foot waves drench us pleasantly and we see
a dead dog bloated as a fraise lolling beside the quai
and slowly pulling out to sea

                              to Irún and Biarritz
we go, sapped of anxiety, and there for the first time
since arriving in Barcelona I can freely shit

and the surf is so high and the sun is so hot
and it was all built yesterday as everything should be
what a splendid country it is
                                full of indecision and cognac
and bikinis, sens plastiques (ugh! hooray!); see the back
of the head of Bill Berkson, aux Deux Magots, (awk!) it gleams
like the moon through the smoke of the Renfe as we passed
through the endless tunnels and the silver vistas
of our quest for the rocher de la Vierge and salt spray

BEER FOR BREAKFAST

It's the month of May in my heart as the song
says and everything's perfect: a little too chilly
for April and the chestnut trees are refusing to bloom
as they should refuse if they don't want to, sky
clear and blue with a lot of side-paddle steamers
pushing through to Stockholm where the canals're true-blue

in my spacious quarters on the rue de l'Université
I give a cocktail in the bathroom, everyone gets wet
it's very beachy; and I clear my head staring at the sign
LOI DU 29 JUILLET 1881
                                so capitalizing on a few memories
from childhood by forgetting them, I'm happy as a finger
of Vermouth being poured over a slice of veal, it's
the new reality in the city of Balzac! praying to be let
into the cinema and become an influence, carried through
streets on the shoulders of Messrs Chabrol and Truffaut
towards Nice
                or do you think that the Golden Lion
would taste pleasanter (not with vermouth, lion!) ?
no, but San Francisco, maybe, and abalone

                                                there is
nothing in the world I wouldn't do foryouforyou (zip!)
and I go off to meet Mario and Marc at the Flore

HÔTEL PARTICULIER

How exciting it is
                    not to be at Port Lligat
or learning Portuguese in Bilbao so you can go to Brazil

Erik Satie made a great mistake learning Latin
the Brise Marine wasn't written in Sanskrit, baby

I had a teacher one whole summer who never told me anything
                                and it was wonderful

and then there is the Bibliothèque Nationale, cuspidors,
glasses, anxiety
                    you don't get crabs that way,
and what you don't know will hurt somebody else

how clear the air is, how low the moon, how flat the sun,
et cetera,
              just so you don't coin a phrase that changes
can be "rung" on
                    like les neiges d'antan
and that sort of thing (oops!), (roll me over)!

is this the hostel where the lazy and fun-loving
                      start up the mountain?

EMBARRASSING BILL

Bill is sounding so funny there in the bathtub like a walrus
he is very talkative and smelling like a new rug in a store window
how pleasant it is to think of Bill in there, half-submerged, listening
and when he comes to the door to get some more cologne he is just like a pane of glass
in a modernistic church, sort of elevated and lofty and substantial
well, if that isn't your idea of god, what is?
in these times one is very lucky to get a bath at all, much less
have someone cheerful come over and help themselves to one in your tub

I like to have all the rooms full and I just hope that Bill will get bigger
and bigger and bigger and pretty soon I'll have to get a whole house
or I could always find a pedestal with central heating perhaps
in case he wants to write his poems standing up

now, Bill, use your own towel

HAVING A COKE WITH YOU

is even more fun than going to San Sebastian, Irún, Hendaye, Biarritz, Bayonne
or being sick to my stomach on the Travesera de Gracia in Barcelona
partly because in your orange shirt you look like a better happier St. Sebastian
partly because of my love for you, partly because of your love for yoghurt
partly because of the fluorescent orange tulips around the birches
partly because of the secrecy our smiles take on before people and statuary
it is hard to believe when I'm with you that there can be anything as still
as solemn as unpleasantly definitive as statuary when right in front of it
in the warm New York 4 o'clock light we are drifting back and forth
between each other like a tree breathing through its spectacles

and the portrait show seems to have no faces in it at all, just paint
you suddenly wonder why in the world anyone ever did them
                                                                I look
at you and I would rather look at you than all the portraits in the world
except possibly for the *Polish Rider* occasionally and anyway it's in the Frick
which thank heavens you haven't gone to yet so we can go together the first time
and the fact that you move so beautifully more or less takes care of Futurism
just as at home I never think of the *Nude Descending a Staircase* or
at a rehearsal a single drawing of Leonardo or Michelangelo that used to wow me
and what good does all the research of the Impressionists do them
when they never got the right person to stand near the tree when the sun sank
or for that matter Marino Marini when he didn't pick the rider as carefully
as the horse
                it seems they were all cheated of some marvellous experience
which is not going to go wasted on me which is why I'm telling you about it

SONG

I am stuck in traffic in a taxicab
which is typical
and not just of modern life

mud clambers up the trellis of my nerves
must lovers of Eros end up with Venus
muss es sein? es muss nicht sein, I tell you

how I hate disease, it's like worrying
that comes true
and it simply must not be able to happen

in a world where you are possible
my love
nothing can go wrong for us, tell me

AN AIRPLANE WHISTLE (AFTER HEINE)

The rose, the lily and the dove got withered
in your sunlight or in the soot, maybe, of New York
and ceased to be lovable as odd sounds are lovable
say blowing on a little airplane's slot
which is the color of the back of your knee
a particular sound, fine, light and slightly hoarse

TRYING TO FIGURE OUT WHAT YOU FEEL

I   AFTER STEFAN GEORGE
Only your keen ear
notes what sings deep inside

what so subtly stays afloat
what's already half lost

Only your strong voice
finds the sound of fate there
in what we are losing
hears it as truth and peace

Only your warm soul
can speak so lightly of regret
of one evening taking away
what days had showered on us

2   POEM

At each start, at each sinister moment of light
I feel sand in my crotch, blood flowing out of my skin, thunder
                    in ears
                              where are you where am I
                              where is the night

3   AFTER RENÉ CHAR

All lives fade in the fog
like the cat that gets fucked
purple and white and invisible
aristocrats of love aren't they
yes, and the precious time
slips into the river widening
the flood of death which seems
like a voyage to those who have always
longed for the wide open spaces
of silence and the wonderful
workmanship of the simple cross

4   POEM

House of love house of death
accept this shit as angel
as we do on earth bind up
the light so no one can see
and seeing cling to falsity
be careful that our fate's
identical with our end

5   AFTER TRISTAN CORBIÈRE

Do you really think the earth
produced the stars that you
wove these feelings in me
like a rope
              where do you think

the crystal came from and the
hammering neck
                              a lot of sweat
went into the invention of lipstick
but it was Egyptian not American

and as for the tire I never
'even liked the wheel
                              it is not
cosy being in love with you
and we are not together

GLAZUNOVIANA, OR MEMORIAL DAY

I see a life of civil happiness
where the leaves whirl into blossoms
and everything is tingling and icy as a smile
and Maria Tallchief returns to the City Center
in a full-length *The Seasons*
as the true spirit of our times
escaping from my heart the vision
hovers in the air like a cyclone over sordid Kansas
as her breathing limbs tear ugliness out of our lives
and cast it into the air like snowflakes
just as Boston once looked ravishing and ravished
when in the distance through the trees
she rose dawning and tender from her shell
as Sylvia with the Public Gardens in her arms

ODE TO TANAQUIL LECLERCQ

Smiling through my own memories of painful excitement your wide eyes
stare
        and narrow like a lost forest of childhood stolen from gypsies

two eyes that are the sunset of
$\qquad$ two knees
$\qquad$ two wrists
$\qquad$ two minds
and the extended philosophical column, when they conducted the dialogues
$\qquad$ in distant Athens, rests on your two ribbon-wrapped hearts, white
$\qquad$ credibly agile
$\qquad$ flashing
$\qquad$ scimitars of a city-state

where in the innocence of my watching had those ribbons become entangled
$\qquad$ dragging me upward into lilac-colored ozone where I gasped
$\qquad$ and you continued to smile as you dropped the bloody scarf of my life
$\qquad$ from way up there, my neck hurt

$\qquad$ you were always changing into something else
$\qquad$ and always will be
$\qquad$ always plumage, perfection's broken heart, wings

$\qquad$ and wide eyes in which everything you do
$\qquad$ repeats yourself simultaneously and simply
$\qquad$ as a window "gives" on something

it seems sometimes as if you were only breathing
$\qquad$ and everything happened around you
because when you disappeared in the wings nothing was there
$\qquad$ but the motion of some extraordinary happening I hadn't understood
the superb arc of a question, of a decision about death

$\qquad$ because you are beautiful you are hunted
$\qquad$ and with the courage of a vase
$\qquad$ you refuse to become a deer or tree
$\qquad$ and the world holds its breath
$\qquad$ to see if you are there, and safe

$\qquad$ are you?

FIVE POEMS

I
Well now, hold on
maybe I won't go to sleep at all
and it'll be a beautiful white night

or else I'll collapse
completely from nerves and be calm
as a rug or a bottle of pills
or suddenly I'll be off Montauk
swimming and loving it and not caring where

2
an invitation to lunch
HOW DO YOU LIKE THAT?
when I only have 16 cents and 2
packages of yoghurt
there's a lesson in that, isn't there
like in Chinese poetry when a leaf falls?
hold off on the yoghurt till the very
last, when everything may improve

3
at the Rond-Point they were eating
a oyster, but here
we were dropping by sculptures
and seeing some paintings
and the smasheroo-grates of Cadoret
and music by Varèse, too
well Adolph Gottlieb I guess you
are the hero of this day
along with venison and Bill

I'll sleep on the yoghurt and dream of the Persian Gulf

4
which I did it was wonderful
to be in bed again and the knock
on my door for once signified "hi there"
and on the deafening walk
through the ghettos where bombs have gone off lately
left by subway violators
I knew why I love taxis, yes
subways are only fun when you're feeling sexy
and who feels sexy after *The Blue Angel*
well maybe a little bit

5
I seem to be defying fate, or am I avoiding it?

Some days I feel that I exude a fine dust
like that attributed to Pylades in the famous
Chronica nera areopagitica when it was found

and it's because an excavationist has
reached the inner chamber of my heart
and rustled the paper bearing your name

I don't like that stranger sneezing over our love

COHASSET

I see you standing
there on a rock
in my light mind
your body's smiling
as a tern plummets
and gulps fishward
from hot rocks
to freezing water
clambering up
swooping down
golden like last
year always golden
your tender eyes
pull me into the
water like a lasso
of seaweed green
and I fall there
the huge rocks
are like twin beds
and the cove tide
is a rug slipping
out from under us

POEM

O sole mio, hot diggety, nix "I wather think I can"
come to see *Go into Your Dance* on TV—*HELEN MORGAN!? GLENDA FARRELL!?*
1935!?
          it reminds me of my first haircut, or an elm tree or something!
or did I fall off my bicycle when my grandmother came back from Florida?

          you see I have always wanted things to be beautiful
          and now, for a change, they are!

SONG

          Did you see me walking by the Buick Repairs?
          I was thinking of you
          having a Coke in the heat it was your face
          I saw on the movie magazine, no it was Fabian's
          I was thinking of you
          and down at the railroad tracks where the station
          has mysteriously disappeared
          I was thinking of you
          as the bus pulled away in the twilight
          I was thinking of you
          and right now

BALLAD

Yes it is sickening that we come
                          that we go that we dissembling live
          that we leave that there is anywhere in the world someone like us
it is that we are always like a that never that

why we it is me

why is it that I am always separated from the one I love it is because of
some final thing, that is what makes you a that, that I don't do
though everyone denies it who loves you

that makes you a that too

why is it that everyone denies it it's apparent as the air
you breathe and you don't want to be breathed do you

why don't you

because it would make you that air

and if you were that air you
would have to hear yourself

no I will never do that

so when you speak to me I will always be other

it will be like the strains of an organist on a piano
you will hate certain intimacies which to me were just getting to know

you
and at the same time

you know that I don't want to know you
because the palm stands in the window disgusted
by being transplanted, she feels that she's been outraged and she has
by well-wisher me, she well wishes that I leave her alone and my self alone
but tampering

where does it come from? childhood? it seems good

because it brings back the that

that which we wish that which we want

that which a ferry can become can become a bicycle if it wants to get

across the river
and doesn't care how
though you will remember a night
where nothing happened

and we both were simply that

and we loved each other so
and it was unusual

FLAG DAY

I've advised Maxine what to get you
what will I give you myself
it's already given
I'm having a beer

I'd like to start with the Prado
I'd give you open-faced Rome or wall-eyed Toledo
not the Seine or the Tagus, rivers are always flowing away
something that stays in love, the Tuileries Gardens
the colonnade house in Bridgehampton minus the gas pumps
or all of Berlin, at last united by us for today
or Katanga Province, which wants to be owned by you
perhaps an enormous banjo in a big glass house, we could both go naked

you shared the first year of your manhood with me
it seems that everything's merely a token
of some vast inexplicable feeling
your face on a postage stamp (airmail)
your body carved out of Mount Rushmore
a menu and on it you've made a drawing of Garbo
the shudder of your left leg as you fall asleep

our life's like a better flag
floating over the Conte Restaurant in front of a crescent moon
soon again to be full of your upturned smile
I'll give you a small piece of linen to cover my heart with
if we ever truly anger each other

HOW TO GET THERE

White the October air, no snow, easy to breathe
beneath the sky, lies, lies everywhere writhing and gasping
clutching and tangling, it is not easy to breathe
lies building their tendrils into dim figures
who disappear down corridors in west-side apartments
into childhood's proof of being wanted, not abandoned, kidnapped
betrayal staving off loneliness, I see the fog lunge in
and hide it
                    where are you?
                                        here I am on the sidewalk
under the moonlike lamplight thinking how precious moss is
so unique and greenly crushable if you can find it
on the north side of the tree where the fog binds you
and then, tearing apart into soft white lies, spreads its disease
through the primal night of an everlasting winter

which nevertheless has heat in tubes, west–side and east–side
and its intricate individual pathways of white accompanied
by the ringing of telephone bells beside which someone sits in
silence denying their own number, never given out! nameless
like the sound of troika bells rushing past suffering
in the first storm, it is snowing now, it is already too late
the snow will go away, but nobody will be there

police cordons for lying political dignitaries ringing too
the world becomes a jangle
                              from the index finger
to the vast empty houses filled with people, their echoes
of lies and the tendrils of fog trailing softly around their throats
now the phone can be answered, nobody calling, only an echo
all can confess to be home and waiting, all is the same
and we drift into the clear sky enthralled by our disappointment
              never to be alone again
                                        never to be loved
sailing through space: didn't I have you once for my self?
                                        West Side?
      for a couple of hours, but I am not that person

STEPS

How funny you are today New York
like Ginger Rogers in *Swingtime*
and St. Bridget's steeple leaning a little to the left

here I have just jumped out of a bed full of V-days
(I got tired of D-days) and blue you there still
accepts me foolish and free
all I want is a room up there
and you in it
and even the traffic halt so thick is a way
for people to rub up against each other
and when their surgical appliances lock
they stay together
for the rest of the day (what a day)
I go by to check a slide and I say
that painting's not so blue

where's Lana Turner
she's out eating
and Garbo's backstage at the Met
everyone's taking their coat off
so they can show a rib-cage to the rib-watchers
and the park's full of dancers with their tights and shoes
in little bags
who are often mistaken for worker-outers at the West Side Y
why not
the Pittsburgh Pirates shout because they won
and in a sense we're all winning
we're alive

the apartment was vacated by a gay couple
who moved to the country for fun
they moved a day too soon
even the stabbings are helping the population explosion
though in the wrong country
and all those liars have left the U N
the Seagram Building's no longer rivalled in interest
not that we need liquor (we just like it)

and the little box is out on the sidewalk
next to the delicatessen
so the old man can sit on it and drink beer
and get knocked off it by his wife later in the day
while the sun is still shining

oh god it's wonderful
to get out of bed
and drink too much coffee
and smoke too many cigarettes
and love you so much

AVE MARIA

Mothers of America
                    let your kids go to the movies!
get them out of the house so they won't know what you're up to
it's true that fresh air is good for the body

                                            but what about the soul
that grows in darkness, embossed by silvery images
and when you grow old as grow old you must
                                        they won't hate you
they won't criticize you they won't know
                                   they'll be in some glamorous country
they first saw on a Saturday afternoon or playing hookey

they may even be grateful to you
                              for their first sexual experience
which only cost you a quarter
                        and didn't upset the peaceful home
they will know where candy bars come from
                              and gratuitous bags of popcorn
as gratuitous as leaving the movie before it's over
with a pleasant stranger whose apartment is in the Heaven on Earth Bldg
near the Williamsburg Bridge
                              oh mothers you will have made the little tykes
so happy because if nobody does pick them up in the movies
they won't know the difference
                          and if somebody does it'll be sheer gravy
and they'll have been truly entertained either way
instead of hanging around the yard
                        or up in their room
                                hating you
prematurely since you won't have done anything horribly mean yet
except keeping them from the darker joys
                             it's unforgivable the latter
so don't blame me if you won't take this advice
                             and the family breaks up
and your children grow old and blind in front of a TV set
                              seeing
movies you wouldn't let them see when they were young

TO MUSIC OF PAUL BOWLES

Dear Bill I think it was very nice of you to have me
for spaghetti and meatballs and champagne
                              and is very nice
to read *History II* and *Hat* which previously hadn't been finished
    and TV is not superior, though a comfort

yes, and I liked the fruit and the nuts too and the sky
paling and purpling, voluble between two skyscrapers
as symmetrical as a humped back and an ass and as blue

now, I thought you were in a little trouble at rehearsal
with your *terrible* temper and the dirt on the floor and the bossing
but I asked Larry and he said wait till he gets back in Paris
and then we'll send him to the apothecary and Maxine said WAIT
which meant another vodka and campari
                                        yes Bill it is like that
with your friends in the theatre, Maxine leaning over the balcony
and all that, especially that the balcony is made of wood and shaky
and I ask you what would happen if you fell over onto a sculpture

the venomous strength of welded steel
                                        is making of our decade
quite a different thing from plaster and putty, but if you come back
from your shower you will find the movie already half finished
and the phone ringing and the moss growing on the window ledge
bright as a hatless burr or a glass of byrrh, but do you know
that we will be late for Judy Garland if we don't beat it
and we've got to get on the trail and we've got to stand those people
up or we'll miss Myrna Loy and William Powell
                                        get that soap out of your ass!

THOSE WHO ARE DREAMING, A PLAY ABOUT ST. PAUL

"Et celles dont la nuque est un nid de mystère . . ."

He gets up, lights a cigarette, puts fire
under the coffee and dials on the telephone.
Where is he? he is everywhere, he is not
a character, he is a person, and therefore general.
He has no tic, unless someone else is observing him
and no one is. He is allowed to look at the windows
but not out them because the shades are drawn.
He picks up some dry leaves from a bouquet
of autumn leaves on the floor and puts them around
the roots of two philodendron plants so they will rot
into richness and enrich the vines. He reflects
mindlessly on the meaning of philodendron, then
on philo-, then on the nature of fondness, of love.
It is then that he dials the phone.

                              He says hello
this is George Gordon, Lord Byron, then he just
listens because he didn't call to talk, he wanted
to hear your voice.
                    Then you tell me what you did
last night and I am happy to hear it, Lord or no Lord.
Poet or no poet. It is because you're you. That's why
I called. And for once it is not three in the morning,
and I am not from Canada either:
                              Behind, in his actual
mind, he has a vague desire to write a long beautiful poem
like *The Night of Loveless Nights* but he has not known
a loveless night for so long, each night has been filled
with love. And it might mean bad luck, to imagine
such a thing. And he ponders the meaning of loveless,
to be alone is not to be loveless, if you love. It
is a frontier the lover has no desire to pass, that
question. He's not just fond, even when alone.
It's more likely that he's fond in front of people.
Then, if they leave the room he takes you in his arms
for a few minutes terminated physically by footsteps.

But the feeling of your body to his arms, to his heart,
remains for the rest of the evening through conversational
troubles, he looks across at you and sees your face
grow pale with sleepiness, and your eyes gleam abstractedly
and your eyelids are the color of Rembrandt's *Polish Rider,*
a color nature has taken the same infinite pains to achieve
and has achieved nowhere else. He feels his lips
pressing lightly against your closed eyes, though they are
not closed.
               He thinks of the hard beige hills of Spain,
of Morocco (where he has never been, Byron or no Byron),
of certain poems which linger in his mind as essences
of what he is, and each thought feels familiar, each object
because you are familiar and have lingered as the hills
still linger outside Madrid, through harsh rains, through
the base rolling drought of daily sun as infinitely
boring as a drunken conversation, through
the civil wars which rage continually as one continues
to try to make something appear between divided selves
clear and abstract as the word *thing* preceded by
another word, so you have lingered. And in the color
of your eyelids is hidden, as are your eyes, the meaning
of abstraction, a color of general significance and beauty,
but appearing only in your flesh, belonging only to you.
And, like abstraction, not so overwhelmingly and unbearably

important because your lids part and reveal the even
greater beauty of your eyes, which was not necessary,
which is extra, he was so completely satisfied before.

And now he is aroused, and dreads the mechanism which
has brought to him your voice, but not your self. Has brought
him an abstraction of your love. He realizes he has not yet
spoken, he has put the silent burden of his feelings
on your throat. He does not speak and cannot. There's
a pounding at the door. Someone has come to take something
from him. He is alone, protected only by your love.

TONIGHT AT THE VERSAILLES,
OR ANOTHER CARD ANOTHER CABARET

I am appearing, yes it's true
accompanied by my criminal record
my dope addiction and my sexual offenses
it's a great blow for freedom
the Commissioner said when he gave me
my card, you have proved that Society
contaminated you, not you it
and we're proud to have you on the boards
not to say the records, again
but try not to spread the infection
like Billie and Monk and the others
be a good whatever-you-are and keep clean
and I'll pick you up after the show

A WARM DAY FOR DECEMBER

57th Street
street of joy
I am a microcosm in your macrocosm

and then a macrocosm in your miscrocosm
a hydrogen bomb too tiny
to make an eye water
and yet I toddle along
past the reverential windows of Tiffany
with its diamond clips on paper bags
street of dreams painterly
Sidney Janis and Betty Parsons
and Knoedler's so Germanesquely full
you don't notice me
except that I am isolated by my new haircut
and look more Brancusi than usual
so I get in a phone booth on a corner
like a space ship
I like the people passing noisily by
blasting off
"I love you"
"I love you too"
then I open the door the sounds rush over me the people
but I am in the air
yet I follow 57th
meeting Roy and Bill I drink Vermouth
we talk about the pleasantness distractions of New York
you're almost there
57th Street

VARIATIONS ON SATURDAY

I
As the polka from *Schwanda*
carols over the coffee-making
where's the coffee
                    it's out
waiting there
                    adding a little
will arrest all of the whites
and kill some of them
                    but
de Gaulle walks through
the hostile crowd
                    armed

bandits read *Nine* magazine
you will wait a long time
I tell you
        there's no coffee

2
Up at the gate we waited too
and the tree with its root
in the river
        we climbed up
the steep side to the waterfall
feeling kissy in the cold
forest
      when I pull you away
from the tree to me
          it's not
just to get up the cliff
and rejoin the others that's
a sailor's grasp   fingernails
your lips are so different
from your palms

3
             Swan Lake ca-
scading water plunging through
the bank   where there's a heart
there's money   accepting walls
accepting bed and a pet giraffe
when you're not here I pet
the giraffe it's like sitting under
a waterfall giggling   the divine Schumann
as Benois said
          or did he say Diaghilev
liked Schumann   what a wide
street to have so many children
what a day to be born Florestan-tree

4
In Joe's deli the old lady
greets me Sonny   the man with
the rolls is my son, Sonny, how
are you today in the cold out? fine
and coffee too and Camels
               well
a saucepan smells of eggs soft sour
Tanya   the Barone Gallery

tomorrow   the light broke
before I even got out of bed
and then it got put together again
you discard your jacket
                    and go
sweatered into the afternoon
wait for me
            I'm staying with you
fuck Canada

5
In a crevice in the rocks
there's a little tree we noticed
I guess it was like us
                    the icy
water takes it and it topples
racing over the rocks towards the
fall   and we raced
with it   how excitement
engenders sex how can we be so alike
and still love each other?
                        wait
till the *Liebeslieder Walzer* are all
over
        and we'll have that regret too
to hold us and cheer us

6
I went to the same strange passport
office
        to get to the woods the wet
not everyone gets one
                        you were
sitting on an American Regency sofa
eating apples
                you tasted wonderful
it was snowing   tomorrow
I will take all this green
                        and put it
around your shoulders like a cave

Don't remember nothing   interesting
isn't it   well what is childhood
a hardon maybe   yes it's that exquisite
what movie is good as the movies of childhood
none   you're goddamned right   what
a way to eat cereal   you seem awfully
quiet   what are you trying to do control
our thoughts   yes and I still am
with my divine verse   ah shit well
why don't you walk right   I don't
feel like it   a ballerina at heart
on your toes   lose weight   straighten your
oh never mind   who am I anyway   I'm
five foot two eyes of blue broken record glug
what's it to you   you're who I   forget
when the snow   I don't   falls
expect anything if our Sundays aren't   well
that's   oh shit   a typical Monday
followed by a typical Tuesday   Flash Gordon
no clothes   Guadalcanal   my friend did it
you really think you're something don't you
yes I am   is there any toast left   a
short way from the station   dropped rucksack
are you kidding   so I'm irritating and
boring am I   the sins of the fathers is
gravy   what about Saturday   oh I know
splash splash flash flash   gordon
Dolores Del Rio   Yma Sumac   Eisenhower
what do you mean you don't play golf intella
at the stock   I mark it   student of thighs
curve   slip   light   slurpings H D
N D   what's the idea   do you feel a small
arrow at the base of your neck   it's life
I smile because I'm doubtful I eat   not much
and yet   what is disturbing is this   and
where did you find that long long trail winding to
I didn't find it   it found me   I packed my
bandana my egg-cup   an old stirrup   and
an LP of sugar   I baked a blue cake I ate it
I set out   at the time there was nothing but
necking   and yet   that was prepping and at the
same time that was the end   goodbye
blue curls   my life begins   again

LIEBESLIED

I came to you
from out of the *boue*
what did we do
I ate you up

You saw me there
standing alone
I was the bone
you were the marrow

and then one day we walked through a field
I didn't think you would yield
but you did   ugh!

and later that day we swam in the rain
you were causing me pain
you couldn't   swim

I came to you
wearing one shoe
what could I do
the other one was on my prick

WHAT APPEARS TO BE YOURS

The root   an acceptable connection
ochre   except meaning-dream partly
where the will falters   a screw polished
a whole pair of shutters   you saw it
I went in the door   the umbrella
apart from the hole you see a slide   up
two blue   yes the wind mutters
it slides and gulps   it is the snow
where   your breast pocket   exception
to the rule   whenever the beast moves
a lion   is the same at lunch as at dinner

tow-head   your heaviness is rather exciting
ai-ai   driving the taxi into the ai
where to   whereto   yet an appendix
stops the trip   on the East River Drive
zooming downtown to Jap's   eating
later a bevy of invitations   a Chinese bar
what done   undone   a long wait for rain
you were under the settee   eating cough drops
I mean nougatines   where are you now
whose hand   behind the pale Housatonic   I
waited   wait   will wait
and what fun it is   Great Northern Hotel
and the sole of a foot   substantial in the snow
warm   through a hole in the stocking   the sky

THE MOTHER OF GERMAN DRAMA

Two major documents   the documents released
the report was made at no time   travesties
the working people   if the danger   not to produce on its
the law when formally promulgated   last week
only now   the trade unions   only now after ten years
on Sunday   if they are hard-pressed   this
message gas not yet been   it is being assumed however
that   Protestant leaders have especially asked
towards those in their care   the idea of a stolid
in my office   the two bands   at that time misused
5 to 21   what they actually feared   where
their hobby originated   a far-reaching event
after some delay   it looks as if more up-to-date means
Germany never had a Shakespeare nor even a Ben Jonson
though his pieces were meticulously constructed   what
after some delay   the full set   anniversary
lenged his absolute   all weathers
and was allowed to settle down   the exception of her
playfellow   the first stationary   the whole of
careful and precise professor submit   standards of Corneille
all out on a purely abstract plane   superior
brain not only   abilities are of course   named
with her innate sense   with a peasant who in the long ago

have been laid at its base   deeply offended the vain
that the worst was over   with a peasant who in the long ago
with the end mitigated by   over the years countless
was at a low ebb   the gas used in Munich
called that of a guardian   discuss was the civic
forbidden   not only offered samplings of the
long-range dislocations that might   that have sometimes

AS PLANNED

After the first glass of vodka
you can accept just about anything
of life even your own mysteriousness
you think it is nice that a box
of matches is purple and brown and is called
La Petite and comes from Sweden
for they are words that you know and that
is all you know words not their feelings
or what they mean and you write because
you know them not because you understand them
because you don't you are stupid and lazy
and will never be great but you do
what you know because what else is there?

POEM

It was snowing and now
it is raining the slush
is all the mud
Manhattan can hope for
yet if it holds
we may have flowers all
over the sidewalks after

all and our shoes will
decay like the complicated
farmer's as the blossoms
grow up and hide them
then barefoot we'll be
happy
          but the slush is like my
heart leading through
little paths and puddles
to a delicatessen or theatre
where no number of fountains
will make anything grow
or anybody happy except
the idea of a few flowers
to be trodden or run over
grown up and cut
to save the space we need
to walk single file
to keep the streets clear
so we can hurry through life

LINES DURING CERTAIN PIECES OF MUSIC

A faint trace of pain and then a tornado
you smile and a drop of blood trickles down
I think that I am at last svelte
I have at last experienced something like
hearing in Weimar Liszt play the *Romance in C major*
when actually someone has just pulled the ring
out of my ear, and you will never again hear Schumann
without that nervous twitch of your left arm up I don't
care about the blood dripping onto your shoulder
I'm glad because you are so meaningless
to think that ever under a streetlamp that smile
meant more to me than an exciting excursion
into another life a life more peculiar more precious
I know that I need never have heard the *Romance in C*
I'm hysterical from the change from that, from lust

                    *   *   *

how horrible those octaves
when I feel no intensity
when I feel just like Satie
anyway it was the *Fantasia in C major*
I've made a mistake all along the line

        *   *   *

well but if you lust after someone
you must face it
your life, after all, must be real

        *   *   *

the mythological figure a kangaroo
leaping a fence to reach some carrots

I on the contrary have had a very serene existence
I've hardly ever been to bed with anyone
who wanted me to do something I didn't want to do

        *   *   *

the two greatest CHs of our time!
how remarkable, the one with
a great big penis and the other's
I've been told a baby's ring fits over

but the latter practically ruined the world
the other simply made us laugh and cry
but that doesn't make any difference, or it hasn't

        *   *   *

a performance of *The Fairy's Buss* at the City Center
well that's too much! that's all

        *   *   *

FOND SONORE

In placing this particular thought
I am taking up the cudgel against indifference
I wish that I might be different but I am
that I am is all I have so what can I do

as the hero of the hour I might have one strange destiny
but it is all mixed up and I have several
I can't choose between them they are pulling me aloft
which is not to say up like a Baroque ceiling or anything

where is the rain and the lightning to drown or burn us
as there used to be
where are the gods who could abuse and disabuse us often
when am I ever in the country walking along a lane plotting murder

you would think that the best things in life were free
but they're the worst even the air is dirty
and it's this "filth of life" that coats us against pain
so where are we back at the same old stand buying bagels

I think that it would be nice to go away
but that's reserved for TV and who wants to end up in Paradise
it's not our milieu
we would be lost as a fish is lost when it has to swim

and yet and yet
this place is terrible to see and worse to feel
along with the purple you have contracted for an awful virus
and it is Christmas and the children are growing up

YOU AT THE PUMP

(*History of North and South*)

A bouquet of zephyr–flowers hitched to a hitching
post in far off Roanoke

a child watches the hitch tense

here an Indian
there a bag of marbles
here a strange sunrise
there suffused with odors
and behind the restored door
a change of clothing
fresh as baking bread

the child sits quietly
with his nose stuck in a
rose in the village square
where the dust is

and a tall man comes along and spreads water everywhere
for the flowers to drink and enjoy us

it is a small mystery of America

how northerly the wind
sweeping into the square
what icicle of color
reaches the bag
of young sensibility
and makes him think
I love you, Pocahontas
where his feet are

AMERICAN

Had you really been wholly mine at night
the fort wouldn't be sneaking its alarms
across the border like a saffron bite
or the tea lady keep nagging "Love harms"

every minute of the day and damn night.
I told you never to mention my arms
to Moors at Headquarters. My dear, be bright,
and never put your dope in candy charms.

Stay away from the soldiers every night,
try to imagine what it's like on farms,
for in pursuing a Chrysler of white
you'll find tears in solution in your arms.

It was not to be so easily charmed
that we sent you to school to be harmed.

CORNKIND

So the rain falls
it drops all over the place
and where it finds a little rock pool
it fills it up with dirt
and the corn grows
a green Bette Davis sits under it
reading a volume of William Morris
oh fertility! beloved of the Western world
you aren't so popular in China
though they fuck too

and do I really want a son
to carry on my idiocy past the Horned Gates
poor kid   a staggering load

yet it can happen casually
and he lifts a little of the load each day
as I become more and more idiotic
and grows to be a strong strong man
and one day carries as I die
my final idiocy and the very gates
into a future of his choice

but what of William Morris
what of you Million Worries
what of Bette Davis in
AN EVENING WITH WILLIAM MORRIS
or THE WORLD OF SAMUEL GREENBERG

what of Hart Crane
what of phonograph records and gin

what of "what of"

you are of me, that's what
and that's the meaning of fertility
hard and moist and moaning

The light comes on by itself
and just as independently off
it goes into the strange sounds of breathing
> *I am waiting for you to love me*

the grass grows and
ants are clambering laboriously over the windowsill
near the paling clouds
> *I am waiting for you to love me*

now a death enters and dumps
suits and dresses out into the
street where the holes are filled and oil stains spread
> *I am waiting for you to love me*

I have a penchant for sad red bricks
and the sun burning itself out up there
for toll booths and water towers and
> *I am waiting for you to love me*

now these streets are becoming winding
the house is falling down not being torn
while I am looking for a right-angle street avenue boulevard   anything
> *I am waiting for you to love me*

MACARONI

to Patsy Southgate

Voici la clématite around the old door
which I planted, watered, and let die
as I have with so many cats, although *sans une claire-voie*
and it seemed that the whole summer dipped
when it withered, when the leaves did, and the purple
blossoms lingered as if you could smell them eventually

on ne vit pas par l'essence seule, thank you
Patsy, for the dope on *essence de vie* and if I'm not

asleep I'll come tonight to talk about
the old days when my father knocked me into the rose-bed
thereby killing a half dozen of his prized rose plants
yak, yak it's a wonderful life for the plants

when you think of what Shelley did with such a theme
and long afterwards Mallarmé reciting it to himself
far across the channel in all that loneliness and stren'th
you wonder if I shouldn't be back on the phone getting black ear
don't you? well, back to your novel, wench! *assez*

you and Marisol, the Grace Kelly and Maria Callas
of the New York School, I do wish that clematis had growed
I don't know what happened, I guess I just lost interest
which along with the current recession fills me with guilt
and besides I was a kid, as now I can hardly be made responsible
for the money troubles of our nation, almost never
having seen any, but the plant in your life

is the plant that died, *"mourir, c'est ainsi pousser"*

FOR THE CHINESE NEW YEAR
& FOR BILL BERKSON

One or another
Is lost, since we fall apart
Endlessly, in one motion depart
From each other.—D. H. Lawrence

Behind New York there's a face
and it's not Sibelius's with a cigar
it was red it was strange and hateful
and then I became a child again
like a nadir or a zenith or a nudnik

what do you think this is my youth
and the aged future that is sweeping me away
carless and gasless under the Sutton
and Beekman Places towards a hellish rage
it is there that face I fear under ramps

it is perhaps the period that ends
the problem as a proposition of days of days

just an attack on the feelings that stay
poised in the hurricane's center that
eye through which only camels can pass

but I do not mean that tenderness doesn't
linger like a Paris afternoon or a wart
something dumb and despicable that I love
because it is silent oh what difference
does it make me into some kind of space statistic

a lot is buried under that smile
a lot of sophistication gone down the drain
to become the mesh of a mythical fish
at which we never stare back never stare back
where there is so much downright forgery

under that I find it restful like a bush
some people are outraged by cleanliness
I hate the lack of smells myself and yet I stay
it is better than being actually present
and the stare can swim away into the past

can adorn it with easy convictions rat
cow tiger rabbit dragon snake horse sheep
monkey rooster dog and pig "Flower Drum Song"
so that nothing is vain not the gelded sand
not the old spangled lotus not my fly

which I have thought about but never really
looked at well that's a certain orderliness
of personality "if you're brought up Protestant
enough a Catholic" oh shit on the beaches so
what if I did look up your trunks and see it

II
then the parallel becomes an eagle parade
of Busby Berkeleyites marching marching half-toe
I suppose it's the happiest moment in infinity
because we're dissipated and tired and fond no
I don't think psychoanalysis shrinks the spleen

here we are and what the hell are we going to do
with it we are going to blow it up like daddy did
only us I really think we should go up for a change
I'm tired of always going down what price glory
it's one of those timeless priceless words like come

well now how does your conscience feel about that
would you rather explore tomorrow with a sponge
there's no need to look for a target you're it
like in childhood when the going was aimed at a
sandwich it all depends on which three of us are there

but here come the prophets with their loosening nails
it is only as blue as the lighting under the piles
I have something portentous to say to you but which
of the papier-mâché languages do you understand you
don't dare to take it off paper much less put it on

yes it is strange that everyone fucks and every-
one mentions it and it's boring too that faded floor
how many teeth have chewed a little piece of the lover's
flesh how many teeth are there in the world it's like
Harpo Marx smiling at a million pianos call that Africa

call it New Guinea call it Poughkeepsie I guess
it's love I guess the season of renunciation is at "hand"
the final fatal hour of turpitude and logic demise
is when you miss getting rid of something delouse
is when you don't louse something up which way is the inn

III
I'm looking for a million-dollar heart in a carton
of frozen strawberries like the Swedes where is sunny England
and those fields where they stillbirth the wars why
did they suddenly stop playing why is Venice a Summer
Festival and not New York were you born in America

the inscrutable passage of a lawn mower punctuates
the newly installed Muzack in the Shubert Theatre am I nuts
or is this the happiest moment of my life who's arguing it's
I mean 'tis lawd sakes it took daddy a long time to have
that accident so Ant Grace could get completely into black

didn't you know we was all going to be Zen Buddhists after
what we did you sure don't know much about war-guilt
or nothin and the peach trees continued to rejoice around
the prick which was for once authorized by our Congress
though inactive what if it had turned out to be a volcano

that's a mulatto of another nationality of marble
it's time for dessert I don't care what street this is
you're not telling me to take a tour are you

I don't want to look at any fingernails or any toes
I just want to go on being subtle and dead like life

I'm not naturally so detached but I think
they might send me up any minute so I try to be free
you know we've all sinned a lot against science
so we really ought to be available as an apple on a bough
pleasant thought fresh air free love cross-pollenization

oh oh god how I'd love to dream let alone sleep it's night
the soft air wraps me like a swarm it's raining and I have
a cold I am a real human being with real ascendancies
and a certain amount of rapture what do you do with a kid
like me if you don't eat me I'll have to eat myself

it's a strange curse my "generation" has we're all
like the flowers in the Agassiz Museum perpetually ardent
don't touch me because when I tremble it makes a noise
like a Chinese wind-bell it's that I'm seismographic is all
and when a Jesuit has stared you down for ever after you clink

I wonder if I've really scrutinized this experience like
you're supposed to have if you can type there's not much
soup left on my sleeve energy creativity guts ponderableness
lent is coming in imponderableness "I'd like to die smiling" ugh
and a very small tiptoe is crossing the threshold away

whither Lumumba whither oh whither Gauguin
I have often tried to say goodbye to strange fantoms I
read about in the newspapers and have always succeeded
though the ones at "home" are dependent on Dependable
Laboratory and Sales Company on Pulaski Street strange

I think it's goodbye to a lot of things like Christmas
and the Mediterranean and halos and meteorites and villages
full of damned children well it's goodbye then as in Strauss
or some other desperately theatrical venture it's goodbye
to lunch to love to evil things and to the ultimate good as "well"

the strange career of a personality begins at five and ends
forty minutes later in a fog the rest is just a lot of stranded
ships honking their horns full of joy-seeking cadets in bloomers
and beards it's okay with me but must they cheer while they honk
it seems that breath could easily fill a balloon and drift away

scaring the locusts in the straggling grey of living dumb
exertions then the useful noise would come of doom of data

turned to elegant decoration like a strangling prince once ordered
no there is no precedent of history no history nobody came before
nobody will ever come before and nobody ever was that man

you will not die not knowing this is true this year

ESSAY ON STYLE

Someone else's Leica sitting on the table
the black kitchen table I am painting
the floor yellow, Bill is painting it
wouldn't you know my mother would call
up
    and complain?
                  my sister's pregnant and
went to the country for the weekend without
telling her
        in point of fact why don't I
go out to have dinner with her or "let her"
come in? well if Mayor Wagner won't allow private
cars on Manhattan because of the snow, I
will probably never see her again
                        considering
my growingly more perpetual state and how
can one say that angel in the Frick's wings
are "attached" if it's a real angel? now

I was reflecting the other night meaning
I was being reflected upon that Sheridan Square
is remarkably beautiful, sitting in JACK
DELANEY's looking out the big race-track window
on the wet
        drinking a cognac while Edwin
read my new poem it occurred to me how impossible
it is to fool Edwin not that I don't know as
much as the next about obscurity in modern verse
but he
      always knows what it's about as well
as what it is do you think we can ever
strike *as* and *but,* too, out of the language

then we can attack *well* since it has no
application whatsoever neither as a state
of being or a rest for the mind no such
things available
                          where do you think I've
got to? the spectacle of a grown man
decorating
                    a Christmas tree disgusts me that's
where
              that's one of the places yetbutaswell
I'm glad I went to that party for Ed Dorn
last night though he didn't show up do you think
,Bill, we can get rid of *though* also, and *also*?
maybe your
                      lettrism is the only answer treating
the typewriter as an intimate organ why not?
nothing else is (intimate)
                                      no I am not going
to have you "in" for dinner nor am I going "out"
I am going to eat alone for the rest of my life

TO MAXINE

The sender of this letter is a mailman
which is why it has no postage where
is this mailman he is away far far away

I saw you in imagination walking in
the startlingly early spring crying a
little because of the absent flowers

never mind they'll come and I, meanwhile,
am sitting in this dark hole thinking
Siegfried's Rhine Journey is pretty great

to hell with Winthrop Sergeant he's
not enough reason to hate it I'm not
that perverse and thinking how three-line

stanzas are feminine and so are you what
a lovely quality so half of us are Siegfried
and half are the Rhine it's awful but there

it's good not to be the same only the
sky should always be blue it is today (well
almost) it will be coming on blue with

those flowers and whatever new season they
bring, Maxine
you put on lipstick as others put on hats

WHO IS WILLIAM WALTON?

he isn't the English composer
and I'm quite aware that everybody
doesn't have to know who everybody
else is
      but why did he take Mrs Kennedy
to the Tibor de Nagy Gallery worthy
as it is of her attention
          though I'm also
used to the fact that one day someone
called up Charles Egan from Grand Central
and asked if he had a *small* Rauschenberg
and Franz said "that's not a *practical*
joke"
      yes many things can happen in
the "world" of art (look at Malraux!)
but who is William Walton?
          and actually
Jean Dubuffet sent me a drawing which
is even more peculiar than anything else
but who is William Walton?
        I guess it's
even most peculiar that any painting
gets done at all with all these questions
zooming through the head who are you?

TO CANADA (FOR WASHINGTON'S BIRTHDAY)

I shall be so glad when you come down
like a Grand Polonaise out of the ice and strangeness
bringing me out of the strangeness and ice
I am so tired of the limitations of immobility
all of America pretending to be a statue
or an African mask making up cigar-rituals
who gives a damn if we ordered enough cigars from Cuba
before we broke off relations (though we did)
and used them to light those fires in Harlem doorways
(everyone knows who that arsonist is) I am
so sick of the pretensions of their worried faces
that worried look too is a valiant attempt to be blind
and I am so weary of their sexual importance
consisting chiefly in "not being had" oh Poles
I'd rather be leaping off the brink of a precipice
with you or eating terrible herring in Toronto
or merluza in Barcelona that tastes like a sandal
I don't care how dark it gets as long as we can still move!
I can't sit here listening to Chopin for the rest of my life!
oh what's the use I think I will

ON A BIRTHDAY OF KENNETH'S

Kenny!
Kennebunkport! I see you standing there
assuaging everything with your smile
at the end of the world you are scratching your head wondering what is
        that funny French word Roussel was so fond of? oh "dénouement"!
and it is good

I knew perfectly well that afternoon on the grass when you read Vincent
        and me your libretto that you had shot out of the brassière factory
        straight into the blue way ahead of the Russians (what do they know
        now that Pasternak is gone) and were swinging there like a Strad
And that other day when we heard Robert Frost read your poems for the

Library of Congress we admired you too though we didn't like the way
    he read "Mending Sump"
and when Mrs. Kennedy bought your drawing that was a wonderful day too

but in a sense these days didn't add up to a year
and you haven't had a birthday
you have simply the joyous line of your life like in a Miró
it tangles us in your laughter

no wonder I felt so lonely on Saturday when you didn't give your annual
    cocktail party!
I didn't know why

POEM IN TWO PARTS

1   SUNDAY AFTERNOON AT THE RANCH
Waiting willing above the lamp
beatitudes came near to be incendiary
all afternoon young Elmo pressed
his shoulder against a fragile screen
on which Shirley Temple kissed
herself then damp he swam down the
liana
        I saw the end of spectacular
entertainments buried in series so
no one could ask a question of it
or why his back was so green if he
really was swinging there's no use in
that and for a very long time forward
there would not be
                    the air crumpled
came up to his knee then his wrist
which made him leap and giggle
like a pleased zebra hiding the please
but that was fine for a start so
pleased was the air to visit his fist

2   POSTSCRIPT OF TARZAN
Yet a tragic instance may be imminent
or uttered later that same night if a

lost and muscular aggression confines itself
to jokes and strangeness to French
to Métro jocularity about Tanganyika
which in the end is more puzzling than
Tanganyika
                is careless of the green
shoot which must always push forwards
to the sun of the liana Tarzan says
like everyone but follow them barefoot
they are not plants even if we are
and it is all much in the jungle

THE ANTHOLOGY OF LONELY DAYS

I   THE UBIQUITOUS MALLARMÉ
Is it true you said poems are made of words?
that's only one kind of poem that's true of

II   THE SKY-WAS BLUE AND SOMETHING EXTRAORDINARY HAPPENED
Vincent.

III   HOMAGE TO GAUDÍ
Convolutions of volu-consciousness valve-conch lend dong-eth to snails

IV   WAITING AT THE GATE
Ope ope thou stormy spectre of the OP

V   THE END IS IN SIGHT
Rapidly moving towards a self-destructive decision, everyone cheered up
because a narrative was obviously in sight, is sight

VI   THE NARRATIVE
Since when has sight replaced feeling?

VII   I AM THE SPIRIT OF CHRISTMAS PAST
It is enough to eat, in Egypt

VIII   POEM
And by the riverbanks there was hail in a basket

IX   POEM
Why eat the bullrushes just because the bullrushes want to eat you?

X   THE WITNESS FOR THE PROSECUTION
There's no case because you're innocent

XI   NO (POEM)
Algeria is difficult in itself, and not to be attached to, as blue
is the most difficult color to use if you are a painter, even an old one

XII   PAINTER
Meet you at the Frick   please don't wear pants

XIII   FRICK MUSEUM
I'm tired too, of receiving pants, and the pants always say they're tired
of being worn . . .

XIV   ATONALISM
O god that I might be simple (it was my intention) o god that I might be
a sample (of grass) it was my handle (o god) to be numerically idiotic

XV   POEM
Yet I am here, as the grass the idiots and the glass congeal (star)! (wait)!

XVI   POEM
And when you come you will be welcome, as you know

VINCENT AND I INAUGURATE A MOVIE THEATRE

Now that the Charles Theatre has opened
it looks like we're going to have some wonderful times
Allen and Peter, why are you going away
our country's black and white past spread out
before us is no time to spread over India
like last night in the busy balcony I see
your smoky images before the smoky screen
everyone smoking, Bogart, Bacall and her advanced sister
and Hepburn too tense to smoke but MacMurray rich enough
relaxed and ugly, poor Alice Adams so in-pushed and out
in the clear exposition of AP American or Associated

Paranoia and Allen and I getting depressed and angry
becoming again the male version of wallflower or wallpaper
or something while Vincent points out that when anything
good happens the movie has just flicked over to fantasy
only fantasy in all America can be good
because all Alice Adams wanted was a nose
just as long as any other girl's and a dress
just as rustly and a mind just as empty so America
could fill it with checks and flags and invitations
and the old black cooks falling down the cellar stairs
for generations to show how phony it all is
but the whites didn't pay attention that's slaving away
at something, maybe the dance would have been fun
if anyone'd given one but it would have been over
before Alice enjoyed it and what's the difference
no wonder you want to find out about India take
a print of *Alice Adams* with you it will cheer them up

VINCENT,

here I sit in Jager House
where you got so mad at Gem
for picking on Bob
                              over a schnitzel
through the window stains the
funny air of spring tumbles
and over the yellow and green
tables into the brew I sip
waiting for Roy
                              I saw
a very surprising thing this
morning before you were up
a sea of sexual sheets
                              draped
on black steel rods and behind
them the glistening white
hair of Nakian on this strange
warm morning like a
sidewalk phone booth

In Bayreuth once
we were very good friends of the Wagners
and I stepped in once
for Isadora so perfectly
she would never allow me to dance again
that's the way it was in Bayreuth

the way it was in Hackensack
was different
there one never did anything
and everyone hated you anyway
it was fun, it was clear
you knew where you stood

in Boston you were never really standing
I was usually lying
it was amusing to be lying all
the time for everybody
it was like exercise

it means something to exercise
in Norfolk Virginia
it means you've been to bed with a Nigra
well it is exercise
the only difference is it's better than Boston

I was walking along the street
of Cincinnati
and I met Kenneth Koch's mother
fresh from the Istanbul Hilton
she liked me and I liked her
we both liked Istanbul

then in Waukegan I met a furniture manufacturer
and it wiped out all dreams of pleasantness from my mind
it was like being pushed down hard
on a chair
it was like something horrible you hadn't expected
which is the most horrible thing

and in Singapore I got a dreadful
disease it was amusing to have bumps
except they went into my veins

and rose to the surface like Vesuvius
getting cured was like learning to smoke

yet I always loved Baltimore
the porches which hurt your ass
no, they were the steps
well you have a wet ass anyway
if they'd only stop scrubbing

and Frisco where I saw
Toumanova "the baby ballerina" except
she looked like a cow
I didn't know the history of the ballet yet
not that that taught me much

now if you feel like you want to deal with
Tokyo
you've really got something to handle
it's like Times Square at midnight
you don't know where you're going
but you know

and then in Harbin I knew
how to behave it was glorious that
was love sneaking up on me through the snow
and I felt it was because of all
the postcards and the smiles and kisses and the grunts
that was love but I kept on traveling

VINCENT, (2)

this morning a blimp was blocking 53rd Street
as inexplicable and final as a sigh
when you are about to say why you did sigh
but it is already done and we will never
be happy together again never sure and
I felt if I walked all the way to the Hudson
through the electrical (artificial spring) air
I would not be able to pass I
would not be able to meet you on the other shore

but here you are in a gust of wind with
your bronze turn-out smiling shyly in the velvet
light my depression drifts off into the blue theatre
why did you sigh anyway why did I notice
a sheet flaps in the wind a pillow hits the floor
we are laughing as time collapses around us there
on the Palisades-Columbus-Avenue-Love-Bed-Awards

AT KAMIN'S DANCE BOOKSHOP

to Vincent Warren

Shade of Fanny Elssler! I dreamt that you passed over me last night in sleep
was it you who was asleep or was it me? sweet shade
shade shade shill spade agony freak
geek you were not nor were you made of ribbons but of warm moving flesh & tulle
you were twining your left leg around your right as if your right were me
I've never felt so wide awake
I seemed to be wearing tights entwined with your legs and a big sash over my crotch
and a jewel in my left ear for luck
(to help me balance) and you were pulling me toward the floor reaching for stars
it seemed to me that I was warm at last
and palpable not just a skein of lust dipped in the grand appreciation of yours
where are you Fanny Elssler come back!

PISTACHIO TREE AT CHÂTEAU NOIR

Beaucoup de musique classique et moderne Guillaume and not
as one may imagine it sounds not in the ear
what went was attributed to wandering aimlessly off
what came arrived simply for itself and inflamed me
yet I do not explain what exactly makes me so happy today
any more than I can explain the unseasonal warmth
of my unhabitual heart pumping vulgarly the blood
of another I loved another and now my love is other

my love is in the movies downstairs and yesterday
bought ice cream and looked for a pigeon-menaced owl
mais, Guillaume, où es-tu, Guillaume, comme les musiques

and like the set for *Rigoletto* like the set for *Roma*
like so many sets one's heart is torn like Berman's
spacious h unt where tenors walk in pumps and girls
in great big hats or none at all "or perhaps he recorded
the panorama of hills and valleys before the strangely
naked" and rain is turning the set into a dumpling

wherever I see a "while" I seem to lose a little time
and gradually my feet dragging I slow down the damn bus
it is because of you so I can watch you smile longer
that's what the spring is and the elbow of noon walks
where did you go who did you see the children proclaim
and they too gradually fill the sepulchre with dolls
and the sepulchre jumps and jounces and turns pink with wrath

THREE POEMS

DANTE
I could guide you into depravity but I'm not sure I could lead either of us
back out.

MASTURBATION
It's a pause in the day's occupation that is known as the children's hour.

TELEPHONE   *(to Patsy Southgate)*
I sometimes wonder how we all get through this soap opera that is our life.

EARLY ON SUNDAY

It's eight in the morning
everyone has left
the *New York Times* had put itself to bed on Wednesday

or Thursday and arrived
this morning I feel pale
and read the difference between the Masai and the Kikuyu
one keeps and identifies
the other keeps and learns
"newfangledness" in Wyatt's time was not a virtue was it
or should I get up
go out into the Polish sunlight
and riot in Washington Square with Joan with the "folk"
if you like singing
what happened to the clavichord

with hot dogs peanuts and pigeons where's the clavichord
though it's raining
I'm not afraid for the string
they have their hats on across the street in the dirty window
leaning on elbows
without any pillows
how sad the lower East side is on Sunday morning in May
eating yellow eggs
eating St. Bridget's benediction
washing the world down with rye and Coca-Cola and the news
Joe stumbles home
pots and pans crash to the floor
everyone's happy again

POEM

Twin spheres full of fur and noise
rolling softly up my belly beddening on my chest
and then my mouth is full of suns
that softness seems so anterior to that hardness
that mouth that is used to talking too much
speaks at last of the tenderness of Ancient China
and the love of form the Odyssies
each tendril is covered with seed pearls
your hair is like a tree in an ice storm
jetting I commit the immortal spark jetting
you give that form to my life the Ancients loved

those suns are smiling as they move across the sky
and as your chariot I soon become a myth
which heaven is it that we inhabit for so long a time
it must be discovered soon and disappear

ST. PAUL AND ALL THAT

Totally abashed and smiling

                    I walk in
                    sit down and
                    face the frigidaire

        it's April
        no May
        it's May

such little things have to be established in morning
after the big things of night
                    do you want me to come? when
I think of all the things I've been thinking of I feel insane
simply "life in Birmingham is hell"
                            simply "you will miss me
                                but that's good"
when the tears of a whole generation are assembled
they will only fill a coffee cup
                    just because they evaporate
doesn't mean life has heat
                  "this various dream of living"
I am alive with you
                full of anxious pleasures and pleasurable anxiety
hardness and softness
                listening while you talk and talking while you read
I read what you read
              you do not read what I read
which is right, I am the one with the curiosity
        you read for some mysterious reason
                    I read simply because I am a writer
the sun doesn't necessarily set, sometimes it just disappears
        when you're not here someone walks in and says
                                "hey,
there's no dancer in that bed"

O the Polish summers! those drafts!
those black and white teeth!
you never come when you say you'll come but on the other hand you do come

FOR A DOLPHIN

When at the open door
an instant of green fire-escapes
to avoid deglutting
I take up *Fantômas* and start
dourly reading and debating with
myself in the sense of strife
of disorder and dismay

        order is only the
        butterfly on the beach
        of dis—
        where I lie sunning
        the month long
        and drinking daiquiris

razor of sun through
the milky fluid and
the sharp little floes of ice
capsizing near the sand
a little spills on my crotch
like a kiss-nibble
what hair is in this glass

        let me see
        through these borrowed shades a
        nice-looking dolphin I
        overhear him quoting Shelley to
        the mellifluous fish al-
        ways eating their plankton not
        hearing a watery syllable
        surfeited with it

whaddaya think Thomas
Mann meant by rouge I go
back to *Fantômas* and murders with a
lot of satisfaction and begin
to enjoy the sandy irritation of
my nature as it gets more

and more itchy and red and infected
and won't lie still

it's all blue and white
here in the surf and won't heal
while the noisy green death is
piling up it's not like
grass that's to eat and the fish
come in closer feel marvelous
against my skin   my eyes

a whole nation is
ordered to be sea-faring and to
go
but I being privileged may go
while lying still
and reading *Fantômas*
and I must go too

DRIFTS OF A THING THAT BILL BERKSON NOTICED

April's over is May too June
and thundershowers tomorrow
you wouldn't want those tears to
stick to your cheeks long
and the grass all growing greasy
and strange in the dark light
of too early summer all too

yesterday the stamp became a
pendulum and politenesses
multiplied into emotions of
oh never mind what emotions
but they're the one you think they
are just as the weather is hotter

but actually people shouldn't
cry in the street I'm glad I don't
know her even if it was winter
it's even more dangerous then and
especially not over someone else
that's sort of like the fall of

Leningrad if it had fallen or
perhaps it should have
                             no that's
too mean a thought it's making me cry
why not give up the streets I wonder

F.Y.I. (THE BRASSERIE GOES TO THE LAKE)

Up at Borton-Smergens, the little town by the sea, you went
berserker
              faster than a coot-catcher creams over kites
Lou said you reminded her of Rilke (that one time he smiled) but
       you reminded me of Patsy Kelly
                                        "Holy Cow" the cenotaph read, and
"Jeepers Creepers," indicating a fate of more than usual charm
but you kept shouting "Help! I'm a nut!" until the villagers
                                    attacked me too: OUCH!
(but I loved it, I love camaraderie at any cost)   o then

                    we were eating lambs'-balls paté on the green
                    (odd dish) and you kept demanding rosé
                    and humming the old song of the Camargue:
                    "Billet doux, comme une rose tisonné"
                    god we were happy for a minute or two!

but I didn't like your aunt
                            from Tchad Lake muttering over and over
"Lordy,
          the country drives that poor boy wild the country drives that
poor boy wild the poor country drives the wild boy the the poor wild
country drives the boy the wild country drives the boy poor, it
certainly does, have you noticed it"
                                      where were you when I struck her?

                    at a certain season
                    the dandelions fluffed out
                    breathing became impossible
                    that was country living
                    red as a nose before summer

                              then it was we discovered
                              that they *had* put the rosé
                              in the hamper (under
                              the portable bedpan all
                              sprayed with ant-repellent)!
                              how happy we were for
                              another couple of seconds!

you waited for me once for 10 minutes
and a half and I want you to know
the memories of that expensive afternoon
will keep me eating grass with you

                              forever!
                              lying on the charming cenotaph
                              reading silently to each other

F.M.I. 6/25/61

Park Avenue at 10:10
P.M.
fragrant after-a-French-movie-rain is over
                              "and shine the stars"
        Kupka buildings aren't being built, damn it
and I'm locked up in this apartment outdoors for a good reason, Mario
Mario? there are 20 of em in this neighborhood
                                        in your blue sweater
            excepting there's a staggering grid   of . . .
air cooling, rushing along   out of the Astor
                                      out of the Ritz, Godfrey
                                      out of the Broadhurst-Plaza
            I'll have an omelette aux fines herbes
      like after *Dolce Vita*
                                  like after a whole day of it
I respond to your affection like a tuning fork which makes me feel
                                              pretty queer
            no ketchup no sugar
            a plain unadorned piece of meat
                              you think of doom
                              but you don't give a damn
and the moon
so often on Park Avenue it is out and shining

even on foggy days, days, nights, PMs and paper leaves
with long English invitations on them to crownings
gee, quite what one didn't expect, no? yum yum

      you find the point of your life
      heading in the wrong direction
      like a compass out of whack, fun!
      because that's the way it goes

oops! no oysters because of the epidemic, for example
                             I want
      you to be very very happy like Central Park
      what a wonderful city you have here I never
      dreamt until we'd been together two weeks straight
              there's the fish again
      staring at us, I love that fish & I love Jean Arthur
            & I love publicity
      to read about and think about and dream awake

this train is going away from the Guggenheim
                          a hot "dog"
                worrying rent already paid
                Joe? he's in the sack
you know,
      your eyes are the color of that Miró's back it's
a marvellous happening of Frank L. Wright
    the great accidental architect
                    who gives life?
                    who taketh away?
                    who's kidding?
                    who's for real?
              wow! (Westminster Abbey!)

F.O.I.

(A Vision of Westminster Abbey)

Yet while   eat   possible   exact   slap
        wilt   acceptable   moan   adverse   creep
    cannever wait   whereof   revolt   struck
          cat   whender   maintenant   brent
butatfirst whenyouwerestriving   quickly   meet   part
                   lallumpherousbreak tendency so

slight   foreign   blue   treat   teat
       ofatempo   fairlytobruise
still   exact   nevertohurt
hit   hitohit   sooftrepeatedhit   sooftponderedanddreadedhit
sopersonalhit   obsession   almostly
           pearly gate   presentedatcourtnight
pat   farthingaleola   peramble
    feather   farfle   quandparfoisalorszut
tobeornottobenot   cajun   fort   framboise
      severalsybillant   bunt   paradeese
    quandvousavezlemaitredeschosestueslemarteaudesmaitres

                                           start
ofadie   sendover   thethermosoteaballs
scantaccomplishment   skimp   saronayasay

        sell the pup
        in jars of dolly
        falalalala
        fa dong bush kep

instrument of sale   cancerectomy   homonymphalis
    tenderisthenight   andalltheheart   thenorevenge
space   electricity   flipping   stains
    frent   caressonut   collapse   goodbye
vaniverisax   vanitoutlemonde   vanivisceral   vanistartto

SUMMER BREEZES

(*F.Y.*(*M.*)*M.B.I.*)

An element of mischief contributed
                          to the float
                          in the lake
              the pool stood on its ear, dripping aqua
                                irritating eyes
they swam all day in the torrid cool
             and at night they sunned each other
it was idyllic
           there was a lot of space between them
                       it was not a grave
then Uncle Ned came and ruined everything
Lois said she was pregnant
the gardener said he was guilty
Lois said he wasn't

                    what an eruption!
                                        (everyone knew it was Cherry
                                        he played basketball winters)
            mother flew in from Des Moines
                                        with her dog
        the whole damn vacation was really ruined!
                                        it wasn't so much
        what happened as having all those people around, I thought

                    yet when Lois got fired I was sorry
                    I was very fond of Cherry

                        (AND OTHER BREEZES)
        which made me think a lot
                        (that *Gone With the Wind* must be right) and
        I looked and looked, but there was nobody for me to do anything with
        what a summer!
                    so I lay on the float on my belly and thought of
        Indians (Eastern and Western, but mostly Western—Apache and Iroquois,
        that is)
            Zanzibar   shishkebab   South Seas   sharks
        ridingboots   lotusleaves   whippings   lipstick   unicorns
            panthers (preferably black panthers, no, preferably blonde panthers)
        tigersandleopardstoo   champagneandothermoviedrinks   blood
        pearls   snow   windycrevasses   a gigantic tornado followed
        immediately by the eruption of the biggest volcano in the world and
        the crash of an oversized comet!
                            and that summer my swimming improved
                                        a lot

MUY BIEN

(*F.Y.S.C.*)

I like to make changes in plans
                            as long as the cook
            doesn't get upset, or blamed for poisoning me
        "well, if it's a buffet that's different
                                let's go"
        and we'll already be stocked up on tunafish and stars
        "WARNER BROTHERS STARS" she screeched (Ruby Keeler)
            and I'd rather be up there (with you) than
        (with somebody else)   down there

I always think of you when *printanière*'s on the menu
"a wasted life," but with spinach

                         I don't think
Popeye is strictly Faulkner's property, do you? do
John Crowe and Allen T.?   pass the noodles . . .
          what were you fingering last 4th of July?
I remember having sand on my balls
                         and a Bloody Mary
              in my hand (pretty pure, hein?)

      what is good is always derogatory, namely: (I),
(selfish), (proud), (bitchy), (cold), (heedless), (sucky),
      (witless), (overbearing), (cavalier), (infatuated)
whereas what is worthless is humble and darling, is
      absent, goes straight up and seems "to make the flowers grow"

                                   BUT on the sunny
side, that photograph of us came out something
cavelike and classical, flat as a platypus's kisser
(rigorous), but with a mysterious CHARGE as we sat
in the Georges de la Tour Room waiting to go see Mia
Slavenska
          did you ever have a Bar Mitzvah? I had a perfectly
agonizing Confirmation   I almost hit the Bishop back
      but he was so like Queen Flab, I knuckled under, biting
my tongue so badly I could never again take Communion (it
stuck to the roof of my mouth anyway) cha cha cha

          ,,,,,,,,,,,,,,,,,,,,,,,,,,,,,,,,,   whew! I needed a push!
          hey! halt! (I mean) stop! hurry up! the corner
                    of Madison and 57th is a very confusing place!
      (waiting for you to call I thought your cook had died)

BILL'S SCHOOL OF NEW YORK

(*F.I.R.*)

He allows as how some have copped out
but others are always terrific, hmmmmmm?
Then he goes out to buy a pair of jeans,
moccasins and some holeless socks. It

is very hot. He thinks with pleasure that
his first name is the same as de Kooning's.
People even call him "Bill" too, and
they often smile. He feels rather severe

actually, about people smiling without a
reason. He is naturally suspicious, but
easily reassured, say by a pledge unto death.
He likes to think of windows being part

of life, you look at them, they look at
you, why not? Passing the huge white Adam
sculpture in the Musée d'art moderne he
was heard to fart. He likes walls to be

white, sculpture to be colored. He provides
his own noise. He is kissy and admires
Miró. Though his head is feathery, his
chronologies are very serious. He has a

longer neck than you might think. About
Courbet he seldom thinks, but he thinks a lot
about Fantin-Latour. He looks like one.
Corner of a Table. At the Frick Museum he

seems rather *apache.* He likes tunafish
and vodka, collages and cologne, and
seeing French movies more than once.
He is most at home at the Sidney Janis Gallery.

BILL'S BURNOOSE

Bathed burnt skin gin tonic
                              Daily Mirror conversation
"prestige talks, darling
"but nobody hears it
"you hear money though, honey" " "

and the train growls on with a $100 bill holding the seat
and the silly cunt didn't even recognize Marcia! (MARCIA!)

                        munching cress
                        dreaming of Hundertwasser
                        pressing the cool moist bread
                        to my burning foots

        in the station
        you avow
        you hate care
        for sunburns
        by eithers

                    there is no TV Guide in this station!
                    there is no yesterday's paper in this station!
                    there is nobody at home at John Button's!

        did you see the duck in the tent
        then another head appeared
        they were doing dirties in the afternoon
        it's called Long Island Duckling

I feel just like Whitman said you should
    and the train burrs and treadles on
    diddleydiddleyGREENHORNETdiddleydiddley

    I wish we weren't sitting on these Long Island asterisks, though

                                did you have a clam?
                                I had a cob of corn

    O the dark!
    I the TV!
    O the various marvellous lotions each costing $12 per ounce of plankton!

                I wrap my grease
                in a big purple towel
                and lie shivering and contented
                as a hunk of dry ice

1
What I once wanted is you
and it is gone
                    so
why blame me the disappearance
over
        it is a sense that gives pause
an ultimate sense
                        that's
gone
        something that never was there
can't
        disappear
                        nor can I
regret nothing
                    in a way
you were everything once
                                that
died of its falsity
                        and I was
to blame
            but you didn't care
that something
                    very beautiful
went
        even if it was only an illusion

2
Where the image
                    of the end
                                hits you
no one can gauge
                        not whether it matters
not whether it stays
                        the (general) (only)
idea
        is that ideas are bad
                                but what
if they are kind and generous
                                in a world
of shits
            would you think that sentimental
no you wouldn't
                        because you're weaker than I am

you didn't try
                you didn't know
that the dark
                was sitting in your lap
                                    not me
I always said I was a shit
                        forearmed
is foredefeated
                that's what Sherman really said

ON RACHMANINOFF'S BIRTHDAY #158

I am sad
I better hurry up and finish this
before your 3rd goes off the radio
or I won't know what I'm feeling
tonight
tonight
anytime
or
ever
kiss me again
I'm still breathing
what do you think
I think
that
the Tratar (no, that would be too funny)
the Tartar hordes
are still advancing
and I identify with them
how do you like that
for a dilemma
how do you like hatred
                cruelty
                sadism
                self-interest
                selfishness
                self-pollution
                self

perhaps you
mistake it for health
as I once did
but you get stuck in a habit
of thinking about things
                                and realize they are all you
that's amusing, hein?
so think

ON RACHMANINOFF'S BIRTHDAY #161

1
Diane calls me so I get up
I wash my hair because
I have a hash hangover then
I noticed the marabunta have walked into the kitchen!
they are carrying a little banner
which says "in search of lanolin"
so that's how they found me!
crawling crawling they don't know
I never keep it in the frigidaire the little dopes
there's something wrong with everyone
that's how we get by at all keep going
and maybe you'll find it you little creeps

2
Darkness and white hair
everything empty, nothing there,
but thoughts how awful
image is, image errrgh
all day long to sit in a window
and see nothing but the past
the serpent is coiled thrice
around her she is dead

3
How are things on the stalinallee
behind the façades is there despair
like on 9th Street behind the beer
and all that life that must be
struggling on without a silence
despair is only the first scratch
of death on the door and a long wait

I'm getting tired of not wearing underwear
and then again I like it
                                strolling along
feeling the wind blow softly on my genitals
though I also like them encased in something
firm, almost tight, like a projectile
                                                at
a streetcorner I stop and a lamppost is
bending over the traffic pensively like a
praying mantis, not lighting anything,
just looking
                        who dropped that empty carton
of cracker jacks I wonder I find the favor
that's a good sign
                                it's the blue everyone
is talking about an enormous cloud which hides
the observatory blimp   when you
ride on a 5th Avenue bus you hide on a 5th
Avenue bus I mean compared to you walking
don't hide   there you are trying
to hide behind a fire hydrant   I'm
not going to the Colisseum I'm going to
the Russian Tea Room fooled you didn't I
well   it is nicer in the Park
with the pond and all that   okay
lake   and bicyclists give you
a feeling of being at leisure in the open
air lazy and good-tempered   which is
fairly unusual these days   I liked
for instance   carrying my old Gautier book
and *L'Ombra* over to LeRoi's the other
pale afternoon through the crowds of 3rd
Avenue and the ambulance and the drunk

"We've got a lot of what it takes to get along."
                    —Ginger Rogers

Plank plank   tons of it
                plank plank
marching   the streets
            up and down
                                    and it's all ours

2

what we all want is a consistent musical development heh heh
                    tappety-tap drrrrrrrrrrrp!

3

Just as aloha means goodbye in Swahili
                                    so is it 9:05
and I must go to work   roll OVER dammit
                                    (see previous FYI)
            hip? I haven't even coughed yet this morning

4

so then I lurch out into the sun to do some
            shop(foralltheworldlike DianeDiPrima)ping
I buy
        eggs mushrooms cheese whitewine grapes
                                    and then
I feel less apprehensive so I cook it all up and we eat
            and we talk all afternoon about death
            which is spring in our hearts
                            LET'S GET OUT OF HERE

5

I had just finished the last chapter of my biography of the
Buddha, *The Yoghurt and the Revolution,* and I was GLAD to eat.
It was raining
            your letter never arrived
                        I opened it, though . . .

6

The wheat jeans were banging back and forth in the toilet
            an apple   a stiff handkerchief
                three tons of plank
        "this dreadful cold"
                            have I ever done anything to hurt
                                you, she said, I said no
            coughcough
                coughcoughcoughcough
                            good morning,

darling,

      how do you like the first snow of summer?

                                       your
           plant in   your window

CAUSERIE de A.F.

"If you don't think that's funny, you better not go to college."
         —Jo Van Fleet

Cracked up on the green
     stretched out like laid out
                   "time is nutting you just shit
get old, sick, crazy, fucked-out"   now the pale prick
     stands in the dawn with a lot of hands around it
they think it's May Day, actually it's beet-red but the sun
                     isn't up yet
"life is awful"
              boy you're not kidding everyone's handled it
by now it may as well be made into a table leg or a lamp base
     where were you last night
                 underneath the stairs playing cops
        and robbers with a fellow public "servant"
     why are you thrashing around so much
                  I'm having a cauchemar
          it's the only thing I ever gave birth to
     you're awfully nice you know that
             so is ground glass
SO for weeks we kissed each other only on the back of the head
             it was hair-raising
             I was so unhappy I began to love it
and Jesus Christ how can anyone be happy
            just because I'm shaving and
     on swoops the *Leonore* Overture No. 3! I'm a tough cookie I guess
     that's why
         so gulp down that vodka and orange juice
          and maybe things will clear up a little
     catch that train tote that luggage get that lanolin and Vitamin B-1
and think of me as a taxi, a plain ordinary taxi
               with a rear view
you were tailing me all those blocks
           and it didn't even make me feel funny
then we drank ourselves into a happy state
           face to face at last

"these are the stairs
from *Funny Face*"

But I would like to see
the three Zenobius bits
before I die of the heat
or you die of the denim
or we fight it out without
lances in the obscure public

"I don't think Houdon
does the trick"

and I could walk through ex–
changing with you through the
exchanging universe tears
of regretless interest tears of
fun and everything being temporary
right where it seems so permanent

"when I saw you coming
I forgot all about Breughel"

no we love us still hanging
around the paintings Richard Burton
waves through de Kooning the
Wild West rides up out of the Pollock
and a Fragonard smiles no pinker
than your left ear, no bigger either

"let's go by my place
before the movies"

I don't really care
If I have a standard or not
or a backless coat of mail
since I never intend to back
up or out of this
whether not is something

"but I think there's
a lot of sin going on"

a long wait in the lists
and the full Courbets like

snow falling over piles of shit
such sadness, you love all
the Annunciations you are feeling
very Sunday take axe to palm

"they weren't just Madonnas,
they were skies!"

so if we take it all down
and put it all up again differently
it will be the same elsewhere
changed as, if we changed we would
hate each other so we don't change
each other or others would love us

"oh shit! a run"

I see the Bellini mirror and this
time you follow me seeing me in it
first, the perfect image of my
existence with the sky above
me which has never frowned on me
in any dream of your knowledge

F.Y.I. (PRIX DE BEAUTÉ)

"Et peut-être je t'aimerais encore."
        —Louise Brooks

Lightly swaying as if clear and torn
                    the leaves float all over the sky
like the green under-edge of foam's boating
                                    a smile very black
like a diamond eating into glass a bullet burning
            its smile into the white fur through the smoke

                jealousy   cigar   projection

what you left on
            the bird cage regrettably
                                is the locked door
shouldn't it go too?
                it appears to be clear
                            then an emblem

finds itself being clutched around the standard in fear
to grow pale at your own image
                                        fear of the doppelgänger
feat of the gang toppling into the sea off the yacht bullets

that bright smile
                        is not going to turn out as brave as a factory
it just can't
                it's a matter of being handled
                                        "How many thousands
of pounds
            of flesh have to be given away"
                                    "I suppose so"
and you Miss Urop
                    to find dessert wrapped in your own face
say "no no no no no no" except for diamonds, then "peach juice"
        for eating there is no substitute like starving   it
appears to be
                finally given away for nothing
                                        knowledge regret icicles
                                    and shoes with sequins nails-heels

when   doubt   cloud   taste   forlorn   eyes   apt
    three   quarters   brows   black   dawn

                            you will send the engine
for the children over the children
                                in their bathing suits
"they are learning to water ski"
                            "they are learning to eat whale meat"
repos repos et repos
                    du calme du calme et encore du calme
your face is a snowball with a rock in it
                                    you are not to blame
            it appears to be a smile
                            it appears to be
death   brilliant   final   out

MADRID

Spain! much more beautiful than Egypt!
better than France and Alsace and Livorno! or Théophile Gautier!

nothing but rummies in Nice
                              and junkies in Tunis
but everything convulses under the silver tent of Spain
the dark
            the dry
                        the shark-bite sand-colored mouth
of Europa, the raped and swarthy goddess of speed! o Spain
to be in your arms again
                              and the dung-bright olives
bluely smiling at the quivering angulas
                                          smudge
                              against the wall of mind

where the silver turns
against the railroad tracks
                              and breath goes down
and down and down
                        into the cool moonlight
where the hotel room is on wheels
and there all buttocks are black and blue
                                          dun
is the color of the streets and sacks of beer
where dopes lead horses with a knight on each

            do you care if the rotunda is sparrowy
caught behind the arras of distaste and sorrow
                                          did you
                  wait, wait very long
                  or was it simply dark and you standing there

      I saw the end of a very long tale
      being delivered in the Rastro on Sunday morning
      and you were crying, and I was crying right away too

the Retiro confided in us
all those betrayals
                        we never meant but had to do, the leaves
            the foolish boats like High School
                              before the Alhambra
                              before the echo of your voice
I have done other things but never against you

            now I am going home
            I am watering the park for La Violetera
            I am cherishing the black and white of your love

426

Connais-tu peut-être la chanson ancienne "C'était un étranger"
in troubadour times it was very popular and made people act promiscuous
even though there were no subways then
elle continuait, cette chanson
"tu as tué mon coeur, 'tit voyou"
which is strange when you think of it
I don't believe the Church would have sanctioned that sort of thing
and besides it was sung to the air which later became
"Connais-tu le pays
où le citron fleurit"
an unimaginable sentiment
for Mignon! a voyou yet!

cherishing these reflections as I walked along, I came to a garbage dump
the poured concrete dome of which
was covered with children's inscriptions
the most interesting of which
was "I ate you up"
it was not a very interesting dump
so I pursued my "course" of thought
"tu es mon amour depuis . . ." oh no, not
that, and then "Ich fühle ein kleiner . . ."
unh unh
yet simply to walk, walk on, did not seem nearly enough for my rabid nerves
so I began to hum the Beer Barrel Polka
hopping and skipping along
in my scarf which came to my heels
and soon caught on a door knob

I was back in town!
what a relief!
I popped into the nearest movie-house and saw two marvelous Westerns
but, alas! this is all I remember of the magnificent poem I made on my walk
why are you reading this poem anyway?

MOZART CHEMISIER

For instance you walk in and faint
you are being one with Africa
I saw the soda standing next to the bay stallion
it was still foaming it had what is called a head on it
then I went and had a double carbonated bourbon on the porch
in the moonlight the poplars looked like aspidistra
over the unexperienced lake
wait, wait a while it all kept murmuring
but I know that always makes me so sad
there was a lot of tinselly sky out which irritated me too
and my anger is strictly European plan plan
now why would I get up and dance around
you see it is all very beautiful
the emphasis being on suds, suds in the lake, suds in my heart
luckily when the lake the tree was tempting me
I didn't have any white toreador pants
back at the ranch they were serving bubbly gin so I ran down the trail
so short a trail
so sweet a smell hay in your ears it's hot
oh world why are you so easy to figure out
beneath the ground there is something beautiful
I've had enough of sky
it's so obvious
everyone thinks they're going up
in these here America
put on your earrings we're going to the railroad station
I don't care how small the house they live in is
you don't have any earrings
I don't have a ticket

POEM EN FORME DE SAW

I ducked out of sight behind the sawmill
nobody saw me because of the falls the gates the sluice the tourist boats
the children were trailing their fingers in the water

and the swans, regal and smarty, were nipping their "little" fingers
I heard one swan remark "That was a good nip
though they are not as interesting as sausages" and another
reply "Nor as tasty as those peasants we got away from the elephant that time"
but I didn't really care for conversation that day
I wanted to be alone
which is why I went to the mill in the first place
now I am alone and hate it
I don't want to just make boards for the rest of my life
I'm distressed
the water is very beautiful but you can't go into it
because of the gunk
and the dog is always rolling over, I like dogs on their "little" feet
I think I may scamper off to Winnipeg to see Raymond
but what'll happen to the mill
I see the cobwebs collecting already
and later those other webs, those awful predatory webs
if I stay right here I will eventually get into the newspapers
like Robert Frost
willow trees, willow trees they remind me of Desdemona
I'm so damned literary
and at the same time the waters rushing past remind me of nothing
I'm so damned empty
what is all this vessel shit anyway
we are all rushing down the River Happy Times
ducking poling bumping sinking and swimming
and we arrive at the beach
the chaff is sand
alone as a tree bumping another tree in a storm
that's not really being alone, is it, signed The Saw

YESTERDAY DOWN AT THE CANAL

You say that everything is very simple and interesting
it makes me feel very wistful, like reading a great Russian novel does
I am terribly bored
sometimes it is like seeing a bad movie
other days, more often, it's like having an acute disease of the kidney
god knows it has nothing to do with the heart

nothing to do with people more interesting than myself
yak yak
that's an amusing thought
how can anyone be more amusing than oneself
how can anyone fail to be
can I borrow your forty-five
I only need one bullet preferably silver
if you can't be interesting at least you can be a legend
(but I hate all that crap)

WEATHER NEAR ST. BRIDGET'S STEEPLES

You are so beautiful and trusting
lying there on the sky
                              through the leaves
            you seem to be breathing softly
you look slightly nude, as if the clouds had parted

when the wind comes
                        you speak of an itch or a tickle
you are very gentle
                  I want to kiss you and I do
and look slightly shaggy and perfectly carved

when the sun sets you have two
red dots in the inner corner of each eye
and you smile
            look Buddha being fully sensual
                              and calm
having the gift of touching others beautifully

when the moon opens
                  my mind races with it
my body is asleep under you tingling
                              there is no
love, being the joining and the joining without memory
                              or fault

430

POLOVTSOI

white

                                        blood
                        dead
        when

                                ate
            fear
                    yes   red

            scare

                        pearl

    die   gay

        black
                    fit

        saturdaynight

                            parse

            fend

                    flame

        contend

                        disperse

LET'S GET OUT

Ouch! help. the helicopter is zooming down
it has stripes all over it
                it's the AAAAAAARMY

431

hate hornets wasps some waists and all wimples
make me blue
                unless I'm talking to you on the phone
not everyone can talk through their bellybutton
up we go

                how strong it all seems again
                how do I know you went I was outside
                with my nose pressed against the bronze

we will never be rich, unless you are
                            the sun says it's okay
down the hatchet in leather jackets
up the boulevard in a burnooses
at the Flore in foulards

what odd "future" is limping towards Idlewild

                pushing a lawnmower
                eating an orange
                limping along
                        though spastic

        later, that's it that's always it
        the only way not to leave is to go

SEVEN NINE SEVEN

A disgusting sun
                trying desperately to look lonely
walks over the asphalt shivering sky
a bottle of bleach
                when were you in Times Square
last do you miss it
                perhaps a bat will turn into
several women on a lawn with their arms twined

the cadaver draped over the quarry the leaves, oil
passing the dumb windmill
                               humping and wheezing
            little pieces of straw in the driveway
and in your hat and on your head
                                      that's right
be grumpy manwithahead manwithahand handwithahead a
boom   city   testicles flopping
serving the silence, swooning
                              I am a mural
you are two big cows hanging your head
                                           I am
a liver an orator
                  spook drawing window letters piled
drawing figure sticks bugs fatness circleness cats
cradles
          there is no ghost there is no wall there is
no people
              a formula for an elegy for a duchess drawn
drawn out
              cantering Moses-like through the monument
the snarl is buried
                  in a field of grain
                                      it is the
profile of a city
                  exploding against the old dull bed

          MEMOIR OF SERGEI O. . . .

      My feet have never been comfortable
      since I pulled them out of the Black Sea
      and came to your foul country
      what fatal day did I dry them off for
      travel loathsome travel to a world
      even older than the one I grew up in
      what fatal day meanwhile back in France
      they were stumbling towards the Bastille
      and the Princesse de Lamballe was
      shuddering as shudderingly as I
      with a lot less to lose I still hated
      to move sedentary as a roach of Tiflis

never again to go swimming in the nude
publicly little did I know how
awfulness could reach perfection abroad
I even thought I would see a Red Indian
all I saw was lipstick everything cov-
ered with grass or shrouds pretty
shrouds shot with silver and plasma
even the chairs are upholstered to a
smothering perfection of inanity
and there are no chandeliers and there
are no gates to the parks so you don't
know whether you're going in them or
coming out of them that's not relaxing
and so you can't really walk all you can
do is sit and drink coffee and brood
over the lost leaves and refreshing scum
of Georgia Georgia of my heritage
and dismay meanwhile back in my old
country they are renaming everything so
I can't even tell any more which ballet
company I am remembering with so much
pain and the same thing has started
here American Avenue Park Avenue South
Avenue of Chester Conklin Binnie Barnes
Boulevard Avenue of Toby Wing Barbara
Nichols Street where am I what is it
I can't even find a pond small enough
to drown in without being ostentatious
you are ruining your awful country and me
it is not new to do this it is terribly
democratic and ordinary and tired

METAPHYSICAL POEM

When do you want to go
I'm not sure I want to go there
where do you want to go
any place
I think I'd fall apart any place else
well I'll go if you really want to

I don't particularly care
but you'll fall apart any place else
I can just go home
I don't really mind going there
but I don't want to force you to go there
you won't be forcing me I'd just as soon
I wouldn't be able to stay long anyway
maybe we could go somewhere nearer
I'm not wearing a jacket
just like you weren't wearing a tie
well I didn't say we had to go
I don't care whether you're wearing one
we don't really have to do anything
well all right let's not
okay I'll call you
yes call me

ADVENTURES IN LIVING

How can you start hating me when I'm so comfortable in your raincoat
the apples kept bumping off the old gnarled banged-up biddy-assed tree
and I kept ducking and hugging and bobbing as if you were a tub of water
on Hallowe'en it was fun but you threw yourself into reverse like a tractor
hugging the ground in spring that was nice too more rain more raincoat

now the issue at stake seems to be
                        how am I going to get
                        my ripped raincoat collar repaired
              when yours is not around me keeping me warm and wet
              or should I get some money and buy
                        a big hooked-up military pocket deal
                              of my own
        well that's no paper doll you're talking about think it over
                        besides I'd be lonely
                        but besides I'd be safe and dry
                              oh let's play it by ear
                              there isn't any money anyway

here on the Esperanto River it's pretty mucky so I get out your suede
heeled pukka fatigue boots from the green box you left them in and put

my feet in them standing there like a Colossus in front of the sandbags
and the vines and the drownding water serpents stilled by my glare
drat those natives they never warned of sludge but I came prepared ho ho ho
oops my toe got stuck in your toe-print a little too big but comfy as hell

there you are
                    it's great to be back under the raincoat
                              shaking the vines off and stomping on the kitchen tiles
                              your breath feels like a radiator made of clouds
                              and the river has subsided and the rain is ystopped
                                             they weren't apples they were plums

FOR BILL BERKSON
(ON AGAIN LOOKING INTO *SATURDAY NIGHT*)

What you hope is beneath your skin

                                   is beneath your skin.

BIOTHERM (FOR BILL BERKSON)

The best thing in the world   but I better be quick about it
better be gone tomorrow
                              better be gone last night and
                    next Thursday better be gone
better be
                    always   or what's the use the sky
        the endless clouds trailing we leading them by the bandanna, red

you meet the Ambassador   "a year and a half of trying to make him"
        he is dressed in red, he has a red ribbon down his chest he
             has   7   gold decorations pinned to his gash

he sleeps a lot, thinks a lot, fucks a lot, impenetrable and Jude-ish
      I love him, you would love him too   if you could see outside

          whoops-musicale (sei tu m'ami) ahhahahahaha
       loppy di looploop   which is why   I suppose
Leontyne Price asked Secretary Goldberg to intervene with Metropera
it's not as dangerous as you think
           NEVERTHELESS (thank you, Aristotle)

    I know you are interested in the incongruities of my behavior, John
just as Bill you are interested in the blue paint JA Oscar Maxine Khnute
perhaps you'd better be particularly interested   POOF

               extended vibrations
ziggurats ZIG I to IV   stars of the Tigris-Euphrates basin
   leading ultimates such as kickapoo joyjuice halvah Canton cheese
in thimbles
        paraded for gain, but yet a parade kiss me,
             Busby Berkeley, kiss me
you have ended the war by simply singing in your Irene Dunne foreskin
"Practically Yours"
        with June Vincent, Lionello Venturi and Casper Citron
     a Universal-International release produced by G. Mennen Williams
               directed by Florine Stettheimer
               continuity by the Third Reich
after "hitting" the beach at Endzoay we drank up the liebfraumilch
       and pushed on up the Plata to the pampas
    you didn't pick up the emeralds you god-damned fool you got
       no collarbone you got no dish no ears
               Maurice Prendergast
               Tilly Losch
       "when the seizure tuck 'im 'e went" — Colette
besides, the snow was snowing, our fault for calling the ticket
         perhaps at the end of a very strange game
         you won   ? (?) ! (?)
    and that is important (yeah) to win (yeah)

bent on his knees the Old Mariner said where the fuck
    is that motel you told me about mister I aint come here for no clams
I want swimmingpool mudpacks the works carbonateddrugstorewater hiccups
fun a nice sissy under me clean and whistling a donkey to ride rocks
        "OKAY (smile) COMING UP"
   "This is, after all," said Margaret Dumont, "the *original* MAIN CHANCE"

(fart) "Suck this," said the Old M, spitting on his high heels
which he had just put on to get his navel up to her knee

but even that extended a little further,
            out into the desert, where
            no flash tested, no flashed!
            oops! and no nail polish, yak
                                yak, yak, Lieut.
            no flesh to taste no flash to tusk
            no flood to flee no fleed to dlown flom the iceth loot
"par exemple!"

out of the dark a monster appears full of grizzly odors which exhale through
him like a samovar belches out the news of the Comintern in a novel by
Howard Fast
        BUT
                    the cuckoo keeps falling off the branch so everything's okay
nobody worries about mistakes disasters calamities so long as they're "natural"
sun sun bene bene bullshit   it's important to be sensitive in business and
insensitive in love because what have you if you have no "balls" what made
the French important after all if not: jeu de balles, pas de balles and,
for murderers of Algerians, règle de balles   may I ask
                    "do you love it?"

    I don't think I want to win anything I think I want to die unadorned

                the dulcet waves are
                sweeping along in their purplish
                way and a little girl is
                beginning to cry and I know
                her but I can't help because
                she has just found her first brick
                what can you do what

does that seem a little too Garboesque? now Garbo, a strange case. oh god

keeping them alive
                there are more waves with bricks in them than there are
                        well-advertised mansions in the famous House
but we will begin again, won't we
                                well I will anyway or as 12,
        "continuez, même stupide garçon"

"This dedelie stroke, wherebye shall seace
The harborid sighis within my herte"

and at the doorway there is no
                              acceptable bong except stick mush
room for paranoia comme à l'heure de midi moins quatre
                                        et pour
JOUR DE FÊTE j'ai composé mon "Glorification" hommage au poète américain
                lyrique et profond, Wallace Stevens
                                          but one
                of your American tourists told me he was a banker
                              quels délices
        I would like to tell you what I think about bankers but . . .
                except W. C. Fields

what do you want from a bank but love   ouch
                but I don't get any love from Wallace Stevens no I don't
I think délices is a lot of horseshit and that comes from one who infinitely
                                    prefers bullshit
                        and the bank rolled on
                        and Stevens strolled on
                        an ordinary evening alone
                        with a lot of people

                "the flow'r you once threw at me
                socked me with hit me over the head avec
                has been a real blessing let me think
                while lying here with the lice
                                    you're a dream"

AND

                "measure shmeasure know shknew
                unless the material rattle us around
                pretty rose preserved in biotherm
                and yet the y bothers us when we dance
                                        the pussy pout"
                        never liked to sing much but that's what being
                                a child means   BONG

le bateleur! how wonderful
I'm so so so so so so so so so so so happy
so happy I make you happy
like in the s- s- s- s- soap opera wow
        what else I mean what else do you need (I)

                                        then you
                          were making me happy otherwise I
                          was staring into *Saturday Night* and flag
                          pink shirt with holes cinzano-soda-grin
                          unh. it is just too pleasant to b.w.y.

hey! help! come back! you spilled your omelette all over your pants!
oh damn it, I guess that's the end of one of our meetings

"vass hass der mensch geplooped
that there is sunk in the battlefield a stately grunt
and the idle fluice still playing on the hill
because of this this this this slunt"
                                        it's a secret told by
                                        a madman in a parlor car
                                        signifying chuckles
                                            * Richard Widmark *
                                            * Gene Tierney *
                                            * Googie Withers *

            I hate the hat you are not wearing, I love to see your narrow head

there in the dark London streets
                              there were all sorts of murderers
                        gamblers and Greek wrestlers
                "I could have had all of wrestling in London in my hand"
                        BANG
                                        down by the greasy Thames shack
                                            stumbling up and over

            (PROKOFIEVIANA)

One day   you are posing in your checkerboard bathing trunks
    the bear eats only honey   what a strange life

is the best of mine impossible   what does it mean

                  that equally strange smile it's like seeing the moon rise
                            "keep believing it"
            you will not want, from me

    where you were no longer exists
    which is why we will go see it to be close to you how could it leave

440

I would never leave you
if I didn't have to

                    you will have to too
                    Soviet society taught us that
                    is the necessity to be "realistic" love is a football
                              I only hear the pianos
               when possession turns into frustration
               the North Star goes out will it
               is there anyone there
the seismograph at Fordham University says it will
                                  so it will not

                        we are alone no one is talking it feels good
              we have our usual contest about claustrophobia
              it doesn't matter much
              doing without each other is much more insane

                      okay, it's not the sun setting it's the moon rising
                      I see it that way too

        (BACK TO SATIE)

when the *Vitalità nell' arte* catalog came in the mail I laughed
              thinking it was *Perspectives USA* but it wasn't it
              was vitality nellie arty ho ho that's a joke pop
              "I never had to see I just kept looking at the pictures"
                          damn good show!
                          don't I know it?
                          take off your glasses
                          you're breaking my frame
                          sculptresses wear dresses

    Lo! the Caracas transport lunch with George Al Leslie 5:30 I'll
be over at 5
               I hope you will I'm dying of loneliness
               here with my red blue green and natch pencils and the erasers
               with the mirror behind me and the desk in front of me
               like an anti-Cocteau movement
"who did you have lunch with?" "you" "oops!" how ARE you

              then too, the other day I was walking through a train
             with my suitcase and I overheard someone say "speaking of faggots"
             now isn't life difficult enough without that
             and why am I always carrying something
             well it was a shitty looking person anyway
             better a faggot than a farthead

or as fathers have often said to friends of mine
"better dead than a dope" "if I thought you were queer I'd kill you"
you'd be right to, DAD, daddio, addled annie pad-lark (Brit. 19th C.)

well everything can't be perfect
you said it

I definitely do not think that Lobelia would be a suitable name
for Carey and Norman's daughter if they have a daughter
and if they have a son Silverrod is insupportable by most
put that back in your pipe Patsy and make pot out of it honey

you were there I was here you were here I was there where are you I miss you
(that was an example of the "sonnet" "form") (this is another)
when you went I stayed and then I went and we were both lost and then I died

oh god what joy
you're here
sob and at the
most recent summit
conference they
are eating string
beans butter
smootch slurp
pass me the filth
and a coke pal
oh thank you

down at the box-office of Town Hall I was thinking of you in your no hat
music often reminds me of nothing, that way, like reforming

September 15 (supine, unshaven, hungover, passive, softspoken) I was
very happy
on Altair 4, I love you that way, it was on Altair 4 "a happy day"
I knew it would be
yes to everything
I think you will find the pot in the corner
where the Krells left it
rub it a little and music comes out
the music of the fears
I reformed we reformed each other
being available
it is something our friends don't understand
if you loosen your tie
my heart will leap out
like a Tanagra sculpture
from the crater of the Corsican "lip"

and flying through the heavens
                              I am reminded of Kit Carson
and all those smiles which were exactly like yours
but we hadn't met yet
                         when are you going away on "our" trip
why are you melancholy
                           if I make you angry you are no longer doubtful
if I make you happy you are no longer doubtful
                                        what's wrong with doubt

it is mostly that your face
is like the sky behind the Sherry Netherland
blue instead of air, touching instead of remote, warm instead of racing
you are as intimate as a "cup" of vodka
                    and when yesterday arrives and troubles us you always say NO
                    I don't believe you at first but you say no no no no
                    and pretty soon I am smiling and doing just what I want
                    again
                              that's very important
                              you put the shit back in the drain
                              and then you actually find the stopper

take back September 15 to Aug something
I think you are wonderful on your birthday
                              I think you are wonderful
        on all your substitute birthdays
                         I am rather irritated at your being born
                              at all
                         where did you put that stopper
                    you are the biggest fool I ever laid eyes on
                    that's what they thought about the Magi, I believe

first you peel the potatoes
then you marinate the peelies
in campari all the while playing
the Mephisto Waltz on your gram
and wrap them in grape leaves
and bake them in mush ouch
that god damn oven delicacies
the ditch is full of after dinner
                              what sky
                              out there in between the ailanthuses
                              a 17th Century prison an aardvark
                              a photograph of Mussolini and
                              a personal letter from Isak Dinesen
                              written after eating

the world of thrills! 7 Lively Arts! Week-in-Review! whew!
if you lie there asleep on the floor after lunch
what else is there for me to do but adore you
I am sitting on top of Mauna Loa seeing thinking feeling
the breeze rustles through the mountain gently trusts me
I am guarding it from mess and measure

                        it is cool
                        I am high
                        and happy
                        as it turns
                        on the earth
                        tangles me
                        in the air

the celestial drapery salutes an ordinary occurrence
the moon is rising I am always thinking of the moon rising
                      I am always thinking of you
                      your morality your carved lips
on the beach we stood on our heads
I held your legs it was summer and hot
the Bloody Marys were spilling on our trunks
but the crocodiles didn't pull them
it was a charmed life full of
innuendos and desirable hostilities
I wish we were back there among the
irritating grasses and the helmet crabs
the spindrift gawk towards Swan Lake Allegra Kent
those Ten Steps of Patricia Wilde
unison matches anxious putty Alhambra
bus-loads of Russians' dignity desire
when we meet we smile in another language

               you don't know the half of it
               I never said I did
               your mortality
               I am very serious

ENDGAME WAITING FOR GODOT WATT HAPPY DAYS which means I love you
what is that hat doing on that table in my room where I am asleep
        "thank you for the dark and the shoulders"
        "oh   thank you"

okay I'll meet you at the weather station at 5
we'll take a helicopter into the "eye" of the storm
we'll be so happy in the center of things at last
now the wind rushes up nothing happens and departs
L'EUROPA LETTERATURA CINEMATOGRAFICA ARTISTICA 9-10

444

your back the street   solidity   fragility erosion
why did this Jewish hurricane have to come
and ruin our Yom Kippur

favorites: vichyssoise, capers, bandannas, fudge-nut-ice, collapsibility,
    the bar of the Winslow, 5:30 and 12:30, leather sweaters, tunafish,
    cinzano and soda, Marjorie Rambeau in *Inspiration*
                    whatdoyoumeanandhowdoyoumeanit

        (MENU)
     Déjeuner Bill Berkson
      30 August 1961

Hors-d'oeuvre abstrait-expressionistes, américain-styles, bord-durs, etc.
Soupe Samedi Soir à la Strawberry-Blonde
Poisson Pas de Dix au style Patricia
Histoire de contrefilet, sauce Angelicus Fobb
La réunion des fins de thon à la boue
Chapon ouvert brûlé à l'Hoban, sauce Fidelio Fobb
Poèmes 1960-61 en salade

       Fromage de la Tour Dimanche 17 septembre
       Fruits des Jardins shakspériens
       Biscuits de l'*Inspiration* de Clarence Brown

Vin blanc supérieur de Bunkie Hearst
Vin rouge mélancholique de Boule de neige
Champagne d'*Art News* éditeur diapré
Café ivesianien "Plongez au fond du lac glacé"
              Vodka-campari et TV

as the clouds parted the New York City Ballet opened Casey Stengel was there
with Blanche Yurka, "Bones" Mifflin, Vera-Ellen and Alice Pearce, Stuts
"Bearcat" Lonklin and Louella "Prudential" Parsons in another "box," Elsa
"I-Don't-Believe-You're-a-Rothschild" Maxwell wouldn't speak to them
because she wasn't "in" the party and despite the general vulgarity Diana
Adams again looked exactly like the moon as she appears in the works of
Alfred de Musset and me
            who am I? I am the floorboards of that zonked palace

after the repast the reap (hic) the future is always fustian (ugh)
    nobody is Anglican everybody is anguished

"now the past is something else the past is like a future that came through
you can remember everything accurately and be proud of your honesty you can

lie about everything that happened and be happily reminiscent you can alter
here and there for increased values you can truly misremember and have it
both ways or you can forget everything completely the past is really something"

            but the future always fall' through!
            for instance will I ever really go live
            in Providence Rhode Island or Paestum Lucania
            I doubt it   "you are a rose, though?" (?)

a long history of populations, though
the phrase beginning with "Palms!" and quickly forgotten
in the pit under the dark there were books
being written about strange rites of the time
the time was called The Past and the books were in German
which scholars took to be Sanskrit or Urdu
(much laughter) which later turned out to be indeed
Sanskrit or Urdu (end of laughter, start of fight)
and at the same time the dark was going on and on
never getting bluer or greener or purpler just
going on and that was civilization and still is
nobody could see the fight but they could hear what
it was about and that's the way things were and stayed
and are except that in time the sounds started to
sound different (familiarity) and that was English

                        well, that Past we have always with us, eh?
                        I am talking about the color of money
                        the dime so red and the 100 dollar bill so orchid
                        the sickly fuchsia of a 1 the optimistic
                        orange of a 5 the useless penny like a seed
                        the magnificent yellow zinnia of a 10
                        especially a roll of them the airy blue of a
                        50 how pretty a house is when it's filled with them
                        that's not a villa that's a bank
                        where's the ocean
now this is not a tract against usury it's just putting two and two together
                              and getting five (thank you, Mae)

     actually I want to hear more about your family
                           yes you get the beer

I am actually thinking about how much I love Lena Horne
I never intended to go to New Hampshire without you
you know there's an interesting divinity in Rarotonga that looks sort of like you

"I am a woman in love" he said
the day began with the clear blue sky and ended in the Parrot Garden
the day began and ended with my finding you in the Parrot Garden
Lena Horne had vanished into a taxi and we were moreorless alone together
of course it wasn't Lena Horne it was Simone Signoret we were happy anyway

      "As if a clear lake meddling with itself
        Should cloud its pureness with a muddy gloom"

      "My steeds are all pawing at the threshold of the morn"

favorites: going to parties with you, being in corners at parties with you,
          being in gloomy pubs with you smiling, poking you at parties when
          you're "down," coming on like South Pacific with you at them,
          shrimping with you into the Russian dressing, leaving parties with
          you alone to go and eat a piece of cloud

        YIPE! 504 nails in *The Gross Clinic*!
        it's more interesting to see a Princess dance
        with a Bluebird than just two bluebirds
        dancing through diagonal vist' together

at the flea circus there was a bargain-hunter
at the end of the road a bum, the blue year
commenced with an enormous sale of loneliness
and everyone came back with a little something
one a baby, one a tooth, one a case of clap
and, best of all, a friend bought a medical dispensary
there were a lot of limbs lying around so
of course someone created a ballet company, oke
the barely possible snow sifted into a solid crystal·
I sometimes think you are Mozart's nephew: "Talk
to me Harry Winston, tell me all about it!"

        "from August to October
        the sun drips down the sign
        for eating at midnight ask Virgo
        to be lost outside the cafeteria"

I went to Albania for coffee and came back for the rent day
"I think somebody oughta go through your mind with a good eraser"
meanwhile Joe is tracing love and hate back to the La Brea tar-pits

        hear that rattling?
those aren't marbles in my head they're chains on my ankles

why do you say you're a bottle and you feed me
the sky is more blue and it is getting cold
last night I saw Garfinkel's Surgical Supply truck
and knew I was near "home" though dazed and thoughtful
                    what did you do to make me think
                    after we led the bum to the hospital
                    and you got into the cab
                    I was feeling lost myself

                    (ALWAYS)

never to lose those moments in the Carlyle without a tie

endless as a stick-pin barely visible you
drown whatever one thought of as perception and
let all the clouds in under the yellow heaters
meeting   somewhere over St. Louis
call me earlier because I might want to do something else
except eat   ugh

endlessly unraveling itself before the Christopher Columbus Tavern
quite a series was born   as where I am going is to
Quo Vadis for lunch
out there in the blabbing wind and glass   c'est l'azur

perhaps
marinated duck saddle with foot sauce and a tumbler of vodka
picking at my fevered brain
perhaps
letting you off the hook at last or leaning on you in the theatre

oh plankton!
"mes poèmes lyriques, à partir de 1897, peuvent se lire comme un journal intime"

yes always though you said it first
you the quicksand and sand and grass
as I wave toward you freely
the ego-ridden sea
there is a light there that neither
of us will obscure
rubbing it all white
saving ships from fucking up on the rocks
on the infinite waves of skin smelly and crushed and light and absorbed

POEM

Lana Turner has collapsed!
I was trotting along and suddenly
it started raining and snowing
and you said it was hailing
but hailing hits you on the head
hard so it was really snowing and
raining and I was in such a hurry
to meet you but the traffic
was acting exactly like the sky
and suddenly I see a headline
LANA TURNER HAS COLLAPSED!
there is no snow in Hollywood
there is no rain in California
I have been to lots of parties
and acted perfectly disgraceful
but I never actually collapsed
oh Lana Turner we love you get up

POEM

Dee Dum, dee dum, dum dum, dee da
here it is March 9th 1962
and JJ is shooting off to work
I loll in bed reading *Poets of Russia*
feeling perfectly awful and smoking

hey wait a minute! I leap out of bed
it's Sam Barber's birthday and they
are going to play *Souvenirs*! turn it up!
how glad I am I'm going to be late that's
starting the day with rose-colored binoculars!

CLYTEMNESTRA

"Oh thou inspiring scepter of my spoon"
we have a lot of raisin bread in the house
and Garfinkle's is cleaning up its marquee
you think you are pretty hot stuff but
you are just he she and me her are you

he walked to the store and came back
a better barrel of pickle dream green and yellow
you would guess he was Mr. Saperstein or you

you would feel that the wall came
down because snow the blinking staring wink-eyed flippy-lipped white-up went
you are always drawing conclusions that he she me and you wouldn't ordinarily
or wow the spangle said of your bandanna hanging on your door in your bathroom
all, alas, limp and sticky with your steam your lanolin plus your whip
your Nazi dirk and your dirty nuts, she said you
I mean you damn it which was the first time she ever used I
in anger wouldn't you guess it of course you would being you
you will be smiling on the other side of your smiling other side in a minute

meanwhile back in Reno
in a minute was taking over the you
and you were so irritated you
threw your rubbers at the two of them
you having two to throw, you
are often lucky having two
when you feel like a throw lucky you

ice has caught in my heart   you will tell her but she
has deafened your doornail   will never believe you
your towel is black with kisses   but she will defend to the death
"a bee sleeps in the briars of my heart" your right to tell her
you believe it don't you   and there is some end in that

when Millicent leaked tomato juice onto Marge
you said turn over the toast or we're done for
that's all you all right all you all over again
I don't mind being only the second time this time

your time is my   ouch is the balloon
something is fading blooming   is it a fart or a departure

POEM

Signed "The Seeing Eye"
you walk under the falsely constructed viaduct
and I hold your arm because you are reading
other people think we are blocking the way
not me
I think it is real service
like in Sophie Tucker

where are you
I have your arm I feel your muscle
but I don't know where "you" are
oh there you are
you are reading
what an odd thing to do while walking
well anyway it makes me a seeing eye

did you know that the snow in Irkutok
is building-high and
did you know you could get high on buildings
you can get stoned out of your head
that's construction for you

well I am leading you on
to a pleasant meal
put the bones in your adjacent serving dish
and have a good time

FOR DAVID SCHUBERT

"Best of all—an aviator on a fire net."

I am Gabriel (dressed in corduroy) am
not listed in the Manhattan phone directory
but am in Edwin Denby's New York cycle
of poems
            we live here in the falling
plaster and get this way that way
going to Gorky shows and looking at

"ink and chalk forms" all the time it is
simpler to be by the sea or in a boat
then you can jump
                              in
                    I miss you
but I never knew you anyway so there
you are or do I know you better than I
would have at 42nd Street and 8th Avenue

well you go up we follow you but you
go up we follow you but you go up we are
following you but you are gone last
Saturday I saw *The Knights of the Round Table*

CAPTAINS COURAGEOUS

"He fell off a barn on his head
and he played with rag dolls for 30 years"

                    do you really think they fish in heaven"

hey! my heart! I find it a great comfort to read this cable
        made of paper and rolled like a cigarette
but the walk took a long time
                    rude snow fell and Lavoris-colored rain
            I was bored on board a ship at sea and walk

"passing a barn there was a thump
but the dazzling end came full of papers flushed with hash and pot"

                    a step at a time and flopped"

I neglected worldliness
                    it did not make me a pure extirpated brother
I wonder what the geography is I hope the fish don't cry
    I remember the Green Banks your invisible hat the Flying Swan
    I remember you
                    that Rudyard Kipling knew what he was walking about

                    there was a dinge
                    holed up in the
                    hold thought death
                    was near Cape Hook

        Now I am entirely enclosed within this pine tree
    and no magical spirit sweeps forward into the latterly
                    the trident shook deservedly I must obey his art is of such
                    when you have remembered

    batfowling I saw thine eye and cheek proclaim a matter which is not
                    what anything's about and
                    yet crown face head imagination our shoulders are reveries
                    of afternoons in Pied Ninny

    I like to pull horsehairs out of lapels of jackets
    the easy emptiness of Ella Cinders
                                        "as rootedly as I"
    and the cannon usurps the sidewalk during a heated argument
            so that the end will not justify a benevolent need, so tall

    LEGEND

    "You give me money happy days"
    the little Chinese girl said
                            to the American soldier before
                            he threw the package of rice at her
    that is differential calculus
    I don't care ha ha I love 32 fouettés more than anything whoopee

    and passed on toward the derelict schooner
                            it was May and the gulls
                            were (swoop) out (swoon)
    yet the Captain told the little Chinese girl to stay in her cabin
    or he'd goose her

perilous days! Sun Yat
and the Yankee pirates
                                    I was a temple bell
when did you come out East
I was sent
well then, the Arctic!
                        when the ranch was blown up
                        pa told me ma did it
                        but she couldn't have she'd run away
I tell you this only so you'll understand why I'm difficult sometimes

and the earrings kept jangling
emeralds earrings
and the soldiers kept saying "Lotus blossom lotus beam"

                        the very next dinner at the country club
                        Madame was unmasked she was
                        really Visionary Puce "the Cocktail Hour Strip"
Hughie had brought her
so he was shipped out
still looking for his Canton Camilla
                        but the war was on this time

        oh god how we fought
        but the sirens sang
        their edaneres which
        is serenade (in Laotian)

                                            so
                                            at least a month
                                            passed
                                            and the camels
                                            spit on us
                then the nurses came
                we'd been interned in the water
                and one swam down with
                a white blossom in her teeth

I was looking for treasure
it was her all right
because if you can just lay your hands on a little gilt you can survive

                        so as a murderer
                        I came to be known as The Drowner
                        that is my story

MAUNDY SATURDAY

Why must all Russian composers   try to be brave
one more trombone and I'll go out of my mind   like Canadian
poets try to be honest   honest for the love of god how boring
yet I will always value that moment when I hated you   the
drawing by Stravinsky   and the *Paris Review*
already white impatience makes night "fall"   down
Fantômas   as if Traviata had fucked everyone
in New York   I guess that's a little too neat
"Franck O'Hara"   Marceline Pleynet   ego
Niki de St Phalle   a long drunken talk with Maxine
"these are my jewels"   don't you
hate to think really think   "croce delizia" what it means
yeah "mysterioso" all right   ahahahahoh ahah   or O'Hara
I suppose (blah)   "palpito"   a season
of nuts   well they're interesting to lick
I think continually of Francis Robinson   Texas *is* Texaco
"Fritz Reiner discovered me"   not quite I was still underage
but Ilya Mourometz   and the dull air over Agatha's prayer
why is it that Verdi is closer to us than Aristotle
what difference does it make   (Texas?) corraggio
my beautiful Cavallon seems to promise something   but
it will never arrive   and I will never leave   if
I could destroy my ego   but I might end up with only an id
Mozart was the first   and with Elizabeth Rethberg
yipe   and the strange dark girl looking at me all
last night I think she is strange   looking
is exhausting   "Monsieur"   mysiremylord
and you will always   no, you never will   *in der fremde*
the rice is still on the floor   and I am still

NEW PARTICLES FROM THE SUN

From Canada   Leningrad Kirov   Saint-Saëns   ex-Maryinsky
"from which he had saved them in '46"   she went screaming into the ditch
aloha oe   a passing fit of masturbation swept over the land of firtrees
it passed, shining bluely in the rain they stood up to be counted on

455

three minutes after one thirteen to go   your 47th cigarette
they ate you in a dream, the ants that are reconnoitring my leg
              and the passage of night
              and the passage of beard
              what a weight what a wound

                        the apple tingling
a panoramic licentiousness of taste   a tambourine of byrrh
                        my Armenian eyes
         sand everywhere in my head strands   frantic scratches the
         of mirror and saint armpit face lips   calm honeyness of hair
         and the amber sky stretching the dune
         's protective smile into Nijinsky

                        le terrain vague
                        sperme cheminée
                        joint-ownership
                        la stangue . . . (of all that)

joined here by the Minister of Spain
I found a very touching aperitif being prepared
ozone poured out of the ear to which my own
match was being applied in front of a Picasso
still life of 1924, OR in almost any movie
as the lost wax process results in bronze masterpieces
I accept Juan Carlos and the Divinity of Princes

               what presented itself as pregnant
               fell out
               became a parade
               the "vast" European "continent"

               Leningrad Kirov ex-Maryinsky dream continuity space disgust
               "Because only once does prosperity let you get away"
               the seeming eventuality of a misunderstood conversation
               "there is a praint steeming in the Rathbone" pix
               a logical *doyouordontyoupleasepleasebangcrashwhyspook*
               to the deserted isle   to the deserted isle
                     chiffonier*   balustrade*   cotillon*

when the magical change approached the end (during a performance of *Mazeppa*)
we thrust ourselves into a canoe and made for the rapids which had dried
up during the spring torrents and washed away most of our kinsmen there
on the heather blanket of Rib Reek, a continent rose swellingly to the
admiration of all pressurecookersalesmen since it was living proof of
the products they'd been giving away their bran-stamps for all along and
the Mistress of Coventry appeared inlaid with dams (as in Boulder) sighed
almost asphyxiated and danced almost anguished because of certain unasked-
for sideburns curly crinkly and wet on the glass out of which she was
looking towards the New World of watches, a specific sentient change . . .

Not the grey stranded end of a raffish explosion (and not the not either)
you will find a querulous skunk ending his strand somewhere else (or not?)
no, there is a definite end
      the caprice tends to coagulate, dinner to cool
querulosity has its own answers
        the lofty din of mushrooms assumes an identity
quite apart from omelettes and shirtfronts
         O Saratoga Day Train where are you?
where is Chesapeake Cumberland and Gap Express? the sky is blue but there
is nothing in it, nothing but flies, mere flies, O Egypt, O Aldebaran!

    one day I was walking down the turnpike
    with my glass of tools in my left hand
    and I spied an obstetrical case on the
    squeeze-ahead to which I nodded "Twins"
    squeezing my heels into the flanks of my
    mother bringing her to a quick gaited trot
    which took me off the pike and into the center
    there I purchased a spanking new Fiat
    and set out for more purchases it was dawn

  the theory of calisthenics is tiring
      the orgone is a bust
when a man has worked all his life for something he hardly knows what it is
   that is called technique in the books
        and in the trade tricks
  I wish I were a trickster instead of a machinist (I am not a machinist)
the Empire I am most interested in is Han (which is a dynasty)
  I hate the idea of dynasties, let alone children, I am a machinist
you don't want a machine to give birth to a machine, but to itself again
  my theory being that an exact other is better than another one
it is a great trouble keeping the parts straight even science doesn't understand

    the way to the mint was paved with terror
    I was sure everyone knew what we were about
    which was to straighten everything out
    and start afresh somewhere else (afresh, hmmmm)
    and the motor failed and then the driver's
    nerves (inexplicable, one would have thought
    the opposite), so we stole the gold on foot
    weary and heartsore we trudged on the first mile
    a grand hole appeared in the leather and then

on the other foot a bleeding welt on my great
toe later an abortive water on my other knee
a strange doctor bandaged my calf bitten
by cacti and then we were home our country collapsed

the duty each man has to his country is similar
                                        to that of a stock car
"spare the driver" so that "one at least remains to tell thee"
                                                    that's what
        I was taught in machining school and that's what I believe
old as I am and spleenish as a brook trout at dusk when fingers look like worms
        they've looked like worms all along
                            put them in a manifold (what are they)
                            well I guess I've had my say

FIRST DANCES

1
From behind he takes her waist
and lifts her, her lavender waist
stained with tears and her mascara
is running, her neck is tired
from drooping. She floats she steps
automatically correct, then suddenly
she is alive up there and smiles.
How much greater triumph for him
that she had so despaired when his
hands encircled her like a pillar
and lifted her into the air
which after him will turn to rock-
like boredom, but not till after
many hims and he will not be there.

2
The punch bowl was near the cloakroom
so the pints could be taken out of the
boys' cloaks and dumped into the punch.
Outside the branches beat hysterically
towards the chandeliers, just fended
off by fearful windows. The chandeliers
giggle a little. There were many

introductions but few invitations. I
found a spot of paint on my coat as
others found pimples. It is easy to
dance it is even easy to dance together
sometimes. We were very young and ugly
we knew it, everybody knew it.

3
A white hall inside a church. Nerves.

POLITICAL POEM ON A LAST LINE OF PASTERNAK'S

'A certain person's epoch's burning'
religious philosophy would like assurances
there are lesser problems which
minimum number of standees exhortations
and analyses the irony is that despite
ernment partnership
                    Mr. Meyer is on the
in some degree the movement   and again
at the moment 163 countries
microwave (wireless) or land line or
can A T & T be regulated?
                              yet
at this moment Marburg is forgotten
the light drifts slowly through
vinelike curtains of white while up
the stairs someone is pouting in tangled
sleep across the grass and boring little
red breasts trot and thump on worms
the grass soothes itself and purrs onward
into the street under the house over the
studio the wind reaches for where
lucid blossoms where in spring the
Polish pain of snow has melted the
statistics have become keyboards and
scratches on an old Chabrier record
though the death is dressing as always before
an enormous mirror which isn't the sea
how do you get to Spain and eat grapes and only grapes

Warm plantains and chilled light radishes
of morning, the Wildean dawn comprehensive and
chilling, instantly finishing a sentence before
the sentence has begun. So clear and astute,
the day under the catbird has already done with
all my meanings that I got up to see, cares
only for the trees and grass, even the house
shivers and moans in the early light.

         All
those insomniac decisions are gone because
the day is already over, so I go in to sleep.
Not without feeling betrayed and hating it.

I wake up at 10:30 and the telegrams start
arriving and the phones start ringing, for
though here in the villa I have only one room
I have several phones. And a dictograph.
One would imagine that Giulia had gone insane
but never mind that. The day is over, there
is no more insanity.

       When I think of that
bastard swimming that dreary creek in his
irregular fashion, at least I assume so since
he walks that way, it makes my blood boil.
The last a metaphor for breakfast, which I
soon valiantly consume.

        And now at last I am
alone again and night, at last, has come.
I shall find again those solutions which the
day has took, and make my history into a hat.

BALLADE NUMBER 4

A man in a beige suit walks
down the street with a woman
grey in a blue print dress

it is mournful, agonizing even
perhaps she is his mother
did she commit suicide or die
just incidentally, full of
mazurkas you will wait a long
time
      what the ship knew when
it banged into the port or
your mystique of selfness
what a strange preoccupation
for an adult
              I will grant you
this little lullaby this lily
that's been shat-upon and its
delicate mouth will open to
the starless world of my dreams
I want, too, to go to Missolonghi
pouring out the whenever part
of my life
          a countess described
herself in terms of damask
that will be a very short wall
covered with cloth a short view
of the Hebrides when you arrived
I took it for granted you were
leaving so you left a long story
ending in the shallows
                 where
is the kismet of this TV night
"oriental dream" bacon rind
I walked along in the sun looking
for the pelican
          a court dance
how fortunate that the 20th Century
can still muster up enough
charlatans to perform it well
that is the art of it all the
mustering towards the dead I
conceive of this ballad as
a parable closer to Tarzan than
the Bible do you end in fun
or do you hate everything red
and alive

1
When the wheat got out of the can
a seascape
    tumbling with sunny pines
your rib against my nose
      gasping
on the towel-roughened rocks
the rock-pool warmly
     smiling out
what the summer thunk
     I do not
care if we never get back there
  but we are
    in new shorts not
quite as comfortable
     and the tree
still bending over the inlet
as we hang
   then drop into the freeze

2
Out of the mild pleasantness of disaster
an acorn
    you think you know what it means
it's sort of phallic or foolish, has a value

but you can't stuff a turkey with that or a goose
it's not truffles
    it doesn't break your heart
it doesn't even lean over and smile, has no waist

I want you to take that cup down off the shelf
and break it against the window
     then I will
wash the window and the sun will shine through

that's the way things happen between people
though the roles get reversed
     like when a flower
comes up too early in the spring and gets bitten
and dies off
   summer is still in its troika, belting
along the dirt road raising a crowd of dust
    to hide everything disagreeable

now I am going to open the hydrant and when the fountain
of ice is formed
                    I'm going to run in and out of it

as if it were a tree
and I'm a noose
                    hello, here's your morning paper
                    Kennedy is in Colombia, cheers

GALANTA

A strange den or music room
                              childhood
dream of Persian grass configured distilled
first hardon milky mess
                         the about-to-be
dead surrounding the already surrounded folk-
hero with a veil of automobile accidents
broken cocktail glasses
                         oh Sally
is still acting the mise en scène of her
great grandmother's embroidered graveyard
while I
            my asiatic tendencies have taken me
to the Baghdad of neurasthenia and
false objectivity
                    faint hope for a familial
contrast for a far-reaching decadence
which presupposes unnatural unselfishness
your sweet yellow hair
                         among the mosques
the faint tribal twitch of your altered
blue eyes
            when Canaan was reached you
called me France we threw sand in our eyes
and ran naked
                    down the street of our awful
progenitors
                    when life is fantastic there

is no chance for make-believe how lucky
the French bourgeois pain
                              could be if we
were children again and everything uninteresting
you never had a chance to be
                              Emma Bovary
nor I Julien Sorel in that attic in the States
and now
                    I remember you only through American
Folk Art opening near the Fonda del Sol
where are you Sally with your practicality
and bottles of fireflies
                              blinking on
and off for footlights

BIOGRAPHIA LETTERARIA

GERTRUDE STEIN
She hated herself because she wrote prose.

JAMES JOYCE
He was a very lovable person, though thorough.

RONALD FIRBANK
I will not go home with you, so perhaps I shall.

IVY COMPTON-BURNETT
My grandfather's lap was comfortable and becoming speaking is not becoming a cactus.

PHILIP ROTH
How do you do, Mr. Rahv; I hope you will print my friend.

CLEMENT GREENBERG
How Orphic?

CHARLES DICKENS
He hated pretense. He was the founder of Social Security.

LAWRENCE OF ARABIA

Cognac is not KY.

TERESA OF AVILA

My ink is hardly dry upon the page.

SAINT PAUL

The light that failed.

GROVER WHALEN

A hoot he had. A crease he did not. The water crusheth, the booth notth.

PIERRE BOULEZ

In a sense I have not really arrived into your country, yet.

BARON HAUSSMANN

As I see it, everything is at right angles, like the flowers, Kenneth.

ARCHIBALD MACLEISH

I heard a creep swimming by me in the lighthouse.

LINES FOR THE FORTUNE COOKIES

I think you're wonderful and so does everyone else.

Just as Jackie Kennedy had a baby boy, so will you—even bigger.

You will meet a tall beautiful blonde stranger, but you will not say hello.

You will take a long trip and you will be very happy, though alone.

You will marry the first person who tells you your eyes are like scrambled eggs.

In the beginning there was YOU—there will always be YOU, I guess.

You will write a great play and it will run for three performances.

Please phone *The Village Voice* immediately: they want to interview you.

Roger L. Stevens and Kermit Bloomgarden have their eyes on you.

Relax a little; one of your most celebrated nervous tics will be your undoing.

Your first volume of poetry will be published as soon as you finish it.

You may be a hit uptown, but downtown you're *legendary!*

Your walk has a musical quality which will bring you fame and fortune.

You will eat cake.

Who do you think you are, anyway? Jo Van Fleet?

You think your life is like Pirandello, but it's really like O'Neill.

A few dance lessons with James Waring and who knows? Maybe something will happen.

That's not a run in your stocking, it's a hand on your leg.

I realize you've lived in France, but that doesn't mean you know EVERYTHING!

You should wear white more often—it becomes you.

The next person to speak to you will have a very intriguing proposal to make.

A lot of people in this room wish they were you.

Have you been to Mike Goldberg's show? Al Leslie's? Lee Krasner's?

At times, your disinterestedness may seem insincere, to strangers.

Now that the election's over, what are you going to do with yourself?

You are a prisoner in a *croissant* factory and you love it.

You eat meat. Why do you eat meat?

Beyond the horizon there is a vale of gloom.

You too could be Premier of France, if only . . . if only . . .

1

If only more people looked like Jerry Lieber we would all be a lot happier, I think.

2

It is May 17th, 17 is a strangely sonorous number, and I haven't made out my income tax yet.

3

There is a man going by with his arm in a sling. I wish men could take care of themselves better.

4

Mahler is great, Bruckner is terrible.

5

Listen, I have to go out to get food. If you want some cigarettes, I'll go out with you.

6

Where they've come from. We're not even up to 23rd Street yet. Sings a little song in middle. "I hate driving."

7

There are certainly enough finks in the world without going to a German restaurant.

8

Listen, I have to go on foot. Would you mind lending me your snow (hic) shoes?

9

I saw T.S. on the telly today. I find that he is one of the most intelligent writers of our "day."

10

If you have to see *Sporting Life* it helped to make sense out of that movie. Read *Radclyffie,* he said.

11

Part 9 is an imitation of Joe Brainard.

12

We are tired of your tiresome imitations of Mayakovsky
we are tired
          of your dreary tourist ideas of our Negro selves
our selves are in far worse condition than the obviousness
of your color sense
            your general sense of Poughkeepsie is
a gaucherie no American poet would be guilty of in Tiflis
thanks to French Impressionism
                we do not pretend to know more
than can be known
            how many sheets have you stained with your semen
oh Tartars, and how many
             of our loves have you illuminated with
your heart your breath
             as we poets of America have loved you
your countrymen, our countrymen, our lives, your lives, and
the dreary expanses of your translations
                   your idiotic manifestos
and the strange black cock which has become ours despite your envy

we do what we feel
            you do not even do what you must or can
I do not love you any more since Mayakovsky died and Pasternak
theirs was the death of my nostalgia for your tired ignorant race
since you insist on race
            you shall not take my friends away from me
because they live in Harlem
             you shall not make Mississippi into Sakhalin
you came too late, a lovely talent doesn't make a ball
    I consider myself to be black and you not even part
where you see death
          you see a dance of death
                which is
imperialist, implies training, requires techniques
our ballet does not employ
            you are indeed as cold as wax
as your progenitor was red, and how greatly we loved his redness
in the fullness of our own idiotic sun! what
"roaring universe" outshouts his violent triumphant sun!
    you are not even speaking
               in a whisper
Mayakovsky's hat worn by a horse

the sunlight steams through the cold
making a glassy melancholy into sound
ping ping ping where are you
if she is jealous of me still
she's not as jealous as she's going to be
as the acid tests produce lignum vitae
stretched over weeks and the sands
of Rachmaninoff sea cold as cocktails
and my thighs crisp as my breath

hello Frank O'Hara how are you!
I take back everything I said about
Friday night and Saturday morning
life can be beautiful as a deserted
street a strong wind and trench coats
flapping against sacred and profane love
as against the neon and swinging keys
how lucky we'd just gone home and
changed our shoes well-tested plot

your thoughts are like the train stops
in the country where strangers pause and
watch the death of someone you will
die for in the future want to die
though the sweeping present can't seem
to bend our solitudes apart or break
or break into something quite different
from a foregone conclusion though again
the feeling is foregone and so beautiful

POEM

for J.-P. Riopelle

At the top of the rung
            at the scream
                        the blood clots

then bursts freshly again ultimately fresh again
      like anger like death
      the bull is only awake once.

The rug wept. The sun accepted a diversion
      as precious as opal
      but smelling of butter
            it was the stain.

when when oh god will it be done
          the duty the effort the diversion.
In the sun the sand seemed to sail.
        not a blood effort
        but the death of anger
     a scent of wool
           gleaming like frost
    neither an animated wasp
     nor a whiff of dawn.
To climb! to climb! to touch the lintel of God!
          the dwarf
  rose sated from the ladder
       onto the roof
and picked his teeth with a harmonica.
      he wrapped himself in the rug.
      he hid from the air.
    it was wood it didn't smell at all
  but the sea rose delicately around its feet and sucked.

[DEAR JAP,]

Dear Jap,

    (my eyes clouded with my cold
    and from looking at lots of watermelons)

I just came back from the Poulenc Memorial Concert
a Riopelle watercolor I have had fallen off the wall
I miss my drawing which I think you are still looking at

yesterday I saw Matisse's great study for *La Danse*
today is colder, but

today I read a beautiful poem out loud
today also I felt confident by being busy
today also I missed Larry a lot

     tonight the moon is not in this house
     which I intend to leave

               I want someday
               to have a fire-escape

            in 1951 I became crazy for fire-escapes
            as you remember

when I think of you in South Carolina I think of my foot in the sand

     do you at some strange distance
     think of glass boxes full of weeds
     and weeds filling bodies aromatically
        and the strange distance between each blade of the eye

               for Easter
               John Myers says
               you should have a hard-boiled egg
               stuffed with ham
               baked in milk
               representing the desert

       this would mean, I think, that summer need never come
       that small insufferable things become culinary
       that accidental simplicity has become a horrible law

in 1951 I never thought I would find mush around the fire-escape
               (just an apprehensive thought before I go to sleep)
               my brother has been bothering me a lot lately

AGAIN, JOHN KEATS, OR THE POT OF BASIL

Just when I was getting completely through
dried out, balled up, anxious and empty
like a gulch in a John Huston movie
I went to see *Strange Interlude* and began
to go away for a weekend on the beach

into that theatre again and again
now I have a pot of basil a friend gave
me and am reading Keats again and realize
that everything is impossible in a different way
well so what, but there's a difference
between a window and a wall again

POEM

The Cambodian grass is crushed
guess what just happened
I almost dropped my sunglasses into the toilet bowl
the grey Cambodian grass

it was there was it
and in the end a scientist
and in the end a sadist
I am so sick of the Bossa Nova

where were you
in the Cambodian grass all brown
you waited
in your amber skin

a long visit
to Cambodia predicted by the euristhenist
but I was not born yet
I have always wished for a truly intellectual club

FOR POULENC

My first day in Paris I walked
            from Saint Germain to the Pont Mirabeau
in soft amber light and leaves
            and love was running out

city of light and hearts
        city of dusk and dismay
the Seine believed it to be true
        that I was unloved and alone

how lonely is that bridge
        without your song
the Avenue Mozart, the rue Pergolèse
        the tobaccos and the nuns

all Paris is alone for this
        brief leafless moment
and snow falls down upon
        the streets of our peculiar hearts

BATHROOM

So that the pliant
and persuadable map
will appeal to you I'll
imagine that my skin
is infinitely extensible
like a sewer or a skyline
the smog of which is lint

of which of which dear god
it is difficult to be an Indian
in a bar wahoo a hud
among hoods there is no
land that's not a land
of asparagus nasturtium
chewing gum and ire

"It's terrible under Kay Francis's armpits"
and I remove the pot of basil from the sink
the borrowed cat gets into the suitcase I am
almost packing here in the harrowing white wine

I think I am about to read MyLifeWithCleopatra
byWalterWanger, O World. as the past sneaks up
and over. What strange fluency invalidates
the desperate? Basil Rathbone. The clothes

are in the patient cat's way. But she is lying
on them, sniffing the crotch of a bathing suit.
Now she is mixing her hairs with mine. Who is
she? She certainly isn't Sylvia who just got fired.

Soon I will fall drunken off the train into
the arms of Patsy and Mike and the greenish pain.
Obliterate everything, Neapolitan seventh!
It will be a long hard way to the railway station,

and Anna Karenina never wore dungarees. I
cannot finish my piece on Arshile Gorky, either.
O Willem de Kooning, you are a very great man
for saying what you said about him and I love you.

Why do gnats always get into white wine?

[THE CLOUDS GO SOFT]

The clouds go soft
                              change color and so many kinds
              puff up, disperse
                                            sink into the sea
the heavens go out of kilter
                      an insane remark greets
                                            the monkey on the moon
              in a season of wit

                    it is all demolished
or made fragrant
                    sputnik is only the word for "traveling companion"

here on earth
                    at 16 you weigh 144 pounds and at 36

          the shirts change, endless procession
                              but they are all neck 14 sleeve 33

              and holes appear and are filled
the same holes   anonymous filler
                    no more conversion, no more conversation

          the sand inevitably seeks the eye
                                        and it is the same eye

          [THE LIGHT PRESSES DOWN]

              The light presses down
              in an empty head the trees
              and bushes flop like
              a little girl imitating
              The Dying Swan the stone
              is hot the church is a
              Russian oven and we
              are traveling still

              you come by to type
              your poems and write a
              new poem instead on my
              old typewriter while I sit
              and read a novel about
              a lunatic's analysis of
              a poem by Robert Frost
              it is all suffocating

              I am still traveling
              with Belinda Lee where
              does she take me Africa
              where it is hot enough

even to make the elephant
angry and the grass is
all withered and TV color

why do I always read
Russian exile novels in
summer I guess because
they're full of snow
and it is good to cry a
little to match your sweat
and sweat a little
to match their tears

WALKING

I get a cinder in my eye
                        it streams into
        the sunlight
                        the air pushes it aside
and I drop my hot dog
                        into one of the Seagram Building's
fountains
                it is all watery and clear and windy

the shape of the toe as
                        it describes the pain
of the ball of the foot,
                        walking walking on
asphalt
        the strange embrace of the ankle's
lock
        on the pavement
                                squared like mausoleums
but cheerful
                moved over and stamped on
slapped by winds
                        the country is no good for us
there's nothing
                to bump into
                                or fall apart glassily

there's not enough
                    poured concrete
                                   and brassy
reflections
              the wind now takes me to
The Narrows
               and I see it rising there
                                       New York
greater than the Rocky Mountains

POEM

for Mario Schifano

I to you and you to me the endless oceans of
                                        dilapidated crossing
everybody up
              the stench of whoopee steerage and candy
                                              cane, for
never the cool free call of the brink
                              but cut it out this
is getting to be another poem about Hart Crane

                                  do you find
the hot dogs better here than at
                         Rosati's, the pepper mills
lousier, the butter softer
                      the acrid dryness of your paper
already reminded me of
                  New York's sky in August before the
nasal rains
            the soot comes down in a nice umber for the scalp

and when the cartoon
                 of a pietà
                          begins to resemble Ava Gardner
in Mexico
          you know you're here
                            welcome to the bull ring
and Chicago and the mush in the enclosures
                                     so brave

so free so blind

         where the drawings are produced on skin, not
forever
    to stay under
        it's not the end
           but for tattoos, you will
like it here, being away and walking
          turning it into sky again

AT THE BOTTOM OF THE DUMP THERE'S SOME SORT OF BUGLE

No matter where I send you remember
          you're still working for me.
Get him a job in Tombstone Gulch.
       He needs a job.
He's just a jerk but he can ride
      herd on the Senate.
Need any help?

       The young Joel McCrea has just ridden
into the gulch on a bicycle.
      It's taxes, the Sheriff says.
Those fellows will never pay taxes without a fight,
you can't tax rustlers.
      Why do they want all that cattle?
Joel says reasonably
     because they weren't in World War I.
Well who was?
     We're not our own grandfathers, are we?
Maybe we are,
    we all have old saddles and old horses
and old loves.
    I think it's disgusting in this saloon which
is so much like the rest of America.
      You go first.
And let's see who hits the dust.
     I just got eaten by a saddled horse.
But the sunset is still beautiful over the Grand Canyon.

CHICAGO

Death is the Dashiell Hammett idea of idiocy
but Gide agrees with it
                              it's red, isn't it?
and rough and ready?
                         it's ready all right
and it isn't over
                    not by a long "shot"

but there's always the alienation of distance
at least from
                  detonation
                               "what, may I ask,
was that?"
              That was the Walled City and if
anyone sees through my merchant drag
                                         I'll
go out tomorrow morning
                            with the garbage
it won't be an explosion
                           I'll be just a package

ENEMY PLANES APPROACHING

to Terry Southern

Ha ha it's fun to run around the deck and see
them going down down
                        boom boom splash splash into
the desert where the camels have just
                                        gotten out
of the way
              it's wonderful to be blond
                                         and it's
marvelous to hear it all so clearly
                                    on the floor
of the Senate they read me
                            into the Congressional
Record boom boom

and you have just twenty minutes
to blast them out of it and pick
                              up the submarine
and make it into my birthday cake
                              boom boom
I am so happy in all this lead
                    the bullets are
lead the sea is lead
                    pewter is my favorite color
Rheingold is my favorite beer
                              Terry Southern
is my favorite writer
                    always going down on
the Twentieth Century like Jonathan Swift gas

HERE IN NEW YORK WE ARE HAVING A LOT OF TROUBLE WITH THE WORLD'S FAIR

A million guys in this
                    town, and you have to shoot
the Crime Commissioner.
                         You loved it tonight
because for the first time the audience treated you
like a lady, a real lady.
                    Well, I guess that squares me
with both of you.

                    On the first pull-out
tense your muscles from head to toe. No blackout!
Something went wrong
                    but I think we're on the right
track.
          Maybe next time we better try ski-jumping.
If every Negro in New York
                              cruised over the Fair
in his fan-jet plane
                    and ran out of fuel
                              the World
would really learn something about the affluent
                                        society.

The stink of the fire hydrant drifts up
                                    and rust
flows down the streets.
                        The Shakespeare Gardens in
Central Park
            glisten with blood, waxen
                                        like apple
blossoms and apples simultaneously. We are happy
here
        facing the multiscreens of the IBM Pavilion.
We pay a lot for our entertainment. All right,
                                        roll over.

I LOVE THE WAY IT GOES

to Tony Towle

Just start writing
                    it's plenty powerful yet so lightweight
my wife . . .
            she likes her shrub and hedge trimmer and her
thirsty lawn

there's a Norwegian cargo vessel in this vicinity

I don't want to fire on the *Pleiades*
        before the iceberg has a chance to sink them

        anything yet, sir? post double lookouts!

it's not a ship, sir, it's too big. It's a lawn! it's
her, my addled wife, she's limping and writing again.

She sank, finally,
                she didn't want to, but she sank
she drowned her shrubs
and sank her lawn
                    and then she saw a Negro bum getting
kicked out of a church
                later he ate her
                            he was handsome

it was almost completely satisfying

                       and the *Pleiades*

sailed on

          in her tight mind, in her grotesque print dress

the album as usual contained a pubic hair

SHOULD WE LEGALIZE ABORTION?

Now we have in our group a lot

                   of unscrupulous

doctors. As they do

             in any profession. Now

(again) at the present time

              a rich person can

always get an abortion,

               they can fly to Japan

or Sweden.

              Not any more, I was in Sweden lately

and they don't like

             the idea that an American

would visit their country

                just for an abortion!

What about the patient?

                I think in the case where

a person has been raped or is insane

                  it definitely

should be allowed.

             But the decision is not up

to the patient.

             Would you like the exact wording

of the penal code?

            I don't think so.

                  I will always

go along with therapeutic abortions,

                golf tournaments

and communion breakfasts.

              And pot. Pot and hash

are very relaxing and worthwhile.

                If you wanted

to go the Scandinavian way

                              it would be a terrific
socio–economic mess!
                    Strange . . .
                                those eyes again!
and they're radioactive!
                        So stop thinking about how
badly you're hurt . . . Stop coddling yourself. You *can*
do something about all this and I'm here to help
you do it! I'll start by getting your clothes off . . .

What the . . .
                THERE'S NOBODY AT THE CONTROLS!
                                            Forget
we ever met.

THE BIRD CAGE THEATRE

What did she give you for your
                                birthday?
I've given up smoking.
                        You know she has to
reject them twice a month.
                            How extraordinary.
Is this what you're looking for?
                        He'll be back
in a couple of weeks.
                        I'm a bung-hole bandit,
baby.
        A wandering man is too old for almost
everybody.
                What do we care whether we're rich or
poor?
        Ain't it the truth, tastes like an expensive
spread but it's important.
                            Marriage! it's something
they slipped over on us while we were in the trenches.

                    You can't have much of a
revolution on three dollars.

THE GREEN HORNET

to J.J. Mitchell

I couldn't kill a man when he was drunk
                                        or shoot him
when he's unarmed, could I?
                              You sure couldn't, kid.
Well give me the money.
                          More of your funny business!
Talk fast, kid. You've got just one minute more. Yipe!
Turn that stage team loose.
                              Do you mind waiting for me
in my office? I've got some papers for Judge Hawkins to sign.
You look mighty pretty.
                          So Wyatt Earp wrote you a letter?
Told you a lot of bad things about me?
                                        A girl wants a man
worth sticking to.
                    I'm sorry you came all the way from
Emporia for nothing.
                        You're the same Johnny I forgot about:
arrogant, stupid and bull-headed.
                                    Well, I got stuck on this
cowboy, baby, and as far as I can see it depends on what
you want to ride.
                    Lock him up, boys, I'll press charges tomorrow.

    "She is more to be pitied than censured,
      she is more to be helped than despised . . ."

A man was the cause of it all. An unarmed man with a weapon.

THE JADE MADONNA

I'll give him two more days
                              and if he don't think of
a way to get Wyatt Earp out here by then
                                            I'm going to
plant some corpses.

You mean that you want that I
should go along?
            I knew it was, Colonel, with all that money
after all that hard work.

I got $820. $820? Yeah dollars. I kind of like having property.

Possession is better than
                a ranch. That's why I collect
all these things that have nothing to do
                            with cows
with dollars or with the great open range.
                    Smell that?
that's my cows thinking about my money.
                        I think too.

THE SHOE SHINE BOY

in memory of John Garfield

Jimmy I got an errand for you to do.
                    What took you so long
I got into a little trouble I ran into a spastic-magic
machine.
            I was trying to earn a few extra bucks. Why? why?

He took out a match and set fire to her eyebrows. He
        called it BRUSHFIRE.
                    Being a Jew turned him bitter
before his time.
                And then to a cold hallway where he could
warm his freezing hands.
                    Just some bum looking for
a haircut.
        I just don't want one of my boys looking
like a bum.
            Oh Frank, you know better than that!
I've never been anyone's girl but yours, Frankie!
                            and
though we kissed a thousand times we were strangers still.

Never love a stranger
                    for strangers always part.
                                        Oy!
why did you take me to this restaurant.
                                        Is it because
you're a Jew?
                    watching your baby grow stronger.
                                                It's
a clip
        a straightener
                        a finish you might want,
                                        you
want.
        I'm sure you don't know what I want here in Trinidad.
Moishe Moscowitz never squealed on anyone in his whole
life,
        and he ain't going to start at the age of sixty-two,
because we get greedy.
                            You just sneak out of town quiet.
I'm against it. No more killings.
                            Remember what it was like
before, Cain?
                Breakfast. How are you, boy?
                                        Frankie. It isn't
like that at all. Don't anybody move.
                                    A three year old angel
from Queens showed up in Flushing unarmed.
                                        My Red friends will
pass among you. One dollar a bottle.

TRIRÈME

to Arnaldo Pomodoro

    The strangeness of palaces for a cowboy
            treachery, flowers, another kind of transiency and disgust
the parallel of cactus
                        the pungency of peyote,
a list
        of forgotten blessings and no disguises
                                        it is ancient
the feeling of disability with a mission and on the march

just before I went off duty I had
                                 a visitor
                                            not in the usual sense
Alamogordo was once important to us, you can understand that, but
                                            you can't forgive it
                                            you can't see it
      any more than a forgotten slave can forgive

                        the essence is not important, it's merely perfume
          but the whole bloody mess exists and is perfunctory and powerful

the prong escapes its function in a storm and surges into the sky reddened

                  "Yf ever man might ons your herte constrayne" remember
Alamogordo
                  and the poor little cat that tried to give birth on the boat
I think those claws are clawing the ocean now towards Carthage
      seeming to be upside down she was having her way
                                            bumping
                              her head against the hawsers

      yet an exemplary situation was in store for all
                                            tri-state
                  advocacy of immoral intent immortal success
                  that was in the slave quarter lunging with birth

Alamogordo and the tawdry desert town
                                            which made an oasis on the map
it's wonderful the way tools seem to come alive in your hands
      you seem to come alive too
                        he's been that way since he got out of
                                    the service
                  that lets Mom out of it
                                      Alamogordo Sierra Trena
is there anything you don't know?
                              yes, what does San Francisco have
      that we don't have
                        a volunteer Fire Department and a Skid Row
you're like a wall that shuts out all the sunshine from the park

            I don't want to be but I am

FANTASY

(dedicated to the health of Allen Ginsberg)

How do you like the music of Adolph

                    Deutsch? I like
it, I like it better than Max Steiner's. Take his
score for *Northern Pursuit,* the Helmut Dantine theme
was . . .

          and then the window fell on my hand. Errol
Flynn was skiing by. Down

                  down down went the grim
grey submarine under the "cold" ice.

                    Helmut was
safely ashore, on the ice.

              What dreams, what incredible
fantasies of snow farts will this all lead to?

                  I
don't know, I have stopped thinking like a sled dog.

The main thing is to tell a story.

              It is almost
very important. Imagine

             throwing away the avalanche
so early in the movie. I am the only spy left
in Canada,

       but just because I'm alone in the snow
doesn't necessarily mean I'm a Nazi.

              Let's see,
two aspirins a vitamin C tablet and some baking soda
should do the trick, that's practically an

             Alka
Seltzer. Allen come out of the bathroom

               and take it.
I think someone put butter on my skis instead
of wax.

      Ouch. The leanto is falling over in the
firs, and there is another fatter spy here. They
didn't tell me they sent

         him. Well, that takes care
of him, boy were those huskies hungry.

             Allen,
are you feeling any better? Yes, I'm crazy about
Helmut Dantine

       but I'm glad that Canada will remain
free. Just free, that's all, never argue with the movies.

CANTATA

How could I be so foolish as to not believe
that my great orange cat Boris (*Armed with Madness*)
Butts loves me when he runs to the door like a dog
each night when I come home from work and
probably isn't even particularly hungry
                                        or lays
his conspicuous hairs on my darkest clothes
out of pure longing for my smell which they do have
because he looks like my best friend my constant lover
hopelessly loyal tawny and apt and whom I hopelessly love

CHEYENNE

I'll skin you alive for this
                    I'm sure you would
"John Derek is the most beautiful man who ever hit Hollywood,"
          she said, "but I've just killed Don Diego."
I've always loved the good things in life: good art
              good food, good coffee.
                            Nature copied this,
          copied John Derek. I don't like Don Diego.

Listen, Jelly-Belly. Back down a little, will you?

We're looking at the most advanced apparatus ever recalled.
It's called a Dixie Cup. I love you. The Tootsie-Roll wrapper
drifts up onto the window ledge
                              ready to jump, inflamed
by all the banalities of positive experientialism
                              diabolical suggestion
that we should all go, go out, so abstract
                                        so it's beautiful,
is it? yeah, it's about as beautiful as Hiroshima and
      Harlem and that movie by Ben Hecht

                                            one murder
and one suicide in one week
                              is a great score for the Yankees

I'll skin you alive for this
                    I'm sure you would
if you don't see me tomorrow don't be surprised I'm doing
          the prairie dog bit
                              it's called the Dixie Cup
don't shit in it
                what's that chef doing going down that manhole

HISTORICAL VARIATIONS

    O Fort Savannah! do you remember Ann Bailey
and how she rode a hundred miles to raise the siege at Fort Lee?
for that matter, do you remember Joanna Baillie?

unfortunately Juan Manuel de Rosas didn't reach English exile
until a year after her death, but she thought doubtless of his
dreaded *Mazorca* and her Argentina-dreams were troubled ones
as were her dreams of Ebenezer Zane and his splendid defense of
Fort Henry from the Indians, but then, when they called it a fort
they knew it would be attacked, or so thought Joanna, and
how boring are men of deeds to the wild passions of fugitive verse

in the middle of a rather tendentious movie on Kant
dreams of chocolate-cream pie are a relief
but if only *Justine* would turn into *The Poet in New York*!
which I am desperately anxious to read today, no substitute!
I guess I'll have to read *The Deer Park* instead, oops!
I just picked up a glass of whiskey left over from last night, ugh!
I guess I must have loaned it to Dave Reiff, well he needs it
more than I do, he's in Florida, ugh, that whiskey again

LITTLE ELEGY FOR ANTONIO MACHADO

Now your protesting demons summon themselves
    with fire against the Castilian dark
and solitary light
                your mother dead on the hearth
and your heart at rest on the border of constellary futures

no domesticated cemeteries can enshroud your flight
    of linear solarities and quiescent tumbrils
vision of the carrion
                past made glassy and golden
to reveal the dark, the dark in all its ancestral clarity

where our futures lie increasingly in fire
    twisted ropes of sound encrusting our brains
your water air and earth
                  insist on our joining you
in recognition of colder prides and less negotiable ambitions

we shall continue to correct all classical revisions
    of ourselves as trials of ceremonial worth
and purple excess
              improving your soul's expansion
in the night and developing our own in salt-like praise

[NOTES ON *SECOND AVENUE*]

These notes which I'm attaching to the excerpts sometimes indicate, because you requested it, a more detailed identification of the subject matter (in some cases just a last name) than I wanted in the poem itself because it is beside the poem's point in most cases; elsewhere the remarks are explanatory of what I now feel my *attitude* was toward the material, not explanatory of the meaning which I don't think can be paraphrased (or at least I hope it can't).

> This thoroughness whose traditions have become so reflective,
> your distinction is merely a quill at the bottom of the sea
> tracing forever the fabulous alarms of the mute
> so that in the limpid tosses of your violet dinginess
> a pus appears and lingers like a groan from the collar
> of a reproachful tree whose needles are tired of howling

To put it very gently, I have a feeling that the philosophical reduction of reality to a dealable-with system so distorts life that one's "reward" for this endeavor (a minor one, at that) is illness both from inside and outside.

There are several scenes in the poem with characters, for instance (briefly) a flier in his plane over the ocean:

> "Arabella" was the word he muttered that moment
> when lightning had smelled sweet over the zoo of the waves
> while he played on and on and on and the women grew hysterical.

a little Western story, beginning:

> The western mountain ranges were sneaking along "Who taps wires and why?" like a pack of dogies and is there much tapping under the desert moon? Does it look magical or realistic, that landing? And the riverboat put in there, keeps putting in, with all the slaves' golden teeth and arms, self-conscious without their weapons, Joe LeSueur, the handsome Captain who smuggles Paris perfumes, tied up at the arroyo . . .

> (Joe LeSueur is a friend of mine, a novelist not published yet.)

a newspaper clipping report of Bunny Lang's trip in the Caribbean:

> *"Nous avons eu lundi soir, le grand plaisir de rencontrer*
> *à l'Hôtel Oloffson où elle est descendue, la charmante*
> *Mlle. Anne R. Lang, actrice du Théâtre Dramatique de Cambridge . . .*

a true description of not being able to continue this poem and meeting Kenneth
Koch for a sandwich while waiting for the poem to start again:

> Candidly. The past, the sensations of the past. Now!
> in cuneiform, of umbrella satrap square-carts with hotdogs
> and onions of red syrup blended, of sand bejewelling the prepuce
> in tank suits, of Majestic Camera Stores and Schuster's,
> of Kenneth in an abandoned storeway on Sunday cutting ever more
> insinuating lobotomies of a yet-to-be-more-yielding world
> of ears . . .

> (He was continuing to write his long poem as he waited)

a talk with a sculptor (Larry Rivers, who also sculpts) about a piece in progress:

> Your feet are more beautiful than your father's, I think,
> does that upset you? admire, I admire youth above age, yes,
> in the infancy of the race when we were very upset we wrote
> "O toe!" and it took months to "get" those feet. Render. Pent.
> Now more features of our days have become popular, the nose
> broken, the head bald, the body beautiful, Marilyn Monroe.
> Can one's lips be "more" or "less" sensual? . . .

a description of a poetry critic and teacher: (tirade?)

> A chicken walked by with tail
> reared, looking very personal, pecking and dribbling, wattles.
> You suddenly got an idea of what black and white poetry
> was like, you grinning Simian fart, poseur among idiots
> and dilettantes and pederasts. When the chips are in,
> yours will spell out in a wealth of dominoes, YOU, and you'll
> be stuck with it, hell to anybody else, drowning in lead,
> like your brain, of which the French poets wrote, "O fat-assed
> configurations and volutions of ribbed sand which the sea
> never reaches!" Memories of home, which is an island, of course,
> and historical, of course, and full of ass, of course. Yes,
> may you . . .

a description of Grace Hartigan painting:

> and when the pressure asphixiates and inflames, Grace destroys
> the whirling faces in their dissonant gaiety where it's anxious,
> lifted nasally to the heavens which is a carrousel grinning
> and spasmodically obliterated with loaves of greasy white paint

and this becomes like love to her, is what I desire
and what you, to be able to throw something away without yawning
"Oh Leaves of Grass! o Sylvette! oh Basket Weavers' Conference!"
and thus make good our promise to destroy something but not us.

Oh, I forgot to excerpt something else, a little description of a de Kooning WOMAN which I'd seen recently at his studio:

You remained for me a green Buick of sighs, o Gladstone!
and your wife Trina, how like a yellow pillow on a sill
in the many-windowed dusk where the air is compartmented!
her red lips of Hollywood, soft as a Titian and as tender,
her gray face which refrains from thrusting aside the mane
of your languorous black smells, the hand crushed by her chin,
and that slumberland of dark cutaneous lines which reels
under the burden of her many-darkly-hued corpulence of linen
and satin bushes, is like a lone rose with the sky behind it.
A yellow rose. Valentine's Day . . .

Actually, I am rather inaccurate about the above, since it is a woman I saw leaning out a window on Second Avenue with her arms on a pillow, but the way it's done is influenced by de K's woman (whom he thinks of, he once said, as "living" on 14th St.).

I don't know if this method is of any interest in taking little pieces of it. You see how it makes it seem very jumbled, while actually everything in it either happened to me or I felt happening (saw, imagined) on Second Avenue. Where Mayakovsky and de Kooning come in, is that they both have done works as big as cities where the life in the work is autonomous (not about actual city life) and yet similar: Mayakovsky: "Lenin," "150,000,000," "Eiffel Tower," etc.; de Kooning: "Asheville," "Excavation," "Gansevoort Street," etc.

As I look this over, it seems quite a batty way to give information about the poem, but the verbal elements are not too interesting to discuss although they are intended consciously to keep the surface of the poem high and dry, not wet, reflective and self-conscious. Perhaps the obscurity comes in here, in the relationship between the surface and the meaning, but I like it that way since the one is the other (you have to use words) and I hope the poem to *be* the subject, not just about it.

Sincerely,

Everything is in the poems, but at the risk of sounding like the poor wealthy man's Allen Ginsberg I will write to you because I just heard that one of my fellow poets thinks that a poem of mine that can't be got at one reading is because I was confused too. Now, come on. I don't believe in god, so I don't have to make elaborately sounded structures. I hate Vachel Lindsay, always have; I don't even like rhythm, assonance, all that stuff. You just go on your nerve. If someone's chasing you down the street with a knife you just run, you don't turn around and shout, "Give it up! I was a track star for Mineola Prep."

That's for the writing poems part. As for their reception, suppose you're in love and someone's mistreating (*mal aimé*) you, you don't say, "Hey, you can't hurt me this way, I care!" you just let all the different bodies fall where they may, and they always do may after a few months. But that's not why you fell in love in the first place, just to hang onto life, so you have to take your chances and try to avoid being logical. Pain always produces logic, which is very bad for you.

I'm not saying that I don't have practically the most lofty ideas of anyone writing today, but what difference does that make? They're just ideas. The only good thing about it is that when I get lofty enough I've stopped thinking and that's when refreshment arrives.

But how can you really care if anybody gets it, or gets what it means, or if it improves them. Improves them for what? For death? Why hurry them along? Too many poets act like a middle-aged mother trying to get her kids to eat too much cooked meat, and potatoes with drippings (tears). I don't give a damn whether they eat or not. Forced feeding leads to excessive thinness (effete). Nobody should experience anything they don't need to, if they don't need poetry bully for them. I like the movies too. And after all, only Whitman and Crane and Williams, of the American poets, are better than the movies. As for measure and other technical apparatus, that's just common sense: if you're going to buy a pair of pants you want them to be tight enough so everyone will want to go to bed with you. There's nothing metaphysical about it. Unless, of course, you flatter yourself into thinking that what you're experiencing is "yearning."

Abstraction in poetry, which Allen [Ginsberg] recently commented on in *It Is*, is intriguing. I think it appears mostly in the minute particulars where decision is necessary. Abstraction (in poetry, not in painting) involves personal removal by the poet. For instance, the decision involved in the choice between "the nostalgia *of* the infinite" and "the nostalgia *for* the infinite" defines an attitude towards degree of abstraction. The nostalgia *of* the infinite representing the greater degree of abstraction, removal, and negative capability (as in Keats and Mallarmé). Personism, a movement which I recently founded and which nobody knows about, interests me a great deal, being so totally opposed to this kind of abstract removal that it is verging on a true abstraction for the first time, really, in the history of poetry. Personism is to Wallace Stevens what *la poésie pure* was to Béranger. Personism has nothing to do with philosophy, it's all art. It does not have to do with personality or intimacy, far from it! But to give you a vague idea, one of its minimal aspects is to address itself to one person (other than the poet himself), thus evoking overtones of love without destroying love's life-giving vulgarity, and sustaining the poet's feelings towards the poem while preventing love from distracting him into feeling about the person. That's part of Personism. It was founded by me after lunch with LeRoi Jones on August 27, 1959, a day in which I was in love with someone (not Roi, by the way, a blond). I went back to work and wrote a poem for this person. While I was writing it I was realizing that if I wanted to I could use the telephone instead of writing the poem, and so Personism was born. It's a very exciting movement which will un-doubtedly have lots of adherents. It puts the poem squarely between the poet and the person, Lucky Pierre style, and the poem is correspondingly gratified. The poem is at last between two persons instead of two pages. In all modesty, I confess that it may be the death of literature as we know it. While I have certain regrets, I am still glad I got there before Alain Robbe-Grillet did. Poetry being quicker and surer than prose, it is only just that poetry finish literature off. For a time people thought that Artaud was going to accomplish this, but actually, for all their magnificence, his polemical writings are not more outside literature than Bear Mountain is outside New York State. His relation is no more astounding than Dubuffet's to painting.

What can we expect of Personism? (This is getting good, isn't it?) Everything, but we won't get it. It is too new, too vital a movement to promise anything. But it, like Africa, is on the way. The recent propagandists for technique on the one hand, and for content on the other, had better watch out.

I am mainly preoccupied with the world as I experience it, and at times when I would rather be dead the thought that I could never write another poem has so far stopped me. I think this is an ignoble attitude. I would rather die for love, but I haven't.

I don't think of fame or posterity (as Keats so grandly and genuinely did), nor do I care about clarifying experiences for anyone or bettering (other than accidentally) anyone's state or social relation, nor am I for any particular technical development in the American language simply because I find it necessary. What is happening to me, allowing for lies and exaggerations which I try to avoid, goes into my poems. I don't think my experiences are clarified or made beautiful for myself or anyone else; they are just there in whatever form I can find them. What is clear to me in my work is probably obscure to others, and vice versa. My formal "stance" is found at the crossroads where what I know and can't get meets what is left of that I know and can bear without hatred. I dislike a great deal of contemporary poetry—all of the past you read is usually quite great—but it is a useful thorn to have in one's side.

It may be that poetry makes life's nebulous events tangible to me and restores their detail; or conversely, that poetry brings forth the intangible quality of incidents which are all too concrete and circumstantial. Or each on specific occasions, or both all the time.

ABOUT ZHIVAGO AND HIS POEMS

We are used to the old saw that poets cannot write great novels or indeed any novels. The adherents of this cliché, hoping to perpetuate a mystery-distinction between two kinds of writing, are cheered on by the novelists who hate "poetic" novels and the poets who hate "prosaic" poems. Virginia Woolf gets hers from one quarter and William Carlos Williams gets his from the other. The argument is usually bolstered by phrases like "Joyce *turned to* prose," which would have been an amusing scene, but never occurred. For what poetry gave to Joyce, as to Pasternak, is what painting gave to Proust: the belief that high art has a communicability far superior in scope and strength to any other form of human endeavor. The Nobel Prize committee was correct in making the award include Pasternak's poetry as well as the novel. To admirers of his poetry *Doctor Zhivago* is the epic expression of many of the themes first found in individual lyrics and short stories; the present epic form is the poet's response to the demand of his time for its proper expression.

With one prose masterpiece behind him, *Safe Conduct* (1931), Pasternak insists in *Doctor Zhivago* on identifying poetry with truth to the supreme extent: in no other work of modern literature do we wait for the final revelation of meaning to occur in the hero's posthumous book of poems. The political ramifications of the novel's publication have thrust the poet (author *and* hero) into dramatic relief for a vast international public and established the efficacy of the poet's stance in realms far beyond personal lyricism. The clamor over *Doctor Zhivago* has been denounced by various literary figures as damaging to Pasternak personally, but let there be no mistake about this clamor: it comes not from anything Pasternak has said in the press, nor from the phrasing of the Nobel Prize citation, nor from Western or Soviet political commentaries on the novel's content, it comes from the nature of the work itself. Of the critics only Edmund Wilson has seen this quality in its proper perspective. Pasternak has written a revolutionary and prophetic work which judges contemporary society outside as well as within the Iron Curtain. And if Pasternak is saying that the 1917 Revolution failed, he must feel that the West never even made an attempt. Far from being a traitorous work, *Doctor Zhivago* is a poem on the nobility of the Soviet failure to reconstruct society *in human terms,* and it is not without hope. The two disillusioning heroes of *Safe Conduct,* Scriabin and Mayakovsky, give way to the triumphant hero of *Doctor Zhivago.*

It is plain that this hero must be an artist; to Pasternak the artist is the last repository of individual conscience, and in his terms conscience is individual perception of life. This is not at all a counterrevolutionary attitude based on an intellectual-aristocratic system. It has not to do with a predilection for "culture." The lesson comes from life. Zhivago himself becomes a doctor, but he finds that his usefulness to society is everywhere stymied, that his social efficacy is incomplete and does not contribute to his understanding of his own predicament. To be a twentieth-century hero Zhivago must leave for subsequent generations a living testament. It does not suffice that he "live in the hearts of his countrymen" by remembered deeds alone. It is a question of articulation: the epic events of *Doctor Zhivago* demand from their participants articulate perception or mute surrender. Pasternak's epic is not the glorification of the plight of the individual, but of the accomplishment of the individual in the face of almost insuperable sufferings which are personal and emotionally real, never melodramatic and official. And it is the poet's duty to accomplish this articulation.

Everywhere in the work of Pasternak published in English, we saw this meaning growing. It is a world very like that of Joyce's characters as we meet them in *Dubliners* and *The Portrait of the Artist as a Young Man* and find them later older, clearer, changed, in *Ulysses* and *Finnegans Wake*. Obviously the young Larisa Feodorovna bears this kind of resemblance to the adolescent Zhenia Luvers of the early story (mistakenly printed as two distinct stories under separate titles by New Directions); several scenes in "Aerial Ways" anticipate events in the novel, and indeed Pasternak draws attention to this aspect of his writing in the opening passages of "A Tale" (called "The Last Summer" in English). It is the writer of the "Letters to Tula" who bears the strongest resemblance to Zhivago himself: "Everything that happens happens from the nature of the place. This is an event on the *territory of conscience*, it occurs on her own ore-bearing regions. There will be no 'poet.'" In this passage Pasternak reveals early (1918) his belief that the poet must first be a person, that his writings make him a poet, not his acting the role. I cannot agree with Elsa Triolet when she recently attacked Pasternak for having betrayed Mayakovsky in writing *Doctor Zhivago*. On the contrary, the principles which were later to seduce Mayakovsky had been exposed in "Letters to Tula" already:

> . . . I swear to you that the faith of my heart is greater than ever it was, the time will come—no, let me tell you about that later. Tear me to pieces, tear me to pieces, night, burn to ashes, burn, burn brilliantly, luminously, the forgotten, the angry, the fiery word "Conscience"! Burn maddening, petrol-bearing tongue of the flame . . .
>
> This way of regarding life has come into being and now there is no place on earth where a man can warm his soul with the fire of shame: shame is everywhere watered down and cannot burn. Falsehood and dissipation. Thus for thirty years all who are singular live and drench their shame, old and young, and already it has spread through the whole world, among the unknown . . .
>
> The poet, henceforward inscribing this word, until it is purged with fire, in inverted commas, the "poet" observes himself in the unseemly behavior of actors, in the disgraceful spectacle which accuses his comrades and his generation. Perhaps he is only playing with the idea. No. They confirm him in the belief that his identity is in no way chimerical . . .

This passage is like a rehearsal of the talks Zhivago has with his uncle when they discuss principles. That it also bears on Pasternak's relationship with Mayakovsky is witnessed by the following passage from *Safe Conduct*:

> But a whole conception of life lay concealed under the Romantic manner which I was to deny myself from henceforth. This was the conception of life as the life of the poet. It had come down to us from the Romantics, principally the Germans.
>
> This conception had influenced Blok but only during a short period. It was incapable of satisfying him in the form in which it came naturally to him. He could either heighten it or abandon it altogether. He abandoned the conception. Mayakovsky and Esenin heightened it.
>
> In the poet who imagines himself the measure of life and pays for this with his life, the Romantic conception manifests itself brilliantly and irrefutably in his symbolism, that is in everything which touches upon Orphism and Christianity imaginatively. In this sense something inscrutable was incarnate both in the life of Mayakovsky and in the fate of Esenin, which defies all epithets, demanding self-destruction and passing into myth.
>
> But outside the legend, the Romantic scheme is false. The poet who is its foundation, is inconceivable without the nonpoets who must bring him into relief, because this poet is not a living personality absorbed in the study of moral knowledge, but a visual-biographical "emblem," demanding a background to make his contours visible. In contradistinction to the Passion plays which needed a Heaven if they were to be heard, this drama needs the evil of mediocrity in order to be seen, just as Romanticism always needs philistinism and with the disappearance of the petty bourgeoisie loses half its poetical content.

What then, after rejecting the concept of the Romantic "pose" in relation to his own life and art, does Pasternak's position become? He had already moved towards this decision in the poems written previous to 1917 and in a later volume he chooses the title from a poem, "My Sister, Life." This expresses very clearly his position: the poet and life herself walk hand in hand. Life is not a landscape before which the poet postures, but the very condition of his inspiration in a deeply personal way: "My sister, life, is in flood today . . ." This is not the nineteenth-century Romantic identification, but a recognition. In the later work Zhivago says to the dying Anna Ivanovna:

> . . . But all the time, life, one, immense, identical throughout its innumerable combinations and transformations, fills the universe and is continually reborn. You are anxious about whether you will rise from the dead or not, but you rose from the dead when you were born and you didn't notice it . . .
>
> So what will happen to your consciousness? *Your* consciousness, yours,

not anyone else's. Well, what are you? There's the point. Let's try to find out. What is it about you that you have always known as yourself? What are you conscious of in yourself? Your kidneys? Your liver? Your blood vessels? No. However far back you go in your memory, it is always in some external, active manifestation of yourself that you come across your identity—in the work of your hands, in your family, in other people. And now listen carefully. You in others—this is your soul. This is what you are. This is what your consciousness has breathed and lived on and enjoyed throughout your life—your soul, your immortality, your life in others. And what now? You have always been in others and you will remain in others. And what does it matter to you if later on that is called your memory? This will be you—the you that enters the future and becomes a part of it . . .

There is every reason to believe that Pasternak's recognition of self was accompanied by great pain. He adored Mayakovsky at the time and indeed was forced to this decision of self by Mayakovsky's presence in that time, ". . . because poetry as I understand it flows through history and in collaboration with real life." Mayakovsky made a fatal error and became a tragic hero. Like Strelnikov in the novel, he succumbed to a belief in the self-created rhetoric of his own dynamic function in society. That society needed him and benefited from this rhetoric is obvious. But both he and the character in *Doctor Zhivago* ended in suicide when their usefulness in this function came to an end, and while their response to social demand seems shortsighted to Pasternak, he also condemned society for the temptation:

> The great Soviet gives to the highest passions
> In these brave days each one its rightful place,
> Yet vainly leaves one vacant for the poet.
> When that's not empty, look for danger's face.

The chair of poetry must remain empty, for poetry does not collaborate with society, but with life. Soviet society is not alone in seducing the poet to deliver temporary half-truths which will shortly be cast aside for the excitement of a new celebration of nonlife. The danger is that life does not allow any substitute for love.

It is not surprising then that this sense of poetry and its intimate connection with his relationship to life is one of the strongest elements in Zhivago's nature. It makes of Zhivago one of the most original heroes in Western literature, a man who cannot be interpreted by nineteenth-century standards, which I suspect Lionel Abel attempts to do when he says, writing in *Dissent,* ". . . how can he not have understood that in yielding to the impulse to write of his beloved immediately after his loss of her, he was taking a practical attitude toward his grief, trying to get something out of it, literature, maybe even glory?" What Mr. Abel misses finding here is the grief-expression of the romantic hero, which had been eschewed by Pasternak himself in an early poem which fits oddly well into the present scene of loss:

> . . . O miraculous orbit, beckon, beckon! You may
> Well be astonished. For—look—you are free.
>
> I do not hold you. Go, yes, go elsewhere,
> Do good. *Werther* cannot be written again,
> And in our time death's odor is in the air;
> To open a window is to open a vein.

Far from shallow or opportunistic in his grief (being left alone in the Urals with the wolves closing in would hardly raise hopes for literary fame), Zhivago weeps, drinks vodka, scribbles poems and notes, is subject to hallucinations, and begins the decline which will end in his death. But at this crucial period of his life in which he unexpectedly suffers the ultimate loss, that of Larisa Feodorovna, the period in which he had hoped to accomplish his poetic testament, his creativity does not desert him. We must remember that the events of the post-Revolution period have robbed him of the time to think, the time to write. He saves his sanity by crowding the writing and the speculations of a lifetime into these days of isolation, coming to conclusions about certain events, and thus approaching once again, after this interval of grief, his "sister, life":

> . . . Mourning for Lara, he also mourned that distant summer in Meliu-zeievo when the revolution had been a god come down to earth from heaven, the god of the summer when everyone had gone crazy in his own way, and when everyone's life had existed in its own right, and not as an illustration for a thesis in support of the rightness of a superior policy.
>
> As he scribbled his odds and ends, he made a note reaffirming his belief that art always serves beauty, and beauty is delight in form, and form is the key to organic life, since no living thing can exist without it, so that every work of art, including tragedy, expresses the joy of existence. And his own ideas and notes also brought him joy, a tragic joy, a joy full of tears that exhausted him and made his head ache.

He decides to forego the virtual suicide of his retreat in the snowy wilderness, in the abandoned house which has offered him, for the first time since he was a student, the solitude for his poetry, and to return to Moscow. The inverted commas have been purged from the word poet. And unlike Chekhov's *Three Sisters* he does reach Moscow. And there he has a tangible reality even after his death, as recognized by his two childhood friends as they read at dusk the posthumous poems which Zhivago's mysteriously angelic half brother Evgraf has collected:

> . . . And Moscow, right below them and stretching into the distance, the author's native city, in which he had spent half his life—Moscow now struck them not as the stage of the events connected with him but as the

main protagonist of a long story, the end of which they had reached that evening, book in hand.

Although victory had not brought the relief and freedom that were expected at the end of the war, nevertheless the portents of freedom filled the air throughout the postwar period, and they alone defined its historical significance.

To the two old friends, as they sat by the window, it seemed that this freedom of the soul was already there, as if that very evening the future had tangibly moved into the streets below them, that they themselves had entered it and were now part of it . . .

And the book they held seemed to confirm and encourage this feeling.

This is Zhivago's triumph over the terrible vicissitudes of love and circumstance which we have witnessed, the "active manifestation" of himself—his soul, his immortality, his life in others.

Though the greatness of scale in *Doctor Zhivago* bears a resemblance to Tolstoy's achievement, this is not a massively documented and described war-novel like those we have had from Americans, French, and Russian neo-Tolstoyans, where the scheme is that of nineteenth-century prototypes swamped by the events of their time. On the contrary, one of the great beauties of Pasternak's technique is that of portraying events through the consciousness of principal and minor characters. In this he resembles Joyce and Proust; often we hear of an event from a character *after* it has changed him, so that we apprehend both the event and its consequences simultaneously. The intimacy which this technique lends to the epic structure, particularly when the character is relatively unknown to us, and the discretion with which it is handled, reminds one of two other works of perfect scale, Lermontov's *A Hero of Our Times* and Flaubert's *A Sentimental Education*.

Nowhere in the novel is this method more rewarding than in the presentation of the hero, and here it is varied beyond what I have described. Of Yurii Andreievich Zhivago we know a great deal as we progress through the novel. We not only know his feelings and his response to and attempted evaluation of events, but also his longings. We even know what he considers the most important elements in his life and how he intends to evaluate them in his work. But here Pasternak's devastating distrust of the plane of action in human affairs becomes clearest and makes its strongest point. In the post-epilogue book of poems we find that Zhivago has not written the poems he wanted to, nor the poems we expected (except for the one on St. George); in the course of creating the poems he has become not the mirror of the life we know, but the instrument of its perceptions, hitherto veiled. This is the major expression of a meaning which Pasternak has implied often in the novel proper. The human individual is the subject of historical events, not vice versa; he is the repository of life's force. And while he may suffer, may be rendered helpless, may be killed, if he has the perceptiveness to realize this he knows that events require his participation to occur. In this context we find another revolutionary reinterpretation of the human condition: Strelnikov, the "active" Red Army Commissar, is rendered passive by his blind espousal of principles whose needful occasion has passed; Zhivago, passively withdrawn from action which his conscience cannot sanction, finds the art for which an occasion will continue to exist. This qualitative distinction between two kinds of significance is as foreign to our own society as it is to that of the U.S.S.R.

The poems with which the novel culminates are truly Zhivago's own, not Pasternak's. They deliver us a total image of the hero's life which is incremented by details of that life from the prose section. While we recognize the occasions of many, we find their expression different from what we, or Zhivago, expected. As an indication of how different they are from Pasternak's own poems, we need only compare two poems on a similar theme, Pasternak's lyric "If only when I made my début" and Zhivago's "Hamlet." In the one, Pasternak deals with one of his central themes which is mentioned above in relation to Mayakovsky. The poem is full of the tragedy of human involvement, but in a pure, nonsymbolic manner; it is the role taking over the actor, of course, but it is also the word consuming the poet, the drama of the meaning, which the poet has found through the act of creating this meaning, transporting him to an area of realization beyond his power, where he has been joined to the *mortal* presence of life:

> A line that feeling sternly dictates
> Sends on the stage a slave, and, faith,
> It is good-bye to art forever
> Then, then things smack of soil and Fate.

How different is Zhivago's poem on this theme. Not only does he assume a "masque," that of Hamlet, but before we are through the second stanza he has made the symbolic connection of Hamlet with the Hebraic-Christian myth of father-and-son positive by reference to Christ in the Garden of Olives. The poem ends on a reference to Zhivago's own physical circumstance, a personal note that has saved many a Symbolist poem:

> I stand alone. All else is swamped in Pharisaism.
> To live life to the end is not a childish task.

Because of the novel, we cannot resist the idea that this poem was written in the snowy forests of Varykino after Lara's departure, where Zhivago endures his agonizing "vigil" and decides to forego suicide and to return to Moscow.

The Christian poems are extraordinary achievements as poems, and also reveal how complicated the structure of the novel is. In reading them we realize for the first time how enormously influential on Zhivago was the interpretation of Christ's significance by a minor character who was speaking to Lara and overheard by him from the next room. It becomes clear that Zhivago's Christianity is no hieratic discipline, but a recognition of social change: ". . . you have a girl—an everyday figure who would have gone unnoticed in the ancient world—quietly, secretly bringing forth a child . . .

"Something in the world had changed. Rome was at an end. The reign of numbers was at an end. The duty, imposed by armed force, to live unanimously as a people, as a whole nation, was abolished. . . . Individual life became the life story of God . . ." For those who have interpreted *Doctor Zhivago* with some smugness as a return to Christianity as the Western World knows it, it should be pointed out that this historical interpretation bears roughly the same analogy to Protestantism and Catholicism as they are practiced that Marxism does to Capitalism. It is not only based on historical distinctions, but "faith" is further set aside by the distinctions made in the poems between human life and nature, and the ambiguities of this relationship as they affect the Christ legend. When the fig tree is consumed to ashes in "Miracle," Zhivago writes:

> If at that point but a moment of free choice had been granted
> To the leaves, the branches, to the trunk and roots
> The laws of nature might have contrived to intervene.

And in "Holy Week" our dependency on nature becomes the rival of God:

> And when the midnight comes
> All creatures and all flesh will fall silent
> On hearing spring put forth its rumor
> That just as soon as there is better weather
> Death itself can be overcome
> Through the power of the Resurrection.

It is not difficult to ascertain that for Pasternak the interdependency of man and nature is far from theological. It is in these clarifications of feelings and thoughts, in these poems, that Zhivago becomes a true hero. Here we find his inner response to his wife's moving letter from exile which also contains his reasons for not joining her outside Russia ("Dawn"), in other poems his ambivalences and his social nobility. In the most revealing of all, the love poems to Lara (including the superb "Autumn," "Parting," "Encounter," and "Magdalene"), we find the intensity which had so moved her and which Zhivago himself reveals nowhere else except in the secrecy of their own intimate hours. Her greatness in responding to this love becomes even more moving in retrospect than it was when one first read her thoughts at his bier, one of the greatest scenes in literature:

> . . . Oh, what a love it was, utterly free, unique, like nothing else on earth!
> Their thoughts were like other people's songs.

They loved each other, not driven by necessity, by the "blaze of passion" often falsely ascribed to love. They loved each other because everything around them willed it, the trees and the clouds and the sky over their heads and the earth under their feet. Perhaps their surrounding world, the strangers they met in the street, the wide expanses they saw on their walks, the rooms in which they lived or met, took more delight in their love than they themselves did.

And the posthumous response to her love is on as grand a scale:

> You are the blessing in a stride toward perdition,
> When living sickens more than sickness does itself;
> The root of beauty is audacity,
> And that is what draws us to each other

It is this inevitability which makes *Doctor Zhivago* great, as if we, not Pasternak, had willed it. And if love lives at all in the cheap tempestuousness of our time, I think it can only be in the unrelenting honesty with which we face animate nature and inanimate things and the cruelty of our kind, and perceive and articulate and, like Zhivago, choose love above all else.

It is very difficult for me to write a statement for Paterson, much as I would find it agreeable to do so if I could. So perhaps it could take the form of a letter? and not be a real statement. Because if I did write a statement it would probably be so non-pertinent to anything you might want to know in connection with my actual poems. The only two starts I have been able to think of since you first asked me for one, are (1) to begin with a description of what I would like my poetry to be, or hope it is (already? in the future? I don't know). This would be a description of the effect other things have had upon me which I in my more day-dreamy moments wish that I could effect in others. Well you can't have a statement saying "My poetry is the Sistine Chapel of verse," or "My poetry is just like Pollock, de Kooning and Guston rolled into one great verb," or "My poetry is like a windy day on a hill overlooking the stormy ocean"—first of all it isn't so far as I can tell, and secondly even if it were something like all of these that wouldn't be because I managed to make it that way. I couldn't, it must have been an accident, and I would probably not recognize it myself. Further, what would poetry like that be? It would have to be the Sistine Chapel itself, the paintings themselves, the day and time specifically. Impossible.

Or (2) if I then abandoned that idea and wrote you about my convictions concerning form, measure, sound, yardage, placement and ear—well, if I went into that thoroughly enough nobody would ever want to read the poems I've already written, they would have been so thoroughly described, and I would have to do everything the opposite in the future to avoid my own boredom, and where would I be? That's where I am anyway, I suppose, but at least this way it's not self-induced. Besides, I can't think of any more than one poem at a time, so I would end up with a "poetics" based on one of my poems which any other poem of mine would completely contradict except for certain affections or habits of speech they might include. So that would be of no use for general readers, and misleading for anyone who had already read any of my poems. So, as they say in the Café Flore, it's better to *tas gueule*. I'm not giving up responsibility for the poems. I definitely don't believe that "your idea is as good as anyone's about what it means." But I don't want to make up a lot of prose about something that is perfectly clear in the poems. If you cover someone with earth and grass grows, you don't know what they looked like any more. Critical prose makes too much grass grow, and I don't want to help hide my own poems, much less kill them.

I know you will think of the remarks I made for Don Allen's anthology and that "Manifesto" in LeRoi Jones's *Yūgen*. In the case of the manifesto I think it was all right because it was a little diary of my thoughts, after lunch with LeRoi walking back to work, about the poem I turned out to be just about to write ("Personal Poem," which he published in an earlier issue of *Yūgen*). It was, as a matter of fact, intended for Don Allen's anthology, and I was encouraged to write it because LeRoi told me at lunch that he had written a statement for the anthology. But Don Allen thought it unwise to use it in relation to the earlier poems included, quite rightly, so I wrote another which he did use. This latter, it seems to me now, is even more mistaken, pompous, and quite untrue, as compared to the manifesto. But it is also, like the manifesto, a diary of a particular day and the depressed mood of that day (it's a pretty depressing day, you must admit, when you feel you relate more importantly to poetry than to life), and as such may perhaps have more general application to my poetry since I have been more often depressed than happy, as far as I can tally it up. In the case of either, it's a hopeless conundrum: it used to be that I could only write when I was miserable; now I can only write when I'm happy. Where will it all end? At any rate, this will explain why I can't really say anything definite for the Paterson Society for the time being.

LARRY RIVERS: A MEMOIR

I first met Larry Rivers in 1950. When I first started coming down to New York from Harvard for weekends Larry was in Europe and friends had said we would like each other. Finally, at for me a very literary cocktail party at John Ashbery's we did meet, and we did like each other: I thought he was crazy and he thought I was even crazier. I was very shy, which he thought was intelligence; he was garrulous, which I assumed was brilliance—and on such misinterpretations, thank heavens, many a friendship is based. On the other hand, perhaps it was not a misinterpretation: certain of my literary "heroes" of the *Partisan Review* variety present at that party paled in significance when I met Larry, and through these years have remained pale while Larry has been something of a hero to me, which would seem to make me intelligent and Larry brilliant. Who knows?

The milieu of those days, and it's funny to think of them in such a way since they are so recent, seems odd now. We were all in our early twenties. John Ashbery, Barbara Guest, Kenneth Koch and I, being poets, divided our time between the literary bar, the San Remo, and the artists' bar, the Cedar Tavern. In the San Remo we argued and gossipped: in the Cedar we often wrote poems while listening to the painters argue and gossip. So far as I know nobody painted in the San Remo while they listened to the writers argue. An interesting sidelight to these social activities was that for most of us non-academic and indeed non-literary poets in the sense of the American scene at the time, the painters were the only generous audience for our poetry, and most of us read first publicly in art galleries or at The Club. The literary establishment cared about as much for our work as the Frick cared for Pollock and de Kooning, not that we cared any more about establishments than they did, all of the disinterested parties being honorable men.

Then there was great respect for anyone who did anything marvelous: when Larry introduced me to de Kooning I nearly got sick, as I almost did when I met Auden; if Jackson Pollock tore the door off the men's room in the Cedar it was something he just did and was interesting, not an annoyance. You couldn't see into it anyway, and besides there was then a sense of genius. Or what Kline used to call "the dream." Newman was at that time considered a temporarily silent oracle, being ill, Ad Reinhardt the most shrewd critic of the emergent "art world," Meyer Schapiro a god and Alfred Barr right up there alongside him but more distant, Holger Cahill another god but one who had abdicated to become more interested in "the thing we're doing," Clement Greenberg the discoverer, Harold Rosenberg the analyzer, and so on and so on. Tom Hess had written the important book. Elaine de Kooning was the White Goddess: she knew everything, told little of it though she talked a lot, and we all adored (and adore) her. She is graceful.

Into this scene Larry came rather like a demented telephone. Nobody knew whether they wanted it in the library, the kitchen or the toilet, but it was electric. Nor did he. The single most important event in his artistic career was when de

Kooning said his painting was like pressing your face into wet grass. From the whole jazz scene, which had gradually diminished to a mere recreation, Larry had emerged into the world of art with the sanction of one of his own gods, and indeed the only living one.

It is interesting to think of 1950–52, and the styles of a whole group of young artists whom I knew rather intimately. It was a liberal education on top of an academic one. Larry was chiefly involved with Bonnard and Renoir at first, later Manet and Soutine; Joan Mitchell—Duchamp; Mike Goldberg—Cézanne-Villon-de Kooning; Helen Frankenthaler—Pollock-Miró; Al Leslie—Motherwell; De Niro—Matisse; Nell Blaine—Helion; Hartigan—Pollock-Guston; Harry Jackson—a lot of Matisse with a little German Expressionism; Jane Freilicher—a more subtle combination of Soutine with some Monticelli and Moreau appearing through the paint. The impact of THE NEW AMERICAN PAINTING on this group was being avoided rather self-consciously rather than exploited. If you live in the studio next to Brancusi, you try to think about Poussin. If you drink with Kline you tend to do your black-and-whites in pencil on paper. The artists I knew at that time knew perfectly well who was Great and they weren't going to begin to imitate their works, only their spirit. When someone did a false Clyfford Still or Rothko, it was talked about for weeks. They hadn't read Sartre's *Being and Nothingness* for nothing.

Larry was especially interested in the vast range of possibilities of art. Perhaps because of his experience as a jazz musician, where everything can become fixed so quickly in style and become "the sound," he has moved restlessly from phase to phase. Larry always wanted to see something when he painted, unlike the then-prevalent conceptualized approach. No matter what stylistic period he was in, the friends he spent most time with were invariably subjects in some sense, more or less recognizable, and of course his two sons and his mother-in-law who lived with him were the most frequent subjects (he was separated from his wife, Augusta). His mother-in-law, Mrs. Bertha Burger, was the most frequent subject. She was called Berdie by everyone, a woman of infinite patience and sweetness, who held together a Bohemian household of such staggering complexity it would have driven a less great woman mad. She had a natural grace of temperament which overcame all obstacles and irritations. (During her fatal illness she confessed to me that she had once actually disliked two of Larry's friends because they had been "mean" to her grandsons, and this apologetically!) She appears in every period: an early Soutinesque painting with a cat; at an Impressionistic breakfast table; in the semi-abstract paintings of her seated in a wicker chair; as the double nude, very realistic, now in the collection of the Whitney Museum; in the later *The Athlete's Dream,* which she especially enjoyed because I posed with her and it made her less self-conscious if she was in a painting with a friend; she is also all the figures in the Museum of Modern Art's great painting *The Pool.* Her gentle interestedness extended beyond her own family to everyone who frequented the house, in a completely incurious way. Surrounded by painters and poets suddenly in mid-life, she had an admirable directness with esthetic decisions: "it must be very good work, he's such a wonderful person." Considering the polemics of the time, this was not only a relaxing attitude, it was an adorable one. For many of us her death was as much the personal end of a period as Pollock's death was that of a public one.

I mention these details of Rivers' life because, in the sense that Picasso meant it, his work is very much a diary of his experience. He is inspired directly by visual stimulation and his work is ambitious to save these experiences. Where much of the art of our time has been involved with direct conceptual or ethical considerations, Rivers has chosen to mirror his preoccupations and enthusiasms in an unprogrammatic way. As an example, I think that he personally was very awed by Rothko and that this reveals itself in the seated figures of 1953–54; at the same time I know that a rereading of *War and Peace,* and his idea of Tolstoy's life, prompted him to commence work on *Washington Crossing the Delaware,* a non-historical, non-philosophical work, the impulse for which I at first thought was hopelessly corny until I saw the painting finished. Rivers veers sharply, as if totally dependent on life impulses, until one observes an obsessively willful insistence on precisely what he is interested in. This goes for the father of our country as well as for the later Camel and Tareyton packs. Who, he seems to be saying, says they're corny? This is the opposite of pop art. He is never naive and never oversophisticated.

Less known than his jazz interests are Larry's literary ones. He has kept, sporadically, a fairly voluminous and definitely scandalous journal, has written some good poems of a diaristic (boosted by Surrealism) nature, and collaborated with several poets (including myself) who have posed for him, mainly I think to keep them quiet while posing and to relax himself when not painting or sculpting. The literary side of his activity has resulted mainly in the poem-paintings with Kenneth Koch, a series of lithographs with me [*Stones*], and our great collaborative play *Kenneth Koch, a Tragedy,* which cannot be printed because it is so filled with 50s art gossip that everyone would sue us. This latter work kept me amused enough to continue to pose for the big nude which took so many months to finish. That is one of Larry's strategies to keep you coming back to his studio, or was when he couldn't afford a professional model. The separation of the arts, in the "pure" sense, has never interested him. As early as 1952, when John Myers and Herbert Machiz were producing the New York Artists' Theatre, Larry did a set for a play of mine, *Try! Try!* At the first run-through I realized it was all wrong and withdrew it. He, however, insisted that if he had done the work for the set I should be willing to rewrite to my own satisfaction, and so I rewrote the play for Anne Meacham, J. D. Cannon, Louis Edmonds and Larry's set, and that is the version printed by Grove Press. Few people are so generous towards the work of others.

As I said earlier, Larry is restless, impulsive and compulsive. He loves to work. I remember a typical moment in the late 50s when both Joan Mitchell and I were visiting the Hamptons and we were all lying on the beach, a state of relaxation Larry can never tolerate for long. Joan was wearing a particularly attractive boating hat and Larry insisted that they go back to his studio so he could make a drawing of her.

It is a beautiful drawing, an interesting moment in their lives, and Joan was not only pleased to be drawn, she was relieved because she is terribly vulnerable to sunburn. As Kenneth Koch once said of him, "Larry has a floating subconscious—he's all intuition and no sense."

That's an interesting observation about the person, but actually Larry Rivers brings such a barrage of technical gifts to each intuitive occasion that the moment is totally transformed. Many of these gifts were acquired in the same manner as his talents in music and literature, through practice. Having been hired by Herbie Fields' band in his teens he became adept at the saxophone, meeting a group of poets who interested him he absorbed, pro or con, lots of ideas about style in poetry, and attending classes at Hans Hofmann's school plunged him into activities which were to make him one of the best draftsmen in contemporary art and one of the most subtle and particular colorists. This has been accomplished through work rather than intellection. And here an analogy to jazz can be justified: his hundreds of drawings are each like a separate performance, with its own occasion and subject, and what has been "learned" from the performance is not just the technical facility of the classical pianists' octaves or the studies in a *Grande Chaumière* class, but the ability to deal with the increased skills that deepening of subject matter and the risks of anxiety-dictated variety demand for clear expression. When Rivers draws a nose, it is my nose, your nose, his nose, Gogol's nose, and the nose from a drawing instruction manual, and it is the result of highly conscious skill.

There is a little bit of Hemingway in his attitude toward ability, toward what you do to a canvas or an armature. His early painting, *The Burial,* is really, in a less arrogant manner than Hemingway's, "getting into the ring" with Courbet (*A Burial at Ornans*), just as his nude portrait of me started in his mind from envy of the then newly acquired Géricault slave with the rope at the Metropolitan Museum, the portrait *Augusta* from a Delacroix; and even this year he is still fighting it out, this time with David's *Napoleon.* As with his friends, as with cigarette and cigar boxes, maps, and animals, he is always engaged in an esthetic athleticism which sharpens the eye, hand and arm in order to beat the bugaboos of banality and boredom, deliberately invited into the painting and then triumphed over.

What his work has always had to say to me, I guess, is to be more keenly interested while I'm still alive. And perhaps this is the most important thing art can say.

NOTES ON THE POEMS AND THE ESSAYS

The following abbreviations are used:

ACW   *A City Winter, and Other Poems.* Two Drawings by Larry Rivers.
New York: Editions of the Tibor de Nagy Gallery, 1952.

Audit   *Audit/Poetry* IV:1 "Featuring Frank O'Hara," 1964.

Hopwood The Avery Hopwood and Jule Hopwood Award in Creative Writing,
University of Michigan, granted to Francis O'Hara 1950–1
for his manuscript collection of poems "A Byzantine Place"
(dated Ann Arbor, March 1951, in MS 635).

IMO   *In Memory of My Feelings.* A Selection of Poems by Frank O'Hara.
Edited by Bill Berkson. With "original decorations" by 30 artists.
New York: The Museum of Modern Art, 1967.

Love   *Love Poems (Tentative Title).* New York: Tibor de Nagy Editions, 1965.

Lunch   *Lunch Poems.* San Francisco: City Lights Books,
The Pocket Poets Series No. 19, 1964.

MIAE   *Meditations in an Emergency.* New York: Grove Press, Inc., 1957.
Second edition, 1967.

MS   Numbered manuscripts in the Frank O'Hara archives.

Myers   John Bernard Myers: *The Poets of the New York School.*
Philadelphia: The University of Pennsylvania, 1969.

NAP   *The New American Poetry: 1945–1960.* Edited by Donald Allen.
New York: Grove Press, Inc., 1960.

ODES   *Odes* by Frank O'Hara. Prints by Michael Goldberg.
New York: Tiber Press, 1960.

HOW ROSES GET BLACK
Dated Cambridge, November 1948, in MS 701. Hopwood.

GAMIN
Dated Cambridge, June 1949, in MS 634.

MADRIGAL FOR A DEAD CAT NAMED JULIA
Dated Cambridge, June 1949, in MS 376. Hopwood. First published, without a title, in *Generation*, spring 1951.

ORANGES: 12 PASTORALS
Dated Grafton [Mass.], June–August 1949, in MS 296. This MS, the first draft, gives names of months for eight of the poems: No. 2 "November," No. 3 "February," No. 4 "March," No. 5 "October," No. 6 "July," No. 7 "June," No. 8 "May," No. 9 "August." No. 12, titled "A Prose Poem," is in Hopwood. First published as a mimeographed pamphlet by Tibor de Nagy Gallery in 1953, on the occasion of an exhibition of Grace Hartigan's twelve paintings called *Oranges*, which incorporated the twelve pastorals.

A PRAYER TO PROSPERO
Dated Cambridge, November 1949, in MS 305, with a dedication: "to Thayer David." Hopwood. First published in *Harvard Advocate*, February 1951.

HOMAGE TO RROSE SÉLAVY
Dated Cambridge, November 1949, in MS 208. First published in *Generation*, spring 1951. The title refers to Marcel Duchamp's famous signature.

MELMOTH THE WANDERER
Dated Cambridge, December 1949, in MS 609. Hopwood.

AUTOBIOGRAPHIA LITERARIA
Kenneth Koch believes this poem was written in 1949 or 1950. First published in *Harper's Bazaar*, October 1967; reprinted in Myers.

THE DRUMMER
Probably written in 1949 or 1950. Hopwood. First published in *Harvard Advocate*, September 1950.

THE MUSE CONSIDERED AS A DEMON LOVER
Dated Cambridge, November 1949, in MS 166, and dated Boston, February 1950, in MS x519. Hopwood. "Trouvez Hortense!" is from Arthur Rimbaud's poem "H."

POEM (At night Chinamen jump)
Dated Cambridge, February 1950, in MS 105, which has the earlier title: "A Poem in Envy of Catullus." Hopwood. First published in *ACW*; reprinted in *MIAE*.

POEM (The eager note on my door said "Call me,)
Dated Cambridge, February 1950, in MS 312. Hopwood. First published in *Harvard Advocate*, September 1950; reprinted in *New World Writing* 1, April 1952, in *MIAE* and in *IMO*.

TODAY
Dated Cambridge, February 1950, in MS x415. Hopwood.

CONCERT CHAMPÊTRE

Dated Cambridge, March 1950, in MS 118. Hopwood. First published in *Generation*, autumn 1951.
MS 171 has the last two lines:

> read you my story" I said. "It
> will make you like me better."

revised to read as given in the text.

AN 18TH CENTURY LETTER

Dated May 1950 in MS x608.

MEMORIAL DAY 1950

Mentioned by George Montgomery in his letter to FOH of June 3, 1950. First published in *Paris Review* 49, summer 1970.

V. R. LANG

Dated Boston, July 1950, in MS 181, with an earlier title, "Anne Lang," and deleted last line: "and forget the kitchen's full of knives," which is from the play *Try! Try!*

A SCENE

John Ashbery writes that FOH showed this poem to him in July or August of 1950. "By the way, the inspiration for 'A Scene' came from *The Midtown Journal,* a Boston scandal sheet which got all its material from police night court blotters; it was very funny and written in a zippy style by Harvard graduates, or so the story went." (JA to DA, June 30, 1969.)

A QUIET POEM

Written before August 1950. Hopwood. First published in *Adventures in Poetry* 5, 1970.

A WALK ON SUNDAY AFTERNOON

Dated Boston, September 1950, in MS x259. First published in *Best & Company,* 1969.

LES ÉTIQUETTES JAUNES

Dated Ann Arbor, September 1950, in MS 82. Hopwood. First published in *MIAE.*

A LETTER TO BUNNY

Dated Ann Arbor, October 1950, in MS x276. "Bunny" was V. R. Lang's nickname.

A PLEASANT THOUGHT FROM WHITEHEAD

Dated Ann Arbor, November 1950, in MS x567. Hopwood. First published in *New Republic,* November 29, 1969.

POEM (The flies are getting slower now)

Dated Ann Arbor, November 1950, in MS 627. In MS 289 the poem is titled "October."

POEM (WHE EWHEE)

Dated Ann Arbor, November 1950, in MS 695.

THE SPOILS OF GRAFTON

Dated Ann Arbor, November 1950, in MS x326.

THE CLOWN

Dated Ann Arbor, December 1950, in MS 624. Hopwood.

ODE ON SAINT CECILIA'S DAY

Dated Ann Arbor, December 1950, in MS 108.

POEM (God! love! sun! all dear and singular things!)
Dated Ann Arbor, December 1950, in MS 631. Text from MS 185.

ANIMALS
Dated 1950 in MS x354, which has "Miró—" written below. Hopwood. First published in *Fathar* 1, 1970.

MORNING
Dated Ann Arbor, October 1950 in Ben Weber's MS. Hopwood. First published in *Generation*, fall 1951.

THE THREE-PENNY OPERA
Written in 1950 (FOH) to DA, 1959), Hopwood. First published in *Accent*, summer 1951; reprinted in *MIAE*.

A NOTE TO JOHN ASHBERY
Probably written in 1950.

A NOTE TO HAROLD FONDREN
Probably written in 1950. MS 217 has this canceled epigraph: "'. . . believe me, every one is really responsible to all men for all men and for everything.'—Dostoyevsky." First published in *Poetry*, May 1970.

A CAMERA
Probably written in 1950 or 1951.

A POEM IN ENVY OF CAVALCANTI
Probably written in 1950. Hopwood, titled "An Audenseque Poem." First published in *Art and Literature* 12, spring 1967.

AN IMAGE OF LEDA
Probably written in 1950. First published in *Evergreen Review*, July 1971.

THE POET IN THE ATTIC
Dated Grafton, November 1951.

EARLY MONDRIAN
Probably written in 1950 or 1951. First published in *ACW*.

NIGHT THOUGHTS IN GREENWICH VILLAGE
Probably written in 1950 or 1951. Hopwood. In MS 115 "sea" is substituted for "song" in the last line.

POEM (All the mirrors in the world)
POEM (Although I am a half hour)
These poems were probably written in 1950 or 1951. Hopwood.

POEM (If I knew exactly why the chestnut tree)
Probably written in 1950 or 1951. Hopwood. First published in *Generation*, fall 1951.

POEM (Let's take a walk, you)
Probably written in 1950 or 1951. Hopwood. First published in *ACW*.

POEM (The clouds ache bleakly)
Mentioned in George Montgomery's letter of June 3, 1950.

POEM (The ivy is trembling in the hammock)
Probably written in 1950 or 1951.

POEM (The stars are brighter)
Dated Cambridge June, 1950 in Ben Weber's MS. Hopwood. First published in *Adventures in Poetry* 5, 1970.

SONG FOR LOTTA
Probably written in 1950 or 1951.

THE ARGONAUTS
THE LOVER
THE YOUNG CHRIST
These poems were probably written in 1950 or 1951. First published in *ACW*.

WOMEN
Probably written in 1950 or 1951. First published in *Generation,* spring 1951.

THE CRITIC
Dated Ann Arbor, January 1951, in MS 607. First published in *Art and Literature* 12, spring 1967.

ORIGINAL SIN
Dated Ann Arbor, January 1951, in MS 628, which has a canceled earlier title: "The Python."

POETRY
Dated Ann Arbor, January 1951, in MS 608. First published in *Angel Hair* 6, spring 1969.

TARQUIN
Dated Ann Arbor, January 1951, in MS 107. First published in Myers.

YET ANOTHER FAN
Dated Ann Arbor, January 1951, in MS 561. Hopwood. First published in *ACW.*

A HOMAGE
Dated Ann Arbor, February 1951, in MS 357. First published in *Adventures in Poetry* 5, January 1970.

A POEM ABOUT RUSSIA
Dated Ann Arbor, February 1951, in MS 133.

A PROUD POEM
Dated Ann Arbor, February 1951, in MS 138.

FEBRUARY
Dated Ann Arbor, February 1951, in MS 588.

A RANT
Dated Ann Arbor, February 1951, in MS 216.

INTERIOR (WITH JANE)
Dated Ann Arbor, February 1951, in MS 229, which has "(About Jane)" written below, referring to Jane Freilicher. MSS 524 and x375 are titled "Interior (With Jane)." Hopwood. First published in *Generation,* fall 1951; reprinted as "Interior/*About Jane*" in *Art and Literature* 12, spring 1967.

RENAISSANCE
Dated Ann Arbor, February 1951, in MS 585. Hopwood.

A POSTCARD FROM JOHN ASHBERY
Dated Ann Arbor, March 1951, in MS 590.

POEM (Ivy invades the statue.)
Dated Detroit, March 1951, in MS 104.

DRINKING
Dated Ann Arbor, March 1951, in MS x449. MS 566 has written below: "Delaunay portrait of Apollinaire."

SMOKING
Dated Ann Arbor, March 1951, in MS 584. Hopwood.

PANIC FEAR
Dated Ann Arbor, March 1951, in MS 223.

BOSTON
Dated Boston, March 1951, in MS 227.

A PASTORAL DIALOGUE
Dated Ann Arbor, May 1951, in MS 193, which has a canceled alternate title: "A Natural Dialogue." First published in *ACW*.

POEM (I ran through the snow like a young Czarevitch!)
Dated Ann Arbor, May 1951, in MS 583. First published in *The World* 13, 1968.

A SONNET FOR JANE FREILICHER
From FOH's letter to JF of June 6, 1951. MS 157 is titled: "Communicating with Jane Freilicher."

THE ARBORETUM
Dated Ann Arbor, June 1951, in MS 629. MS 172 has a canceled earlier title: "Revery." First published in *Adventures in Poetry* 5, 1970.

A TERRESTRIAL CUCKOO
Dated Ann Arbor, July 1951, in MS 88. First published in *ACW*; reprinted in *MIAE*.

ON LOOKING AT *LA GRANDE JATTE*, THE CZAR WEPT ANEW
Part 3, which was originally a separate poem and so titled, is dated Ann Arbor, July 1951, in MS 292. First published in *Partisan Review*, March–April 1952; reprinted in *MIAE*.

ANN ARBOR VARIATIONS
Dated Ann Arbor, July 1951, in MS 284. First published in *Poetry*, December 1951; reprinted in *IMO*.

A CHINESE LEGEND
Dated New York, November 1951, in MS 616, with original title: "A Chinese Tale."

AFTER WYATT
Dated New York, November 1951, in MS 293. MS x588 is titled: "Blowing Somebody." First published in *The World* 13, 1968; reprinted in *Paris Review* 49, summer 1970.

THE SATYR
Dated Ann Arbor, December 1951, in MS 139.

THE TOMB OF ARNOLD SCHOENBERG
Dated New York, December 1951, in MS 163. First published in *Poetry*, May 1970.

POET
Dated New York, December 1951, in MS 200, which is titled "The Poet."

A MODERN SOLDIER
Dated Ann Arbor, February 1951, in MS 106, which is titled "Holy Modern Soldier." Dated New York, December 1951, in MS 385.

A MEXICAN GUITAR
Dated New York, September 1951 in Ben Weber's MS. *ACW;* reprinted in *MIAE.*

JANE AWAKE
Written in 1951 (FOH to DA, 1959). First published in *ACW;* reprinted in *MIAE.*

1951
First published in *The Bonacker: A Collection of Eastern Long Island Writing* (East Hampton, 1953).

DIDO
Probably written in 1951. First published in *Poetry,* May 1970.

BROTHERS
Dated New York, January 1952, in MS 522, which has a canceled earlier title: "Dawns and Brothers."

A CITY WINTER
James Schuyler believes that these sonnets were finished before late January or early February of 1952, when he first saw them (JS to DA, August 12, 1969). First published in *ACW.*

ASHES ON SATURDAY AFTERNOON
Dated New York, February 1952, in MS 97. MS 61 has an alternate title: "Poet to Poet." "Ashes" was FOH's nickname for John Ashbery, the poet addressed in the poem.

FEMALE TORSO
Dated New York, February 1952, in MS x311, with "Maillol" written below. First published in *Angel Hair* 6, spring 1969.

IN HOSPITAL
Dated New York, October 1951, in MS 179, and New York, February 1952, in MS 601.

OVERLOOKING THE RIVER
Dated New York, February 1952, in *Locus Solus* MS. First published in *Locus Solus* 1, winter 1961.

POEM FOR A PAINTER
This sonnet is dated New York, February 1952, in MS 135, which has "(Hartigan)" written in alongside the title. Grace Hartigan's MS has a variant title: "Poet Trapped by the Tail," and "play" for "trough" in line 5.

AN ABORTION
Dated New York, March 1952, in MS 633. First published in *Angel Hair* 6, spring 1969.

SUNSET
Dated New York, March 1952, in MS x453.

WALKING WITH LARRY RIVERS
Dated New York, March 1952, in MS 599.

FUNNIES
Dated March 1952, in MS 691.

WASHINGTON SQUARE
Dated New York, April 1952, in MS 356.

ELEGY (Ecstatic and in anguish over lost days)
Dated New York, April 1952, in MS 120. MS x717 has "Beckmann still life with fish" written below. MS 102 has "Mystified" crossed out in the first line and "Ecstatic!" written in. First published in *Angel Hair* 6, spring 1969.

ELEGY (Salt water. and faces dying)
Dated New York, April 1952, in MS 121. MS x716 has "Klee fish still life" written below. First published in *Angel Hair* 6, spring 1969.

COMMERCIAL VARIATIONS
Dated New York, April 1952, in MS x233, with alternate title: "V. on a Radio Commercial," written alongside. First published in *Folder* 1, 1953; reprinted in *C* I:7, 1964.

COLLOQUE SENTIMENTAL
Dated New York, May 1952, in MS x588. First published in *The World* 13, 1968.

PORTRAIT OF GRACE
Dated New York, May 1952, in MS x355, with "Rivers' drawing of Grace as a girl monk" written alongside the title.

JANE AT TWELVE
Dated New York, January 1951, in MS 354, and New York, May 1952, in MS 206.

JANE BATHING
Dated New York, June 1952, in MS 205.

LOCARNO
Dated New York, June 1952, in MS 547b. First published in *Locus Solus* 1, winter 1961.

MOUNTAIN CLIMBING
Dated New York, June 1952, in MS 559, where "Kafka" is crossed out in the second paragraph and "The Author" written in, and "because I won't tell" is deleted from the end. First published in *Semi-colon* I:5 in 1954 or 1955.

OLIVE GARDEN
Dated New York, June 1952, in MS x231, where the earlier title, "The Garden of Olives," is crossed out. First published in *Semi-colon* I:1, 1954.

THE NEXT BIRD TO AUSTRALIA
Dated New York, July 1952, in MS x287, and New York, November 1952, in MS 109. First published in *Art and Literature* 12, spring 1967.

DAY AND NIGHT IN 1952
Dated East Hampton, July 1952, in MS x517, which has "Myers" after "the other John" in the first paragraph and where the last section was originally titled "The Golden Apple of Juno." First published in *Audit*.

POEM (The distinguished)
From FOH's letter to Jane Freilicher of August 8, 1952. First published in *Art and Literature* 12, spring 1967.

BEACH PARTY
Dated East Hampton, August 1952, in MS 578.

EASTER
Dated New York, August 1952, in DA MS. First published in *Ephemeris* 2, May 1969. Kenneth Koch wrote: "Another of his works which burst on us all like a bomb then [1952] was 'Easter,' a wonderful, energetic, and rather obscene poem of four or five pages, which consisted mainly of a procession of various bodily parts and other objects across a vast landscape. It was like Lorca and Whitman in some ways, but very original. I remember two things about it which were new: one was the phrase 'the roses of Pennsylvania,' and the other was the line in the middle of the poem which began 'It is Easter!' (Easter, though it was the title, had not been mentioned before in the poem and apparently had nothing to do with it.) What I saw in these lines was 1) inspired irrelevance which turns out to be relevant (once Frank had said 'It is Easter!' the whole poem was obviously about death and resurrection); 2) the use of movie techniques in poetry (in this case coming down hard on the title in the middle of a work); 3) the detachment of beautiful words from traditional contexts and putting them in curious new American ones ('roses of Pennsylvania')." "A Note on Frank O'Hara in the Early Fifties," *Audit.*

STEVEN
Dated New York, August 1952, in MS x279, which has the earlier title: "Steven Rivers."

POEM (The hosts of dreams and their impoverished minions)
Dated August 1952, in James Brodey's MS. First published in *Clothesline* 2, 1970.

CHEZ JANE
Dated New York, September 1952, in MS 86. First published in *Poetry,* November 1954; reprinted in *MIAE,* in *NAP,* and in *IMO.*

DUCAL DAYS
Dated New York, September 1952, in *Locus Solus* MS. Jane Freilicher recalls saying "the day was ducal" when she joined FOH in the Cedar Tavern and that he then took a small piece of paper out of his pocket and wrote this poem. (JF to DA, November 1969.) First published in *Locus Solus* 1, winter 1961.

TWO SHEPHERDS, A NOVEL
Dated New York, September 1952, in MS x268.

OCTOBER 26 1952 10:30 O'CLOCK
The title dates the poem.

AUBADE
Dated New York, October 1952, in MS 361, where the title is canceled.

BAARGELD
Dated New York, October 1952, in MS 489.

BIRDIE
Dated New York, October 1952, in MS 207, which was originally titled "Birdie, a Meditation."

BLOCKS
Dated New York, October 1952, in MS x219, which has a canceled earlier title: "Curiosity." First published in *Folder* 1, 1953; reprinted in *MIAE* and *IMO.*

POEM (He can rest. He has blessed him and hurt him)
Dated October 1952, in MS x536.

OCTOBER

Presumably written in October of 1952. In line 19 of MS 151 "without" has been altered to "with."

SNAPSHOT FOR BORIS PASTERNAK

Dated New York, October 1952, in MS 153, which has a canceled earlier title: "Letter to Boris Pasternak."

THE BATHERS

Dated New York, October 1952, in MS 93. First published in *Art and Literature* 12, spring 1967.

ALMA

Dated 1952 in MS 426. First published in *Lunch*.

EAST RIVER

Dated 1952 in *Locus Solus* MS. First published in *Locus Solus* 1, winter 1961.

HATRED

Dated 1952 in MS 44. "Frank's most famous poem during that summer [1952] was 'Hatred,' a rather long poem which he had typed up on a very long piece of paper which had been part of a roll." Kenneth Koch, "A Note on Frank O'Hara in the Early Fifties," *Audit*. First published in *Folder* 2, 1954; reprinted in *C* I:8, 1964.

HIERONYMUS BOSCH

Dated 1952 in MS 565.

INVINCIBILITY

Dated 1952 in MS 426. MS 225 indicates it was written in Southampton, and has an earlier title, "Razors at Twilight," crossed out and an alternate title, "The Tears of Invincibility," written in and "The Tears of" crossed out. First published in *MIAE*.

RIVER

Dated New York, February 1953 in Ben Weber's MS. First published in *MIAE*.

SAVOY

Dated 1952 in DA MS.

SONNET ON A WEDDING

Dated New York, 1952, with a query in MS 98, which has an earlier title: "Epithalamium."

TO A FRIEND

Dated 1952 in MSS 523 and x624.

WALKING TO WORK

Dated 1952 in MS x535. First published in *Poetry*, February 1969.

GLI AMANTI
JOVE

These poems were probably written in New York in 1951 or 1952. First published in *ACW*.

STUDY FOR WOMEN ON A BEACH

Probably written in 1951 or 1952.

THE STARVING POET

Probably written in New York in 1952. In line 3 "must" is crossed out in MS 364.

3RD AVENUE EL

Probably written in New York in 1951 or 1952. The text is from MS 290, where the last line originally read: "and behind, my life, the open sea."

BARBIZON

Dated New York, January 1953, in MS 488, with "Delvaux" written below.

SONNET (Lampooning blizzards, how your ocularities)

Dated New York, January 1953, in MS x612, where FOH has labeled the substitution of "cuffed" for "culled" in line 7 "Dick Mayes' addition."

HOUSE

Dated New York, February 1953, in MS x454. First published in *Locus Solus* 1, winter 1961.

MANIFESTO

Dated New York, February 1953, in MS 142, which has an earlier title: "Franklin, a journal of the arts."

POEM (When your left arm twitches)

Dated New York, February 1953, in MS 549, which has an earlier title: "To Larry." First published in *Paris Review,* winter 1968.

THE OPERA

Dated New York, February 1953, in *Locus Solus* MS. First published in *Locus Solus* 1, winter 1961.

[THEN THE WEATHER CHANGED.]

Dated New York, February 1953, in MS 579.

TWO VARIATIONS

Dated New York, February 1953, in MS 80, which has a canceled earlier title: "To Edwin." First published in *MIAE.*

VERY RAINY LIGHT, AN ECLOGUE

Dated New York, May 1952, in MS 636, and New York, February 1953, in MS 195. FOH told James Schuyler that the initials of the title refer to V. R. Lang (JS to DA, August 12, 1969). First published in *The Ant's Forefoot* 7 & 8, winter–spring 1971.

POEM (As you kneel)

Dated Southampton, March 1953, in MS 604. "Do you think there should be a reference in the title to my idea in beginning it which was something like 'how to be a Chinese poet'?" (FOH to Larry Rivers, June 27, 1953.)

RENT COLLECTING

Dated New York, March 1953, in MS x450. A somewhat different version was first published in *Clothesline* 2, 1970.

SONNET FOR LARRY RIVERS & HIS SISTER

Dated New York, March 1953, in MS x704.

ROUND ROBIN

Dated New York, January 1953, in MS x260, and New York, April 1953, in MS 571, which has FOH's footnotes.

SECOND AVENUE

Dated New York, March and April 1953, in MS x356, which has a canceled dedication: "To

Willem de Kooning." Larry Rivers' MS has this quotation from Mayakovsky as the epigraph: "In the church of my heart the choir is on fire."

Larry Rivers wrote: "His long marvelous poem *Second Avenue*, 1953, was written in my plaster garden studio overlooking that avenue. One night late I was working on a piece of sculpture of him. Between poses he was finishing his long poem. Three fat cops saw the light and made their way up to make the 'you call this art and what are you doing here' scene that every N.Y. artist must have experienced." "Life among the Stones," *Location*, spring 1963. See FOH's "Notes on *Second Avenue*," pages 495–7.

Section 9 was first published in *Measure* 1, 1957. The whole poem was first published by Totem Press and Corinth Books in 1960. Sections 7, 8, and 11 were reprinted in *IMO*.

DOLCE COLLOQUIO
Dated New York, April 1953, in MS 493. First published in *Poetry*, May 1970.

3 POEMS ABOUT KENNETH KOCH
Dated New York, April 1953, in MSS x226 and x227.

TWO EPITAPHS
Dated New York, May 1953, in MS x441.

POEM (He sighted her at the moment of recall.)
Dated Nyack, July 1953, in MS x542.

HOMAGE TO ANDRÉ GIDE
Dated Southampton, July 1953, in MS x320, which has three canceled alternate titles: "Weeping," "The Rain," and "Apology to André Gide." First published in *Voices*, May–August 1954.

LIFE ON EARTH
Dated July 1953 in MS 183, which has a canceled earlier title: "The Stars." "Pole" in line 1 was originally "Pollack" in MS 177, then changed to "poet" in MS 183, and to "Pole" again in the text first published in *Folder* 4, 1956. Part 4, line 9 reads "blank" in MSS 177 and 183 and *Folder*; but in the latest version (DA MS) it reads "bland."

ON RACHMANINOFF'S BIRTHDAY (Quick! a last poem before I go)
Dated New York, July 1953, in MS x406, which has the earlier title: "Poem." First published in *Evergreen Review* I:3, 1957; reprinted in *Lunch*.

TO MY MOTHER
Dated Sneden's Landing, August 1953, in MS 603.

TO MY DEAD FATHER
Possibly a pair poem to the preceding.

SNEDEN'S LANDING VARIATIONS
"Frank wrote the Variations you ask about at Sneden's Landing in 1953, in late August or September." (James Schuyler to DA, July 22, 1969.)

APPOGGIATURAS
Dated Sneden's Landing, August and October 1953, in MS 188.

POEM (I am not sure there is a cure,)
Dated Sneden's Landing, October 1953, in MS 366, which has the alternate title "Chopiniana." First published in *Poetry*, May 1970.

ROMANZE, OR THE MUSIC STUDENTS

Dated Sneden's Landing, October 1953, in MS 87, where these two lines are deleted following line 5 of stanza 4:

> O distances, how you emulate their stance!
> Peaks, how gleefully you accept their rigidity!

MS 350 has a canceled earlier title: "Coral Beads." First published in *Poetry*, November 1954; reprinted in *MIAE* and in *IMO*.

THE HUNTER

Dated 1953 in MS 426. "Written at Sneden's Landing in September or October 1953. We were sitting under a paulownia, which has leaves of a notable size, when I said they were falling like pie-plates, which found its way into the poem." (James Schuyler to DA, August 12, 1969.) First published in *Folder* 2, 1954; reprinted in *MIAE*.

LINES TO A DEPRESSED FRIEND

Dated New York, November 1953, in MS x239, which has these earlier titles: "To Joe" and "Umber of the sweetest evocation." First published in *Angel Hair* 6, spring 1969.

GRAND CENTRAL

Dated 1953 in MS x331. First published in *Fathar* 1, 1970.

LARRY

Dated 1953 on verso of MS 161.

LEBANON

Dated 1953 in MS 487. First published in *Locus Solus* 5, 1962.

POEM (Now it is light, now it is the calm)

Dated 1953 in MS 521, which is so titled. First published in *Poetry*, October 1955.

THE APRICOT SEASON

Dated 1953 in MS 518, which has "Picabia: Udnie" written below.

NEWSBOY

Dated 1953 in MS x394.

THE SPIRIT INK

Dated 1953 in MS 496.

THE AFTERNOON

MS x511 has the title "The Afternoon, or My Penis," with the subtitle crossed out. First published as "My Penis" in *Clothesline* 2, 1970, where it is dated 1953.

TO THE POEM

Probably written in 1952 or 1953. MS 435 has a canceled earlier title: "To a Reader."

ANACROSTIC

This acrostic poem is dated New York, January 1954, in MS 568, which has an earlier title: "To Elaine" [de Kooning] written above, and "René Bouché" written below.

ON A PASSAGE IN BECKETT'S *WATT* & ABOUT GEO. MONTGOMERY

Dated New York, January 1954, in MS x300.

UNICORN
Dated New York, January 1954, in MS x613. First published in *Poetry,* May 1970.

POEM (The little roses, the black majestic sails)
Dated New York, January 1954, in MS x322.

LINES WRITTEN IN *A RAW YOUTH*
Dated Southampton, February 1954, in MS 560. MS x313 has an earlier title: "Lines Written on the Beach at Southampton," revised to final title. First published in *Voices,* January/April 1957.

SOUTHAMPTON VARIATIONS
Dated Southampton, February 1954, in MS 557.

THE PIPES OF PAN
Dated Southampton, March 1954, in MS 612, which has "Keats 'As from the darkening gloom a silver dove'" written below.

MRS BERTHA BURGER
Dated Southampton, March 1954, in MS 610. Mrs. Burger was Larry Rivers' mother-in-law.

HOMOSEXUALITY
Dated March 1954 in MS x353, where it is numbered "5," and has "Ensor Self portrait with Masks" written below. In MS x334 it is titled "The Homosexuals" and numbered "I," which is crossed out. First published in *Poetry,* May 1970.

TO JANE; AND IN IMITATION OF COLERIDGE
Dated Southampton, March 1954, in MS x422. First published in *C* 7, 1964.

TO A POET
Dated April 10 and 11, 1954, in MS x242, which has the following written below:

> Ich weiss: am sengendheissen bergeshange
> Bei schweiss und mühe nur gedeih ich recht
> Da meine seele ich nur so empfange;
> Doch bin ich niemals undankbar und schlecht.
> —Stefan George, Die Seele des Weines

AUS EINEM APRIL
Dated Southampton, April 1954, in MS 317. The title is from a poem by Rilke. First published in *Poetry,* November 1954; reprinted in *MIAE.*

DEATH
Dated Southampton, April 1954, in MS 304, which has a canceled earlier title: "After Charms Have Fed."

SPLEEN
Dated Southampton, April 1954, in MS 189. First published in *Adventures in Poetry* 5, January 1970.

LINES WHILE READING COLERIDGE'S "THE PICTURE"
Dated Southampton, April 1954, in MS x607.

KITVILLE
First published in *Clothesline* 2, 1970, where it is dated April 1954.

ON RACHMANINOFF'S BIRTHDAY (Blue windows, blue rooftops)
Dated New York, April 1954, with a query in MS 314. First published in *Poetry*, March 1956; reprinted in *MIAE*.

ON RACHMANINOFF'S BIRTHDAY (I am so glad that Larry Rivers made a)
Dated April 10, 1954, in MS 491. First published in *Paris Review*, winter 1968.

POEM IN JANUARY
Dated Southampton, April 1954, in MS 316, which has a canceled last stanza:

> Navigator! assemble your Moors and move
> them towards the magician as if March were a meat
> grinder, with its opacity and gnashing moods.

First published in *Poetry*, November 1954; reprinted in *MIAE*.

TO JANE, SOME AIR
Dated Southampton, April 1954, in MS 516.

THREE RONDELS
They are dated Southampton, May 1954, in MSS 300, x531, and x532.

MY HEAT
Dated Southampton, May 1954, in MS 515. MS x338 has "(after Corbière)" written beside the title.

HOMAGE TO PASTERNAK'S CAPE MOOTCH
Dated 1953 in MS 519 and New York, June 1954, in MS x451, which have the earlier title: "Debussy." "Cape Mootch" is the title of a poem in Pasternak's *My Sister, Life*.

ODE (An idea of justice may be precious)
Dated June 18, 1954, in MS 235, which is titled: "To . . ." First published as "An Ode" in *Folder* 3, 1955; reprinted in *MIAE*, *NAP*, and *IMO*.

MEDITATIONS IN AN EMERGENCY
Dated June 25, 1954, in MS 315, which has the earlier title: "Meditations on Re-emergent Occasions." ". . . as you remember Kenneth [Koch] had to talk me out of 'Meditations on an Emergency' and into 'Meditations in an Emergency.' " (FOH to John Ashbery, February 1, 1961.) First published in *Poetry*, November 1954; reprinted in *MIAE* and *IMO*.

TO THE MOUNTAINS IN NEW YORK
Dated July 1, 1954, in MS 444.

3 REQUIEMS FOR A YOUNG UNCLE
Dated July 11, 1954, in MS x702.

MAYAKOVSKY
Part 1 is dated New York, June 1954, in MS x497. Part 2 is dated July 12, 1954, in MS x498 and is titled "To Someone Gone"; it has this epigraph: " 'Oh Rodney! dese wounds ve have inflicted on each odder are a bond.'—Greta Garbo, *The Fall and Rise of Susan Lenox*." Part 3 is dated New York, July 1954, in MS x572; and Part 4 is dated Southampton, February 1954, in MS 77.

The stanza breaks in Part 2 follow MSS 352 and 378.

James Schuyler wrote: "Two of these poems were 'found' by me at 326 East 49th—one in a book. Frank said he had forgotten about it when I produced it. I wanted him to include them in *MIAE*, but he didn't think them substantial enough to stand by themselves. I suggested he make one poem of them, and he dug out of his MSS pile the other two stanzas, which I don't think I'd seen before. He liked the result and said that since it was 'my' poem I had to think up a title—which I easily and instantly did—Frank had (again) been reading Mayakovsky and the book was on his desk. The other of the two poems—or verses—I found was 'My heart's aflutter!' of which Frank said, 'You *think* you know who that's about—and you're wrong! It's about Gandy Brodie. . . .' The 'bricks' he was carrying were the supports of a John Ashbery bookcase, which he and Fairfield [Porter] helped John with; I recall Fairfield complaining that one went to see John and ended up carrying bricks around the city. . . ." (JS to DA, August 12, 1969.) First published in *MIAE*.

FOR JANICE AND KENNETH TO VOYAGE
Dated July 20, 1954, in MS 349, which has "Alphonsine" canceled in line 2 and "honeymoon" substituted. First published in *Poetry,* March 1956; reprinted in *MIAE*.

TWO BOYS
Dated July 28, 1954, in MS x295.

A HILL
Dated New York, July 1954, in MS 611. First published in *Evergreen Review,* July 1971.

[I KISS YOUR CUP]
Dated New York, July 1954, in MS x556.

PORTRAIT
Dated New York, July 1954, in MS x402, which has an alternate title, "Heroin," and "de Chirico Song of Love" written below.

ON THE WAY TO THE SAN REMO
Dated New York, July 1954, in MS 480. The San Remo was a famous Greenwich Village cafe. First published in *Lunch Poems;* reprinted in *IMO*.

IN THE MOVIES
Dated Southampton, August 18, 1954, in MS x432. First published in *Fuck You/A Magazine of the Arts* V:5, April 1964, which combines lines 27 and 29.

[JULY IS OVER AND THERE'S VERY LITTLE TRACE]
Dated Southampton, August 1954, in MS 283.

MUSIC
Dated October 2, 1954, in MS 535, which has "Ilaria del Carretto" written below. First published in *Yūgen* 4, 1959; reprinted in *Lunch* and in *IMO*.

TO JOHN ASHBERY
Dated October 11, 1954, in MS x350. First published in *Angel Hair* 6, spring 1969.

POEM (Tempestuous breaths! we watch a girl)
Dated November 26, 1954, in MS 415, where the heavily scored out original title appears to be "Lana's Skirt."

CHRISTMAS CARD TO GRACE HARTIGAN
"Frank did give me 'Christmas Card,' I have a copy in my journal of 1954–55 so it must have been the Christmas of 1954." (GH to DA, September 3, 1970.)

2 POEMS FROM THE OHARA MONOGATARI
Dated December 30, 1954, in MS 544, which has three additional poems (of which No. 3 is crossed out):

3
Tendentious parrot, signal for burning.

4
The mare mirrors my switching wishes under her tail
as I gather the "Harvest of Leisure" on horseback.

4
Since I left Court
it's become increasingly more difficult
to stand on my hands
Oh Eastern shore! oh mud!

In 1959 FOH sent DA a typescript of the 2 POEMS with this note: "A little souvenir I found (of seeing *Sayonara* at the Academy of Music). F." First published in *Lunch*.

TO GIANNI BATES
Dated December 31, 1954, in MS 127.

FOR GRACE, AFTER A PARTY
Written in 1954 (FOH to DA, 1959). First published in *MIAE*.

LOVE (A whispering far away)
Dated 1954 in MS x288. First published in *Paris Review* 49, summer 1970.

POEM (I watched an armory combing its bronze bricks)
Dated 1954 in MS 479. First published in *Lunch*.

POEM (There I could never be a boy,)
Written in 1954 (FOH to DA, 1959). First published in *MIAE*.

TO THE HARBORMASTER
In 1959 FOH told DA this poem about Larry Rivers was written in 1954. First published in *MIAE*.

HERMAPHRODITE
Written in 1954 or earlier. First published in *Folder* 3, 1955.

POEM (Pawing the mound with his hairy legs)
Possibly written in 1954.

THE STATE OF WASHINGTON
Possibly written in 1954. MS x351 has "Tobey Red Man etc" written below.

ON SAINT ADALGISA'S DAY
Dated April 20, 1955, in MS 141.

CHOSES PASSAGÈRES
Dated May 6, 1955, in MS 552, which has "Magritte" written below. MS x99 has original line 7: "Néamoins, il y a fagots et fagots," and written below: "Picabia: Je revois en souvenir ma chère Udnie." First published in *Locus Solus* 2, summer 1961.

SONNET (The blueness of the hour)
Dated June 14, 1955, in MS 510, which has an earlier title: "To Joe," and "bluenesses" for "blueness" in line 1. First published in *Angel Hair* 6, spring 1969.

POEM (The eyelid has its storms. There is the opaque fish-)
Dated June 21, 1955, in MS 509, which has "Pollock / Masson" written below. First published in *Poetry*, October 1955.

AT THE OLD PLACE
Dated July 13, 1955, in MS x527, which has an earlier version of the last line: "How ashamed they are of us! There's the music!" The Old Place was a dance-bar in Greenwich Village. First published in *New York Poetry*, November 1969.

A WHITMAN'S BIRTHDAY BROADCAST WITH STATIC
Dated July 14, 1955, in MS 512. First published in *Clothesline* 2, 1970.

NOCTURNE
Dated August 8, 1955, in MS 513. First published in *Adventures in Poetry* 5, 1970.

POEM (Johnny and Alvin are going home, are sleeping now)
John Button remembers this poem as being written in September or October 1955. (JB to DA, December 1970.)

GOODBYE TO GREAT SPRUCE HEAD ISLAND
Probably written in early autumn of 1955 on the island.

TO AN ACTOR WHO DIED
Probably written in late summer or early autumn of 1955 on Great Spruce Head Island off the coast of Maine. This text follows Grace Hartigan's MS. MS x599 has a canceled earlier title, "To Laura Riding," and epigraphs: "I have set poetry aside" and "Heaven susteyne thy course in quietness"; it also has two final lines:

> sea, star, nor swell; and I now move away from love as from
> a lobster- and berry-laden table, not hungry for my time.

WITH BARBARA AT LARRÉ'S
Dated October 3, 1955, in MS 511, the earlier version is given below to show how FOH cut a poem. The deletions are italicized.

> WITH BARBARA AT LARRÉ'S
> Fall faces who have lunched on other
> Wednesdays at the flattering, *burning*
> bar. They are not turned by a change
> of suit not touched by noon, they could be
> *dining, they are here, we're here again,*
>
> oscillating with hope, its cigarette-ish
> pallor. We pour Martinis in our ears, listening
> for the other's silence. *"There's a flame*
> *on orioles in just such weather."*
> "I ate here with an Englishman
>
> who ordered skate." Demitasses bang together
> in the Fall behind the door.
> *A French lady shrieks "Monsieur Larré!"*
> It is the scene of many disasters, how
> we wait, as stamps pile up in postal boxes.
>
> "This is quite an aërial table,
> isn't it?" *"I'm waiting for miraculous London*
> *broil."* To such a tryst we cannot come

so frequently, guarding the effervescent from
the air, the air from all the burning conversation.

Larré's is a popular French restaurant in midtown Manhattan.

FOR JAMES DEAN
Dated October 5, 1955, in MS 78, which has an earlier title: "Elegy for James Dean." First published
in *Poetry*, March 1956; reprinted in *MIAE* and *NAP*.

THINKING OF JAMES DEAN
Dated October 11, 1955, in MS x515. Grace Hartigan's MS is titled "Thoughts."

MY HEART
Dated November 1, 1955, in MS 247. First published in *Paris Review* 49, summer 1970.

TO THE FILM INDUSTRY IN CRISIS
Dated November 15, 1955, in MS 323, which has "mother" crossed out in line 9 and "starched
nurse" written in. First published in *MIAE*; reprinted in *Hasty Papers* 1960 and in *IMO*.

PEARL HARBOR
Dated November 21, 1955, in MS 514, which has the earlier title crossed out: "On Seeing *From
Here to Eternity*." First published in *Paris Review*, winter 1968.

ON SEEING LARRY RIVERS' *WASHINGTON CROSSING THE DELAWARE* AT THE
MUSEUM OF MODERN ART
Dated November 29, 1955 in MS 322. First published in *Poetry*, March 1956; reprinted in *MIAE*.

RADIO
Dated December 3, 1955, in MS 325. Kenneth Koch wrote: "RADIO is perfect. I was in the
Cedar Tavern last night and Bill de Kooning was there, so I asked him if he'd seen your poem
about his picture. He said, Yeah, is that right? He said, Yeah, but how can you be sure it's about
my picture, is it just about a picture? I quoted him 'I have my beautiful de Kooning / to aspire
to. I think it has an orange / bed in it . . .' He said, 'It's a couch. But then it really is my picture,
that's wonderful.' Then he told me how he had always been interested in mattresses because they
were pulled together at certain points and puffed out at others, 'like the earth.'" (KK to FOH,
March 22, 1956.) First published in *Poetry*, March 1956; reprinted in *MIAE*.

STATUE
Dated December 3, 1955, in MS 441. MS x352 has "Rivers statue" written alongside the title
and is dated 1956.

SLEEPING ON THE WING
Dated December 29, 1955, in MS 321. James Schuyler wrote: "The day this was written I was
having breakfast (i.e. coffee) with Frank and Joe [LeSueur] at 326 East 49th Street, and the talk
turned to Frank's unquenchable inspiration, in a teasing way on my part and Joe's. The cigarette
smoke began jetting from Frank's nostrils and he went into the next room and wrote SLEEPING
ON THE WING in a great clatter of keys." (JS to DA, August 12, 1969.) First published in
MIAE; reprinted in *IMO*.

AIX-EN-PROVENCE
Probably written in 1955. MS x447 revises "wistful" to "restless" in line 3. First published in
The Ant's Forefoot 7 & 8, winter–spring 1971.

POEM (All of a sudden all the world)
Dated 1955 in MSS x164 and x238, which have this subtitle: "'Drunk as I have often been.'"

JOSEPH CORNELL
Dated 1955 in MS 569, which has FOH's direction "print like boxes" written below. First published in *Art and Literature* 12, spring 1967.

EDWIN'S HAND
Edwin Denby believes this acrostic poem dates from "about 1955" (letter to DA, June 15, 1969). It was first printed in the invitation to a dinner at 791 Broadway celebrating ED's sixtieth birthday on March 15, 1963. First published in *C* I:4, 1963.

CAMBRIDGE
Dated January 12, 1956, in MS 507. Larry Rivers' MS has an earlier title: "Massachusetts." First published in *Poetry*, May 1957; reprinted in *Lunch*.

THE BORES
Dated February 12, 1956, in MS 124.

DIALOGUES
Dated March 27, 1956, in Larry Rivers' MS.

STAG CLUB
MEMORIES OF BILL
These poems are dated April 3, 1956, in MS 483.

KATY
Dated November 1953 in Robert Fizdale's MS.

LISZTIANA
Dated April 7, 1956, in MS 505. First published in *Poetry*, May 1957.

ON A MOUNTAIN
Dated April 11, 1956, in MS 503. First published in *Poetry*, May 1957.

POEM (And tomorrow morning at 8 o'clock in Springfield, Massachusetts,)
Dated April 17, 1956, in MS x333.

POEM (Instant coffee with slightly sour cream)
Dated April 20, 1956, in MS 502. First published in *Poetry*, May 1957; reprinted in *Lunch*.

SPRING'S FIRST DAY
Dated May 4, 1956, in MS x431, where "William" is substituted for "Willard" in line 12.

RETURNING
Dated May 5, 1956, in MS 484, where the last line originally read: "know what's expected of the dark."

LIKE
Dated May 12, 1956, in MS 485, where this line following line 10 is canceled: "ready for dress rehearsal,"

TO JOHN WIENERS
Dated May 12, 1956, in MS x281. First published in *Paris Review*, winter 1968.

FOUR LITTLE ELEGIES
No. 1 is dated October 9, 1955, in MS x285; No. 2 is dated October 31, 1955, in MS x549; No. 3 is dated October 6, 1955, in MS x216; and No. 4a is dated April 30, 1956, in MS x710,

while Nos. 4b, c, and d are dated February 21, 1956, in MS x709 and June 21, 1956, in MS x550. Nos. 1 and 3 were first published in *Audit;* No. 2 was first published in *Fathar* 1, 1970.

HUNTING HORNS

Dated June 30, 1956, in Larry Rivers' MS. Larry Rivers recalls that this poem was inspired by the musical *Pal Joey* revival of that year (LR to DA, December 1969).

IN MEMORY OF MY FEELINGS

Dated June 27–July 1, 1956, in *NAP.* First published in *Evergreen Review* II:6, 1958; reprinted in *NAP* and in *IMO.* The following poem, dated June 17, 1955, in MS 149, was incorporated into lines 26–36 of Part 4.

> POEM
> I don't know what blood's in me
> I feel like an African prince
> I am a girl walking downstairs
> in a red pleated dress with heels
>   what land is this, so free?
>
> I am a champion taking a fall
> I am a jockey with a sprained ass-hole
> I am the light mist in which a face appears
> and it is another face of blonde
>   what land is this, so free?
>
> I am a baboon eating a banana
> I am a dictator looking at his wife
> I am a doctor eating a child
> and the child's mother smiling
>   what land is this, so free?
>
> I am a Chinaman climbing a mountain
> I am a child smelling his father's underwear
> I am an Indian sleeping on a scalp
> and my pony is stamping in the birches
>   what land is this, so free?

A STEP AWAY FROM THEM

Dated August 16, 1956, in MS 539b. First published in *Evergreen Review* I:3, 1957; reprinted in *Lunch* and *IMO.*

QU'EST-CE QUE DE NOUS!

Dated October 5, 1956, in MS 567, which has "Mathieu: Montjoie Saint Denis" written below.

A RASPBERRY SWEATER

Dated October 22, 1956, in MS 504. First published in *Angel Hair* 6, spring 1969.

LISZTIANA, MUCH LATER

Dated October 22, 1956, in MS 504. First published in *Paris Review,* winter 1968.

DIGRESSION ON *NUMBER 1, 1948*

Dated December 20, 1956, in MS 506, which has "Pollock, Painting #1" written below. First published in Frank O'Hara: *Jackson Pollock* (New York, 1959).

[IT SEEMS FAR AWAY AND GENTLE NOW]

Dated December 20, 1956, in MS x591, which has this canceled fourth stanza:

> I hit him it fell off and I
> stepped on it so wherever he were
> he'd never again know the time

and written below: "Guston" and "Discipline et personnalité, voilà les limites du style comme je l'entends . . . Apollinaire, Tendre comme le souvenir."

WHY I AM NOT A PAINTER
Dated 1956 in *NAP*. First published in *Evergreen Review* I:3, 1957; reprinted in *NAP*, and in the catalog of Michael Goldberg's show at the Martha Jackson Gallery, March–April 1966.

MILITARY CEMETERY
First published in *i.e., The Cambridge Review* I:6, 1956.

AGGRESSION
Presumably written in 1956.

POEM READ AT JOAN MITCHELL'S
Presumably written February 16, 1957. John Ashbery's MS is titled: "Poem Read at Joan Mitchell's in 1957." The occasion was Joan Mitchell's party for Jane Freilicher and Joe Hazan on the eve of their marriage. First published in *Audit*; reprinted in Ron Padgett and David Shapiro: *An Anthology of New York Poets* (New York, 1970).

JOHN BUTTON BIRTHDAY
Dated March 1, 1957, in MS 500. First published in *C* I:10, 1965; reprinted with a drawing by John Button in *Man-Root* 3, August 1970.

ANXIETY
Dated 1957 in MS 540, with this last line crossed out: "passion." "I also enclose *Anxiety*, which is the most recent of my 'efforts.'" (FOH to John Ashbery, March 27, 1957.) First published in *Ephemeris* 2, May 1969.

WIND
Dated March 31, 1957, in MS 501. First published in *Locus Solus* 3–4, winter 1962.

BLUE TERRITORY
Dated March 31, 1957, in MS 427, which has a canceled earlier title: "For Mary Butts." "Blue Territory" is the title of a painting by Helen Frankenthaler. First published in *Locus Solus* 5, 1962.

POEM (I will always love you)
Dated April 6, 1957, in MS 527. Franz Kline incorporated this poem in FOH's handwriting in an etching he made for the portfolio *21 Etchings and Poems*, published by the Morris Gallery in 1960.

JE VOUDRAIS VOIR
Dated April 29, 1957, in MS x247, which has these two canceled last lines:

> (avanti lui tremava
>   tutta Roma)

and the following on the verso in holograph:

> I thought of my old house
> and the communicability
> of images—and that a house
> can't be just a home
> and I tore up my old poem
> and started on this new one

CAPTAIN BADA

Dated May 16, 1957, in MS 495. The title apparently refers to the play by Jean Vauthier. First published in *San Francisco Earthquake* I:2, 1968.

LOUISE

Dated May 14, 1957, in MS x198. "Louise is a louse I thought I saw in the john of this very museum one day on my immaculate person." (FOH to John Ashbery, January 26, 1959.)

FAILURES OF SPRING

Dated June 17, 1957, in MS x529, which has canceled subtitle: "Bays of 1953–57." First published in *Locus Solus* 1, winter 1961.

TO HELL WITH IT

Dated July 13, 1957, in MS x96. MS x325 is marked "(original restored)," which text is printed here. "The play referred to in 'To Hell with It' [line 17] is *The Compromise* (sob, sob,). . . ." (FOH to JA, January 26, 1959.) John Ashbery's play was produced at the Poets' Theatre in Cambridge in 1956. First published in *Yügen* 4, 1959; reprinted in *NAP.*

TWO DREAMS OF WAKING

Dated September 6, 1957, in MS x438. First published in *Fathar* 1, 1970.

A YOUNG POET

Dated September 23–October 21, 1957, in MS x445, where the title is "John Wieners in 1957." Incorporated in Larry Rivers' lithograph *O'Hara Reading* (1967), which was reproduced in *Lunch Poems* (Cologne, 1969).

SONG OF ENDING

Dated October 29, 1957, in MS x262.

ODE ON NECROPHILIA

Dated November 13, 1957, in MS 10. First published in *Odes,* which omits the epigraph.

ODE TO JOY

Dated November 13, 1957, in MS 11. First published in *Partisan Review,* summer 1958; reprinted in *NAP* and in *Odes.*

POEM (To be idiomatic in a vacuum,)

Dated November 29, 1957, in FOH's letter to DA of December 15, 1961. First published in *Locus Solus* 1, winter 1961.

ODE ON LUST

Written in 1957 (FOH to DA, 1959). First published in *Odes.*

ODE TO WILLEM DE KOONING

Written in 1957 (FOH to DA, 1959). Harold Snedcof points out that line 15 echoes the titles of two paintings by de Kooning: *Gotham News* and *Easter Monday,* painted in 1955 and 1956. First published in *A New Folder* (New York, 1959); reprinted in *Odes* and in *IMO.*

POEM (I live above a dyke bar and I'm happy.)

Dated 1957 in MS x82. The poem refers to FOH's and Joseph LeSueur's apartment on University Place, New York City.

TO EDWIN DENBY

Edwin Denby believes this poem may date from 1957 (ED to DA, June 15, 1969). First published in *Adventures in Poetry* 5, January 1970.

ABOUT COURBET
Dated Southampton, June 1953 in MS 178. First published in *Art News,* January 1958.

STUDENTS
Dated February 27, 1958, "(at Gold & Fizdale concert)" in MS 310, which has original title, "To a Student," and a canceled last line: "it's composition." This poem was incorporated in the *Stones* lithograph "Music" FOH made with Larry Rivers in 1958. Larry Rivers wrote: "One stone was dedicated to Music. This one is a little more old-fashioned: our unintegrated style. Frank decided he wanted to write something first and see how I would respond. He wrote it on paper and when it got to the stone its shape changed. He had to arrange it all somewhere in the bottom third of the stone. I read it through. 'You are someone who is crazy about a violinist in the New York Philharmonic Orchestra' struck me as being very funny. It was hard to see exactly how I might use it to take care of my two-thirds. The rest of the writing was tender and in the realm of feeling. A good poem but for the kind of mind I have, useless. I kept reading the first part over and over and finally the title and violin made me decide to do my own version of Batman. Violinman." "Life among the Stones," *Location,* spring 1963.

ODE TO MICHAEL GOLDBERG ('S BIRTH AND OTHER BIRTHS)
Dated January–March 13, 1958, in MS 6, which has this deleted stanza after line 120:

> Well, Mike, are you still listening?
> and do you still believe a little what I am telling you about my life
> or have I drifted upward into falsehood?
> which is the end of poetry
> the point beyond gravity
> where the free-floating heights of personal ambition
> sail you like a cork in a trough
>   for poetry does drag you down,

DA MS 1 has a deleted final line: "Am I that poet? and the mirage has disappeared." First published in *NAP;* reprinted in *Odes* and in *IMO.*

THREE AIRS
The second is dated New York, January 1954, in MS x300, and the third is dated March 30, 1958, in MS x256. First published in *Evergreen Review* III:9, summer 1959; reprinted in *Lunch.*

GOOD FRIDAY NOON
Dated April 4, 1958, in MS 498, which has a canceled alternate title: "Good Friday Spiel."

ODE (TO JOSEPH LESUEUR) ON THE ARROW THAT FLIETH BY DAY
Dated May 11, 1958, in MS 15. First published in *Odes.* The phrase is from Psalms 91:5. Joseph LeSueur wrote: "But sometimes . . . the details in a poem will remind me of a day I would otherwise have forgotten. Mother's Day, 1958, for example. Frank was struck by the title of a *Times* book review, 'The Arrow That Flieth by Day,' and said he'd like to appropriate it for a poem. I agreed that the phrase had a nice ring and asked him for the second time what I should do about Mother's Day, which I'd forgotten all about. 'Oh, send your mother a telegram,' he said. But I couldn't hit upon a combination of words that didn't revolt me and Western Union's prepared messages sounded too maudlin even for my mother. 'You think of a message for my mother and I'll think of one for yours,' I suggested. We then proceeded to try to top each other with apposite messages that would have made Philip Wylie applaud. Then it was time to go hear a performance of Aaron Copland's *Piano Fantasy* by Noel Lee. 'It's raining, I don't want to go,' Frank said. So he stayed home and wrote 'Ode on the Arrow That Flieth by Day,' which refers to the Fantasy, Western Union, the rain and Mother's Day." "Four Apartments: A Memoir of Frank O'Hara," *The World* 15, March 1969.

TO RICHARD MILLER
Dated May 14, 1958, in MS x263. Richard Miller of the Tiber Press published FOH's *Odes* with silk-screen prints by Mike Goldberg in 1960.

JUNE 2, 1958
First published in *Clothesline* 2, 1970.

ODE ON CAUSALITY
Dated May 21–July 8, 1958, in MS 12, which has this title: "Ode on Causality in the Springs." MS 9 of the first seven lines only is titled "Elegy on Causality (in the Five Spot Cafe)" and is dated May 12, 1958. MS 17 gives the title as "Ode at the Grave of Jackson Pollock." Line 9 refers to Jackson Pollock's grave at the Springs, near East Hampton, Long Island. Line 34 has "lead window" as does *Yūgen,* where *Odes* has erroneous "leaf window." MS 259 has "de mauvaises moeurs" canceled after line 27 and "moelleusement" substituted. First published in *Yūgen* 5, 1959; reprinted in *Odes.*

FANTASIA (ON RUSSIAN VERSES) FOR ALFRED LESLIE
Dated July 8, 1958, in MS x586, where "(TITLES)" is written after the title and "VERSES" substituted for "THEMES."

ODE: SALUTE TO THE FRENCH NEGRO POETS
Dated July 9, 1958, in MS 14, which has an earlier title: "Ode en salute aux poètes nègres françaises." First published in *NAP;* reprinted in *Odes.*

A TRUE ACCOUNT OF TALKING TO THE SUN AT FIRE ISLAND
Dated Fire Island, July 10, 1958, in MS 494. First published in *Paris Review,* winter 1968; reprinted in Ron Padgett and David Shapiro: *An Anthology of New York Poets* (New York, 1970).

PLACES FOR OSCAR SALVADOR
Dated Rome, August 18–19, 1958, in MSS x290 and x600–602. First published in *Poetry,* February 1969.

POEM (Today the mail didn't come)
Dated Berlin, August 26, 1958, in MS x525. In MS x618 this poem and the following one are titled: "Berlin Poems."

TO GOTTFRIED BENN
Dated September 6, 1958, in MS x618 where "void of" in line 14 and line 15 are crossed out.

WITH BARBARA GUEST IN PARIS
Dated Paris, September 12, 1958, in MS x604. The last two lines are canceled in MS x620. First published in *Paris Review,* winter 1968.

FAR FROM THE PORTE DES LILAS AND THE RUE PERGOLÈSE
Dated Paris, September 17, 1958. First published in *Locus Solus* 1, winter 1961.

HEROIC SCULPTURE
Dated October 5, 1958, in MS x329. Published in *Paris Review* 49, summer 1970.

LOVE (To be lost)
BERDIE
Printed as nos. 4 & 5 in the *Stones* lithographs FOH made with Larry Rivers in 1958.

TWO RUSSIAN EXILES: AN ODE
Dated November 8, 1958, in MS 16, which has the original title: "Ode to Sergei Vasilyevich and Boris Leonidovitch." MS 13 has lines 12–13:

> which is not the comfortable abyss that sympathy
> tends toward from humans for their own lost kind

First published in *Odes*.

THANKSGIVING
Dated November 20, 1958, in DA MS.

[MELANCHOLY BREAKFAST]
Dated 1958 in the *Stones* lithographs, where it was first printed.

GREGORY CORSO: *GASOLINE*
Presumably written in 1958, as a review of the book.

THE "UNFINISHED"
Dated January 27, 1959, in MS x95, which has a canceled earlier title: "A Short Story in the Only Form I Can Find." First published in *Ephemeris* 2, May 1969.

DREAM OF BERLIN
Dated February 14, 1959, in MS 175

THE LAY OF THE ROMANCE OF THE ASSOCIATIONS
Dated March 2, 1959, in MS x90. First published in *C* I:7, 1964.

ON RACHMANINOFF'S BIRTHDAY (It is your 86th birthday)
Dated April 2, 1959, in MS x566, which has these canceled last two lines:

> Larry Rivers told me all of this
> when I was seven.

FOR BOB RAUSCHENBERG
Dated May 17, 1959, in MS 572.

[THE SAD THING ABOUT LIFE IS]
Dated April 27, 1959, in MS x621.

IMAGE OF THE BUDDHA PREACHING
Dated June 3, 1959, in MS 541. Bill Berkson believes the poem was inspired by FOH's reading the catalog of an exhibition of Buddhist art in West Germany. First published in *Second Coming*, July 1961; reprinted in *Lunch* and in *IMO*.

ALL THAT GAS
Dated July 15, 1959, in MS 529. First published in *Texas Quarterly*, spring 1962, where Christopher Middleton points out that the last line of the third stanza ends "with half the title of a book of poems by André Breton [*Jeunes cerisiers garantis contre les lièvres*]."

THE DAY LADY DIED
Dated July 17, 1959, in MS x408. First published in *NAP*; reprinted in *Lunch* and in *IMO*.

RHAPSODY
Dated July 30, 1959, in DA MS. "515 is 'off' Madison on 53rd; Frank would have passed it every day to and from the Museum. Its door façade is very beautiful" (Bill Berkson to DA, July 1969).

First published in *City Lights Journal* 2, 1964; reprinted in *C* I:7, 1964, in *Evergreen Review*, October 1966, in *Lunch* and *IMO*.

SONG (Is it dirty)
Dated July 31, 1959, in MS x335, which has this canceled note: "If I called this *Vilanelle* it would seem like Empson but I call it *Hangover*." First published in *Lunch*.

AT JOAN'S
Dated July 31, 1959, in MS x335, where "with me" is crossed out at the end of the last line.

ADIEU TO NORMAN, BON JOUR TO JOAN AND JEAN-PAUL
Dated August 7, 1959, in DA MS. First published in *Locus Solus* no. 1, winter 1961; reprinted in *Lunch*.

JOE'S JACKET
Dated August 10, 1959, in DA MS. First published in *Big Table* 4, 1960.

YOU ARE GORGEOUS AND I'M COMING
This acrostic poem is dated August 11, 1959, in MS x9. First published in *NAP*.

POEM (The fluorescent tubing burns like a bobby-soxer's ankles)
Dated August 13, 1959, in MS x44, which has this canceled last line: "but it is all right to want two things maybe more too." First published in *Paris Review*, winter 1968.

SAINT
Dated August 18, 1959, in DA MS. First published in *Poetry*, May 1960.

"L'AMOUR AVAIT PASSÉ PAR LÀ"
Dated August 19, 1959, in MS x46.

POEM (Hate is only one of many responses)
Dated August 24, 1959, in MS x11, which has a canceled earlier title: "For Another's Fear." First published in *Poetry*, May 1960; reprinted in *NAP* and in *IMO*.

POEM (I don't know as I get what D. H. Lawrence is driving at)
Dated August 24, 1959, in MS L10.

PERSONAL POEM
Dated August 27, 1959, in MS x407. MSS x174 and x407, and *The Beat Scene*, have two final lines:

> it would probably be only the one person
> who gave me a blue whistle from a crackerjack box

First published in *Yūgen* 6, 1960; reprinted in *The Beat Scene* (New York, 1960), and in *Lunch*.

POST THE LAKE POETS BALLAD
Dated August 28, 1959, in MS x47, which deletes the last two stanzas. First published in *Love*.

NAPHTHA
Dated September 3, 1959, in MS x418. Hattie Smith identified "with a likeness burst in the memory" in line 38 as from a statement by Jean Dubuffet reprinted in the catalog for his 1959 show at the Museum of Modern Art. "The most exciting thing that has happened to me recently is that *Big Table* forwarded me an envelope the other day and in it was a drawing from Dubuffet.

It is in India ink on his stationery, about the size of this page, the head of a man, and around it is written, so it fills out the rest of the space—'Salut Frank O'Hara . . . de Paris . . . le jour de Noël 1960 . . . à vous . . . un bon jour . . . d'un ami . . . j'ai lu le poème . . . dans *Big Table* . . . bonne année . . . Jean Dubuffet.' " (FOH to John Ashbery, February 1, 1961.) First published in *Big Table* II:5, 1960; reprinted in *Lunch* and in *IMO*.

SEPTEMBER 14, 1959 (MOON)
Dated September 15, 1959, in MS x29. First published in *Love*.

VARIATIONS ON PASTERNAK'S "MEIN LIEBCHEN, WAS WILLST DU NOCH MEHR?"
Dated September 15, 1959, in Vincent Warren's MS. First published in *Poetry*, May 1960; reprinted in *IMO*.

POEM (Khrushchev is coming on the right day!)
Dated September 17, 1959, in MS x207. First published in *NAP*; reprinted in *The Beat Scene*, in *Lunch* and in *IMO*.

GETTING UP AHEAD OF SOMEONE (SUN)
Dated September 19, 1959, in MS L26. First published in *Love*.

IN FAVOR OF ONE'S TIME
Dated September 24, 1959, in MS x64, which has an earlier title: "Outbreak in Favor of One's Own Time." ". . . it is Marvell's garden we are living outside, and hence the poem is in favor of our own time rather than his, nicher? (as Hans Hofmann says)." (FOH to John Ashbery, October 13, 1959.) First published in *Poetry*, May 1960; reprinted in *NAP*.

TO YOU
Dated September 30, 1959, in MS x181, which has a canceled earlier title, "Painting," and line 23, "as long as our strengthened time allows," canceled and the new line substituted: "The you is you. As you may know." (FOH to Vincent Warren, September 30, 1959.) First published in *Poetry*, May 1960.

LES LUTHS
Dated October 6, 1959, in MS L3, and in FOH's letter to Pierre Martory: "Here is a little poem which you appear in so I am sending it regardless of its soupiness (it was inspired by *Arts* du 16 au 22 Sept which had a picture of a rather boring looking lute on the back page)." First published in *Big Table* I:4, 1960.

LEAFING THROUGH FLORIDA
Dated October 23, 1959, in MS x42.

DANCES BEFORE THE WALL
Dated October 27, 1959, in MS L5, with this footnote: "The title is from the ballet of James Waring."

POEM (Now it is the 27th)
Dated October 27, 1959, in MS x524.

POEM (Now the violets are all gone, the rhinoceroses, the cymbals)
Dated October 27, 1959, in MS L29. First published in *Love*; reprinted in *IMO*.

POEM V (F) W
Dated November 6, 1959, in MS x193. The title refers to Vincent Warren, the ballet dancer. First published in *Texas Quarterly*, spring 1962; reprinted in *Love* and in *IMO*.

CROW HILL
Dated November 10, 1959, in MS x371, where these last two lines are deleted:

> as it fills your lungs with sky
> I wake again happy to be writing under-the-counter works

POEM ("*À la recherche d' Gertrude Stein*")
Dated November 12, 1959, in MS x35, which has the original subtitle: "À la recherche d' Gertrude Stein et d' Vincent Warren" with the second dedication crossed out. "This comes from Gertrude saying a thing continues to exist in the time of its happening even though other things happen before or later—?" (FOH to Vincent Warren, December 12, 1959.) First published in *Love*.

VARIATIONS ON THE "TREE OF HEAVEN" (In the Janis Gallery)
Dated December 2, 1959, in MS x182.

POEM (Light   clarity   avocado salad in the morning)
Dated December 5, 1959, in MS x41, which reads "in a strange" in line 10, as opposed to "on a strange" in *Love*. First published in *Love*; reprinted in *IMO*.

HÔTEL TRANSYLVANIE
Dated December 12, 1959, in MS x10, which has the title: "Ode: Hôtel Transylvanie" with "Ode:" crossed out. First published in *NAP*.

POEM (Wouldn't it be funny)
Dated 1959 in MS 580a. First published in *Lunch*.

POEM (So many echoes in my head)
Dated January 6, 1960, in MS x40. "You once ran naked toward me / Knee deep in cold March surf" in lines 6 and 7 is from Gary Snyder's poem, "For a Far-out Friend" in *Riprap, & Cold Mountain Poems*. First published in *Love*.

PRESENT
Dated January 6, 1960, in MS x183. First published in *The Nation*, December 28, 1964.

POEM (That's not a cross look it's a sign of life)
Dated January 7, 1960, in MS x180. First published in *Sum* 4, April 1965; reprinted in *Love*.

SUDDEN SNOW
Dated January 12, 1960, in MS x77, which has this canceled earlier title: "The Particularization of the World (Day and Night)." MS x77 has this stanza crossed out following line 31:

> I have practically been welded
> to you by a TV set! (floor-butt-ache) so carefully has
> my heart contracted an obligation
> to itself, it's a riot! who's laughing

Line 24 is deleted in MS x171. First published in *Poetry*, February 1969.

AVENUE A
Dated January 16, 1960, in MS x185, which gives this reading for line 16: "everything is too incomprehensible." First published in *Love*.

NOW THAT I AM IN MADRID AND CAN THINK
Dated March 31, 1960, in MS x436, which has a last line crossed out: "and you see and you make me live." First published in *Floating Bear* 2, 1961.

DÉRANGÉ SUR UN PONT DE L'ADOUR
Dated April 13, 1960, in MS 530. First published in *Floating Bear* 34, 1967.

A LITTLE TRAVEL DIARY
Dated Paris, April 14, 1960, in MS x209. First published in *Signal* I:1, autumn 1963; reprinted in *Lunch*.

BEER FOR BREAKFAST
Dated Paris, April 14, 1960, in MS x112. First published in *Floating Bear* 2, 1961.

HÔTEL PARTICULIER
Dated April 14, 1960, in DA MS. First published in *City Lights Journal* 2, 1964; reprinted in *Lunch*.

EMBARRASSING BILL
Dated April 15, 1960, in MS x111.

HAVING A COKE WITH YOU
Dated April 21, 1960, in MS x186, where "the rider as carefully as the horse" is canceled in lines 22 and 23 and "you to ride the horses" inserted. First published in *Love*.

SONG (I am stuck in traffic in a taxicab)
Dated April 27, 1960, in MS x592. First published in *Paris Review* 49, summer 1970.

AN AIRPLANE WHISTLE (AFTER HEINE)
Dated May 5, 1960, in MS x189, where these last four lines are crossed out:

> which is why I love you
> but not roses, lilies, doves or love itself
> except in you
> your mind, your limbs, your hair, your love

First published in *Love*.

TRYING TO FIGURE OUT WHAT YOU FEEL
No. 1 is dated August 5, 1960, and Nos. 2, 3, 4, and 5 are dated August 9, 1960, in MSS x464 and x465. MS x465 has two additional poems also dated August 9, 1960:

> [1]
> I am out of money
> now what do I do
> write some songs?
>
> I'm not Larry Hart
> not Oscar Hammerstein
> of Opera House fame
> not even Galli-Curci
> or Gregory Corso
>
> so I guess I wait here
> till it's time to go
> to a friend's house for
>
> TV and there
> I'll make myself
> a sandwich

Paris, 77 rue de Varenne
I wonder what happened there
it had something to do with hands
and something to do with hair
Paris is always making do
with a little bit of pomade
but so would you I assume
if you were lucky enough to be there

GLAZUNOVIANA, OR MEMORIAL DAY

Dated May 30, 1960, in MS x523. First published in *Fathar* 1, 1970.

ODE TO TANAQUIL LECLERCQ

Dated June 7, 1960, in MS 102. First published in *Paris Review* 49, summer 1970.

FIVE POEMS

Dated November 15–17, 1960, in MS 477. First published in *Lunch*. The stanza numbering is supplied by the editor.

POEM (Some days I feel that I exude a fine dust)

Dated July 19, 1960, in MS 476. First published in *Love*.

COHASSET

Dated July 28, 1960, in MS 528. First published in *Floating Bear* 2, 1961.

POEM (O sole mio, hot diggety, nix "I wather think I can")

Dated July 28, 1960, in MS x21. Vincent Warren points out that "I wather think I can" is FOH's amused imitation of Kay Francis (VW to DA, October 1969).

SONG (Did you see me walking by the Buick Repairs?)

Dated July 29, 1960, in MS 528, which has "Eddie Fisher's" crossed out in line 4 and "Fabian's" written in. First published in *Floating Bear* 2, 1961.

BALLAD (Yes it is sickening that we come)

Dated August 10, 1960, in MS 53. First published in *Audit*.

FLAG DAY

Dated August 30, 1960, in MS x4, which has two earlier titles; "Vincent's Birthday" and "Another Birthday." Vincent Warren (to DA, October 1970) explains some of the references: line 3 shows that the poem was the present; line 9 refers to a Greek Revival building in Bridgehampton which now has a gas station in front; and line 21 refers to the Conte Restaurant on Lafayette Street, New York, which is also in a Greek Revival building. At the bottom of VW's MS, FOH wrote: "Here it is at last! Happy Birthday! Frank."

HOW TO GET THERE

Dated October 4, 1960, in Patsy Southgate's MS. John Button's MS has a notation by FOH indicating that lines 2 and 3 are to be closed up "making one long line":

beneath the sky, lies, lies everywhere, it is not easy to breathe

First published in *Locus Solus* 3–4, winter 1962; reprinted in *City Lights Journal* 2, 1964, and in *Lunch*.

STEPS

Dated October 18, 1960, in MS x18, which has the earlier title crossed out: "Only the Sky Is Still Blue." First published in *Lunch*.

AVE MARIA

Dated October 19, 1960, in MS x404. First published in *Swank*, May 1961; reprinted in *C* I:10, 1965, and in *Lunch*.

TO MUSIC OF PAUL BOWLES

Dated October 29, 1960, in MS x120, where the last 3 words of line 6, lines 7 and 8, and 18–23 are bracketed in ink, suggesting FOH was thinking of deleting them. The poem is apparently addressed to Bill Berkson.

THOSE WHO ARE DREAMING, A PLAY ABOUT ST. PAUL

Dated November 18, 1960, in MS x250, which identifies the epigraph and *The Night of Loveless Nights* as by Robert Desnos. First published in *C* I:7, 1964.

TONIGHT AT THE VERSAILLES, OR ANOTHER CARD ANOTHER CABARET

Dated December 2, 1960, in MS x161.

A WARM DAY FOR DECEMBER

Dated December 5, 1960, in MS x25.

VARIATIONS ON SATURDAY

Dated December 10, 1960, in MS x16, which has two canceled lines: line 7: "pigment to the linseed oil" and line 52: "the coffee pot is filthy and." First published in *Love*.

A SHORT HISTORY OF BILL BERKSON

Dated December 13, 1960, in MS x116. First published in *Angel Hair* 6, spring 1969.

LIEBESLIED

Dated December 13, 1960, in MS 47.

WHAT APPEARS TO BE YOURS

Dated December 13, 1960, in MS L28. First published in *Love*.

THE MOTHER OF GERMAN DRAMA

Dated December 15, 1960, in MS x98.

AS PLANNED

Dated December 16, 1960, in MS x141. The poem is a reply to a poem by Bill Berkson of the same date. First published in *Paris Review* 49, summer 1970.

POEM (It was snowing and now)

Dated December 16, 1960, in MS x24, which has an earlier title crossed out: "A Little Elegy (A Little Pastoral Too)." First published in *Ephemeris* 2, May 1969.

LINES DURING CERTAIN PIECES OF MUSIC

Dated December 14–19, 1960, in MSS x575 and x584.

FOND SONORE

Dated December 22, 1960, in MS x715, which has a deleted third stanza:

> I'm just as narcissistic as the rest
> because it is a pretty flower and what are you to do

there is nothing to keep me from doing anything I don't choose
so I go ahead and do it as I've been taught by others

The reading of line 18 is from MS 550. First published in *Fathar* 1, 1970.

YOU AT THE PUMP (History of North and South)
Dated December 27, 1960, in MS x15, which has the earlier title "Vincent at the Pump" altered to "Vermeer at the Pump." First published in *Love*.

AMERICAN
From *Awake in Spain*, published in *Hasty Papers* 1960. FOH had planned to include this poem in a projected selected poems in 1966.

CORNKIND
Dated 1960 in *Lunch*. First published in *City Lights Journal* 2, 1964; reprinted in *Lunch*.

[THE LIGHT COMES ON BY ITSELF]
Probably written in 1960.

MACARONI
Dated February 1, 1961, in MS x570.

FOR THE CHINESE NEW YEAR & FOR BILL BERKSON
Dated February 14, 1961, in *Floating Bear* and *C*. First published in *Floating Bear* 15, 1961; reprinted in *C* I:9, 1964, in *Lunch* and in *IMO*.

ESSAY ON STYLE
Dated February 19, 1961, in MS x114, which has an earlier title crossed out: "Homage to Edward Dorn."

TO MAXINE
Dated February 19, 1961, in MS 532. First published in *Best and Company*, 1969.

WHO IS WILLIAM WALTON?
Dated February 19, 1961, in MS x412.

TO CANADA (FOR WASHINGTON'S BIRTHDAY)
Dated February 22, 1961, in MS x184. The poem is addressed to Vincent Warren, who was dancing in Canada at the time.

ON A BIRTHDAY OF KENNETH'S
Dated February 28, 1961, in MS x413. "Mending Sump" is Kenneth Koch's superb parody of Robert Frost.

POEM IN TWO PARTS
Dated February 27 and 28, 1961, in MS x115, where "at the ranch" is crossed out in the title of the first part, and "mush" changed to "much" in the last line of the second part.

THE ANTHOLOGY OF LONELY DAYS
Dated February 3, 1961, in MS x405 and February 3–March 6, 1961, in Vincent Warren's MS. MS x405 was originally titled: "An Anthology of Frank O'Hara's Latest and Least."

VINCENT AND I INAUGURATE A MOVIE THEATRE
Dated March 13, 1961, in MS x39. Vincent Warren's MS has "funny" for "phony" in line 22.

VINCENT,

Dated March 27, 1961, in MS x20. First published in *Ephemeris* 2, May 1969.

MARY DESTI'S ASS

Dated April 15, 1961, in MS x194, which has the earlier title crossed out: "Dear Vincent." Vincent Warren had given FOH the autobiography of Mary Desti, Isadora Duncan's great friend. (Joseph LeSueur to DA, July 24, 1969.) First published in *Floating Bear* 21, 1962; reprinted in *Locus Solus* 5, 1962, and in *Lunch*.

VINCENT, (2)

Dated April 17, 1961, in MS x22.

AT KAMIN'S DANCE BOOKSHOP

Dated April 18, 1961, in Patsy Southgate's MS. Vincent Warren's MS is titled "At Kamin's Dance Bookshop Getting a Present." First published in *Lunch*.

PISTACHIO TREE AT CHÂTEAU NOIR

Dated April 25, 1961, in MS 475. First published in *Floating Bear* 28, 1963; reprinted in *Lunch*.

THREE POEMS

Dated April 25, 1961, in MS x330. First published in *Paris Review*, winter 1968.

EARLY ON SUNDAY

Dated May 1, 1961, in MS x416.

POEM (Twin spheres full of fur and noise)

Dated May 6, 1961, in *Locus Solus* MS. First published in *Locus Solus* 5, 1962.

ST. PAUL AND ALL THAT

Dated May 20, 1961, in MS 474. First published in *Floating Bear* 21, 1962; reprinted in *Lunch*.

FOR A DOLPHIN

Dated June 10, 1961, in MS 35.

DRIFTS OF A THING THAT BILL BERKSON NOTICED

Dated June 19, 1961, in MS x118.

F.Y.I. (THE BRASSERIE GOES TO THE LAKE)

Dated June 26, 1961, in MS x127. Bill Berkson wrote: "The F.Y.I. works were written as correspondence between Frank & me & mostly by Frank—he would write the poems, like *Lunch Poems*, at his desk at the Museum of Modern Art. Together, they were supposed to form 'The Collected Memorandums of Angelicus & Fidelio Fobb'—2 brothers (Frank was Angelicus, I was Fidelio) who wrote poems, letters, postcards (all 'memorandums') to each other. The poems, however, don't seem to involve this brother-act too much—they have to do with what our lives in New York were like at the time (1960–61). 'F.Y.I.' comes from the typical heading for office memorandums—'For Your Information'—which was also the title of *Newsweek* magazine's 'house organ,' a little offset journal of employee gossip distributed weekly. I had worked at *Newsweek* the summers 1956–57 and told Frank about it & he picked up on 'F.Y.I.' He was also inspired to ring a lot of changes on the original in titles like 'F.M.I.' ('For My Information'), etc." (BB to DA, August 12, 1970.)

F.M.I. 6/25/61

Dated June 26, 1961, in MS x125. First published in *Locus Solus* 3–4, winter 1962.

F.O.I. (A Vision of Westminster Abbey)
Dated June 26, 1961, in MS x128.

SUMMER BREEZES (F.Y.(M.)M.B.I.)
Dated June 27, 1961, in MS x131.

MUY BIEN (F.Y.S.C.)
Dated June 28, 1961, in MS x132.

BILL'S SCHOOL OF NEW YORK (F.I.R.)
Dated June 30, 1961, in MS x133.

BILL'S BURNOOSE
Dated July 6, 1961, in MS x113. First published in *Evergreen Review,* July 1971.

A CHARDIN IN NEED OF CLEANING
Dated July 6, 1961, in MS x706. First published in *Evergreen Review,* July 1971.

ON RACHMANINOFF'S BIRTHDAY #158
Dated July 6, 1961, in MS 546. First published in *Angel Hair* 6, spring 1969.

ON RACHMANINOFF'S BIRTHDAY #161
Dated July 8–9, 1961, in MS x411. The numbering of the stanzas is supplied by the editor. First published in *The World* 13, 1968.

F. (MISSIVE & WALK) I. #53
Dated July 10, 1961, in MS x135. First published in *Paris Review* 49, summer 1970.

THE LUNCH HOUR FYI
Dated July 11, 1961, in MS x136.

CAUSERIE DE A.F.
Dated July 21, 1961, in MS x137.

FAVORITE PAINTING IN THE METROPOLITAN
Dated July 31, 1961, in MS x107, from which the line divisions have been restored. First published in *Locus Solus* 3–4, winter 1962.

F.Y.I. (PRIX DE BEAUTÉ)
Dated July 31, 1961, in MS x108. *Prix de Beauté* is the title of a French film that starred Louise Brooks. First published in *Audit.*

MADRID
Dated August 1, 1961, in MS 536. First published in *Locus Solus* 5, 1962.

PETIT POÈME EN PROSE
Dated August 4, 1961, in MS x324, which has the last line crossed out. An early draft, MS 533, has this canceled title: "Marchbanks s'en va-t-en guerre."

MOZART CHEMISIER
Dated August 10, 1961, in MS 49. When FOH read this poem in the NET *USA: Poetry* film, he prefaced it by saying: "'Mozart Chemisier' is a poem I wrote after visiting David Smith, the great American sculptor, in his house in Bolton Landing; . . . the Mozart comes in because he was his favorite composer." First published in *Best and Company,* 1969. Reprinted in *Clothesline* 2, 1970, which text is followed here.

POEM EN FORME DE SAW

Dated August 13, 1961, in MS x201, which has in line 5: "a good enough nip." When FOH sent DA a copy of the poem he wrote on it: "this is what Watermill was like last weekend." First published in *C* 7, 1964, which has "Poème" in the title; reprinted in *Lunch*.

YESTERDAY DOWN AT THE CANAL

Dated August 13, 1961, in *C* 7, 1964, where it was first published; reprinted in *Lunch*.

WEATHER NEAR ST. BRIDGET'S STEEPLES

Dated September 9, 1961, in MS x106a, which has a canceled earlier title: "Another Hymn to St. Bridget." "The steeples of St. Bridget's Catholic Church on Avenue B are visible across Tompkins Square Park from 441 East Ninth Street, where FOH lived from 1959 to 1963." (Tom Clark to DA, September 1969.)

POLOVTSOI

Dated August 14, 1961, in MS x147.

LET'S GET OUT

Dated October 25, 1961, in MS x119, which has "strong" substituted for "strange" in line 9 and these stanzas deleted after line 8:

> like in the Atchison-Topeka
> Railway Station when you gave
> me the nut, I'm not hungry
>
> waiter another screwdriver
> because it's raining and we
> don't care if we get wet
>
> > when you think that Louella Parsons
> > Parson is actually given parties

MS L30 has FOH's note to John Myers, who apparently was considering the poem for *Love*: "the 'a burnooses' is the way I want it, not a typo—."

SEVEN NINE SEVEN

Dated December 6, 1961, in MS 531.

MEMOIR OF SERGEI O. . . .

Dated 1961 in *Lunch,* where it was first published.

METAPHYSICAL POEM

Dated January 9, 1962, in MS x149.

ADVENTURES IN LIVING

Dated January 17, 1962, in MS x106b. First published in *Floating Bear* 29, 1964.

FOR BILL BERKSON (ON AGAIN LOOKING INTO *SATURDAY NIGHT*)

Dated January 20, 1962, in Bill Berkson's MS. The poem quotes from "Pasternak: May 28, 1960" in *Saturday Night,* BB's first book of poems.

BIOTHERM (FOR BILL BERKSON)

Dated August 26, 1961–January 23, 1962, in MS x110. "I've been going on with a thing I started to be a little birthday poem for BB and then it went along a little and then I remembered that was how Mike's Ode [ODE TO MICHAEL GOLDBERG ('S BIRTH AND OTHER BIRTHS)] got done so I kept on and I am still going day by day (middle of 8th page this morning). I don't know anything about what it is or will be but am enjoying trying to keep going and seem to have something. Some days I feel very happy about it, because I seem to have been able to keep it 'open' and so there are lots of possibilities, air and such. For example, it's been called *M.L.F.Y.*, *Whereby Shall Seace* (from Wyatt), *Biotherm,* and back and forth, probably ending up as *M.L.F.Y.* The Wyatt passage is very beautiful: 'This dedelie stroke, wherebye shall seace / The harborid sighis within my herte. . . .' *M.L.F.Y.,* I hasten to add, is not like that at all though, so don't get your hopes too high. . . . Biotherm is a marvelous sunburn preparation full of attar of roses, lanolin and plankton ($12 the tube) which Bill's mother fortunately left around and it hurts terribly when gotten into one's eyes. Plankton it says on it is practically the most health-giving substance ever rubbed into one's skin." (FOH to DA, September 20, 1961.) First published in *Audit;* reprinted in Paris Leary and Robert Kelley: *A Controversy of Poets* (New York, 1965).

POEM (Lana Turner has collapsed!)
Dated February 9, 1962, in MS x202, which has a canceled earlier title: "Ode to Staten Island." Bill Berkson writes that the poem "was written on the Staten Island ferry en route to Wagner College, where he read mano / mano with Robert Lowell." (BB to DA, July 1969.) First published in *Lunch.*

POEM (Dee Dum, dee dum, dum dum, dee da)
The poem dates itself: March 9, 1962.

CLYTEMNESTRA
Dated March 19, 1962, in MS 54. First published in *Audit.*

POEM (Signed "The Seeing Eye")
Dated March 22, 1962, in MS x435.

FOR DAVID SCHUBERT
Dated March 29, 1962, in MS 545. David Schubert (1913–1946) was a poet FOH never knew but strongly admired; his posthumous book, *Initial A,* was published in 1962. First published in *Best and Company,* 1969.

CAPTAINS COURAGEOUS
Dated April 2, 1962, in MS x307, which has the earlier title "Bearing Beauteous" canceled and "Captains Courageous & Pre-legendary" written in and then shortened. First published in *Audit.*

LEGEND
Dated April 11, 1962, in MS x304. First published in *Audit.*

MAUNDY SATURDAY
Dated April 21, 1962, in MS 456.

NEW PARTICLES FROM THE SUN
Dated May 20, 1962, in MS 459, which has a canceled earlier title, "Copie d'un Autographe Chez Paul Rosenberg et CIE." and two last lines crossed out:

> *I have never saved you
> and unfortunately I can   not

THE OLD MACHINIST
Dated May 28, 1962, in MS 55. First published in *Audit.*

FIRST DANCES
Dated July 4, 1962, in MS x178.

POLITICAL POEM ON A LAST LINE OF PASTERNAK'S
Dated July 7, 1962, in MS x197. The first line is from J. M. Cohen's translation of Pasternak's "M.T." (Boris Pasternak: *Selected Poems*. London, 1958.) First published in *C* I:7, 1964.

ROGERS IN ITALY
Dated July 28, 1962, in MS x80.

BALLADE NUMBER 4
Dated September 10, 1962, in MS x417. First published in *Audit.*

TWO TRAGIC POEMS
Dated December 18 and 19, 1962, in MS x200. First published in *Nomad / New York* 10/11, autumn 1962.

GALANTA
Dated 1962 in *Lunch,* where it was first published.

BIOGRAPHIA LETTERARIA
Probably written in New York in 1961 or 1962.

LINES FOR THE FORTUNE COOKIES
From an undated MS in the Academic Center Library, The University of Texas, Austin. Probably written in New York in 1961 or 1962.

THE SENTIMENTAL UNITS
Joe LeSueur believes this poem was written in 1963.

ANSWER TO VOZNESENSKY & EVTUSHENKO
Dated January 19, 1963, in *Audit,* where it was first published.

34 MILE WIND
Dated February 16, 1963, in MS x234, which gives line 10 as the original first line and where line 20 originally read: "in *Zhivago* where strangers pause and." First published in *C* I:7, 1964.

POEM (At the top of the rung)
First printed in the Pierre Matisse Gallery catalog for Jean-Paul Riopelle's show of April–May, 1963.

[DEAR JAP,]
Dated April 10, 1963, in his letter to Jasper Johns, to which FOH added this postscript: "I may want to take out the first 2 lines—hope you find something in the rest—Frank." He did delete those two lines in MS 455, where "watercolors" in line 3 is changed to "watermelons" and "by James Brodey" is crossed out after "poem" in line 11.

AGAIN, JOHN KEATS, OR THE POT OF BASIL
Dated June 8, 1963, in MS 463. First published in *Ephemeris* 2, May 1969.

POEM (The Cambodian grass is crushed)
Dated June 17, 1963, in MS 461. FOH sent the poem, like DEAR JAP, to Jasper Johns for possible use in a lithograph, with this note: "Dear Jap, do you think we can do anything with this? If it doesn't interest you particularly, let's not and I'll keep after some more—best, Frank   PS Maybe you would want to spread it around the page? who knows?"

FOR POULENC
Dated June 25, 1963, in Ned Rorem's untitled MS. Set by Ned Rorem for solo voice and piano. He writes: "The poem represents the last of several occasions for which Frank and I conjointly

conceived an idea. In this case it was for a Poulenc Memorial Concert given by Alice Esty. Mrs. Esty invited (and commissioned) the collaboration. . . . The 'tobaccos and the nuns' refer to Poulenc's two operas: one profane, the other sacred." (NR to DA, June 1969.) Published by E. C. Schirmer Music Co. in 1968.

BATHROOM
Dated June 20, 1963, in FOH's letter to Jasper Johns: "Dear Jap, this is that thing I wrote in Ruth Kligman's bathroom after that stunning dinner party, but I think it is too trivial or something to be of use, maybe. Nevertheless I'm sending it just because it did happen."

ON RACHMANINOFF'S BIRTHDAY & ABOUT ARSHILE GORKY
Dated July 3, 1963, in MS x166. First published in *Audit*.

[THE CLOUDS GO SOFT]
Dated July 11, 1963, in MS 452. Jasper Johns reproduced this poem in his lithograph *Skin with O'Hara Poem*, published by Universal Limited Arts Editions in 1965. It was reproduced in *Art in America*, October 1965.

[THE LIGHT PRESSES DOWN]
Dated July 26, 1963, in MS x308. First published in *Best and Co.*, 1969.

WALKING
Dated February 13, 1964, in MS x192, which has these last two lines deleted:

> not a backdrop
> but the middle of the scene

First published in *Poetry*, February 1969.

POEM (I to you and you to me the endless oceans of)
Dated March 2, 1964, in MS 453. First printed in Galleria Odyssia's catalog for Mario Schifano's show in 1964.

AT THE BOTTOM OF THE DUMP THERE'S SOME SORT OF BUGLE
FOH sent this and the following nine poems to Jan Cremer for a projected collaboration. His letter is dated May 8, 1964:

> Dear Jan,
> Forgive me for the long delay in sending you these poems. I hope you like them, but if you don't let me know and I will send you ten older ones which you may like better. But my first idea was to give you new poems which have never been printed before, since you will be doing new drawings. However, don't hesitate to let me know if you don't like them, & I'll send the others. There is no reason for you to do drawings for poems you don't like.
> As for the poems, what do you want to call them? We can call them poems by me drawings by you; I also thought of a couple of other titles, such as THE END OF THE FAR WEST or THE NEW YORK AMSTERDAM SET ("set" as in Jazz set). What do you think? As you will see, for some reason a lot of the poems refer to cowboys, Western outlaw heroes (Wyatt Earp), etc., which is what made me think of the first title (along with a few other elements, like the far west being western civilization—not that the poems are all that serious), but maybe the second title is better, or just calling them poems and drawings. Maybe you have thought of something else, or will when the drawings are done. . . .
>
> > Best, as always,
> > Frank

CHICAGO
ENEMY PLANES APPROACHING
HERE IN NEW YORK WE ARE HAVING A LOT OF TROUBLE WITH THE
    WORLD'S FAIR
I LOVE THE WAY IT GOES
SHOULD WE LEGALIZE ABORTION?
THE BIRD CAGE THEATRE
THE GREEN HORNET
THE JADE MADONNA
THE SHOE SHINE BOY
This last poem is dated May 5, 1964, in Jan Cremer's MS.

TRIRÈME
Dated November 26, 1964, in MS 460c. First printed in the Marlborough Gallery catalog for
Arnaldo Pomodoro's show in October 1965.

FANTASY
Dated 1964 in *Lunch*, where it was first published.

CANTATA
Dated February 18, 1965, in Maureen Granville-Smith's MS, which has the title crossed out.

CHEYENNE
Dated March 20, 1965, in MS x387.

HISTORICAL VARIATIONS
Possibly written in 1964 or 1965.

LITTLE ELEGY FOR ANTONIO MACHADO
Dated March 27, 1966, in MS x358, the original version, which has this stanza before the last:

> you sank the cadavers in the dusk to free the air
> by embracing them and therefore also us
> moving in your space
> accepting your grandeur
> as a necessary condition of the purple correction

A shortened version of the poem was first published in the catalog for John Bernard Myers'
"Homage to Machado" show (a benefit for refugees of the Spanish War) at the Tibor de Nagy
Gallery in 1966. The fuller version was first published in *Harper's Bazaar*, October 1967; it was
reprinted in *Intransit, The Andy Warhol–Gerard Malanga Monster Issue*, 1968, and in Myers.

[NOTES ON *SECOND AVENUE*]

Written in 1953 or later, apparently as a letter to an editor of a literary magazine.

PERSONISM: A MANIFESTO

Dated September 3, 1959, in *Yūgen* 7, 1961, where it was first published. Reprinted in *Audit.*

[STATEMENT FOR *THE NEW AMERICAN POETRY*]

Dated 1959 in *NAP,* where it was first published.

ABOUT ZHIVAGO AND HIS POEMS

Commissioned by DA and written in 1959. First published in *Evergreen Review* II:7, winter 1959.

[STATEMENT FOR PATERSON SOCIETY]

Dated March 16, 1961, in MS x159. It was never sent to the Paterson Society.

LARRY RIVERS: A MEMOIR

Published in *Larry Rivers,* the catalog of the retrospective exhibition of the Poses Institute of Fine Arts, Brandeis University, 1965.

INDEX OF FIRST LINES

Each night plows instead of no head 78
Easy to love, but 238
Ecstatic and in anguish over lost days 83
Elf, forbidden word, heart within me 175
Entraining to Southampton in the parlor car with Jap and Vincent, I 329
Essays, boring conversations and vistas 70
Etruria! 200
Exactly at one o'clock your arms broach 49

Fall faces who have lunched on other 227
57th Street 375
515 Madison Avenue 325
First you took Arthur's porcelain 3
For instance you walk in and faint 428
Free to suffer speechful constraint 133
From behind he takes her waist 458
From Canada   Leningrad Kirov   Saint-Saëns   ex-Maryinsky 455
From near the sea, like Whitman my great predecessor, I call 305
full of passion and giggles 278

God! love! sun! all dear and singular things! 29

Ha ha it's fun to run around the deck and see 479
Had you really been wholly mine at night 386
Hahahahaha! he laughs briefly 67
Harder nails 303
Hate is only one of many responses 333
Have you forgotten what we were like then 30
He allows as how some have copped out 414
He can rest. He has blessed him and hurt him 109
"He fell off a barn on his head 452
He gets up, lights a cigarette, puts fire 373
he isn't the English composer 395
He never, Kenneth, did an effortless thing 151
He paces the blue rug. It is the end of summer, 63
He set out and kept hunting 167
He sighted her at the moment of recall. 153
He waits, and it is not without 45
He was used to guises and masks 127
He'd be wispy in a double feature, 69
Her spinning hair webbed lengthening through 87
"Here he comes now, the big prick-with-ears, 103
Here I am at my desk. The 23
here I sit in Jager House 400
Hey, you! raining, from your dilapidated pier, 164
Homes of aviators suddenly mounting, 116
House of love house of death 362

A NOTE ABOUT THE EDITOR

Donald Allen grew up in northwest Iowa and was educated at the state universities of Iowa, Wisconsin, and California (Berkeley). After wartime service in the Navy in the Pacific, Washington, and London, he worked for ten years in publishing in New York City. Since 1960 he has made his home in San Francisco, where he directs the Four Seasons Foundation and Grey Fox Press. He has translated *Four Plays of Eugène Ionesco,* and has edited the following: (with Francisco García Lorca) *The Selected Poems of Federico García Lorca; The New American Poetry;* (with Robert Creeley) *New American Story* and *The New Writing in the USA;* and (with Warren Tallman) *The Poetics of the New American Poetry.*

A NOTE ON THE TYPE

The text of this book was set on the Fotosetter in a type face called Biretta—the camera version of Bembo, the well-known monotype face. The original cutting of Bembo was made by Francesco Griffo of Bologna only a few years after Columbus discovered America. It was named for Pietro Bembo, the celebrated Renaissance writer and humanist scholar who was made a cardinal and served as secretary to Pope Leo X. It was in recognition of Pietro Bembo's role as cardinal that the name Biretta was chosen for the film adaptation of the face.

Sturdy, well balanced, and finely proportioned, Bembo is a face of rare beauty. It is, at the same time, extremely legible in all of its sizes.

The book was composed by Westcott & Thomson, Inc., Philadelphia, Pennsylvania, and York Graphic Services, Inc., York, Pennsylvania. It was printed and bound by Maple-Vail Book Mfg. Group, Binghamton, New York. Typography and binding design by Betty Anderson.